Situationist Funhouse

Goff Books
Published by Goff Books. An Imprint of ORO Editions
Gordon Goff: Publisher

www.goffbooks.com
info@goffbooks.com

Text by Stephen Zacks
Book design by Pablo Mandel
Proofread by Alejandro Guzman-Avila
Managing Editor: Jake Anderson

10 9 8 7 6 5 4 3 2 1 First Edition

ISBN: 978-1-951541-99-6

Color Separations and Printing: ORO Group Ltd.
Printed in China.

Goff Books makes a continuous effort to minimize the overall carbon footprint of its publications. As part of this goal, Goff Books, in association with Global ReLeaf, arranges to plant trees to replace those used in the manufacturing of the paper produced for its books. Global ReLeaf is an international campaign run by American Forests, one of the world's oldest nonprofit conservation organizations. Global ReLeaf is American Forests' education and action program that helps individuals, organizations, agencies, and corporations improve the local and global environment by planting and caring for trees.

G.H. Hovagimyan: Situationist Funhouse

Stephen Zacks

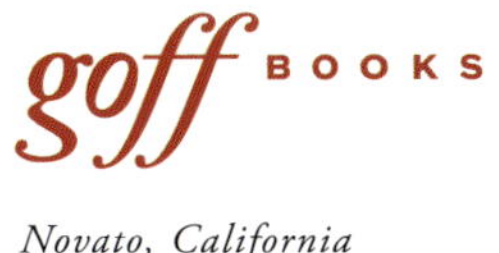

Novato, California

CONTENTS

4

FOREWORD

G.H. Hovagimyan is an absurdist, a strategist, a serial collaborator, and nothing short of a cultural icon in the world of contemporary art, particularly as it relates to how artists have adopted the digital technological tools of our times, adapting them for critique of art, popular culture, and social engagement.

Situationist Funhouse is a joyride through this history. The journey Stephen Zacks so meticulously documents and describes is not only an incredibly comprehensive ride through G.H.'s life work to date—Hovagimyan adopted G.H. as an acronym in the 1990s as a kind of gesture of personal rebirth and to ease others' difficulty with his last name [pronounced ho-va-gim-yan]—it also serves as a document that tracks a particular view on the alternative contemporary art scene of New York from the 1970s to the present day.

G.H.'s background in underground art, punk, and subculture movements of the 1970s made him a shape-shifter, his practice almost impossible to define. The common threads through all of his work are his commitment to collaboration and open conversations, his engagement with new technological tools that interrogates their place in our lives, and a defiantly punk and DIY (Do-It-Yourself, or perhaps even better DIWO—Do-It-With-Others) aesthetic and approach to his art practice.

From his early work with Gordon Matta-Clark to his involvement with collective platforms such as Colab (or Collaborative Projects), a loose collective formed by artists in downtown New York City in 1977, and punk/No Wave band the Communists, to which he belonged in late 1970s, continuing through his work with the very early internet art platform The Thing, established by artist Wolfgang Staehle in the pre-web early 1990s, the *Art Dirt* internet radio program in the late 1990s, and the Artists Meeting collective in the late 1990s, G.H.'s career is full of rich collaborations in the fields of contemporary art, radio, music, internet art, and collective art practices.

Looking back to the early days of internet art, pre-web, I am reminded of my days noodling around with SystemX in Sydney, Australia, a dial-up BBS (bulletin board system) that operated concurrently and in a similar way to The Thing in New York City. These were the halcyon days of the internet, when artists were sharing their work in completely open and radically collaborative ways. The only way to view pieces was to dial up through a modem and download them. At SystemX, artists were experimenting with mods (a modification made to an image-manipulation, sound, or video game software application) and open source—before that term existed—as well as challenging modes of art production, uploading images and sound files, and encouraging other artists to modify and re-upload them, establishing global friendships and collaborations. In New York, G.H. was similarly experimenting with collaborators at The Thing, defiantly holding dear an open approach to the early days of the internet.

By the mid-to-late 1990s, the internet, with the introduction of graphic user interfaces—following the public release of the Mosaic browser developed at University of Illinois at Urbana–Champaign in 1993, and then Netscape, the first attempt to capitalize on the emerging communications platform in 1994—the world wide web as we know it was emerging. In the early years, it was still a space of generosity and sharing, but as the so-called dot-com boom began to take root, open platforms began to recede into the background.

Of the *Art Dirt* internet radio project, Adrianne Worzel, a collaborator, says, "We always had enormous fun," a constant thread through all of G.H.'s collaborations. They interviewed a veritable who's who of artists and cultural activators of the time, from Charlie Ahearn to Martha Wilson, and periodically staged events that, as Zacks points out, became an early aspirational model of the internet start-up lifestyle.

Play and experimentation inside and outside of the art market are evident throughout G.H.'s career. His collaborative installations and video works in the 2000s also set the stage for his most recent explorations in interactive public art projections and his AR (augmented reality) work in the last decade. Not content with commercial explorations of these media, G.H.'s most recent *Space Paintings* and other AR work are both literally and metaphorically an interrogation not only of humanity's exploitation of space and the space junk that now surrounds our planet, they also explore 3D space in radical ways. They operate not like commercial game applications, but as appropriated tools to truly play with perception and 3D space. Once again, he's shape-shifting: Where a majority of AR applications layer 2D virtual objects into 3D real space, his 3D sculptures become the capture points for the AR objects, truly defying spatial logic.

G.H. continues his exploration of new technologies, always staying just ahead of the commercialization of new forms. The work might belong in galleries or museums, but it equally belongs in our parks and public spaces: places ripe for and committed to the kinds of participatory practices, audience engagement, and the wonderful sense of play that G.H.'s entire body of work invites. Although his work continues to morph and change with every new advance in technology, it never deviates from his commitment to participation, nor from his roots in building community. And so his sculptural works, like various iterations of the *Fibonacci Spiral*, operate simultaneously as sculptures, projection surfaces, and community-engaged public artworks.

Situationist Funhouse is thus a joyful ride through G.H.'s history and his work, but it is also a call to action to remind us that we might envision new futures for artistic and cultural practices: ones that are filled with joy and play but which also critique the commercialization of contemporary technologies and demand that we take them back into our own hands to build better creative futures. Long live collaborative DIY cultures. Taking G.H.'s lead, may we continue to play and learn together.

—Amanda McDonald Crowley

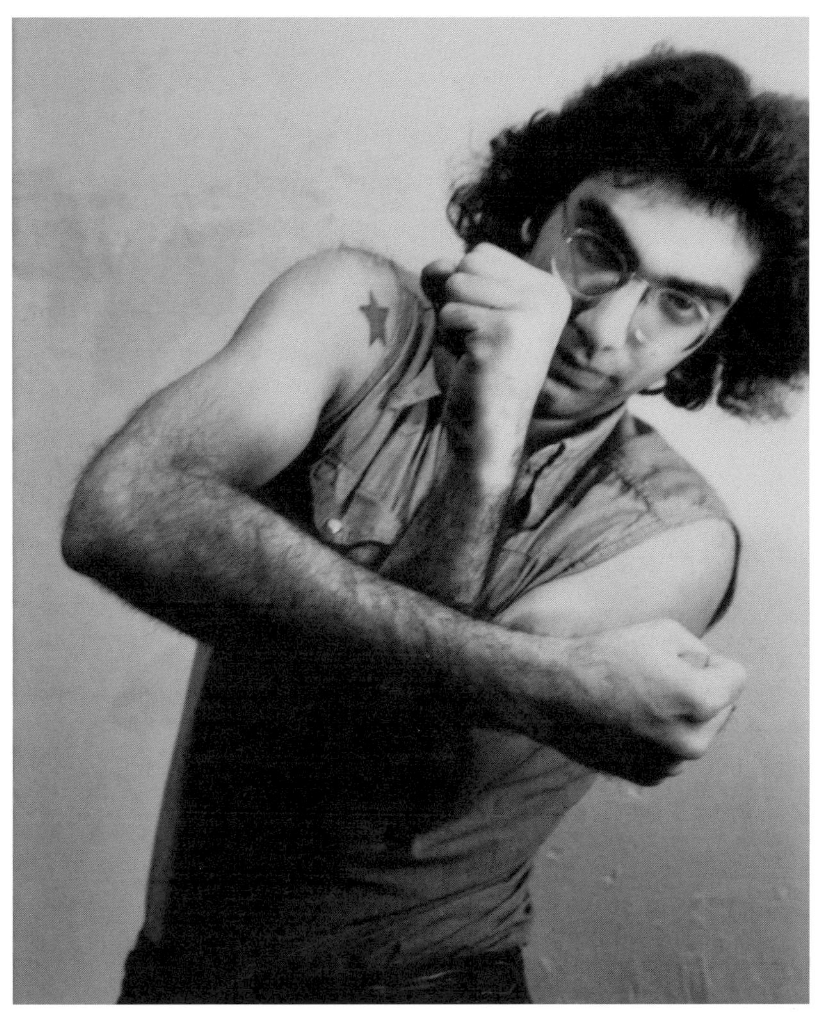

G.H. in 1975. Photo by Scott Billingsley

INTRODUCTION

This project began as a catalog raisonnée of G.H. Hovagimyan, documenting his work over the course of the last 50 years. It evolved into a story spanning five decades of changing media and culture, and seven major periods of activity—a compelling reflection on shifts in technology and consciousness in the last half-century. Hovagimyan's spirit as a critical and fun-loving observer carries throughout: we find him continually embracing new forms of media and collaboration as a kind of freeform aesthetic research. It's a position that allowed him to stay on the cusp of the latest media being developed for representation, information distribution, sharing, and computer-generated altered realities, adapting commercial programs for his own purposes in the manner of hacking or *détournement*, the Situationist method of turning hegemonic cultural products against themselves.

From the start, Hovagimyan had the good fortune to witness and participate in some of the watershed moments, places, and artistic projects of his time. In the early-to-mid 1970s, as a recent graduate of the Philadelphia College of Art (now the University of the Arts), having studied with Cynthia Carlson, Rafael Ferrer, Don Roger Gill, and Rhee Morton, he landed at 112 Greene Street in SoHo as the neighborhood was being transformed by ad hoc artistic activity and the ascendency of the live/work loft and gallery scene. He sat the gallery at 112 Greene and became affiliated with post-minimalist artists who were repurposing discarded materials and buildings, altering the perception of spaces and their use. He visited Gordon Matta-Clark's *Splitting* in Ridgefield, New Jersey, and assisted him in *Day's End* in downtown Manhattan, *Conical Intersect* in Paris, and several pieces in Milan. He showed his own conceptual work at loft shows organized by Fluxus artist Jean Dupuy and at 112 Greene Street, The Kitchen, Idea Warehouse, and P.S. 1.

In the following years, Hovagimyan played drums in the punk band the Communists, which performed at CBGB and Max's Kansas City, and in the famous No Wave show at Artists Space. He participated in the formation of Colab, a group of peers who exhibited works in their lofts—borrowed and squatted spaces to compensate for the lack of commercial galleries for young people in the late 1970s and early 80s. He performed in films of Scott and Beth B. and Charlie Ahearn. He opened an East Village gallery called Virtual Garrison in 1984, when artists leased hundreds of commercial storefronts to exhibit their own work, famously selling out a whole show of John Bowman paintings to the collector Eli Broad.

But Hovagimyan's mature period as an artist begins in the 1990s with his early net art pieces, first distributed through bulletin board systems (BBS) and early internet servers by The Thing and artnetweb. His *Barbie and Ken Politically Correct* inadvertently ended up as a screensaver at the SoHo gallery TZ Art, signaling to him a new approach. He appeared in *Art in America* at the time, and his work received regular coverage in venues for new media art. He won a commission from Creative Time, causing a major stir with his *Hey Bozo!* billboards, which attracted scandal-seeking headlines in the *New York Post*. The pieces from this period had a consistent punk performance ethos that placed them on the edge of any kind of normal art market, yet he likely benefited from the lack of commercial outlets. Over the next 30 years, it pushed him to continually adapt new media platforms at their moments of inception. His catalog is a mini history of media itself.

In the coming decade, Hovagimyan would collaborate extensively with the French Aix-en-Provence-based artist Peter Sinclair on various subversions and *détournements* of Apple computers and software. They rewrote code and redirected software to turn it into a tool for computer performances at new media and avant-garde festivals and modern and contemporary art museums across Europe. Postmasters, run by adventurous gallerists Magda Sawon and Tamas Banovich, became a regular venue in New York City, hosting performances of his hacked interfaces, YouTube *Triptych Parties*, and events and collaborations with the group Artists Meeting until 2012.

Hovagimyan's most recent trajectory, virtual and augmented reality, led to one-person shows at TRANSFER in Brooklyn in 2014 and Delaware Valley Arts Alliance in Narrowsburg, New York in 2019. Rewriting gaming software and freely adapting Kinect cameras, virtual reality headsets, and AR gaming programs, he created immersive environments in 3D *Karaoke, Space Paintings*, AR *Column*, and *Satellites* that operate at the borderline of two-dimensional painting, flattened 3D representation, physical objects, and virtual 3D objects, appropriating technology destined to surface soon as the next mass-entertainment, attention-consuming, hyper-commercialized medium. In his work, new technology is a space of freedom and play.

The interviews with Hovagimyan that formed the background for this project began in 2012, when I was working on an unfinished project on the cultural, physical, and economic transformation of New York City from the 1960s through the 80s. That work was supported by grants from the New York State Council on the Arts, Graham Foundation for the Advanced Studies in the Fine Arts, a Warhol Foundation Arts Writers Grant, and a MacDowell Fellowship, which made it possible to gain access to many of the sources for images and to interview and develop relationships with many of the artists from this period.

Over the following years, I had the opportunity to work with Hovagimyan on several projects that figure into *Situationist Funhouse*, including 3D *Karaoke, Fibonacci Spiral*, *Zipline,* and *Applause Please.* In 2018, we began discussing putting together a catalog raisonnée, and at the end of June 2019, we began an additional series of interviews that resulted in this project. I'm grateful to G.H. for his time and access to his archive and images, and to both he and Joyce Castleberry for their generous support for this effort, as well as for their friendship and encouragement.

This publication also would not be possible without the help of editor extraordinaire Ashley Simone, who pointed us in the direction of Gordon Goff at ORO EDITIONS. Garret Linn beautifully printed an early draft of the manuscript, which helped give the project a tangible form. Michael Sarff and Raphaele Shirley generously hosted me at their OTOA residency house in Callicoon, New York for interviews with Hovagimyan, offering time and space for writing. Amanda McDonald Crowley reviewed the manuscript, and Jane Crawford assisted in providing access to photos from Hovagimyan's work with Matta-Clark. Colab and many of its members kindly allowed us to reproduce images, including Charlie Ahearn, Beth B., Scott Billingsley, Coleen Fitzgibbon, Jenny Holzer, and Alan Moore. Marc Miller of online Gallery 98 also provided images. Thanks also to Leonard Abrams for access to the full archives of the *East Village Eye*, through which I retrieved images of reviews and ads for Virtual Garrison gallery, and to White Columns for images from the archives of 112 Greene Street. Finally, thank you to Laurie Anderson for her encouragement. In some way too, I owe the Covid19 pandemic acknowledgement for the break from regular assignments to devote time to this project.

—*Stephen Zacks*

1

Early Collaborations

Rafael Ferrer, *Three Leaf Pieces*, 1968

While studying at the Philadelphia College of Art, G.H. Hovagimyan was introduced to some of the most prominent post-minimalist artists emerging in downtown New York. It was 1968, and Robert Morris's *Anti-Form* essay appeared that year in the April issue of *Artforum*, helping define what become known as process art, an emerging tendency to move away from durable materials and consistency of form toward softer, pliable fabrics, strings, fibers, wires, and natural elements that decomposed and could be installed in a variety of ways depending on the setting.

Along with process art, performance—or what was then being called body art—was also gaining currency. It was a short train ride to New York City, and Hovagimyan took it to see a performance by his Philadelphia teacher Italo Skanga at 98 Greene Street, one of the first SoHo galleries. These were some of his earliest aesthetic influences as a young artist, plunging him straight into the avant-garde of the time.

> When I was in art school, I was doing essentially a kind of process art, then I started doing performance. It was something like body works at that time, using your body as a material. It was something between Joseph Beuys and Vito Acconci.[1]

In 1968, Hovagimyan participated in a staged guerrilla art action by Rafael Ferrer, who would appear the following year in the Whitney Museum of American Art's annual sculpture exhibition.

> At that point Rafael Ferrer was a teacher at the University of the Arts, and there were several other people—Rhee Morton, Cynthia Carlson, Don Roger Gill—who were all pretty hot up-and-coming artists on the New York scene. Rafael was inviting artists in the New York scene like Robert Morris and Gordon Matta-Clark to come down as visiting artists and lecturers, along with several others.[2]

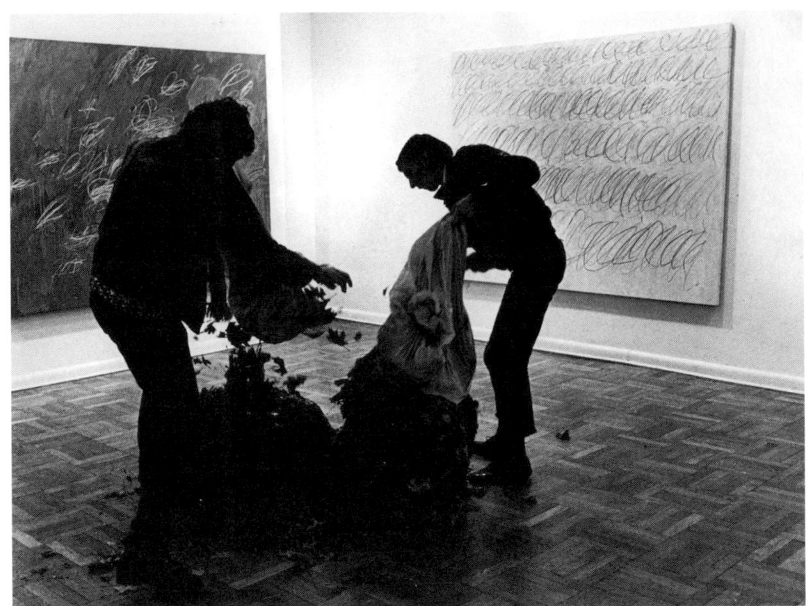

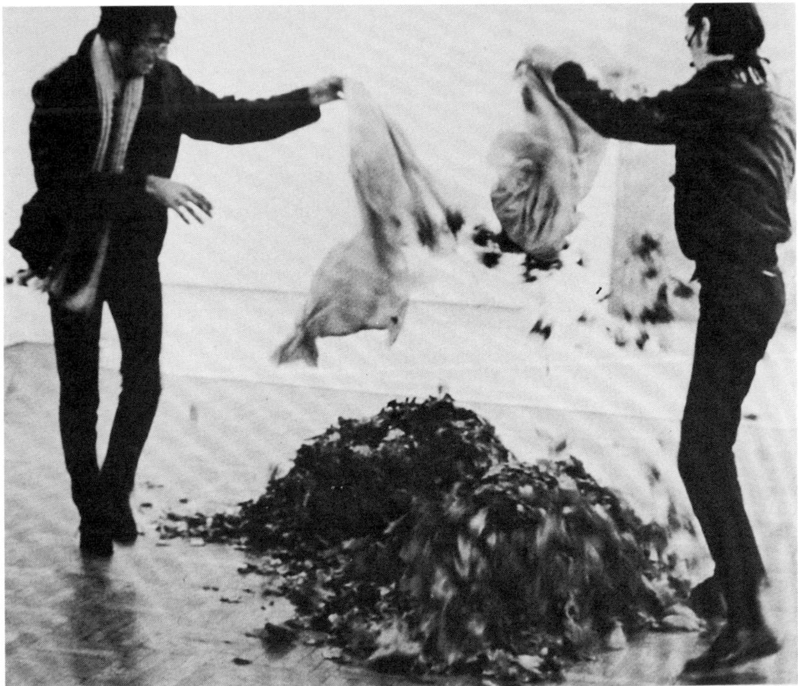

Rafael Ferrer, *Three Leaf Pieces,* 1968. Photos by Ron Miyashiro. © 2020 Rafael Ferrer/Licensed by VAGA at Artists Rights Society (ARS), NY

With two other students, Hovagimyan joined Ferrer in a truck from Philadelphia carrying large bags filled with leaves. They went to Leo Castelli's galleries on 108th Street, 57th Street, and 77th Street and emptied the bags in the elevator, on the gallery floor, and in the stairwell. Castelli was at the time the most important gallerist in New York, representing Andy Warhol, Jasper Johns, Robert Rauschenberg, Frank Stella, and Cy Twombly, among other famous artists.

> Rafael was invited by Robert Morris to be involved in the Castelli Warehouse show, which was a seminal show for Art Povera/process art that had people like Eva Hesse, Bill Bollinger, Richard Serra, Keith Sonnier, Alan Saret. He invited me and two other students to come with him, loaded up these big garbage bags with leaves in the truck, and we essentially filled the staircase in the Castelli Gallery with leaves. It was a seminal process art show, and that was literally after my first year in art school. I was introduced to the avant-garde art scene.[3]

The occasion for *Three Leaf Pieces* was *Nine at Castelli*, a show of nine post-minimalist artists organized by Robert Morris at Castelli's 108th Street warehouse. Though they appeared to be ad hoc, the temporary Ferrer leaf installations were organized with the knowledge and blessings of Morris. It became a portal into the hippest quotient of the downtown scene.

> We went to the gallerist Barbara Rose's apartment for cocktails after the opening, and Keith Sonnier was there and Richard Serra and everybody, and I met them all. Then we went to Max's Kansas City, which is kind of interesting, because Frosty Myers is here in Abrahamsville, Pennsylvania, and he was actually a fixture at Max's. Mickey Ruskin was his patron, and Frosty designed and built every single one of Max's bar and restaurants.[4]

Max's was a famous hangout scene for artists, and Warhol dominated the back room during the period, with his Factory located around the corner on Union Square. It became a legendary venue for the glam bands that were formative for the emergence of punk. Later, Hovagimyan would play shows at

Max's, which reopened under new ownership in 1975, as a drummer for the late 70s punk/No Wave band the Communists.

112 Greene Street

After art school, Hovagimyan moved to New York in 1973 and lived in an apartment in Lower Manhattan at 64 Fulton Street. He got a job at a frame shop on Greene Street in SoHo, Frames Unlimited.

> I was so poor, it was amazing. I was making $75 a week. Rent was $200 a month. I couldn't afford taking the subway. Someone gave me a girl's bicycle, which was two sizes too small for me. I used to ride that to work, from Fulton up to Greene street. Then I wouldn't have to take a subway. I would go to the store and buy $20 worth of groceries. I'd get a pound of hamburger, cut it into four, and freeze it, so I'd have four hamburger meals and a can of peas.
>
> Nobody had credit cards. They didn't exist. At Max's Kansas City and other places, they would have a happy hour. Max's used to have chicken and ribs and things like that, so you could go there and buy a draft beer for a dollar, and then eat the buffet. That's what I used to do, drive my girl's bicycle up.[5]

Working at the nearby frame shop, Hovagimyan regularly dropped into 112 Greene Street and soon got hired to sit the gallery. Initiated in 1970 by Jeffrey Lew in collaboration with Alan Saret in a building Lew owned—and where Lew lived on the top floor—the gallery occupied the ground floor and basement for the next eight years.

> I got a job at 112 Greene Street, which was the hot place at the time. I was introduced to 112 Greene Street by Italo Skanga, and Italo had done a piece at Willoughby Sharp's place on Grand Street where they ran *Avalanche* magazine. We went up to see that piece and hang out, then we went over to Food, which was Gordon's restaurant and a part of that scene. Then when I moved up a year later, I got a job a 112 being the gallery sitter—I was really the manager. I met that whole 112 group.[6]

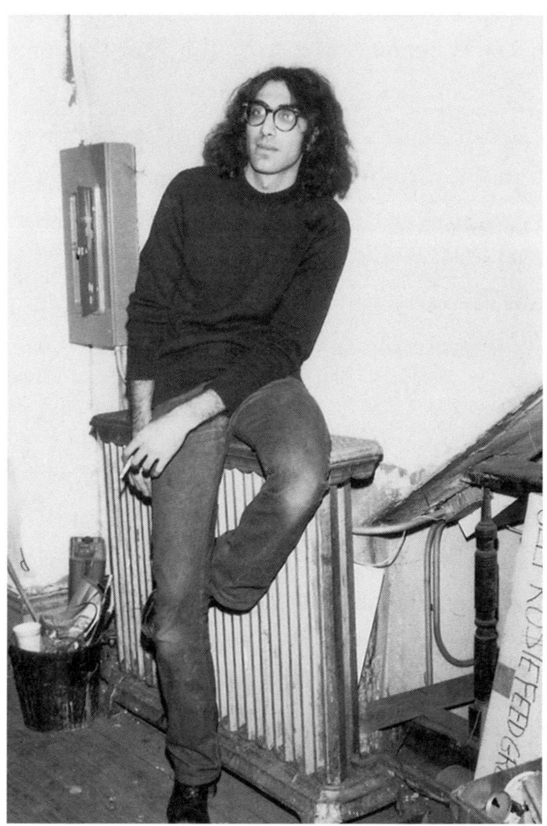

G.H. at 112 Greene Street opening of Ulrike Rosenbach, *Isolation is Transparent,* Jan. 15, 1974. Photo: Cosmos Sarchiapone/Smithsonian Archives of American Art. Charles Denson. Cosmos in Cosmos Appearance Series #371, circa 1979. Cosmos Andrew Sarchiapone papers, circa 1860-2011. Archives of American Art, Smithsonian Institution

112 Greene Street gained a reputation for experimental exhibitions, performances, dance, and social happenings, featuring a group that included Laurie Anderson, Gordon Matta-Clark, Tina Girouard, Suzanne Harris, Jene Highstein, Larry Miller, Richard Nonas, Alan Saret, and Richard Serra. Hovagimyan became the youngest fixture of the pioneering scene, which defined a generation of downtown New York art, participating in performances, assisting in installations, and mounting his first solo show in the gallery in 1974. As Jessamyn Fiore wrote in *112 Greene Street*,

> G.H. Hovagimyan managed the 112 Greene Street front desk for much of its existence. He also staged his own performances at the venue and elsewhere in New York, often involving punk-inspired poetry. Hovagimyan further worked as Gordon Matta-Clark's assistant for several years and helped him on several major cutting projects, including *Day's End* at the Pier 52 in New York and *Conical Intersect* in Paris, both in 1975. His first-person accounts represent some of the only surviving documentation of many aspects of the execution of the projects and complement available film and photography… including the 1974 video-recorded performance at 112 Greene Street, *Prisoner's Dilemma*, by Richard Serra and Robert Bell. Many of his own works from the decade incorporated music.[7]

Robert Bell and Richard Serra, *Prisoner's Dilemma,* 1974

On January 20, 1974, Hovagimyan played opposite actor Spalding Gray—later renowned for his autobiographical monologues—in a performance of *Prisoner's Dilemma* at 112 Greene Street, directed by Robert Bell and Richard Serra. Gallerist Leo Castelli participated as one of the pairs of performers playing out the scenes, which were based on a classic game theory experiment. The event was videotaped live, with an audience watching on four monitors in the gallery as interrogations were conducted behind a screen and in the basement. Programmed as part of the *Video Performance Series* events organized by curator and *Avalanche* co-founder Willoughby Sharp, *Prisoner's Dilemma* was one of the seminal works of the period that Hovagimyan participated in, this time in the genre of early video art.

Richard SERRA & Robert BELL . .

RS: There's one place where Schechner says to Hovagymyan, "You're in trouble." And he says, "I'm not in trouble." And it's obvious that he means, not only am I not in trouble in this program, I'm not in trouble in my life, or in the world, or sitting here in 112 Greene Street. Spalding had a similar double take in that situation.
LB: It's too bad if some people didn't read those layers of ambiguity, because I thought they were very clearly there.
RS: That's not the level of *Dragnet*. That awareness, that take on the process of how the show was being made is not what *Dragnet* does at all. In fact, Schechner even reinforced that by trying to pull himself away and saying to Spalding, "We are making a television program, we're going to send the tapes to your mother in Rhode Island," which then took you one step back into the game, it gave another reason for the presence of the cameras. So I think there were multi-levels within the tape.
LB: In the acting, and also in the interplay between acting and performing, right?
RS: Yes. What happened was that the non-actors had to try to have the same overview of the situation that the professional actors had, rather than just do a Strassberg number. I think there was a kind of raw interphase there between what's documentary, what's acting, what's performing, what's within the TV context. And I'm very interested in the questions the audience ask themselves when those layers of meaning are presented to them. If that's what they consider entertainment, fine. But if they don't understand the multiplicity of the syntax, then it's so much propaganda.
SECOND TAKE.
LB: How did the idea for *Prisoners' Dilemma* develop?
RS: I made an earlier videotape, *Surprise Attack*, which used a game theory that went: If you hear a burglar downstairs, should you pick up a gun or not pick up a gun. It was taken from Schilling's book *The Strategy of Conflict*. About a year and a half ago Robert Bell and I had talked about the possibility of making a film on a train going to Las Vegas which would deal with game theory. And then when I saw him in New York recently he'd just finished a paper on Deterrents which mentioned this specific prisoners' dilemma. I read the paper, and in my trying to dope out the pros and cons of it, what I would do if I were in that situation, I found that my own thinking fascinated me, so much so that I thought it must have an awful lot to do with the way I think about anything . . . I don't know . . .
LB: I think it certainly does!
RS: But anyway, it fascinated me to the point where I wanted to involve myself in making a tape, so I asked Bell if he would like to do it with me and he said yes. So we decided on the format. I was really interested in doing a cops and robbers tape, and he was interested in doing a quiz program. And what was so nice about the thing for me was that all the people who worked on it were very very generous and warm, and the production as a company was one of the better things I've been involved with in my life. I mean, it was just a lot of fun.□

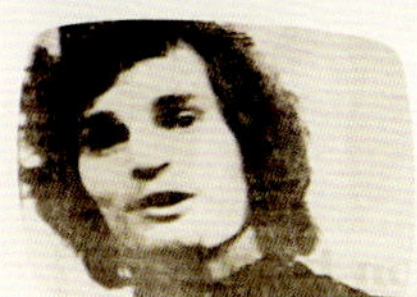

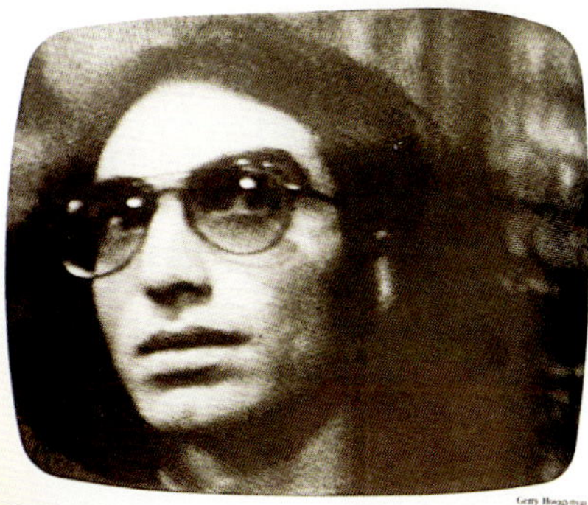

Gerry Hovagymyan

"I'm not in any trouble!"

Schechner: Your record includes armed robbery, attempted rape, and a few drug arrests. You know what the citizens of New York want? They want crime in the streets eliminated! They want goons and beasts and monsters put behind bars!
Hovagymyan: You calling me a goon, man? You telling me, you fat fuck!
Schechner: I'm telling you your ass is in a lot of trouble!
Hovagymyan: I'm not in any trouble.
Schechner: We got the gun, we got the watch, we got you, we got a dead man. We got a few minutes left. You ever heard of plea bargaining? Here's your chance. If you sign the confession which says, "I confess to killing Mr. Angelo Badista on January 20, 1974, and swear that Mr. Spalding Gray did it with me, you'll get off scot free. You going to sign?
Hovagymyan: No, I ain't going to sign nothing.
Schechner: Take him away. Bring the other one back.

An interview with ROBERT BELL

LB: What did you see as your role in *Prisoner's Dilemma?*
RB: Well, this piece was really just a continuation of a lot of work that I've done on that particular problem in game theory since 1965.
LB: Why does that problem appeal to you specially?
RB: Essentially, the prisoner's dilemma is a problem where the theory of games crumbles, where the concept of rational decision making falls apart. Take the version of the game that Castelli and Boice played: if they both chose A, they'd spend four hours together in the basement downstairs. If they both chose B, they'd spend two hours. And if one chose A when the other chose B, the one choosing A would go away free and the other would spend six hours down there. The theory of individual rationality offers two ways of thinking about the problem which arrive at the same conclusion—that the rational choice is for each person to choose A. One way of looking at it claims A is the rational choice because every pay-off associated with A is better than the corresponding pay-off with B. Four hours is better than six and no time is better than two. Looking at it another way, if one person believes the other is going to choose A, he would feel compelled to choose A also to avoid being the fall guy in the game. And once he's made up his mind on these grounds, there's no reason why he would change it. Changing his mind would only increase the punishment. But as we saw with Castelli and Boice, real people may not choose A. They both chose B. And Castelli is one of the theory of games, in this case, is clearly wrong . . .
LB: I'd say there was definitely something deficient about a concept of rationality that presupposed rational decisions are exclusively motivated by immediate self-interest.
RB: The prisoner's dilemma is simply an example of a class of games called non-zero sum games, as opposed to pure conflict games, in which whatever you win, I lose, and vice versa. In the prisoner's dilemma it's possible for both players to win or lose at the same time, or for one to win more than the other loses or vice versa. My contention—which was developed in my PhD thesis—was that the logic behind the prisoner's dilemma problem is a hoax because a key ingredient in the situation had been left out, namely the district attorney, the person who sets the pay-offs.
LB: What's the origin of these games, at least in this form?
RB: The original theory was developed by a Princeton professor, John Von Neumann, who later co-authored the classic book on the subject, *The Theory of Games and Economic Behavior* with Oscar Morgenstern. It was published in 1943. The theory of non-zero sum games is usually associated with John Nash.
LB: You're basically a cyberneticist, aren't you?
RB: Yes, I've made my living as a guest lecturer on it for several years. Game theory is subsumed under cybernetics, which is concerned with goal-directed behavior. But I don't suppose you want a definition of cybernetics?
LB: Well, it wouldn't hurt.
RB: Machines fall apart. Animals rot. They also get confused. To counteract those tendencies all animals and some machines employ principles of self-regulation. The aim of cybernetics is to those principles. For instance, a game

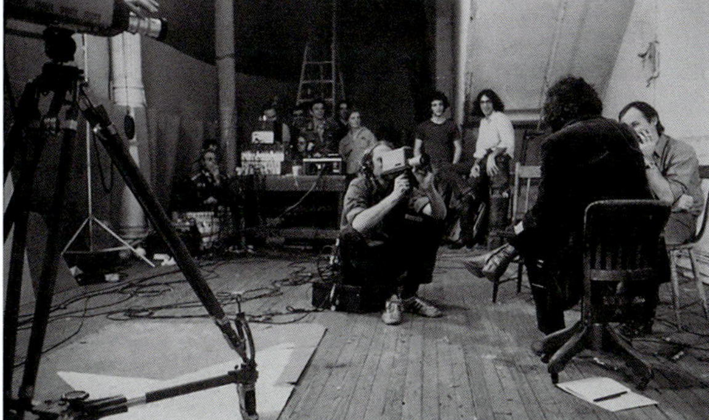

Top: Scan of *Avalanche*, May/June 1974
Above: Robert Bell and Richard Serra, *Prisoner's Dilemma.* Photo: Cosmos Sarchiapone.

> The game is that essentially two people get caught by the police. They're both being questioned individually and told if they rat on their partner, they go free and their partner goes to jail. If both turn on each other, they both go to jail. If neither one of them rats, then they both go free. If one of them rats and the other one doesn't, the one who rats goes free. That was kind of my beginnings of performance and video performance art, which I then picked up again in the 1990s when I started to do digital art performances.[8]

Avalanche published the performance, featuring it on the cover of the May/June 1974 issue, with extensive interviews of Bell and Serra about the piece.

> Liza Bear: Do you think that by having a live TV production in a gallery context you somehow forced people to look at it more seriously?
>
> Richard Serra: I think that television has a psychologically debilitating effect when you're sitting around in your living room. Getting several hundred people jammed together in a confined space where they're being deprived in every way, and the only thing they can do is watch the monitors, is very different. The solidarity of the audience was like a Saturday afternoon matinee, nothing like the casualness of looking at TV in a living room or a bar. I structured the situation so that all the audience could do was watch those four monitors. Hovagimyan helped me a lot with that. We forced the audience away from the set by placing the monitors on the opposite wall, so that their backs were to the cardboard. I feel that in the first half of the evening we had them in the box, I'm pretty sure—take that, B. F. Skinner.[9]

Gordon Matta-Clark, 1975–76

Through his work at 112 Greene Street, Hovagimyan befriended Gordon Matta-Clark and became his assistant in two other seminal artworks of mid-1970s New York City, as well as two other minor projects.

In the meantime, I was working for Gordon Matta-Clark, helping him in terms of doing pieces, and he taught me construction because it was a lot of construction work. I worked on the pier piece which was *Day's End*. I basically hitched a ride with him over to Europe. I bought my own plane ticket and showed up in Paris, and we did the *Conical Intersect*, then we went to Italy and chopped up Salvatore Ala's gallery.[10]

Day's End, 1975

An iconic artwork of the mid-70s New York art world, *Day's End* involved breaking in, changing the door lock, and spending a month cutting through the decommissioned Navy Pier building on the Hudson River, removing the tin siding and cutting a slit through the floor. The result was a crescent that brought an orb of projected sunlight into the pier.

Hovagimyan worked with Matta-Clark, Jene Highstein, and others throughout the process, and attended the small gathering to celebrate its completion on August 27, 1975.

Gordon got this film permit, because he figured he was going to have this public opening with the art scene, I guess it was in August. He didn't want it to get messed up, so he got a film permit from the Mayor's office. So we were in there the day before, because it was like typical, "Oh I have to do a few finishing touches." Gordon was like, "Oh, I could just cut a little bit here or there." We were in there for like two months with chain saws and cutting torches. We were making so much noise, but nobody ever came in. They didn't want to know.

Gordon got a film permit the day before, when we walk in. I bring some tools in, he's looking around, the truck's parked on the side, doors open. I turn around, there's a dock inspector there. "OK. What's going on here?" "Well, we're just looking at this place for a film shoot for tomorrow." And there's a big barricade of beams, right? And the dock inspector goes and looks at it, and he's like, "Holy cow, what's that?" And Gordon says, "I don't know, kind of interesting, we thought we were going to film there." Meanwhile he's

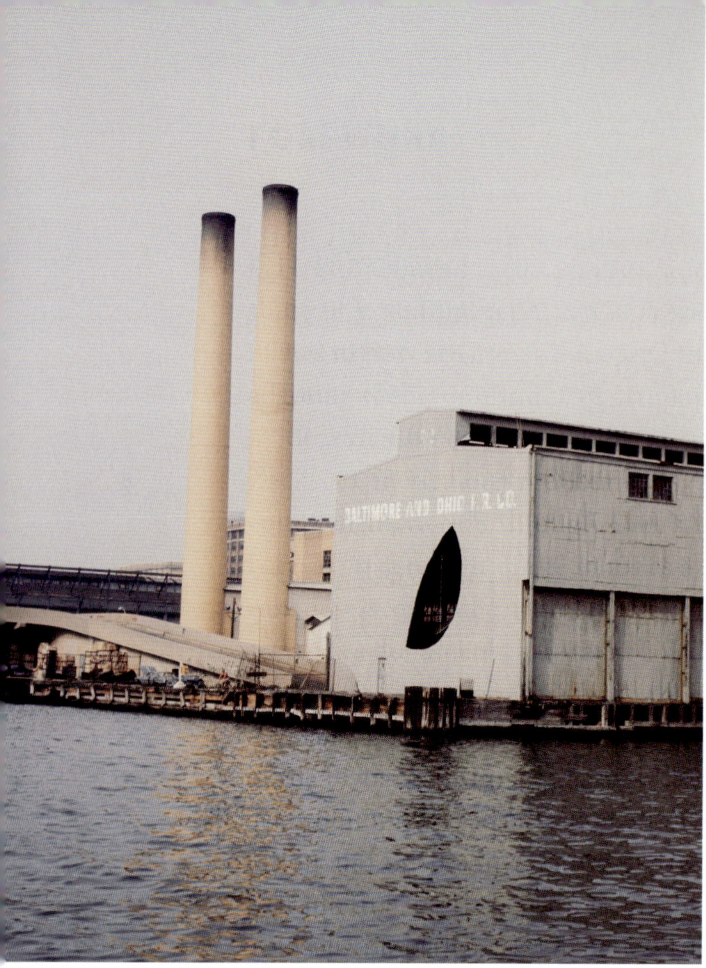

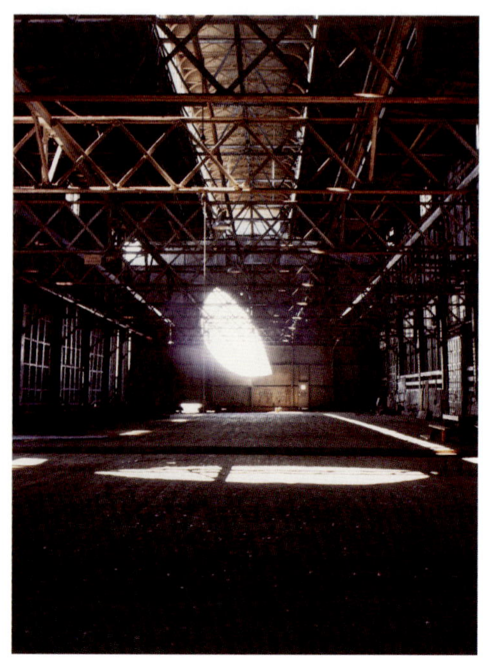

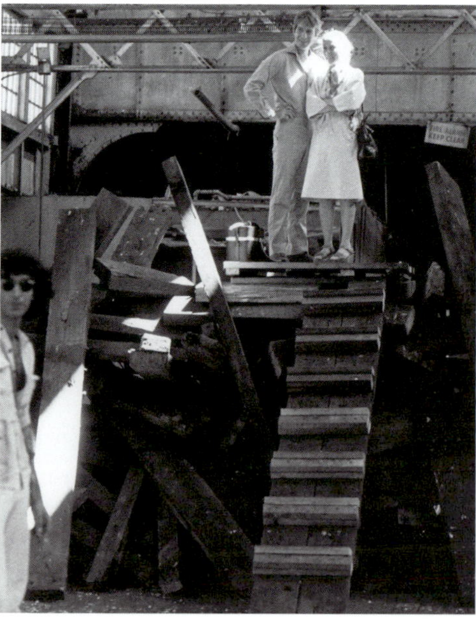

Above: Gordon Matta-Clark, *Day's End* (exterior view) (1975). Photo courtesy of the Estate of Gordon Matta-Clark/Artists Rights Society
Top right: Gordon Matta-Clark, *Day's End* (interior view) (1975). Photo courtesy of the Estate of Gordon Matta-Clark/Artists Rights Society
Right: Holly Solomon posing with William Wegman at *Day's End* opening, with Hovagimyan in the foreground, Aug. 27, 1975. Courtesy of the Estate of Gordon Matta-Clark/Artists Rights Society

like signaling behind his back, "Get the tools out." I'm running and taking and throwing the tools back in the pickup truck. Meanwhile he's grabbed the guy, holds him by his shoulders saying, "You know, this is kind of interesting, don't you think?"

So, the next day, we open up, we put down some picnic tables and food and wine. There was a little bridge across the moat. What happens is, is the whole art scene shows up. And the art scene can fit in like Max's Kansas City, so the whole art scene is not that big. Forty people or whatever. Everybody's talking and hanging out. All the people who worked on the art. The dock inspector comes in, with his boss, with like six policemen who kind of walk in and they say, "OK, who did this?" And the policemen are standing in a line with their hands behind their back. Holly, of course, is looking, and says, "Well, of course, it's Gordon Matta-Clark, the famous artist." He had to cover, and he says, "Look, I just renovated this pier, and now, instead of it being a sad reminder of a bygone era, now people can use it as a park. It's a giant sculpture place, it's my gift to the city."[11]

Conical Intersect, 1975

In 1975, Hovagimyan traveled to Paris with Matta-Clark for three months to work on *Conical Intersect*, cutting out a wide rounded section through the center and side of a 17th century building to be demolished in Beaubourg across from the Centre Pompidou, which was just finishing. His father Roberto Matta had lived in Paris, and Matta-Clark had been specially invited for the Paris Biennale.

We were staying with his step-mother, Millet Matta, so we had a free place to live. Then basically we were just being invited to dinner every night. So it was like, coffee and croissant in the morning, for lunch we had a worker's lunch at a worker's cafe across the street, and then dinners were out. We were basically cutting it. Gordon was trying to finance his trip and try to keep me afloat in some way. I think I made $500 in that trip.

The way Gordon would work, he would try to figure out the social focus of the place. Analyze it. *Conical Intersect* was perfect because it was working class housing. It was being demolished to do this Richard Rogers-designed Pompidou Center. It was in this flux between the old and new Paris. There was a lot of discussion in the press about both sides. "The fascists, this is an insult to our grand France," and the left was saying, "Why is he doing this, this stupid artist, they should just renovate it and give it to the poor people." There was a big debate over that.

The actuality of the piece was that you had to walk through it. You can't sense anything from the photographs. They're just like souvenir postcards. They're nothing compared to the work. The work is just totally visceral...A lot of it is Situationist. That's exactly where Gordon's coming from. You can't put Situationist work into an art gallery, it doesn't make any sense.[12]

Salvatore Ala Gallery and *Arche Du Triomphe for Workers* (unrealized), Milan, 1975

In Milan, during the same trip to Europe, Hovagimyan participated in another project at Matta-Clark's dealer Salvatore Ala's gallery, cutting slices through the walls. Normally he would produce photography and films to correspond with the work and sell them along with the cut-out building pieces.

The other project he pursued in Milan was unrealized and ultimately a failure. He planned to install a "working man's arch" in a closed-down factory being squatted by a group of young Marxists to support them. The presence of the famous artist drew the attention of authorities, and the group was expelled from the factory.

> We were going to do a working man's arch in this kind of Marxist-occupied factory, but the cops got wind of it and chased us out, because there were all these teenagers. They wanted a community center and health care, and some developers wanted to build something, I don't know what—shopping malls, apartments, whatever. That's all documented history. Then we came back to New York. [13]

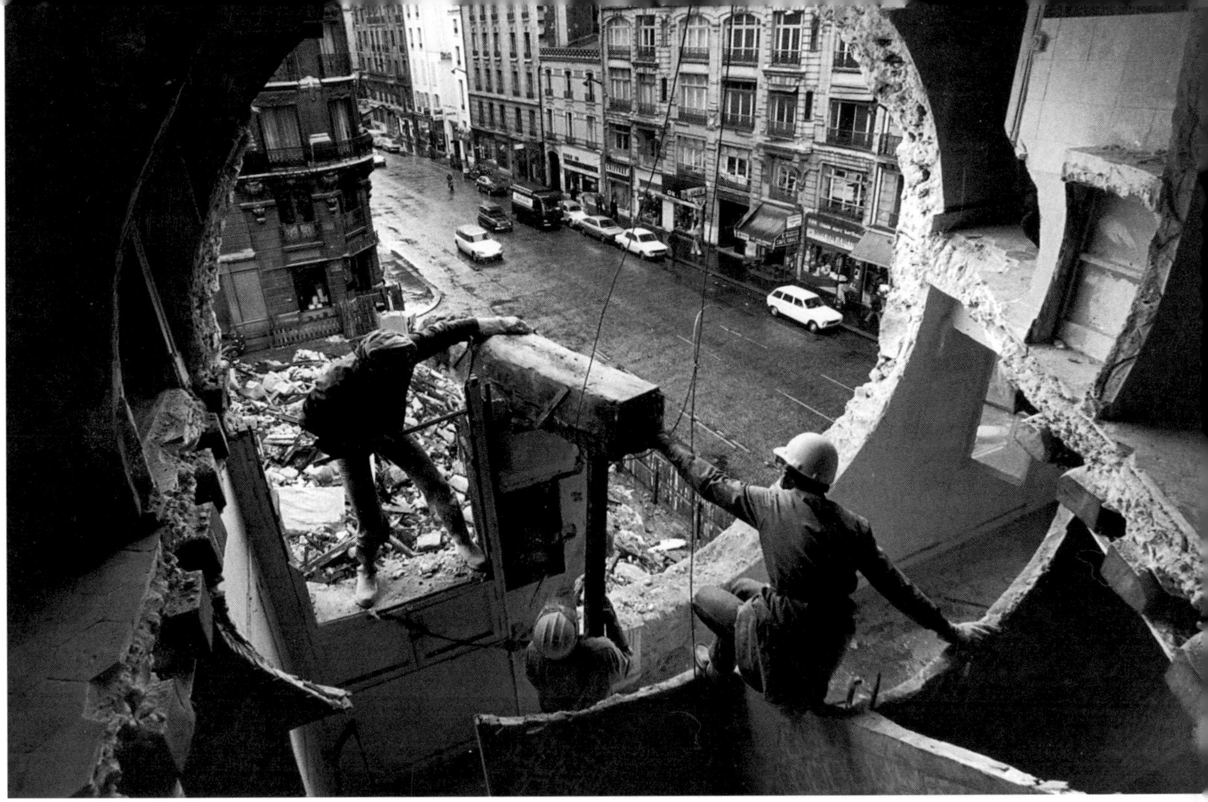

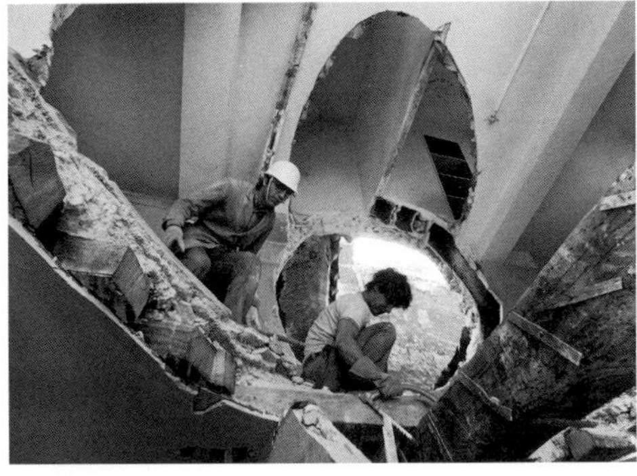

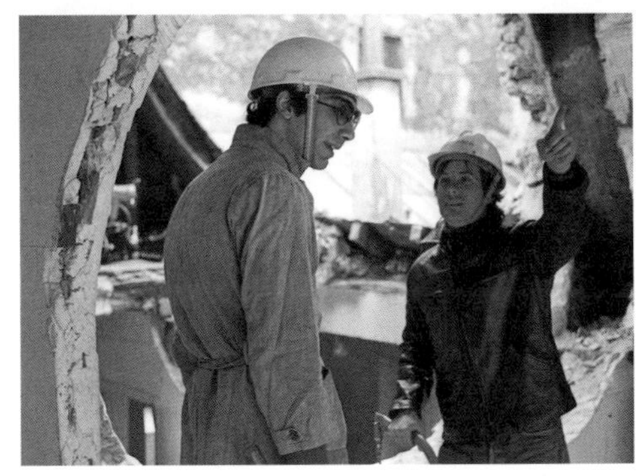

Above: Gordon Matta-Clark, *Conical Intersect,* 1975. Photo: Harry Gruyaert. Courtesy of the Estate of Gordon Matta-Clark/Artists Rights Society
Above right: Gordon Matta-Clark, *Conical Intersect*, 1975. Photo: Harry Gruyaert. Courtesy of the Estate of Gordon Matta-Clark/Artists Rights Society
Right: Gordon Matta-Clark, *Conical Intersect*, 1975. Photo: Harry Gruyaert. Courtesy of the Estate of Gordon Matta-Clark/Artists Rights Society

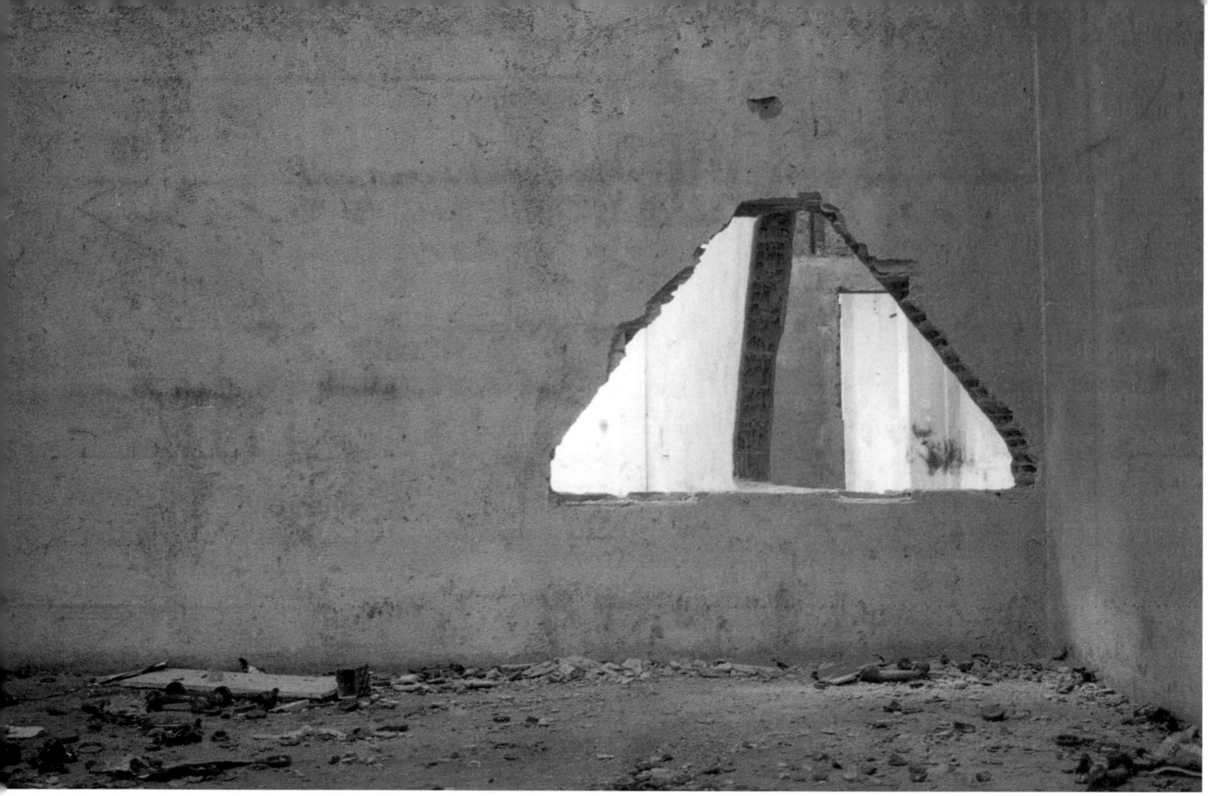

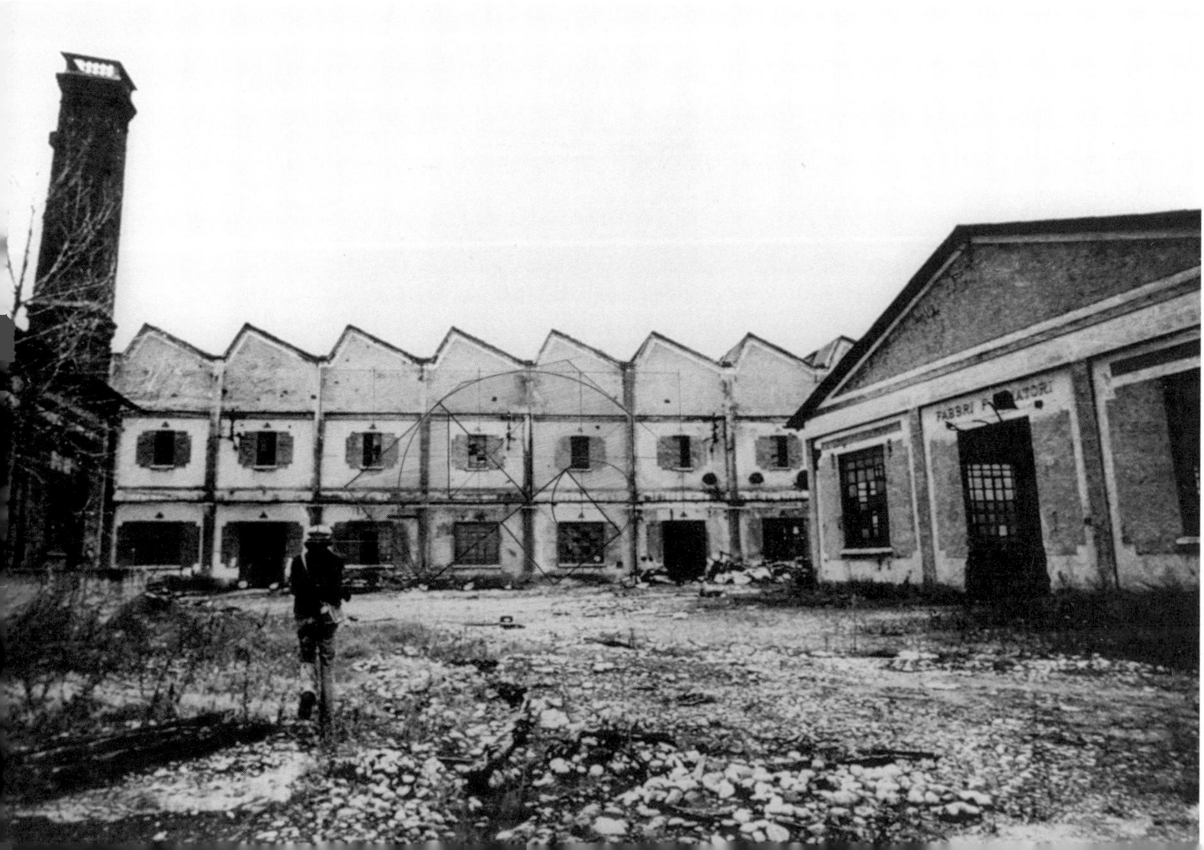

Substrait [Underground Dailies], 1976

Hovagimyan joined Matta-Clark in the filming of underground tunnels in New York City, including the New York Central Railroad tracks, Grand Central Station, 13th Street, and Croton Aqueduct in Highgate. Matta-Clark would die only two years later of pancreatic cancer at the age of 35.

597 Group, 1975

In 1975, Hovagimyan moved into a loft on the top floor of 597 Broadway in SoHo with Scott Billingsley, then a kinetic sculptor with an installation up at the Whitney's downtown space. Billingsley later became known as one-half of the No Wave filmmaking team of Scott and Beth B., in whose films *G Men* and *The Offenders* Hovagimyan would appear.

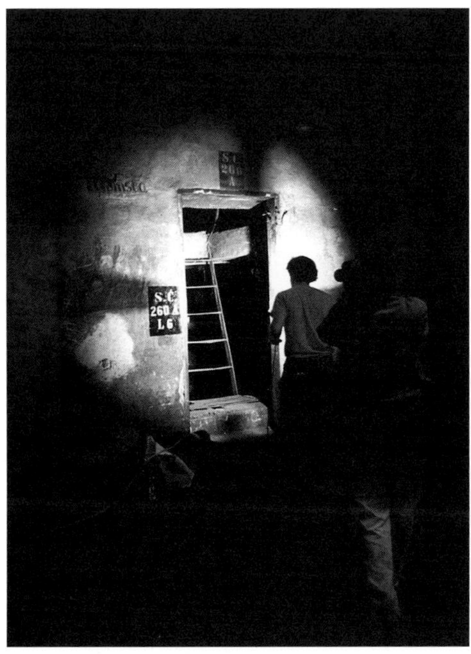

Opposite top: Gordon Matta-Cark, Wall cutting, Salvatore Ala gallery. Photo courtesy of the Estate of Gordon Matta-Clark/Artists Rights Society
Opposite below: Gordon Matta-Cark, Drawing of *Arche Du Triomphe for Workers* on photo. Photo courtesy of the Estate of Gordon Matta-Clark and Artists Rights Society
Right: Hovagimyan filming with Matta-Clark, *Underground Dailies*, still. Photo courtesy of the Estate of Gordon Matta-Clark and Artists Rights Society

> I was roommate with Scott Billingsley who later became Scott B. of the B movies. We had a loft at 597 Broadway. I had a big room: it was the top floor, and I had half the space, so it was like 900 square feet, just a sheetrock box basically, but no window, so I cut a hole in the wall way up by the ceiling. It was one of those pitched roofs slanted above the building next door. I made a window, which was probably illegal because it was a lot line. But I did it: it was one of those things. I had gotten some steel plate from the demolition of a wall, and I built a 16-foot-long ramp that went from zero-to-four feet over 16 feet. It ended where the sunlight streamed down through a right angle in the corner.[14]

They started meeting weekly in their Broadway loft with a group about organizing shows together under the rubric of 597 Group. Billingsley recalled:

> We didn't have any place to show stuff, so it was the same impetus as Colab. What we considered ourselves, the word we used was "disenfranchised"… That was how it felt, all of us. The art scene at the time was almost nonexistent. There was no money at all, so there were no galleries that were showing new artists to speak of. It was a way of generating our own—it was a Do-It-Yourself project, like people in that same era were building their own airplanes or building their own computers from scratch. It had the same Do-It-Yourself ethic, in the same way that punk music and hip hop came out of that era. It's all part of the same genesis really. It was a way for us to have a forum and combine our powers and interests in a way that…for the most part no one was interested in showing the work.[15]

Videotapes and Performances, The Kitchen, February 1975

In February, they organized a series of video screenings and performances at the Kitchen, featuring Billingsley and Hovagimyan along with Dan Graham, Dick Miller, J.B. Cobb, Joost A. Romeo, Julia Heyward, Kirsten Bates, Michael McClard, Susan Ensley, Willoughby Sharp, and Robin Winters. Significantly, the initial group included McClard and Winters, the formative members of Colab in 1977.

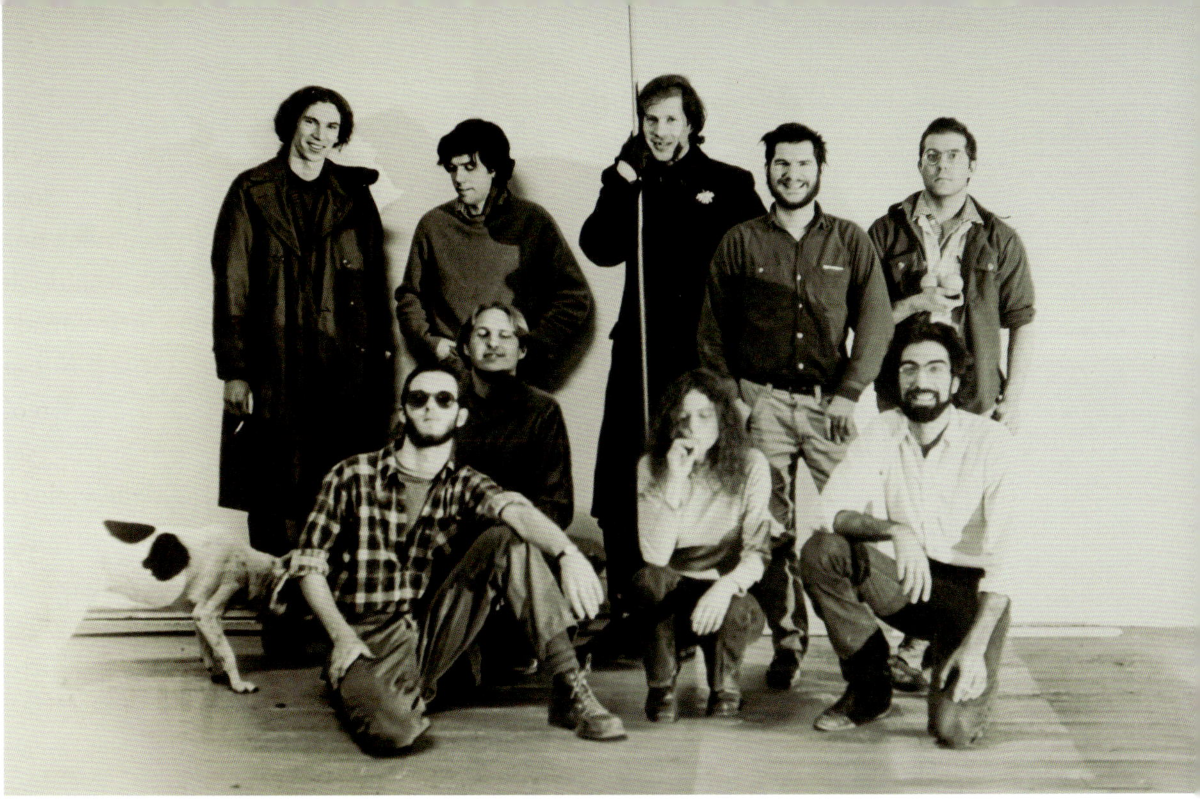

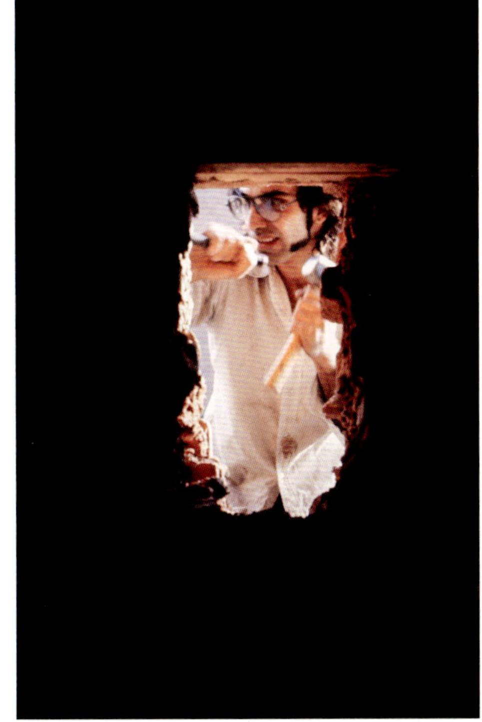

Above: 597 Group. Top, left to right: Alan Moore, Joost Romeo, Willoughby Sharp, Dan Graham, Robin Winters; Bottom: Scott Billingsley, Jim B. Cobb, Lee Lozano, G.H. Hovagimyan. Photo: Scott Billingsley
Right: Hovagimyan cutting a window for his loft at 597 Broadway, 1975. Photo: Scott Billingsley

Loft Show, 597 Broadway, Spring 1975

That spring, 597 hosted a group show featuring work by Hovagimyan and Billingsley, along with Alan Saret, Kirsten Bates, Willoughby Sharp, J.B. Cobb, Scott Johnson, Gianfranco Mantegna, Dick Miller, Stefan Eins, Lee Lozano, Julia Heyward, Dara Birnbaum, Michael McClard, Dan Graham, and Robin Winters.

> I had organized a group of artists, we did a video performance show at the Kitchen for two nights, then we did a physical-objects show at 597 Broadway. These were all younger artists—artists my age in their 20s doing video and performance, including Julia Heyward. That group broke apart and it reformed into Colab a couple of years later.[16]

Lozano, part of the initial organizing group with Billingsley and Hovagimyan, had four years earlier begun a conceptual artwork that involved no longer speaking to women, which ultimately continued for 27 years. Posted in the photo smoking a joint, at the time Lozano was going by the name Lee Fer, rhyming with "reefer," another of her life-as-conceptual-art pieces.

Hovagimyan is quoted in Alan Moore's June 1975 *Artforum* review of the show:

> The gallery structure's become tighter to work in than it had been. 112, Artists Space, and The Clocktower aren't really open to experimentation. In fact, most of the people doing these highlights of younger artists are doing it not for the artists, but to get grants. Most artists in New York are very secluded. They have very little confrontation with other people. That doesn't happen at parties. We were trying to break down this isolation. No more of this crazy garret shit. You can't think you're this individual heroic artist, and you're going to take New York by storm. Instead, you're an artist and you've got to talk to other artists. Otherwise you just fold in on yourself, and that's no good.[17]

Moore also provides a description of Hovagimyan's contribution to the show, a rectilinear shape composed of cardboard, suspended in mid-air by twine,

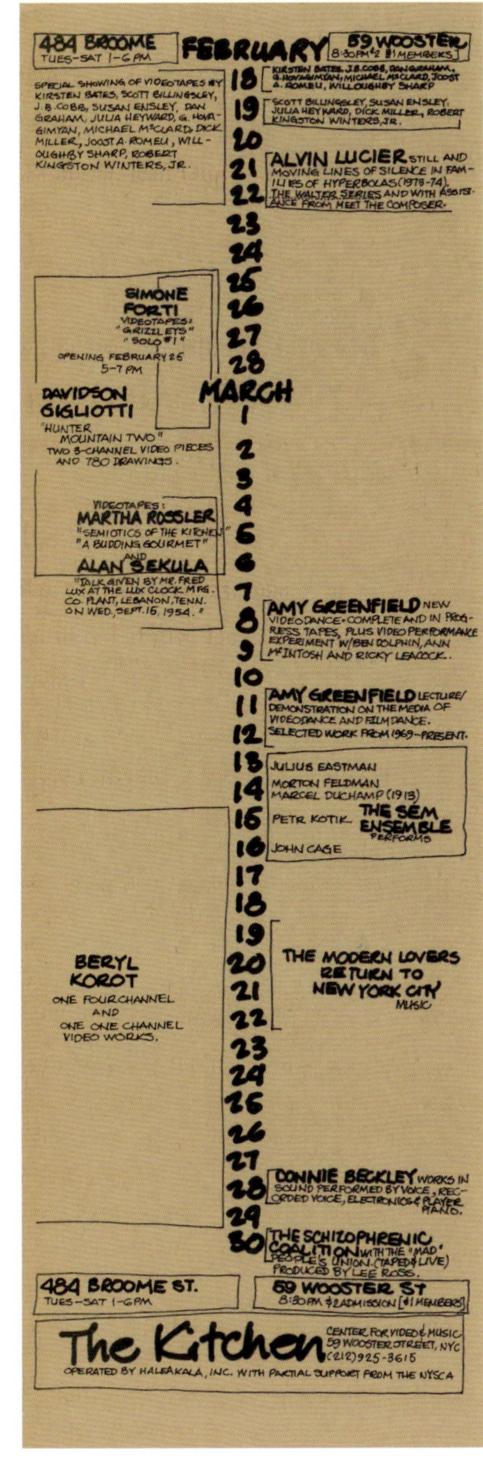

Videotapes and Performances event in the Kitchen's Feb./Mar. 1975 calendar

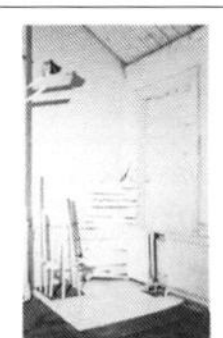

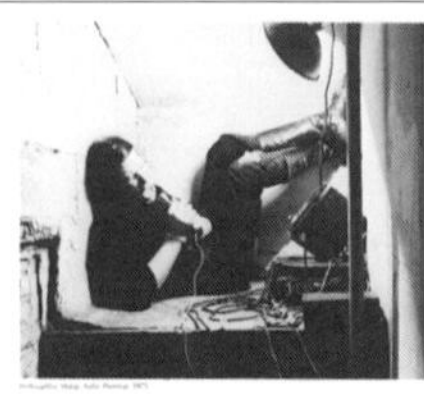

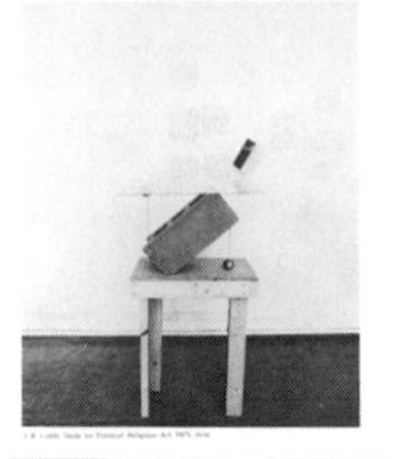

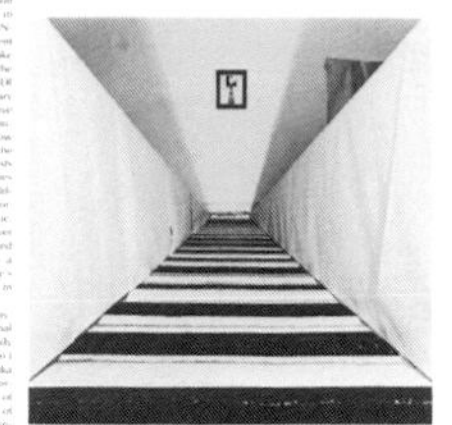

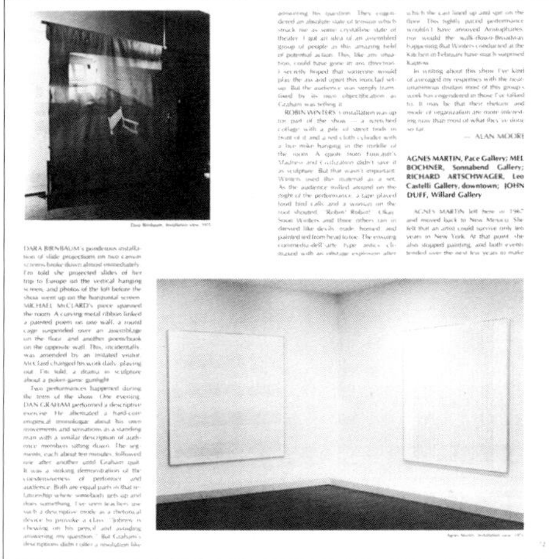

Artforum review, June 1975. Images (clockwise): Paula Longendyke, *White Space #7*; Willoughby Sharp, *False Promesse*; J.B. Cobb, *Study for Political, Religious Art*; Dick Miller, *Broadway Stairwell Piece*; Dara Birnbaum, installation view; Agnes Martin, installation view © 2020 Agnes Martin/Artists Rights Society (ARS), New York with a cardboard model of a pavilion tipped on a shelf above the window. The use of architectural and thought models would be a theme of his early work, reappearing periodically at later stages.

Billingsley sold the loft to the sculptor Jonathan Borofsky around 1976–1977. Billingsley describes their friendship and his work at the time:

> It was a really cool time, and Gerry and I were kind of inseparable for a while. We were really hanging out a lot, besides him living with me there too—even before that…That's how I met his was he was at 112…he was living down at that time by Wall Street in the same building that Charlie Ahearn was in, and Cindy Sherman and Richard Prince. One of my more vivid memories was going down there and seeing the illustrator board sculptures that he was doing: these crystalline transformer-type shape things that he laid out. They were maquette-sized, they were not full-on normal sculpture size, and they were out of cardboard, so they were disposable but beautiful, beautiful stuff… The whole start of Colab was right then.[18]

Colab, 1977–79

A couple of years after the 597 Group shows, Robin Winters and Michael McClard began to organize meetings around a similar set of ideas, expanding from a similar group of colleagues. Many of them were affiliated through the Whitney's Independent Study Program, the San Francisco Art Institute, and the School of the Art Institute of Chicago.

Although many of them had come to the city years earlier, they formed a younger contingent that had not gained a foothold in galleries. A slightly older peer group had already gained recognition.

> All the people were basically my age. We were like the junior generation people. And we all knew, basically, a) there was no place to show, b) all the people who were ten years older than us had gotten just about everything they could get, so we were going to end up just being assistants. A lot of us

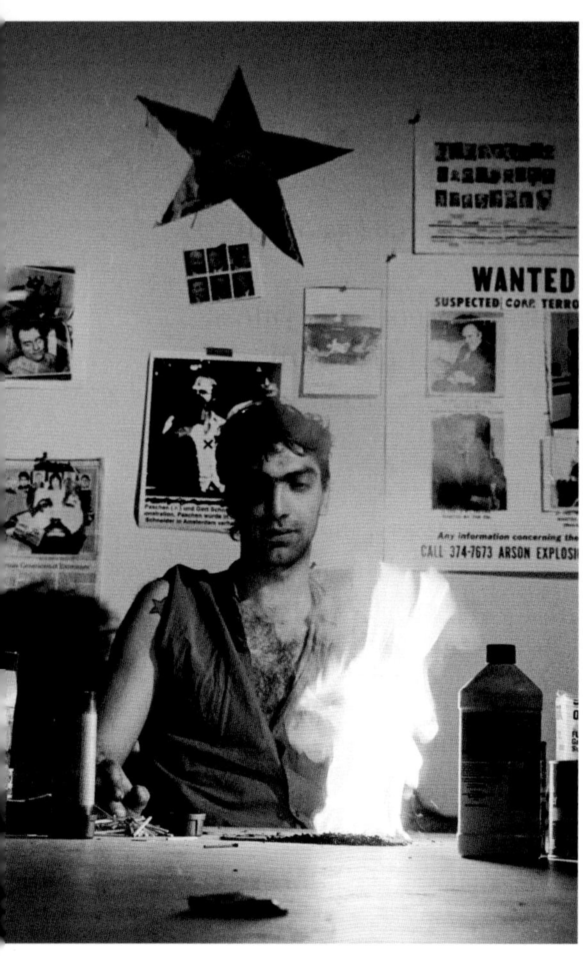

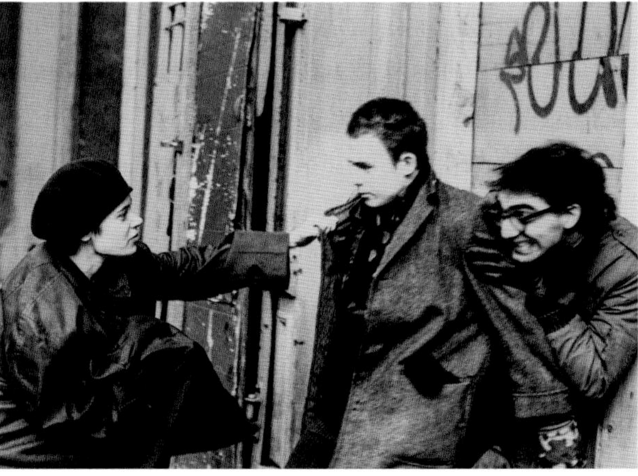

Left: Still from *G-Man*. Copyright Scott B & Beth B
Right: Still from *The Offenders*: Adele Bertei, Robert Cooney, Gerry Hovagimyan. Copyright Scott B & Beth B

started out like that, but we said, "Oh no, no, this is not going to work." You could tell you were being positioned hierarchically.[19]

Hovagimyan would participate in the group's early meetings and display work in its shows, including the 1979 *Manifesto Show* curated by Coleen Fitzgibbon and Jenny Holzer. He also played a small part in *G Men* (1978) and played a role as a terrorist in *The Offenders* (1979), both cult No Wave films directed by Scott and Beth B. At the time, Hovagimyan was a drummer in the punk band the Communists with lead guitarist Bob Mason, who is portrayed in the film being tortured and hung by his wrists by Lydia Lunch, lead singer of Teenage Jesus and the Jerks. Hovagimyan also acted in Charlie Ahearn's first feature film, *The Deadly Art of Survival*, which Ahearn would follow two years later with *Wild Style*, the first narrative feature film depicting the nascent hip hop scene. Colab would later gain renown for its 1980 *Real Estate Show* and *Times Square Show*, establishing the identity of the young punk-and hip hop-affiliated artists. Beth B described *The Offenders* at the time:

The film that I've been collaborating on with Scott B. is about submission and dominance in occupational and private lives. It's going to be a 90-minute feature length film. We've done the first two scenes in which there is a dominance session between a man who is a terrorist investigator and a dominatrix. There is one portion where she has a whip and is standing over him. A woman named Sylvia plays the dominatrix…Bill Rice plays the 46-year-old man. We're now working on the third scene, which has Punk rock and terrorists. The Kommunists [sic] are the Punk rock group…they also play the terrorist in the film.[20]

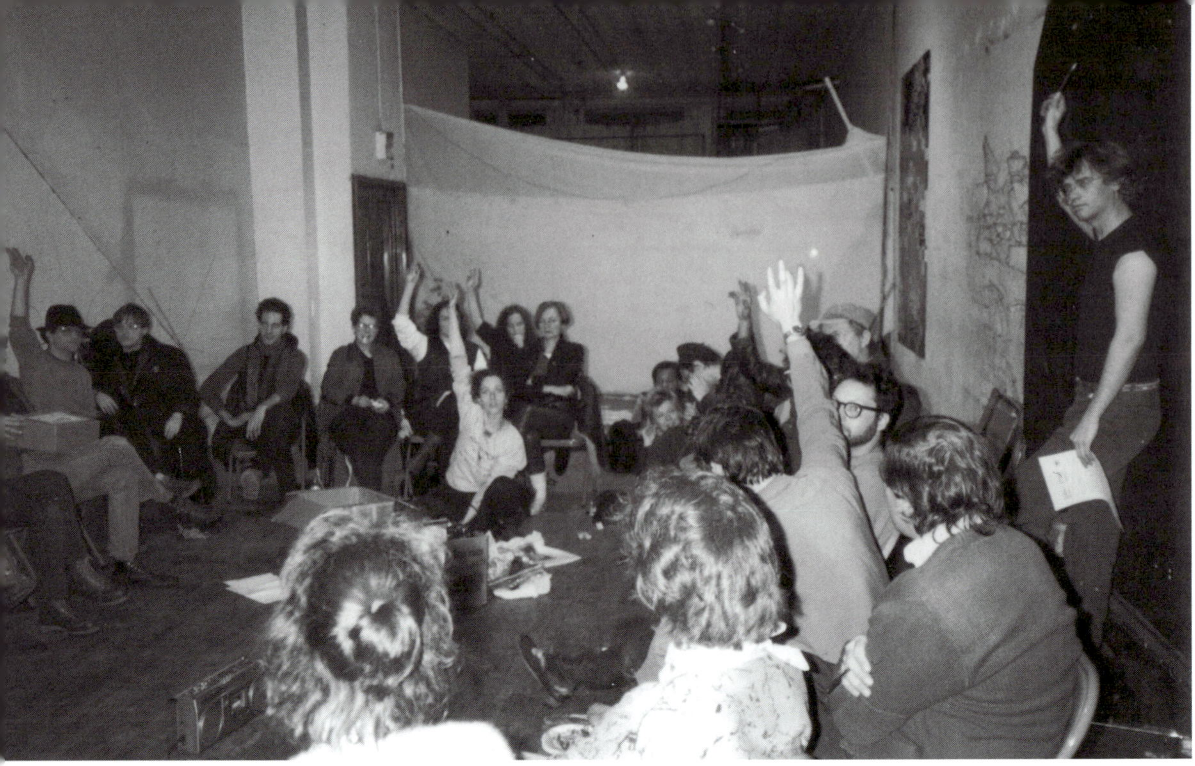

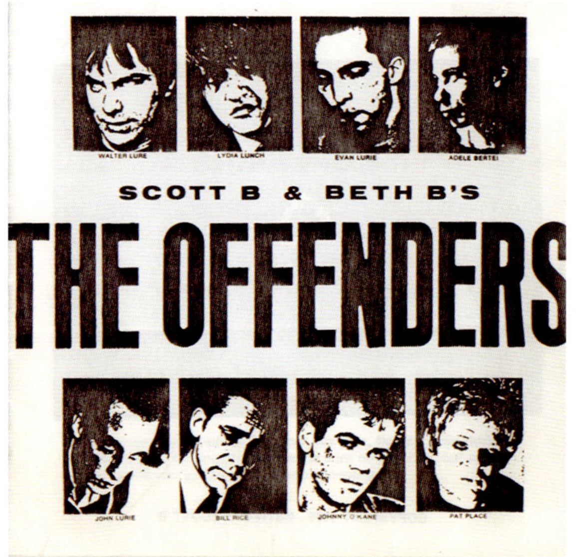

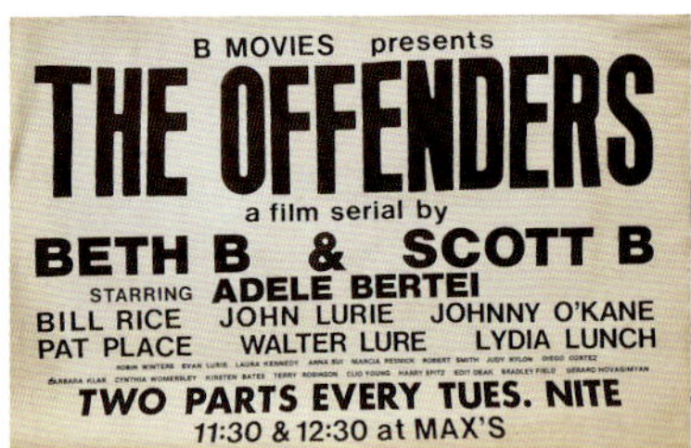

Top: Colab meeting on the second floor of 597 Broadway in Peter Fend's loft, 1983. Photo: Albert DiMartino

Above: Poster and banner ad, Scott and Beth B., *The Offenders*, 1979

Opposite: Colab member list, May 22, 1977. Courtesy of Alan Moore

Katy Kirsten 226-0596

MAY 22 1977

966-625

925 897

an association

Bear, Liza	93 Grand St.	431-6560
Billingsley, Scott	54 Thomas, 10013	962-1365
Burns, Tim	~~235 E. 1st St., 10003~~ 25 Park Pl. 07	[illegible]
Cooney, Robert	~~72 Greene St., 5th Flr.~~	966-3359
Corber, Mitch	10 Stanton St., Apt. 14, 10002	677-7447
Eins, Stefan	3 Mercer St., 10013	226-3169
Ensley, Susan	250 Mulberry St., Apt. 14, 10012	925-0377
Fitzgibbon, Colen	~~5 Bleeck St. (store), 10012~~	~~[illegible]~~
Gilluly, Marcia	133 Chrystie St.	966-7786
Granet, Ilona	281 Mott St., 10002	226-7238
Hanadel, Keith	10 Bleecker St., 10012	3411
Horowitz, Beth	54 Thomas St., 10013	962-1365
Hovagimyan, Gerry	~~[illegible]~~	
Longendyke, Paula	25 Park Pl. 10007	233-7859
McClard, Michael	25 E. 3rd St., 10003	473-2583
Maiwald, Christa	102 Forsyth St., 10002	226-2505
Martin, Katy	307 Mott St. 10003	[illegible]
Mayer, Aline	29 John St., St.	285 1165
Miller, Dick	37 Vestry St., 10013	966-6571
Nares, James	11 Jay St., 10013	226-3719
Ochs, Jackie	591 Broadway, 10012	925-7995
Payne, Lan	102 Forsyth St., 10002	925-1678
Perkins, Gary	14 Harrison St., 10013	925-2291
Slotkin, Teri	37 Vestry St., 10013	966-6571
~~Smith, [illegible]~~	~~38 White St.~~ 10013	966-2974
Sussler, Betsy	246 Mott St. 10002	966-0140
Tillett, Seth	11 Jay St., 10013	~~226-3717~~
Winters, Robin	P.O.B. 751, Canal St. Station. 10013, (73 E. Houston St.)	477-1206
Mass, Steve	at 38 White St.	
DEWYS, MARGARET	54 FRANKLIN ST. 10013	349-8707
John Boroman	15 Jay St, 10013	226 050
Sheri Best	15 Jay St, 10013	2260506
Harry Spitz	~~66 W. Broadway, 10007~~ 732 2587	[illegible]
Julia Harrison	222 Varick St, 10014	691 924
Susan Russell	4 Rivington St, 10002	533-02
Charlie Ahearn	64 Fulton St., 10038	964 24
John Ahearn	150 Franklin St., 10013	925 800
Julius Valiunas	388 BROADWAY, 10013	966-4448
Cara Brownell	168 Mercer St, 10012	966-616
Diego CORTEZ	10 Stanton st 10002	777
Tom Otterness	262 mott st 2554	[illegible]
Gloria Zola	93 Warren St. 10007	962 4870
Valery Taylor	54 Franklin St. 10013	349 8707
Alan Moore	73 E.Houston St. 10012	[illegible]
Cathrine Seopik (Stevenson)	104 W.Broadway	227 7847

431 6 [illegible] 474 Greenwich 4th studio

Leslie Dew

Smith's first name illegible

962 1717

Sheila McClay

PROFESSES ASIATIC REST

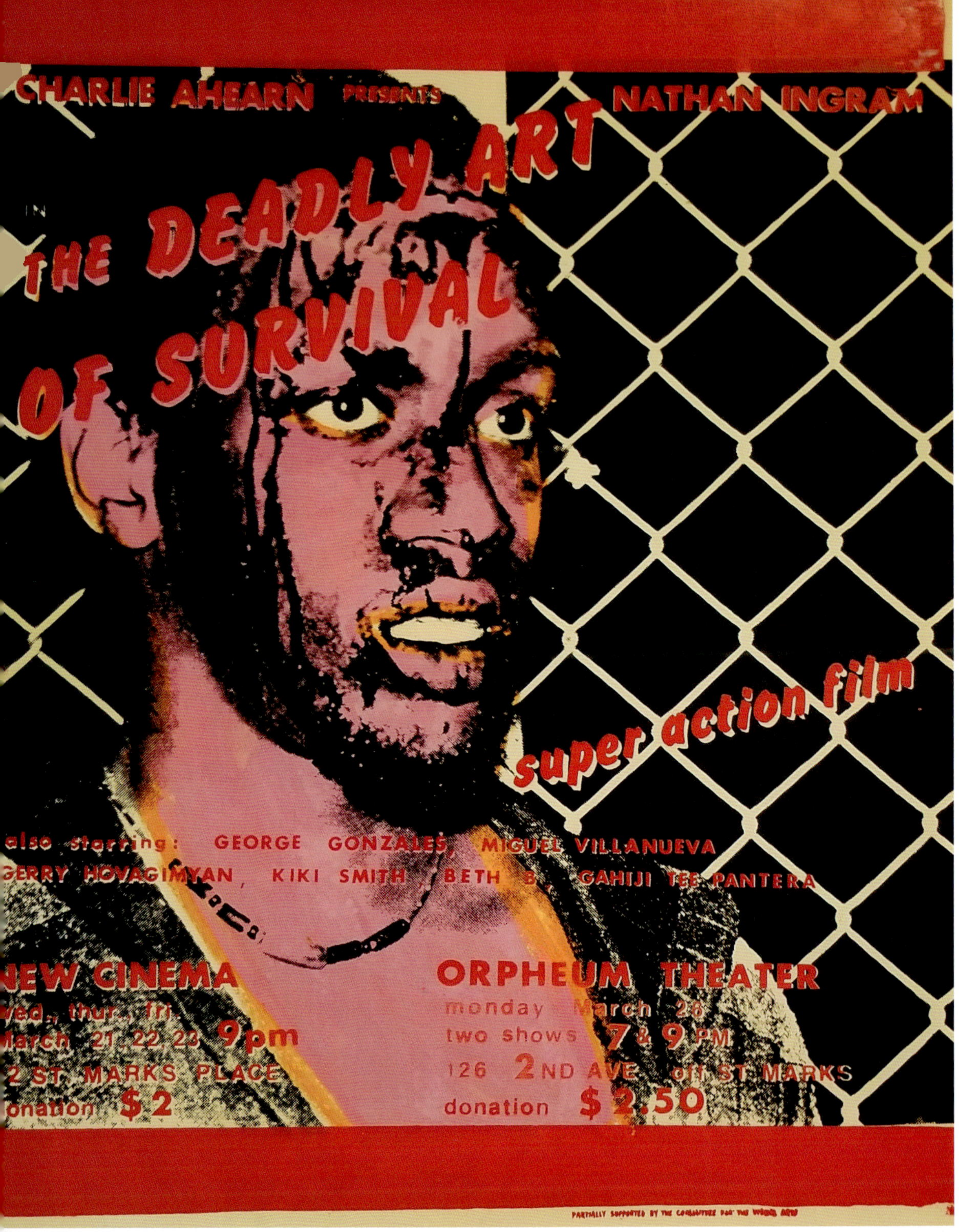
CHARLIE AHEARN PRESENTS NATHAN INGRAM
IN
THE DEADLY ART OF SURVIVAL
super action film
also starring: GEORGE GONZALES, MIGUEL VILLANUEVA
ERRY HOVAGIMYAN, KIKI SMITH, BETH B., GAHIJI TEE PANTERA
EW CINEMA
ed., thur., fri.
arch 21, 22, 23 9pm
2 ST MARKS PLACE
onation $2
ORPHEUM THEATER
monday March 26
two shows 7 & 9 PM
126 2ND AVE off ST MARKS
donation $2.50

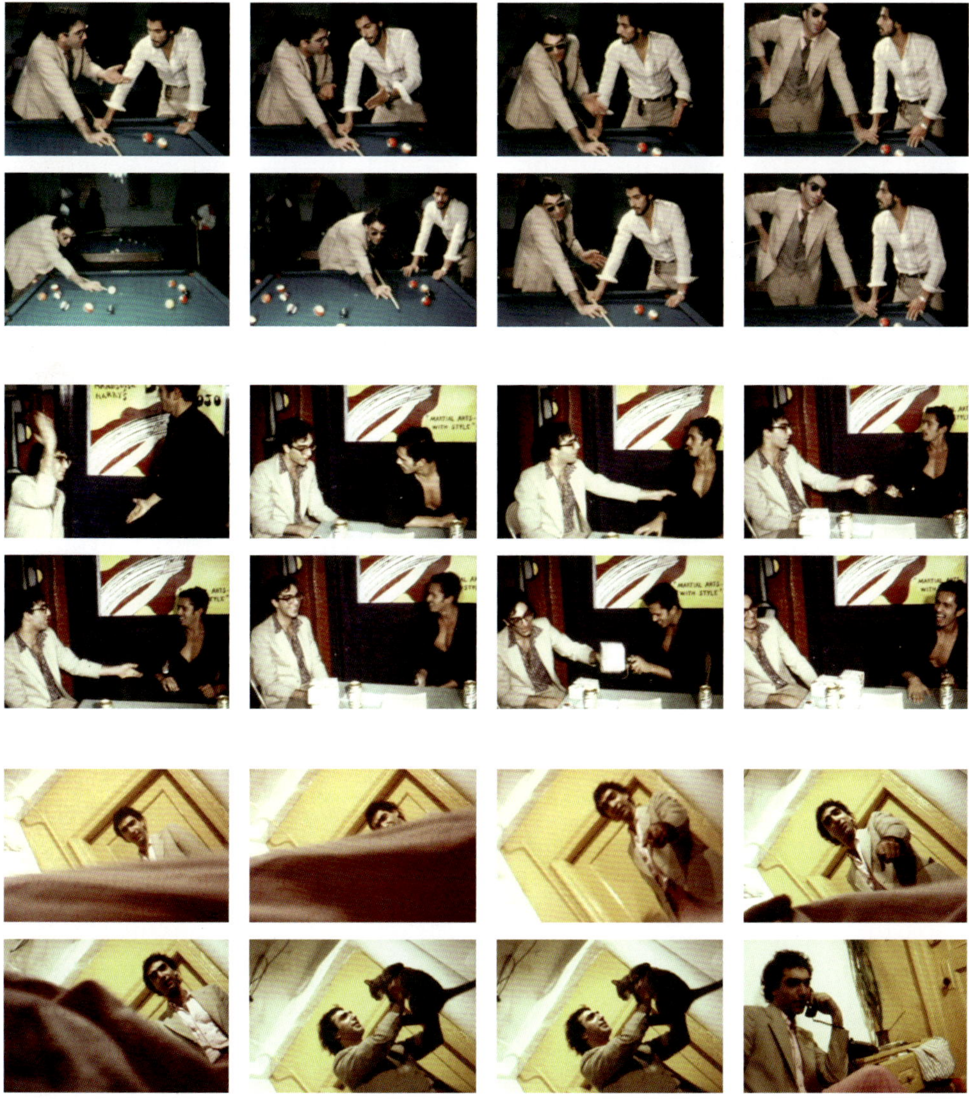

Opposite: Charlie Ahearn, *The Deadly Art of Survival*, 1976 28×23 hand painted silkscreen
Above: Stills from *The Deadly Art of Survival* (Super 8, 75 min., 1978, directed by Charlie Ahearn). Hovagimyan plays the coke dealer of a karate instructor who is pushing drugs to his dojo. His final scene has him coming home to someone fooling around in his bed. The payoff reveals it to be his cat.

The Communists, punk/No Wave band, 1977–1978

Like many artists in the late 1970s and early 1980s, Hovagimyan played in a band as an extension of his artistic work—and, for that matter, better-paid construction labor in the live/work loft trade. Fluxus was immersed in crossovers between minimalist composition and scripted performance, Walter de Maria had played drums with Lou Reed in the Primitives before his conceptual art turn, and Alan Vega was a well-known light sculptor before starting punk/electronic noise band Suicide with Martin Rev. For the Colab generation, punk and No Wave became a primary affiliation, with Diego Cortez ensconcing himself as manager of James Chance and the Contortions, and later a promoter of the Mudd Club and curator of P.S. 1's 1980 *New York/No Wave* exhibition.

The Communists featured poet Iolsta Hatt (Lenny Ducati) as lead singer, Bob Mason—rumored to be in an abusive relationship with Hatt—on lead guitar, and Lou Valentine Ferreiro on bass, with Hovagimyan on drums. They rehearsed on the fourth floor of 474 Greenwich Street in Tribeca—the same building where Richard Hell and the Voidoids, Rhys Chatham, and the Black-and-German punk band the New York Niggers practiced.[21] That year, the Communists played at Max's Kansas City, CBGB, 57 Club, and Artists Space, which had moved from Wooster Street to a Beaux-Arts office tower in TriBeCa known as the Fine Arts Building, which also housed the first Printed Matter bookstore and the first office for Marcia Tucker as she was founding the New Museum. The Communists also played several loft parties at 474 Greenwich organized by the New York Niggers, composed of singer Elliot Harris (aka Aid Hadid), guitarist Leo Faison, and German expat Dieter Runge.

> I was asked by Bob Mason, who was acting in The Offenders and was living in same building as me to join his band the Communists because they needed a drummer. I said, "I don't know how to drum." He said, "Don't worry, I'll teach you in two weeks." So I got my brother's drum set and started drumming. We played at CBGBs, we played at Max's, we played at the battle of the bands at Artists Space, which was the No Wave bands—Teenage Jesus & the Jerks, the Contortions, Mars, and the Communists.[22]

Dieter Runge recalled an especially memorable Communists song, "Let's Blow Up SoHo," an over-the-top fantasy conceived to arouse enthusiasm and offense, premised on committing terrorist acts against bohemians, snobs, and fashionistas on the streets of SoHo.[23]

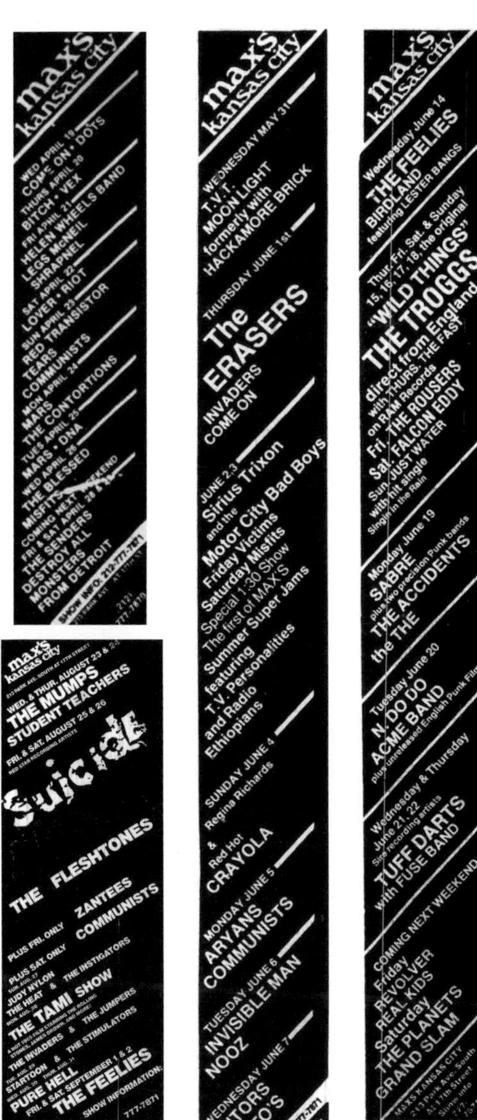

Max's Kansas City banner ads from the *Village Voice*

Let's not wait for a better reason
since every day is tourist season
Let's blow up SoHo
and every fool
Let's blow up SoHo
let's be cool

I'm sick of bohemians
infesting the street
I want to make my city neat
I want some action and I want it now
I'd rather be dead than culture fed
rather unkind than fashionably blind
rather a snake than a fucking fake
Let's blow up SoHo
and watch it shake
Let's blow up SoHo
Get those well-kept bastards awake

Let's get off a bombing high
all those snobs are gonna die
smash those Warhol glasses
burn those fag boots
I gotta kill Vogue models
and polish Prince Street suits
Let's not wait for a better reason
since every day is tourist season
Let's blow up SoHo.

The Communists appear in punk histories most frequently in reference to their May 1978 show at Artists Space, in what was promoted as a battle of the bands—featuring many of the best-known No Wave acts. Robert Christgau picked it as a "Choice" in the May 8th issue of the *Village Voice*, which he might have later regretted.

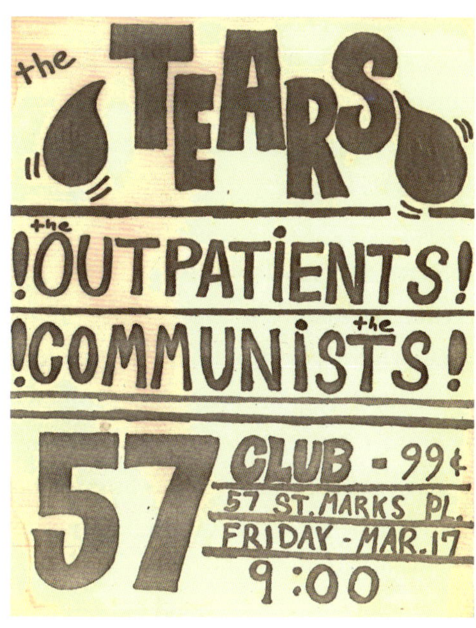

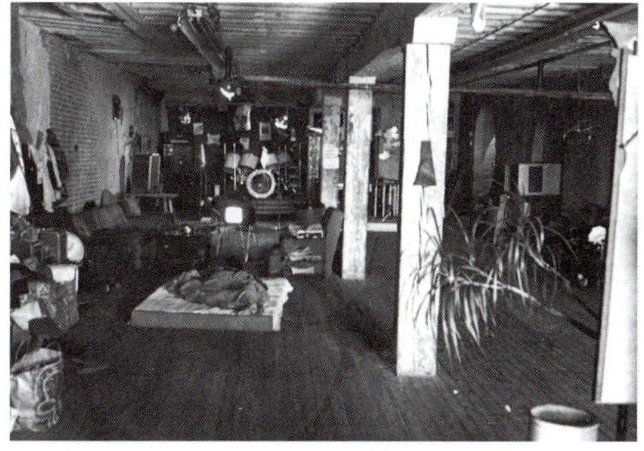

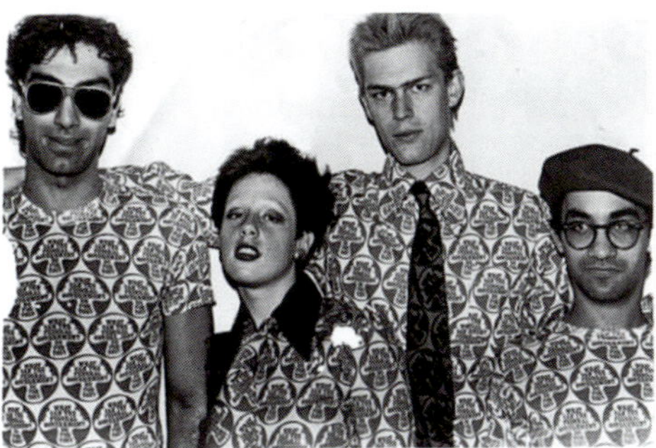

Top left: The Communists flyer at 57 Club
Top right: 747 Greenwich Street, courtesy of Dieter Runge. Photo: Matthus Simons
Above: The Communists band photo

Showcasing some of the horde of third-generation New York bands to have surfaced recently. Schedule: Terminal and the Communists May 2 (before this issue goes on sale); Theoretical Girls and the Gynecologists May 3; Daily Life and Tone Death May 4; DNA and the Contortions May 5; Mars and Teenage Jesus and the Jerks May 6. Except for the May 6 groups (both of whom have struck me as arty and empty), I like all the bands I've seen enough to catch them again, and the word-of-mouth on the others is intriguing. Those who seek finished music should stay away; otherwise, check it out.[24]

James Chance famously cemented his notoriety by getting into a fistfight with Christgau during the Contortions set by insulting Christgau's wife, according to photographer Julia Gorton.[25] Thurston Moore and Byron Coley describe the event in *No Wave: Post-Punk. Underground. New York.*

> Over the course of five nights at Artists Space during May 1978, Terminal, the Communists, Theoretical Girls, the Gynecologists, Tone Death, Daily Life, DNA, the Contortions, Mars, and Teenage Jesus performed to an audience primarily made up of downtown artists. This photograph was taken moments before the legendary tussle between the Contortions' James Chance and *Village Voice* music editor Robert Christgau at Artists Space's 105 Hudson Street location. Soundman Perry Brandston is in a white shirt just behind Chance. His partner Dan Stanger is in glasses to the right of the frame. Though James had created an already legendary stir at the × magazine benefit, his dustup with Christgau represented something new in the dynamic between artist and critic. Overnight the Contortions became one of the hottest tickets in town.[26]

In a blog documenting the Fine Arts Building's history, Megan Govin provided a gloss of the scene:

> Beyond hosting intellectually rigorous exhibitions with lasting historical significance. Artists Space consistently broke the mold with performance, film, video, and audio art exhibitions while in the Fine Arts Building, as well as dipping their toe into hosting punk/New Wave shows typically found at seedy dives like CBGBs on the Bowery or at the Kitchen—a nonprofit space for video, performance and experimental music. In May of 1978, ten New Wave bands performed during a week-long festival in the Fine Arts Building. Bands included James Chance and the Contortions, Daily Life, DNA, the Gynecologists, Mars, Teenage Jesus and the Jerks, Terminal, The Communists, Theoretical Girls and Tone Death. It was remarked that the "weighty aesthetic issues" typically tackled at Artists Space, "almost overshadowed the urge to boogie," but not quite. Experimental musician Brian Eno is said to have "looked on from the front" during the Contortions, while Chance "put on an incredible display of punk rock outrageousness, plunging into the audience repeatedly, picking fights

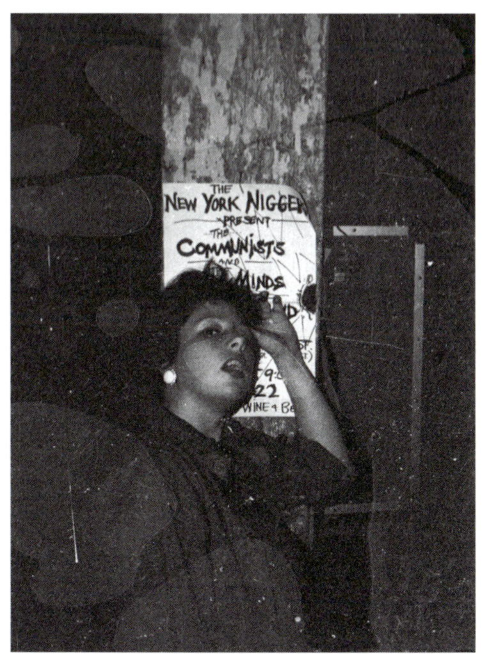

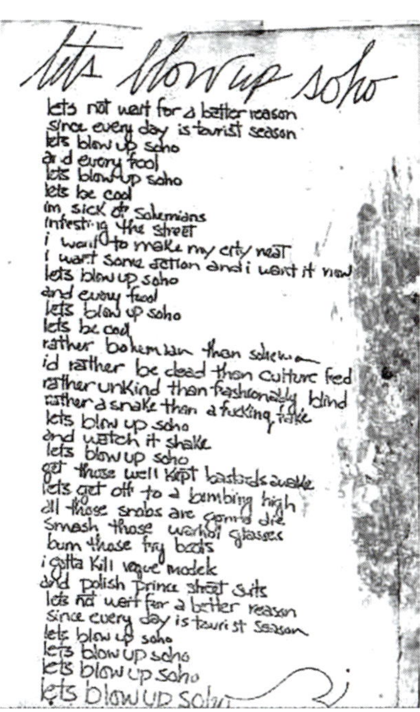

lets blow up soho

lets not wait for a better reason
since every day is tourist season
lets blow up soho
and every fool
lets blow up soho
lets be cool
im sick of sohemians
infesting the street
i want to make my city neat
i want some action and i want it now
lets blow up soho
and every fool
lets blow up soho
lets be cool
rather bohemian than sohemian
id rather be dead than culture fed
rather unkind than fashionably blind
rather a snake than a fucking fake
lets blow up soho
and watch it shake
lets blow up soho
get those well kept bastards awake
lets get off to a bombing high
all those snobs are gonna die
smash those warhol glasses
burn those fry boots
i gotta kill vogue models
and polish prince street suits
lets not wait for a better reason
since every day is tourist season
lets blow up soho
lets blow up soho
lets blow up soho
lets blow up soho

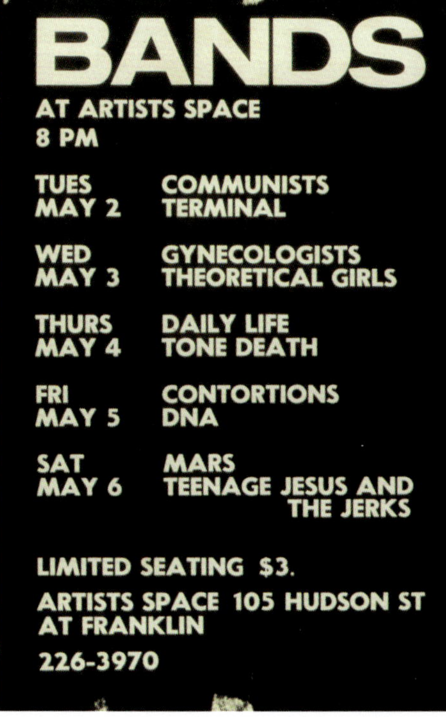

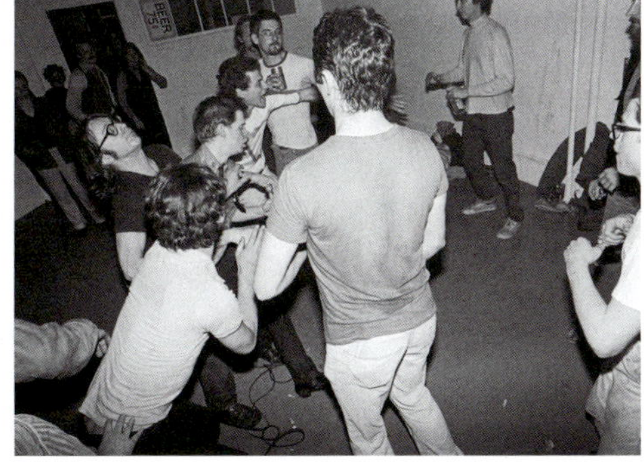

Top left: Iolsta Hatt, courtesy of Dieter Runge. Photo: Matthus Simons

Top: "Let's Blow Up SoHo" handwritten lyrics from Lou Valentine's MySpace page

Left: Artists Space flyer

Above: Chance and Christgau fight at No Wave show. Photo: Julia Gorton along the way" and Lydia Lunch of Teenage Jesus and the Jerks "left the field in shambles with a set of gem-hard brilliance." The *Soho Weekly News* stated the obvious in pointing out that the bands' "avant-garde aspirations limit their audience and make it impossible for them even to consider playing a place like the Palladium," but that was the intention. Their indifference to the mainstream and their dedication to experimentation is what found them to be right at home in the Fine Arts Building.[27]

Mason and Hatt broke up later in 1978, and the Communists disbanded.

Recordings (Possible)

Club 57	Apr., 7, 1978
Artists Space	May 2, 1978

Shows (Incomplete)

Club 57	Apr. 7, 1978
Max's Kansas City	Apr. 23, 1978
Artists Space	May 2, 1978
Max's Kansas City	Jun. 5, 1978
CBGB	Jun. 18, 1978
Max's Kansas City	Jul. 17, 1978
Max's Kansas City	Aug. 26, 1978[28]

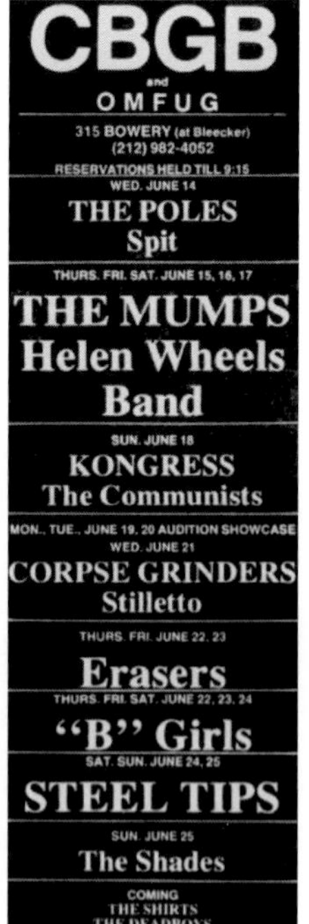

Right: CBGB ad from the *Village Voice*

Virtual Garrison Gallery, 19 2nd Avenue at 1st Street, 1984–1985

In 1980, Hovagimyan married painter Fredda Mekul and moved to the East Village, where the young energy was gravitating in the early 80s. Apart from construction work and appearing in Les Levine's *Deep Gossip,* in which Levine interviewed various denizens of SoHo talking about relationships, with the video showing only their mouths, Hovagimyan's main pastime was running art galleries. From in 1980 until 1983, Hovagimyan worked as director of Manhattan Art at 81 Greene Street, run by Lori Ellen Goodman and Annie Plumb. By 1984, he had opened his own space in the booming East Village gallery scene.

> I got married and moved to the East Village. It was the time when the East Village was beginning to get up a punk scene and an art scene. A lot of times what people were doing was, there was no place to do performance art, so they were performing at the rock venues like the Mudd Club and CBGBS between acts, and there was another place which is this punk club called 8BC. So I was involved in all that, and I was in a punk band, and I opened an art gallery at the same time everybody else opened art galleries in the East Village. Mine was called Virtual Garrison.[29]

Co-founded in 1984 with Bruce Rayvid at 19 Second Avenue at 1st Street, Virtual Garrison figured among the recognized artist-run galleries that eventually numbered in the hundreds in the East Village.

> Everybody had a gallery, and everybody was essentially showing their friends. But the other issue was that you could use the market like a conceptual artwork. Because since there was such a heavy recession, nobody had any money. Then at a certain point, it was like, "You know what, fuck it, do you think it makes any difference to be serious? Don't be serious. Mix styles. Put surrealism with pop art; it doesn't make any difference. Market, so what." We were doing these things like putting paintings up, $500 apiece, little holes in the wall, who cares? It was a joke more than anything else. "Fine, you have an art gallery? I can open an art gallery. What difference does it make? You want a one-person

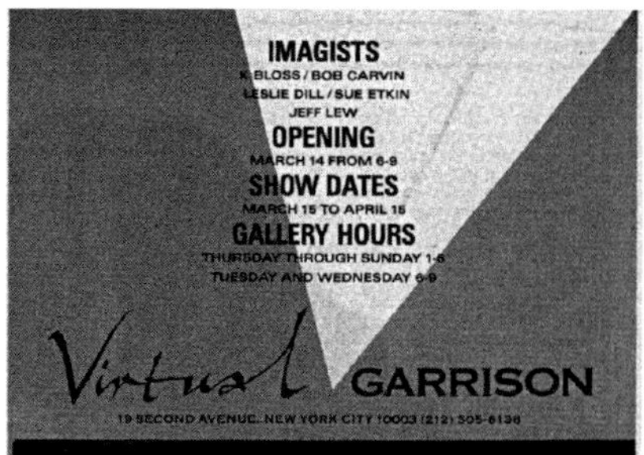

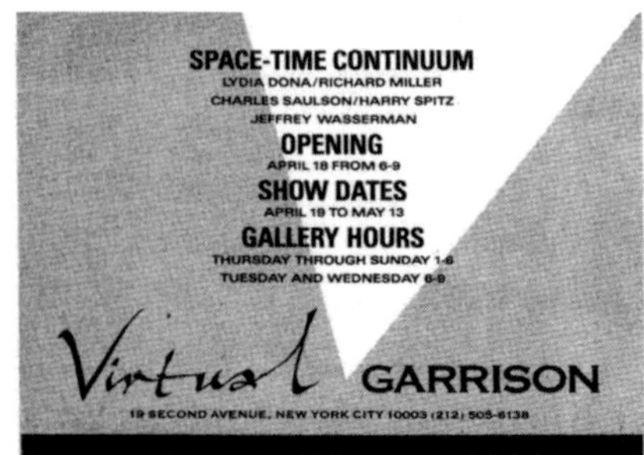

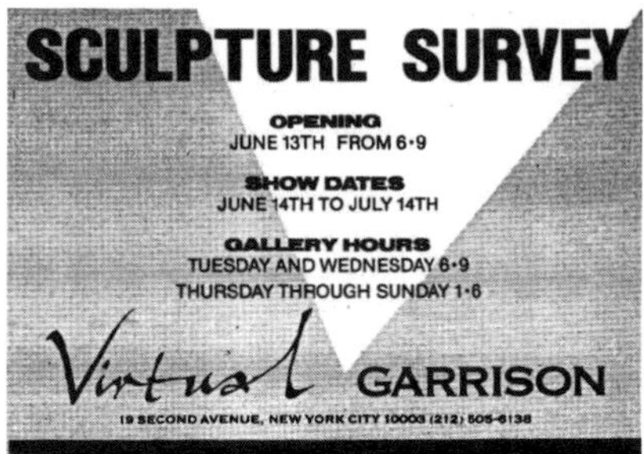

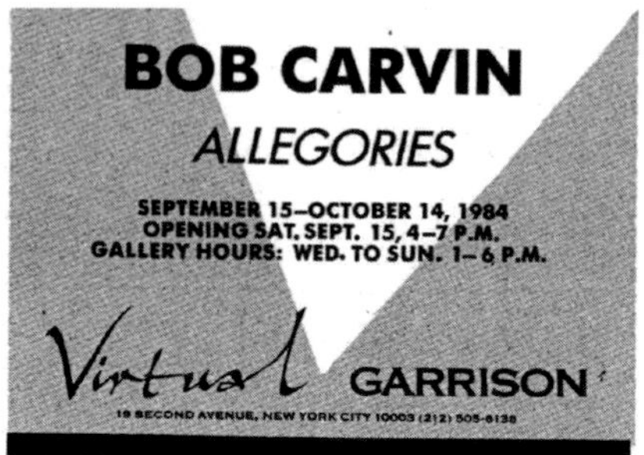

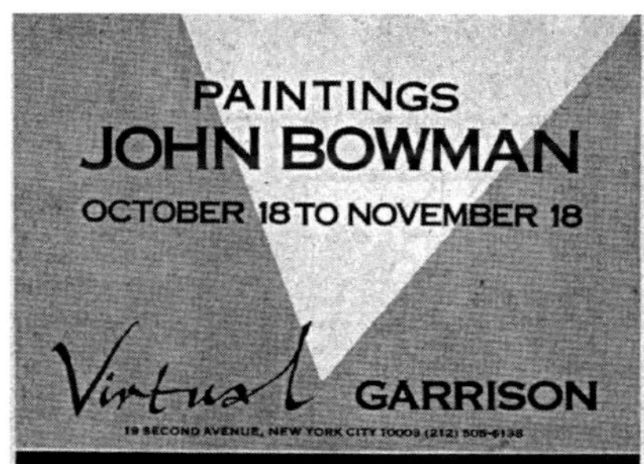

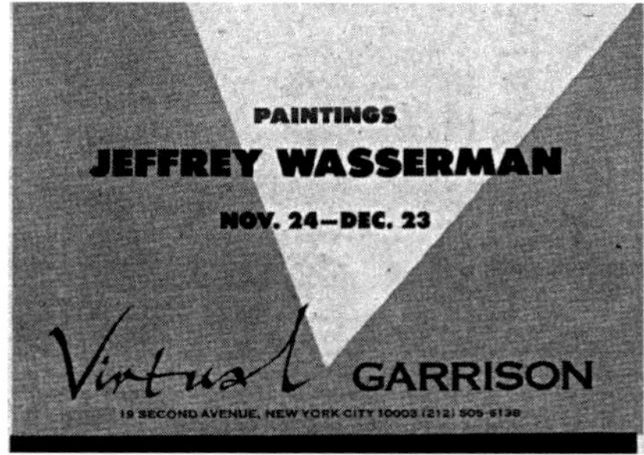

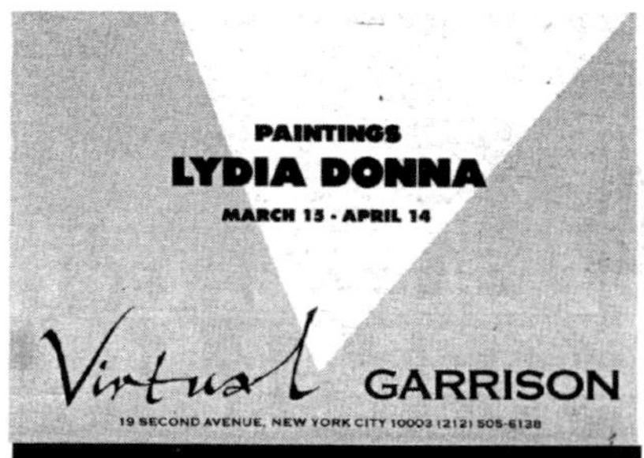

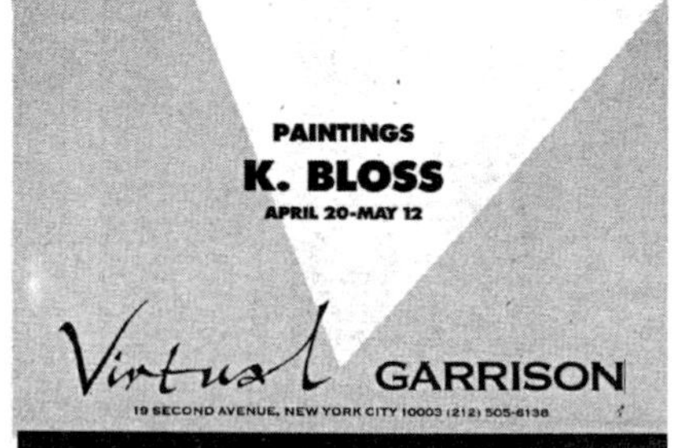

Top to bottom, above, left to right:
Mar. 1984 ad, *East Village Eye;*
Apr. 1984 ad, *East Village Eye;*
Jun. 1984 ad, *Eye Village Eye;*
Sep. 1984 ad, *East Village Eye;*
Oct. 1984 ad, *East Village Eye;*
Nov. 1984 ad, *East Village Eye;*
Mar. 1995 ad, *East Village Eye;*
Apr. 1985 ad, *East Village Eye*

> show? No problem. Everybody can have a one-person show." My rent there was like $75 a month for an 800-square-foot storefront in the East Village.[30]

Some of the more famous venues included Fun Gallery, Gracie Mansion, Civilian Warfare, Mo David, M-13, Piezo Electric, P.P.O.W., International With Monument, Nature Morte, 51X, Pat Hearn, and East 7th Street.[31] Among the artists shown by Virtual Garrison were K. Bloss (Rayvid's wife Kathryn Bloss), John Bowman, Saint Clair Cemin, Lesley Dill, Lydia Dona, Willy Heeks, Robin Hill, Holly Hughes, Jeff Lew, Roger Loft, Fredda Mekul, Charlie Saulson, Randall Schmit, Timothy J. Segar, Ann Shostrom, Richard Thatcher, Jeffrey Wasserman, and Susanne Wibroe-Fost.

Many of their names are recorded in the regular monthly ads placed in the *East Village Eye*, which became the standard tabloid of the scene starting in May 1979, with Carlo McCormick and Walter Robinson penning most of the reviews. McCormick wrote in 1984:

> Last year's theory about the East Village was that it was a bush league SoHo, a post-art-school testing ground. The best artists would be skimmed off the top by the "real" art world as they become ready. But in fact, the opposite is closer to the truth. Not only have artists stayed with their original East Village galleries, but the new vogue (a word I use for its trendy implications) has been for established artists to show here.[32]

When the *East Village Eye* failed to mention Virtual Garrison's shows, Hovagimyan wrote to the tabloid demanding coverage or he would pull its advertising. Robinson, a painter and co-founder of the sceney SoHo publication *Art-Rite*, complied in a typically cheeky fashion. He led off the July 1984 review, "Lumps of All Kinds," with a description of the incident.

Under the nom de plume Walter Winshield, he wrote, "Gerry Hovagimyan, who I know from when I used to live in TriBeCa (a place near New Jersey), wrote my boss demanding 'the acknowledgment of my gallery's existence' lest he be forced to 'put my advertising money elsewhere.' This was all it took. I had been meaning to get around to him (like everybody else), but the temptation to respond to a threat like that was too much to resist!"[33]

Robinson proceeded to poke fun at his machismo. "The East Village isn't just sequins and wimp painters," Gerry Hovagimyan says, "it's also the home of the new macho metalworkers." Mentioned more affirmatively in the sculpture survey were Saint Clair Cemin, Dick Miller, Ann Messner, Joel Fisher, Beriah Wall, Roger Loft, Paola Borgata, Robin Hill, Jim Goss, Kevin Radu, Rebecca Howland, and Taro Suzuki.

The following March, Robinson penned another Virtual Garrison review, this time of a Charlie Saulson exhibition. He partly embraced its blue-collar sensibility and waxed political about the value of art as labor, suggesting more in common with Hovagimyan than he earlier implied:

> Saulson's sculpture speaks eloquently of a process of work, here work in metal, steelwork, a defiantly blue-collar labor, now nevertheless almost as archaic as oil painting or marble carving...this type of labor is noble and ethically allied with the progressive class—but it is rendered anachronistic by contemporary avant-garde theory, which favors white-collar, bureaucratic paper-moving work. The smartest artists position themselves as capitalists: their [a]esthetic identity is their capital, and they hire wage-slaves or craftsmen to handle actual production...In truth, most art labor is "unalienated"—the artist feels compelled to work. The artist "works" but not for wages and doesn't sell his/her labor power...Ideally, we can envision a situation in which labor is valued [a]esthetically, for its own sake, outside...questions of the art's appearance...[or] the distortion of value attendant upon market exchange.[34]

Perhaps the most famous moment for Virtual Garrison, however, came later in 1985, when real estate developer and collector Eli Broad walked in off the street and bought the entire show of John Bowman paintings, a not-unheard-of thing to occur in the go-go East Village scene. The *New York Times* referenced Virtual Garrison among the hot galleries in January 1985 in "East Village Gets on the Fast Track." In October, the *Times* reported on the Bowman sales.

> In a not untypical shopping spree, the Los Angeles home-building tycoon Eli Broad, a major collector of contemporary art, recently dropped by the

OWN A GALLERY!
Established E. Village Gallery For Sale
serious, interested parties contact:
Bruce Rayvid, VIRTUAL GARRISON
(212) 460-5050

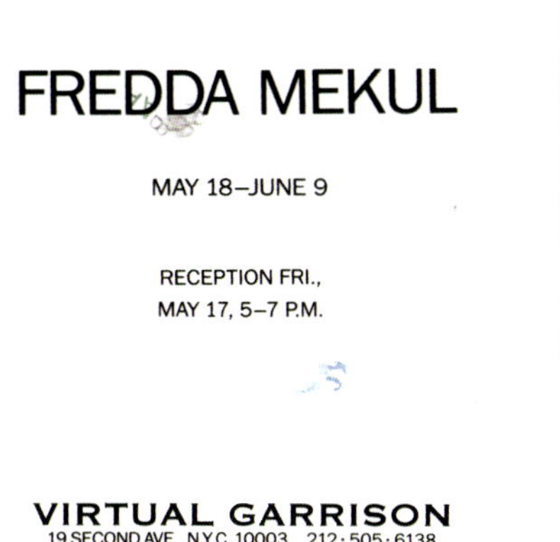

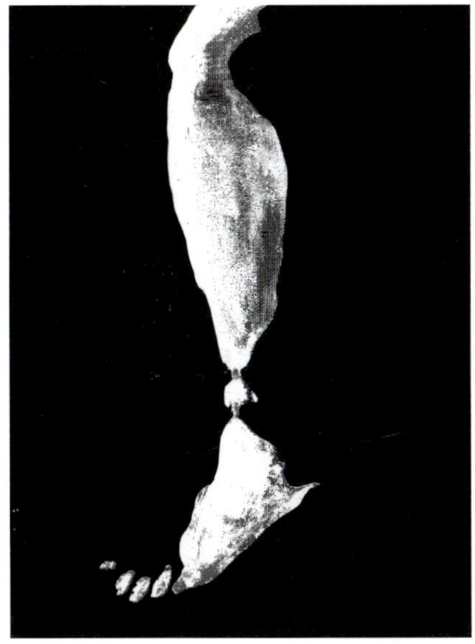

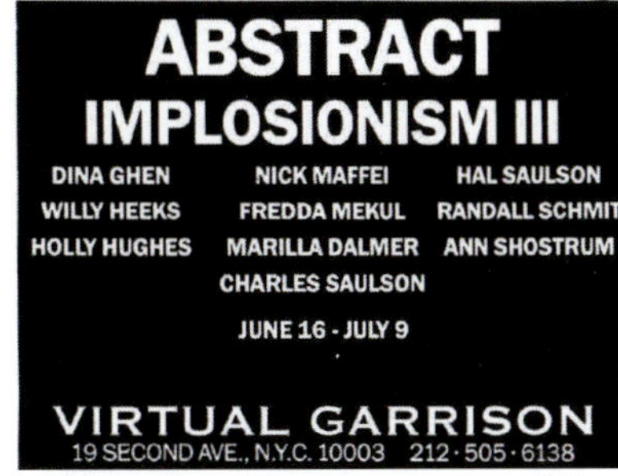

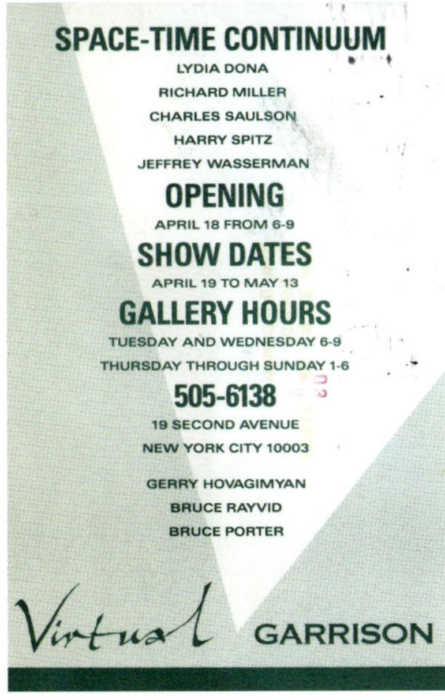

Above top: Sep. 1985 ad, *East Village Eye*
Above middle: Fredda Mekul exhibition postcard, May 1985. Courtesy of online Gallery 98
Above: Suzan Etkin postcard, Feb. 1985. Courtesy of online Gallery 98
Top right: K Bloss postcard, Apr. 1985
Right middle: Jun. 1985 ad, *East Village Eye*
Lower right: Postcard, May 1984. Courtesy of online Gallery 98

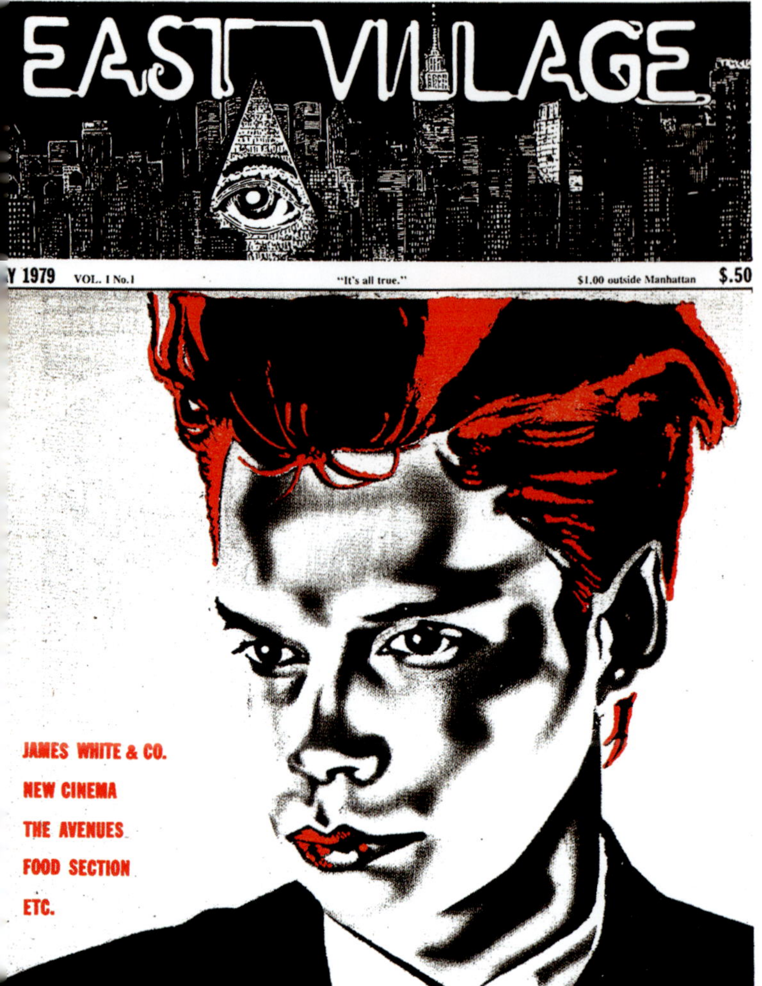

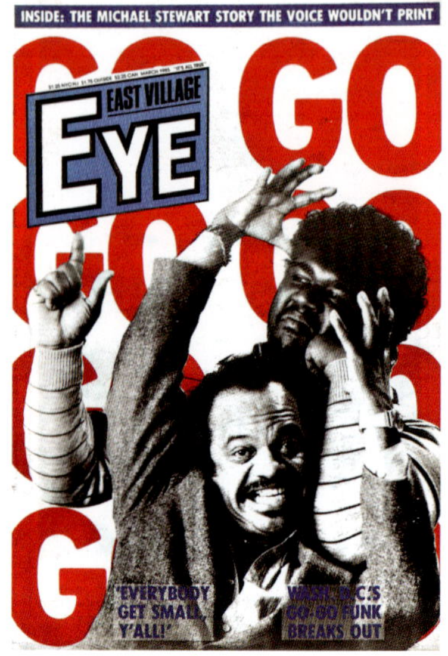

Above: *East Village Eye*'s first cover by Dana Gilbert
Above right: Cover of March 1985 *East Village Eye*, photo by John Eder
Opposite left: Virtual Garrison review
Opposite right: "East Village Gets on the Fast Track" article in the *New York Times*, Jan. 13, 1985

Virtual Garrison Gallery (at First Street and Second Avenue) and bought out nearly the entire show of paintings, elevating the "unknown" artist John Bowman into the "emerging" artist category.[35]

By late 1985, the gallery closed. Its final show in July was titled "Summer Madness." That September, Rayvid, who owned the lease to the city-owned storefront, placed an ad in the *East Village Eye* announcing the gallery was for sale. Within a few years, the East Village scene had fallen into precipitous decline, due to a combination of large rent increases and the rapid spread of H.I.V. in the community. In 1986, Hovagimyan moved to 11 Harrison Street in TriBeCa with Joyce Castleberry, an ad executive at the *New Yorker*. In January 1987, the *East Village Eye* ceased publication, and later in 1987, Hovagimyan and Mekul divorced. Hovagimyan and Castleberry would marry in 1999.

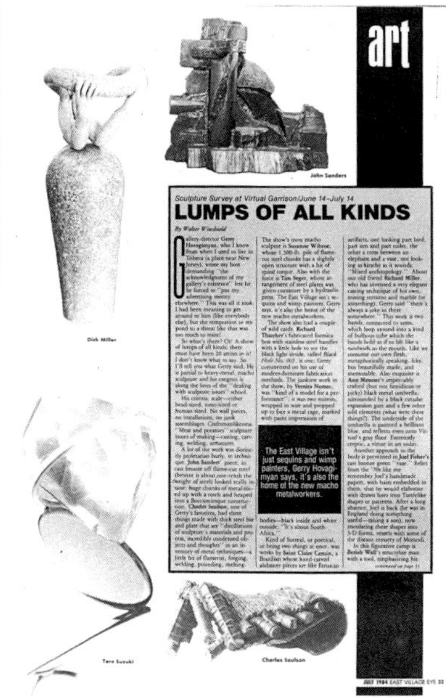

art

John Sanders

Sculpture Survey at Virtual Garrison/June 14–July 14

LUMPS OF ALL KINDS

By Walter Wiesbald

The East Village isn't just sequins and wimp painters, Gerry Hovagimyan says, it's also the home of the new macho metalworkers.

Dick Miller

Taro Suzuki

Charles Saulson

JULY 1984 EAST VILLAGE EYE 33

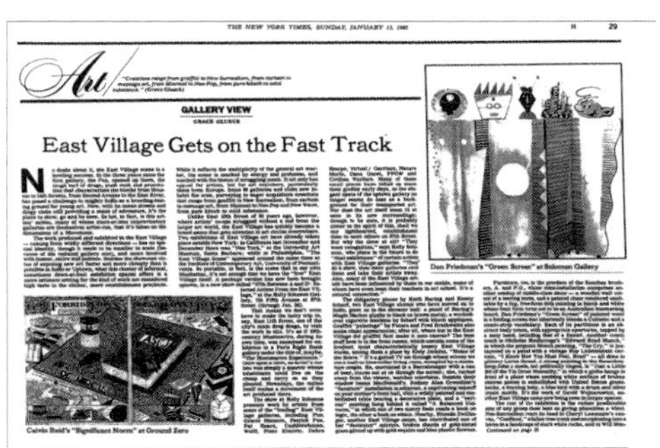

THE NEW YORK TIMES, SUNDAY, JANUARY 13, 1985 H 29

Art

GALLERY VIEW

GRACE GLUECK

East Village Gets on the Fast Track

Calvin Reid's "Significant Noore" at Ground Zero

Dan Friedman's "Green Screen" at Soloman Gallery

2

Early Work

Control Designators, 112 Greene Street, Sep. 21–Oct. 3, 1974

Hovagimyan's first one-man show took place at 112 Greene Street. It's an early glimpse of Hovagimyan's interest in expressing ideas using mathematics and measurement as an alternative language, a rudimentary coding and thought-modeling experiment through which to analyze space. Robyn Brentano describes it extensively in the *112 Greene Street/112 Workshop* catalog of the gallery:

> ...Hovagimyan made use of three types of designators to direct the viewer's experience of the space at 112: 100 number codes indicating the surface topologies of the space, three visual sighting devices functioning like a gun-sight to locate 100 points in the space, and 100 language signs giving directions for the ways to think about the space and move around within the space. The system was based on Jean Piaget's theory of child development as opposed to adult intellectual development. Thus, the basic matrix of the artist's code was related to the progression from undifferentiated surface topology through geometric triangulation to the linear sense of language experienced in reading.[36]

The space of the gallery had been a preoccupation of 112 Greene Street since the beginning—as it was in the downtown milieu generally—but by the time of *Control Designators* it was becoming increasingly explicit as a subject of discussion, with Brian O'Doherty's *Inside the White Cube: The Ideology of the Gallery Space* appearing in 1976, two years later, as a series of three essays in *Artforum.*

The previous year, Jean Dupuy, affiliated with the Fluxus group of neo-Dada conceptual artists, had opened his loft at 405 E. 13th Street to 34 associates, including Hovagimyan, for his first group show on the theme of "spatializing" the elements of the loft. Laurie Anderson, then an emerging sculptor, reviewed it in the September 1973 issue of *Artforum*, noting, "The murky and raw space contributed to the initial impression of casual disarray rather than that of a carefully spotlighted area for the display of discrete objects."[37]

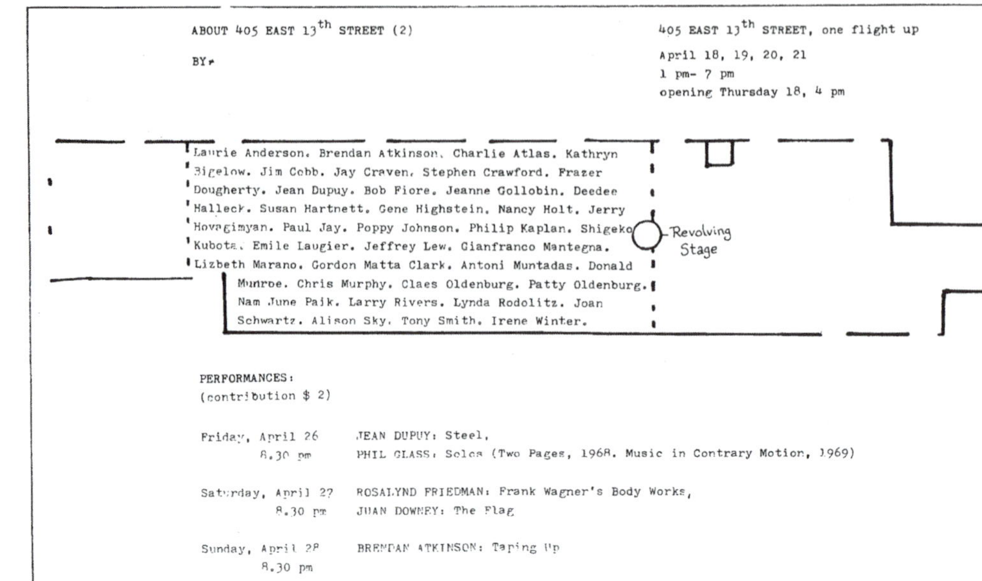

ABOUT 405 EAST 13th STREET (2)

BY:

405 EAST 13th STREET, one flight up

April 18, 19, 20, 21

1 pm- 7 pm

opening Thursday 18, 4 pm

Laurie Anderson. Brendan Atkinson. Charlie Atlas. Kathryn Bigelow. Jim Cobb. Jay Craven. Stephen Crawford. Frazer Dougherty. Jean Dupuy. Bob Fiore. Jeanne Gollobin. Deedee Halleck. Susan Hartnett. Gene Highstein. Nancy Holt. Jerry Hovagimyan. Paul Jay. Poppy Johnson. Philip Kaplan. Shigeko Kubota. Emile Laugier. Jeffrey Lew. Gianfranco Mantegna. Lizbeth Marano. Gordon Matta Clark. Antoni Muntadas. Donald Munroe. Chris Murphy. Claes Oldenburg. Patty Oldenburg. Nam June Paik. Larry Rivers. Lynda Rodolitz. Joan Schwartz. Alison Sky. Tony Smith. Irene Winter.

Revolving Stage

PERFORMANCES:
(contribution $ 2)

Friday, April 26, 8.30 pm — JEAN DUPUY: Steel, PHIL GLASS: Solos (Two Pages, 1968. Music in Contrary Motion, 1969)

Saturday, April 27, 8.30 pm — ROSALYND FRIEDMAN: Frank Wagner's Body Works, JUAN DOWNEY: The Flag

Sunday, April 28, 8.30 pm — BRENDAN ATKINSON: Taping Up

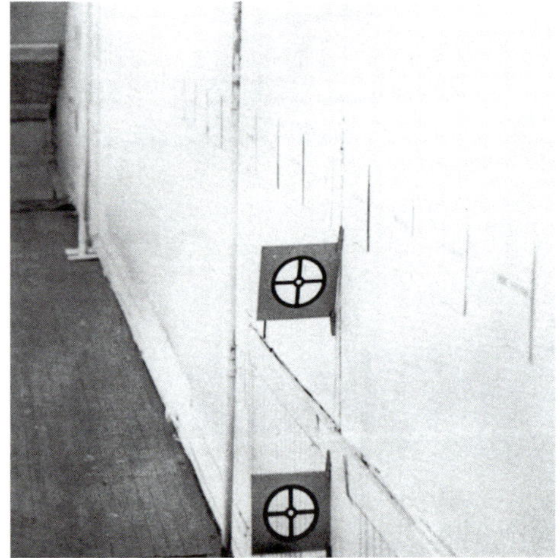

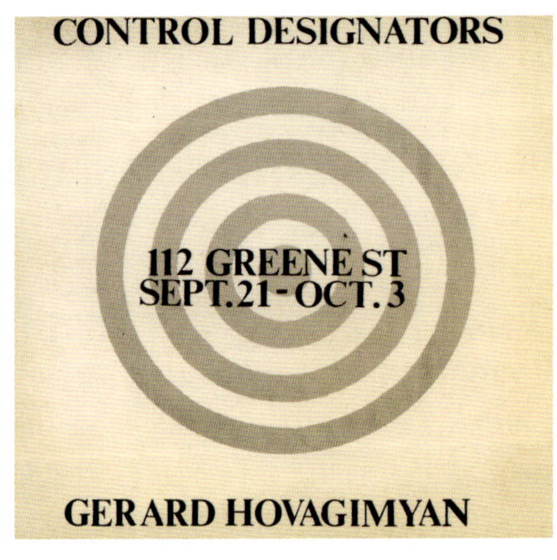

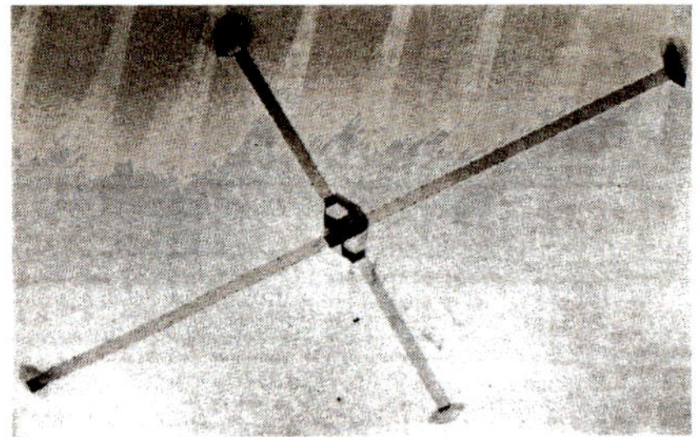

Top: *About 405 E 13th Street* flyer, 1974
Above, left: *Control Designators* installation
Above: Exhibition postcard, courtesy of White Columns
Left: Installation shot

About 405 E. 13th Street, Apr. 18–21, 1974 & Jun. 10–20, 1975

In 1974 and 1975, Hovagimyan exhibited in the second and third of three shows Jean Dupuy organized in his 405 E. 13th Street loft, inviting artists to react to its physical space with conceptual installations. The shows included Fluxus generation artists, associates of 112 Greene Street, and some of Hovagimyan's younger peers. Laurie Anderson reviewed the first edition in *Artforum:*

> "Spatializing" and its implications were the premises of the 34 artists who participated in Jean Dupuy's show *About 405 East 13th Street* early this summer. *About* dealt with various interior, exterior, and interfacial aspects of Dupuy's loft in terms of description and manipulation. Microscopic and telescopic realignments undermined the standard subject-object relationship. The show's site, a living and working loft, dramatized this "spatializing" approach. Psychological and visual conditions imposed on the viewer in gallery space did not exist.[38]

No images survive of Hovagimyan's contributions, but his description appears in the 1980 volume edited by Dupuy, *Collective Consciousness: Art Performance in the Seventies*:

> Placed on a wall were a series of pieces of paper. On the sheets were scrawled messages which were barely legible. Underneath, the messages were typewritten so they could be read. The rape piece was about rape, mental, physical, emotional. For instance, "Look in the mirror as I fuck you up the ass, the pain in your face is my freedom, your tears are the drops of my manhood." The piece was intended to shock and disgust people. Several of the pages were torn from the wall and stepped on by angry viewers; others were amended by an angry feminist. I had no moral position in the piece, I was simply presenting loaded information.[39]

It's the beginning of a trajectory of work that Hovagimyan describes as punk performance, contemporaneous with the first shows of Television, the Ramones, and the Dictators at CBGB. Hovagimyan dates another work with a

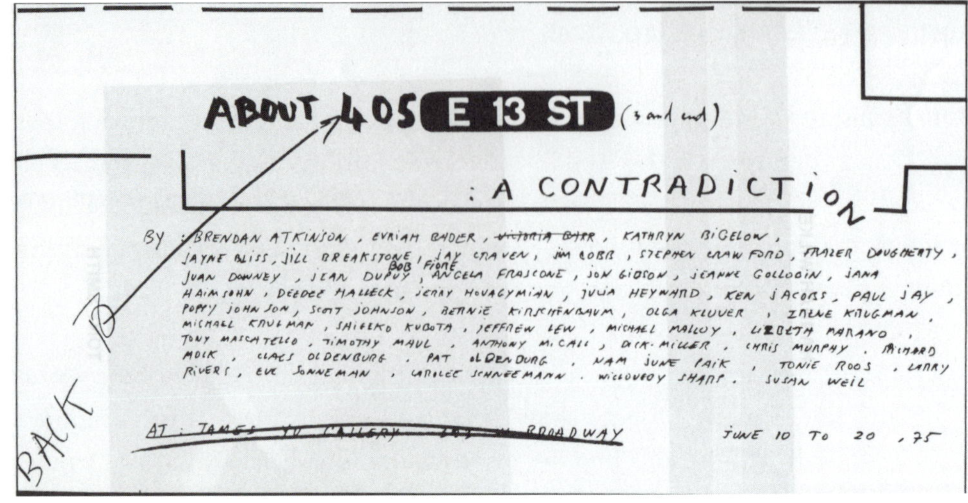

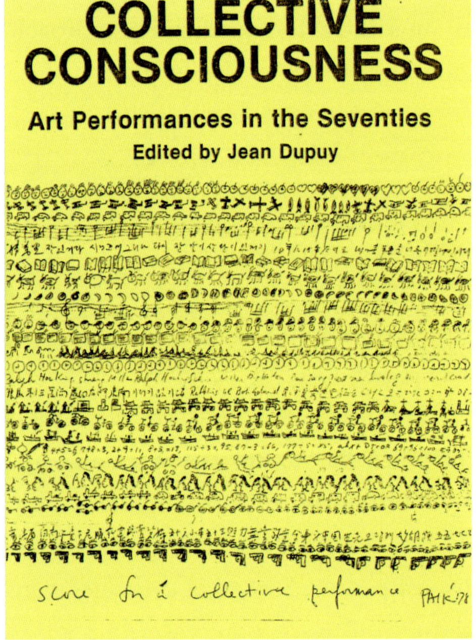

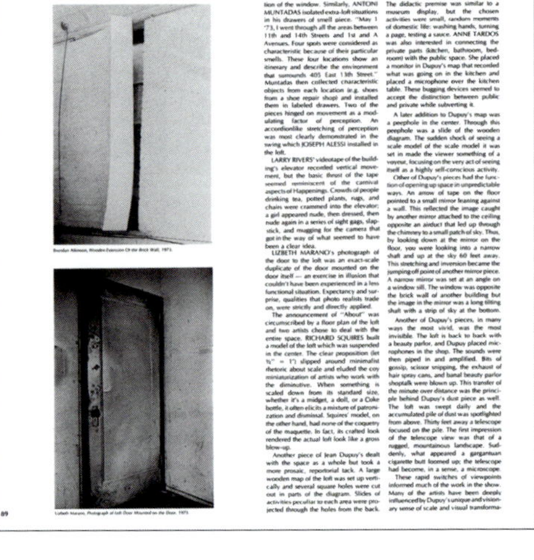

tion of the window. Similarly, ANTONI MUNTADAS isolated extra-loft situations in his drawers of smell piece: "May 1 '73, I went through all the areas between 11th and 14th Streets and 1st and A Avenues. Four spots were considered as characteristic because of their particular smells. These four locations show an itinerary and describe the environment that surrounds 405 East 13th Street." Muntadas then collected characteristic objects from each location (e.g. shoes from a shoe repair shop) and installed them in labeled drawers. Two of the pieces hinged on movement as a modulating factor of perception. An accordionlike stretching of perception was most clearly demonstrated in the swing which JOSEPH ALESSI installed in the loft.

LARRY RIVERS' videotape of the building's elevator recorded vertical movement, but the basic thrust of the tape seemed reminiscent of the carnival aspects of Happenings. Crowds of people drinking tea, potted plants, rugs, and chairs were crammed into the elevator; a girl appeared nude, then dressed, then nude again in a series of sight gags, slapstick, and mugging for the camera that got in the way of what seemed to have been a clear idea.

LIZBETH MARANO's photograph of the door to the loft was an exact-scale duplicate of the door mounted on the door itself — an exercise in illusion that couldn't have been experienced in a less functional situation. Expectancy and surprise, qualities that photo realists trade on, were strictly and directly applied.

The announcement of "About" was circumscribed by a floor plan of the loft and two artists chose to deal with the entire space. RICHARD SQUIRES built a model of the loft which was suspended in the center. The clear proposition (let ½" = 1') slipped around minimalist rhetoric about scale and eluded the coy miniaturization of artists who work with the diminutive. When something is scaled down from its standard size, whether it's a midget, a doll, or a Coke bottle, it often elicits a mixture of patronization and dismissal. Squires' model, on the other hand, had none of the coquetry of the maquette. In fact, its crafted look rendered the actual loft look like a gross blow-up.

Another piece of Jean Dupuy's dealt with the space as a whole but took a more prosaic, reportorial tack. A large wooden map of the loft was set up vertically and several square holes were cut out in parts of the diagram. Slides of activities peculiar to each area were projected through the holes from the back. The didactic premise was similar to a museum display, but the chosen activities were small, random moments of domestic life: washing hands, turning a page, testing a sauce. ANNE TARDOS was also interested in connecting the private parts (kitchen, bathroom, bedroom) with the public space. She placed a monitor in Dupuy's map that recorded what was going on in the kitchen and placed a microphone over the kitchen table. These bugging devices seemed to accept the distinction between public and private while subverting it.

A later addition to Dupuy's map was a peephole in the center. Through this peephole was a slide of the wooden diagram. The sudden shock of seeing a scale model of the scale model it was set in made the viewer something of a voyeur, focusing on the very act of seeing itself as a highly self-conscious activity.

Other of Dupuy's pieces had the function of opening up space in unpredictable ways. An arrow of tape on the floor pointed to a small mirror leaning against a wall. This reflected the image caught by another mirror attached to the ceiling opposite an airduct that led up through the chimney to a small patch of sky. Thus, by looking down at the mirror on the floor, you were looking into a narrow shaft and up at the sky 60 feet away. This stretching and inversion became the jumping off point of another mirror piece. A narrow mirror was set at an angle on a window sill. The window was opposite the brick wall of another building but the image in the mirror was a long tilting shaft with a strip of sky at the bottom.

Another of Dupuy's pieces, in many ways the most vivid, was the most invisible. The loft is back to back with a beauty parlor, and Dupuy placed microphones in the shop. The sounds were then piped in and amplified. Bits of gossip, scissor snipping, the exhaust of hair spray cans, and banal beauty parlor shoptalk were blown up. This transfer of the minute over distance was the principle behind Dupuy's dust piece as well. The loft was swept daily and the accumulated pile of dust was spotlighted from above. Thirty feet away a telescope focused on the pile. The first impression of the telescope view was that of a rugged, mountainous landscape. Suddenly, what appeared a gargantuan cigarette butt loomed up; the telescope had become, in a sense, a microscope.

These rapid switches of viewpoints informed much of the work in the show. Many of the artists have been deeply influenced by Dupuy's unique and visionary sense of scale and visual transforma-

Top: Third *About 405* show flyer, 1975
Above, left: *Collective Consciousness,* 1980 (book cover)
Above, right: *About 405 E. 13th Street* show, *Artforum.* Images: Brendan Atkinson, *Wooden Extension on the Brick Wall, 1973;* and Lizbeth Marano, *Photograph of Loft Door Mounted on the Door,* 1973

similarly aggressive tendency from the same period, *Tactics for Survival in the New Culture,* which would appear in the 1979 Manifesto Show and later be transposed into an early net art piece.

Alan Moore covered the second edition of *About 405 E. 13th Street*, which featured 40 artists, in an October 1974 *Artforum* article on Dupuy. It "amalgamated certain underground tendencies, as an alternative to the strictures of a gallery situation," Moore wrote. "Unlike the galleries—clean, self-effacing marketplaces—the pieces at 405 were crammed together, unidentified, and shown without commercial motive...Most of the works were loosely related, dealing as they did with the space and/or the architectural facts of 405."[40]

Scale 1/1, James Yu Gallery, May 1975

In 1975, Jean Dupuy invited Hovagimyan, with a group that included Jene Highstein, Suzanne Harris, Jeff Lew, and Matta-Clark, to contribute to the *Sculptors' Drawings Show, Scale One to One* at James Yu Gallery. Part of Hovagimyan's *Thought Models* series, *Scale 1/1* was concept to turn Castle Clinton in Lower Manhattan into a shrine for Mao.

> Using designer's board in shades of grey i.e., warm grey, cool grey, and charcoal grey placed on the wall in a rotated cruciform. The piece had four small units at the end of each armature; in the center were two units joined together. The piece was pseudo-architectural, pseudo-painting, pseudo-sculpture, and pseudo-drawing. It was an aerial view placed on a wall and rotated. I imagine people living at the end of each armature and coming together in the central meeting house. The different shades of grey board placed next to each other made the piece shimmer to the eye. It was very funny to produce a retinal painting effect without using paint.[41]

His romanticization of Mao reflected the leftist energy of the moment: Sylvère Lotringer's 1975 *Schizo-Culture* conference and Colab members' 1977 *X Motion Picture Magazine* had glorified the Baader–Meinhof Gang, and double-digit inflation, an oil crisis, high unemployment, and crime produced extreme precarity.

Thought Models, Idea Warehouse, Jun. 11–12, 1975

Before opening P.S. 1 Contemporary Art Center in 1976, curator and arts organizer Alanna Heiss had founded the nonprofit Institute for Art and Urban Resources and gained access to multiple disused buildings for exhibitions.

In 1973, she had a temporary agreement to host studios, exhibitions, and performances in a former municipal storage warehouse at 22 Reade Street. As the 597 Group took shape in early 1975, launching its *Videotapes and Performances*, the Idea Warehouse's expansive space and the interest of a better-established but still nascent curator attracted the group's energy.

Members of the group would participate in the *Ideas at the Idea Warehouse* event series that summer, but before that, Hovagimyan installed his *Thought Models* in the open space for a few days in mid-June. They took some cues from Richard Serra's paint stick drawings.

> What he was doing was taking a rectangle, then he was taking that black oil stick and rubbing the paint into the canvas like Belgian linen, attached directly to the wall. Then what he'd do is, after he put them on the surface, he would squeegee it to get these textures. Then he would drop one corner, snap a chalk line and cut the bottom so that it was level with the floor, but you could tell that it was off. But he was trying to find the exact place of dynamic tension where it was sitting on the wall, no frame or anything. It was relating to the floor and your physical space, but it would create a lot of anxiety.[42]

In *Thought Models*, Hovagimyan used simple geometric shapes—a circle, square, cylinder, triangle, and cone—each about 3 × 1.5 feet, to create an iterative landscape mounted on colored matte boards. Three squares edge-to-edge would create a prism. The top of the prism defined a half-cone "roof." Placing four squares together created a box, with the half-cylinder placed on top. Then he would attach three squares and a cone to the opposite end. Tilting the point of the prism one-half inch off the floor created a gap where it meets the rectangle and half-cylinder, then he would adjust the other shapes accordingly. To add visual interest, he varied the shapes and proportions to create permutations. It anticipates his later works using architectural and sculptural modeling, as well as VR and AR models, to articulate abstract and otherworldly forms.

Ideas at the Idea Warehouse followed, the participants including Kirsten Bates, Bill Beirne, Michael McClard, Jim Cobb, Ralston Farina, Dieter Froese, Coleen Fitzgibbon, Julia Heyward, Virginia Piersol, Judy Rifka, Joost Romeo, Willoughby Sharp, and Robin Winters—all participants in the 597 Group or future members of Colab.

> Julia Heyward did this piece called *Ma I Am.* It was video. I did some kind of terrorist piece. Dick Miller like drank a bottle of Wild Turkey and then brought a live wild turkey and slaughtered it in a cage. Susan Ensley talked to the people in the buildings across the way to have little acting vignettes in the windows, and then she took spotlights and spotlighted the windows, so the performance was going on in the space across the street.[43]

"That what the Times Square Show—the Colab movement—was all about was more formalizing that [people creating their own galleries]," Billingsley recalled. "597 was completely Do-It-Yourself without any idea of 'Yeah, we might be able to get government money to help support it,' which is where the Kitchen and Artists Space and a lot of those nonprofit galleries came into existence in that same era. But they were run by people who had a little more sense of how to get government money. Colab eventually did get some grants, but that was kind of like a toe in the door."[44]

Rubber Room, P.S. 1, Mar. 24–Apr. 10, 1977

In June 1976, Alanna Heiss opened P.S. 1, a closed-down Romanesque Revival public school in Long Island City, Queens, as a European-style Kunsthalle, inviting 78 artists to mount installations in the school's empty classrooms and interstitial spaces. Along with exhibitions, Heiss envisioned temporary residencies that would provide artists with studio space.

Initially P.S. 1 rented space to artists, then showed their work in open studios, but by early 1977, it was promoting special projects. From March 24th to April

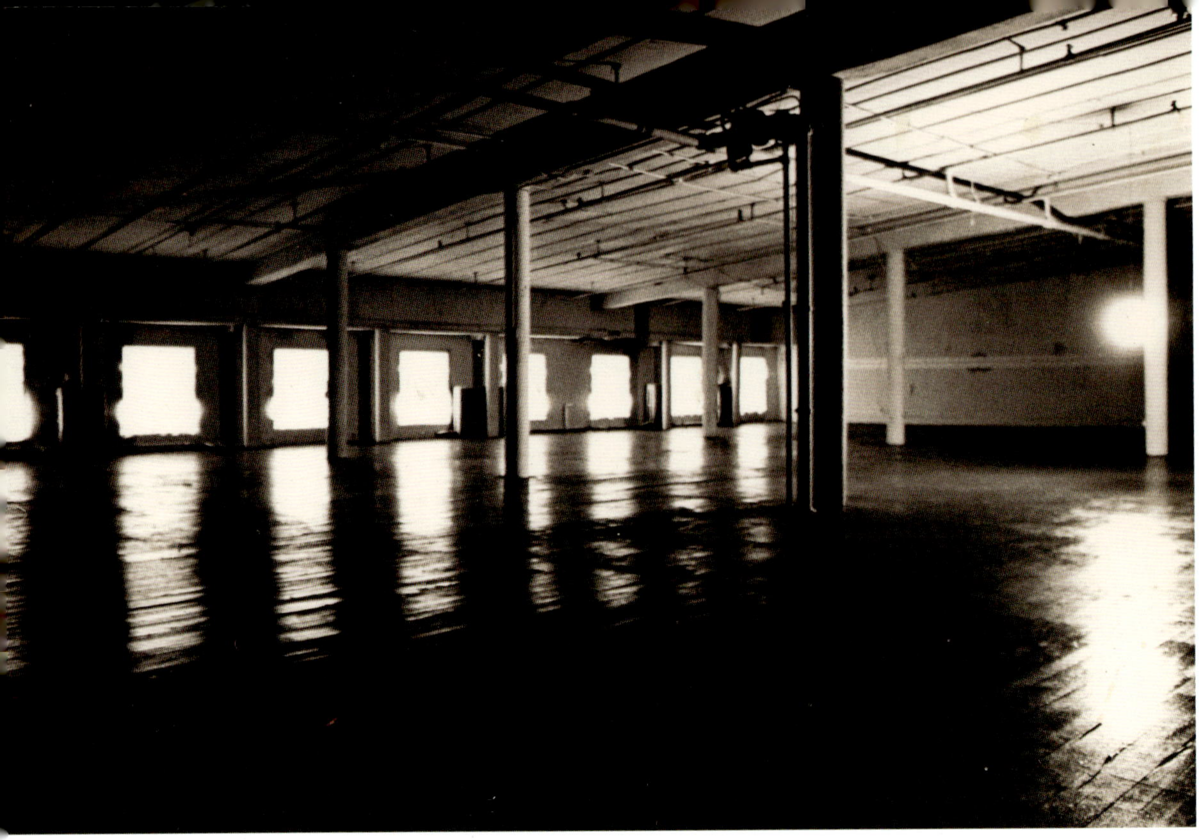

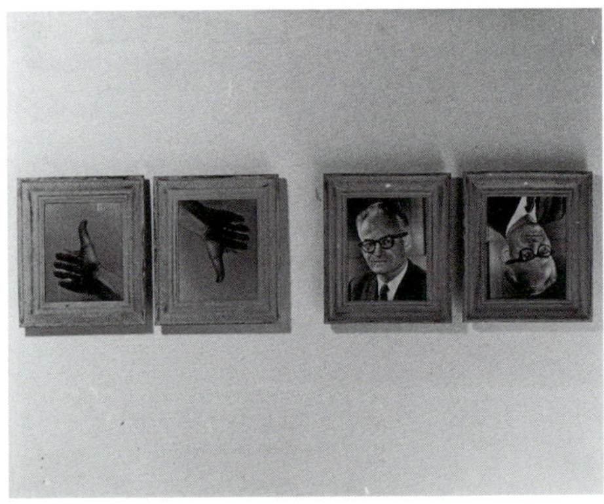

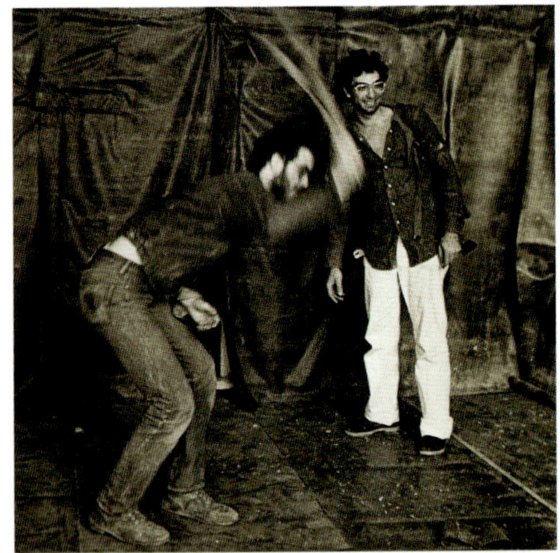

Top: Installation view, "Long Film for Ambient Light" by Anthony McCall in *Ideas at the Idea Warehouse* (Jun. 16–Jul. 11, 1975). MoMA PS1 Archives, I.A.37. Museum of Modern Art Archives. © The Museum of Modern Art/ Licensed by SCALA/Art Resource, NY
Above left: Installation view of work by Julia Heyward in *Ideas at the Idea Warehouse* (Jun. 16–Jul. 11, 1975), MoMA PS1 Archives, I.A.37. The Museum of Modern Art Archives, New York. © The Museum of Modern Art/Licensed by SCALA/Art Resource, NY
Above right: Scott Billingsley and G.H. in *Rubber Room*. Courtesy Scott Billingsley

10th, Hovagimyan's *Rubber Room* installation exhibited concurrently with a show by Richard Nonas. Around that time, Hovagimyan had been working on a demo job around Reade Street cleaning out a rubber warehouse. He used the reclaimed materials to line the walls and floors with black rubber and built a floor-to-ceiling Jacob's ladder (an electrical arc) with two aluminum rods and a high voltage neon transformer that intermittently sparked on a timer. Electrostatic transfers of this piece were exhibited at the club TR3 in 1978.

Rich Sucker Rap, Artists Space, 1977/*Chant à Capella,* Jean Dupuy and Davidson Gigliotti, Museum of Modern Art, 1978

In 1977, Hovagimyan participated in an open mic performance event at Artists Space, the nonprofit gallery that opened in 1972 at 155 Wooster Street in SoHo as a venue for young artists without gallery representation. It moved into the Fine Arts Building at 105 Hudson Street in 1977. For the event, he performed *Rich Sucker Rap*, an aggressive spoken word performance that repeated the lines "Fuck you, rich suckers, give me your money, fuck you, rich suckers, give me your money," "No money, no art, no money, no art," "Whose art whose art whose art?" and "Buy and sell" as fast as possible to a regular beat, in the rhythm of a paradiddle.

Later, Jean Dupuy and Davidson Gigliotti received a grant to videotape young performance artists. They recorded the piece, along with work by Laurie Anderson, Don Cherry, Julia Heyward, Joe Lewis, Nam June Paik, Charlemagne Palestine, Jackson MacLow, and George Maciunas. They showed it at MoMA, which caused a stir.

> I did this piece called *Rich Sucker Ra*p, which was essentially a rant and rap combined. It was very confrontational and punk. They had an open mic at Artists Space, so I did it at the open mic, and maybe six months later I did it with Jean Dupuy. That was shown at the Museum of Modern Art in the *Video Views*. My piece was so punk and offensive that a lot of the rich trustee

* = "Meet the Composer" sponsored	77-78 Sept	Oct	Nov	Dec	Jan	Feb	
Clocktower	TOM ROSE Sept. 21 – Oct 19	BOB MOSCOWITZ Oct 19 – Nov 16	Vito Acconci Nov 16 – Dec 14	Claudia Schwab 14 – Jan 11			
P.S. 1 Exhibition Ctr.	Ten Downtown Sept 11 — Oct 2	Works + Projects of the Seventies 9 — Nov 6	Pattern Painting Nov. 13 – Dec 4	Queens Artists Choose Queens Artists 11 — 25			
Auditorium	Richard Horn Sept 8, 9, 10 (830 PM) Sept 11 (3-6 PM)	Stanley + Wasserman Oct 2 – 30 (access, Sept 12 – Nov 2)	Bill Hellermann * Stephanie Woodard 3-6, Nov 6 perfs. 2 pm, 4 pm	Dan Graham Dec 4 3pm perf RON GORCHOV (access Dec 5) 22 – Jan 8	Jill Kroesen 9-28 Jacki Apple 9-28	Jean Dupuy 2-25	Mar Ric
Studio A		Peter Grass 2-30 Oct 30 2pm perf. Stephanie Woodard Oct 31 – Nov 2 rehearsal	DAN GRAHAM Aud. + Studio A Nov 10 – 4	Dan Graham Dec 4 3pm perf			
Studio B		Bill Hellermann 2-30 Exhibition (access Sept 26)					
S.P. 209	Richard Jackson Sept 11 – Sept 25	Carolyn Conrad Oct 1 – Nov 6 (access, Sept 26)	Poppy Johnson Nov 10-20 (access, Nov 7)	Jim Pavlicovic 4 – Jan 29 (access, Nov 21)		Connie Beckley 2-25	
S.P 208	Sept. access	Skip La Plant Oct 6 – 30 Oct 30, 4pm perf.	Terry Fox 3 – 27 (access Oct. 31)		Bickhard Bottinelli 5-28 (not confirmed)		
S.P. 207	Myrel Chernick Sept 11 – Oct 9	Donald Sultan Oct 20 – Nov 27 (access Oct 10)		Stuart Sherman 15 – Jan 1 (access Dec 1)	Joan Jonas 5 – 29 (not confirmed)		
S.P. 206	Beth Anderson * Sept 25, 3:00 PM (Performance)	Bill Anastasi Oct 2 – Nov 13 (access, Sept 26)		Roberta Allen 3 – Jan 8 (access Nov 14)			
S.P. 205	Krzysztof Wodiczko Sept 11-25	Robert George Oct 6 – 30	Jim Cobb 3 – 27	Susan Russell 8 — Jan 1	Joan La Barbara 4 — 29		
S.P. 204	TANIA MOURAUD Sept 11 – Oct 2	Dennis Ashbaugh Oct 6 – Nov 13		Abigail Gerd 3 – Jan 1 (access Nov 14)			

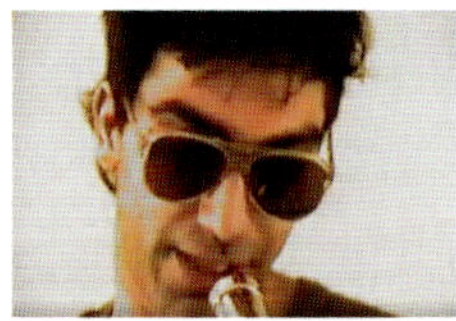
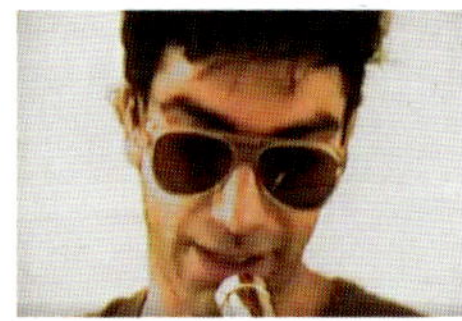
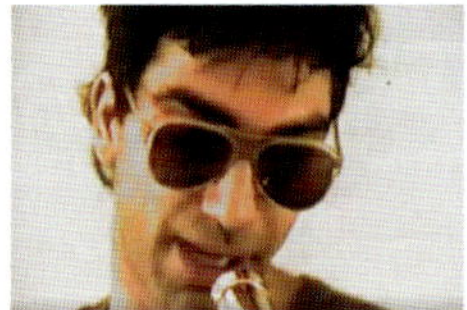
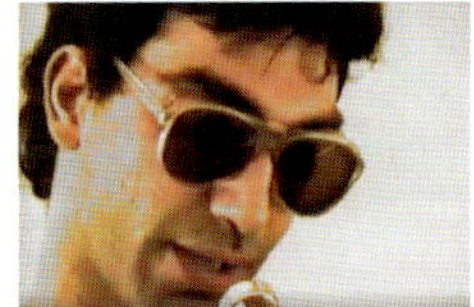

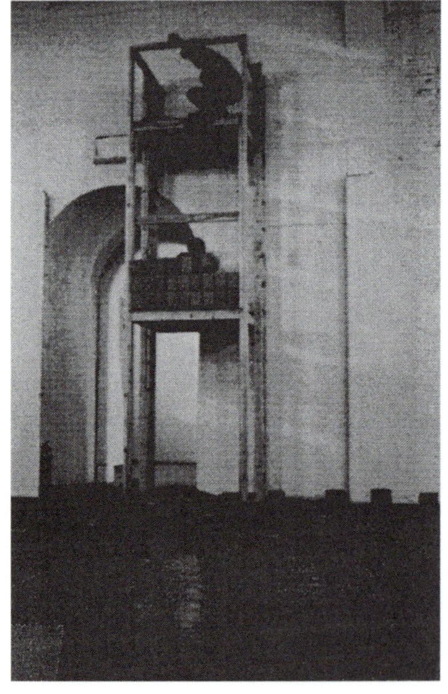

Top: Institute for Art and Urban Resources Programming Spreadsheet of Fall Season for P.S. 1 (now MoMA PS1) and the Clocktower, 1977. MoMA PS1 Archives. The Museum of Modern Art, New York. © The Museum of Modern Art/Licensed by SCALA/Art Resource, NY
Above: *Rich Sucker Rap*, 1978. Video stills: Jean Dupuy and Davidson Gigliotti
Left: *A Tower at P.S. 1.* Photo: *Collective Consciousness*

patrons were asking for it to be removed from the exhibition. They didn't remove it, but it kind of caused this big deal on the art scene. I tried to do it as fast as I could, something like a country auctioneer, but essentially it was punk rap. Subsequently, when I went back to doing performance art, I actually started from that premise in the 1990s.[45]

A Tower at P.S. 1, February 1978

In early 1978, Jean Dupuy built a tower/performance platform in the auditorium at P.S. 1. Every Saturday and Sunday, performances took place on it, including one by Hogavimyan. For the piece, he asked John and Charlie Ahearn, twin brothers and both members of Colab, to pile and assemble one-foot square boxes on Dupuy's tower, while he played a soundtrack of brainwave feedback and radio static in the background.

> Another piece I did was a relational aesthetics piece for a 1978 show *A Tower at P.S.1* organized by Jean Dupuy. In this piece, Jean had built a two-story tower/performance platform and then invited artists to do things on it. I asked Charlie and John Ahearn (identical twins) if they would participate by assembling 100 cardboard boxes each on the two different platforms.[46]

Hovagimyan wrote a text describing it at the time:

> The piece is about a set-up situation. People focusing on work activity, work activity being assembling boxes and piling them or moving matter. The piece then sits on the edge of sculpture and performance both, yet neither. That's why I call it situational. The message is not the material (sculpture) nor a virtuoso activity (performance). It is situational. Another aspect of the performance is sound. The tape played is of brain waves, radio static, and a continuous tone generator. These act as a signal of focus on (thought-work) process of the twins. The sounds are concrete and non-aesthetic. They are not music; they are concrete sound. Sound as a physical aspect of our lives.[47]

75 Warren Street, Jan. 6–Feb. 1, 1979

With Harry Spitz (an associate from Philadelphia College of Art), Chiara (Kiki) Smith, and John Shaw, Hovagimyan obtained a small grant of around $300 from the Committee for the Visual Arts, Inc., a nonprofit established in 1972, which founded Artists Space and provided support for exhibitions, performances, screenings, and installations of challenging art not being shown in commercial galleries. They got permission to use a vacant storefront from the owner of 75 Warren Street in January 1979, extended through February.

Tactics for Survival in the New Culture, Manifesto Show, Colab, Apr. 1979

Tactics for Survival originated as a punk-conceptual text piece to be shown in the storefront window at 112 Greene Street for the gallery's 1974 group show.[48] Jeffrey Lew considered it too controversial, according to Hovagimyan, and it was never shown until the 1979 *Manifesto Show*, organized for Colab by Jenny Holzer and Coleen ("Colen") Fitzgibbon.

The exhibition took place at Fitzgibbon's 5 Bleecker Street studio, one of the two regular venues, along with Robin Winters' Broadway loft—directly next door to Scott Billingsley's 597 Broadway loft—for Colab's series of 1979 theme shows, culminating in its landmark *Real Estate Show* on New Year's Day and *Times Square Show* in June 1980.

> It's like what happens if you're in a very bad place where you don't have any money, where you're a young man with no hope, no future, no anything. You feel suicidal, but at a certain point you say, "Well, why should I kill myself? Why don't I just kill other people? Same difference, right?" Then you start getting into how do you liberate yourself, which is the basis of consciousness. Essentially, you liberate yourself through nihilism. Once you get into the notion of destroying anything that has any meaning, it begins to liberate you. Because you're not tied to commercialism. The market, the art market, so what. Fuck it, it doesn't exist. Now what? The rock market, so what. Fuck it, it doesn't exist. Once all the rules get broken down, they don't exist.[49]

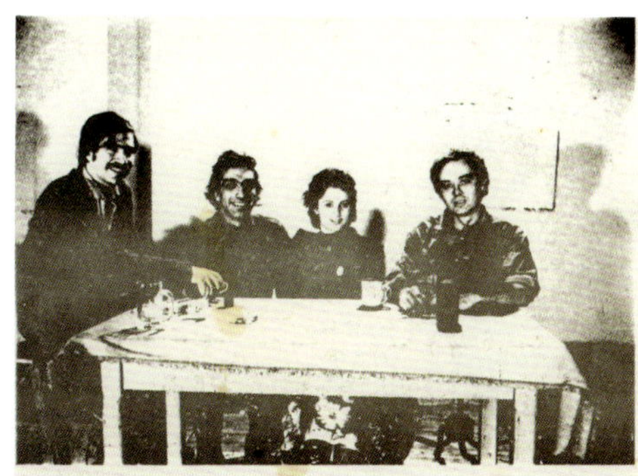

HARRY SPITZ
GERARD HOVAGIMYAN
CHIARA SMITH
AND JOHN SHAW
WILL BE SHOWING WORK
AT 75 WARREN ST.
OPENING JANUARY 6
FROM 1 TO 6 P.M.
AND RUNNING UNTIL
FEBRUARY 1, 1979
HOURS, FROM 1 TO 6 P.M.
WED. THRU SATURDAY.

Committee for the
Visual Arts, Inc.
105 Hudson Street
N.Y.C. N.Y. 10013

Non-Profit Org.
U.S. Postage
Paid
New York, N.Y.
Permit No. 8521

Eve Sonneman
98 Bowery Street
NYC 10013

PARTIALLY SPONSORED BY THE COMMITTEE FOR THE VISUAL ARTS

MANIFESTO

5 BLEECKER ST

THRU APRIL

2-6 PM

THURS-FRI-SAT

OPENS APRIL 7 W/

FILMS AT 8 PM

SHOW

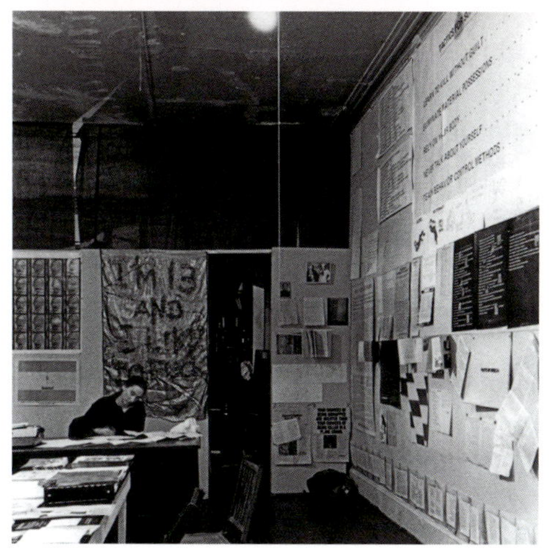

Above: Postcard for *75 Warren Street* exhibition, courtesy of Gallery 98
Above right: *Manifesto Show* poster
Right: Jenny Holzer sitting at desk in the *Manifesto Show*, curated with Colen (Coleen) Fitzgibbon and Collaborative Projects, 1979. Installation: 5 Bleecker Street, New York. © 2020 Jenny Holzer, member Artists Rights Society (ARS), New York

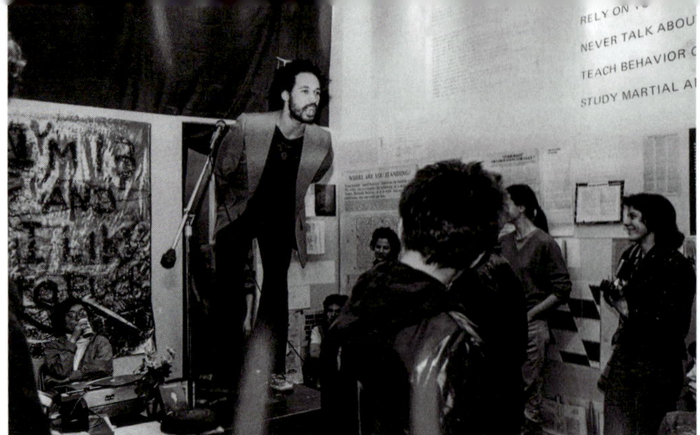

<u>Tactics For Survival in the New Culture</u>

Learn To Kill Without Guilt 1

Eliminate Material Possessions 2

Rely on Your Body 3

Use Sexuality as a Weapon 4

Never Talk About Yourself 5

Choose One Stance:
Passive-Aggressive, Aggressive-Passive,
Passive-Passive, Aggressive-Aggressive . . . 6

Become Pan- Sexual 7

Consider Murder instead of Suicide 8

Believe In No-One 9

Deny History 10

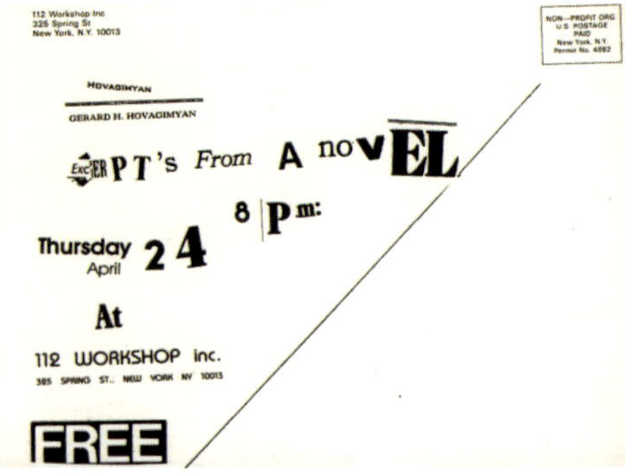

Top: Joe Lewis performing at the *Manifesto Show*.
Photo: Coleen Fitzgibbon
Above: *Tactics of Survival in the New Culture*,
G.H. Hovagimyan, 1979
Right: Postcard for reading at 112 Workshop

Excerpts from a Novel, 112 Workshop, Apr. 24, 1980

In 1979, the cast-iron loft building at 112 Greene Street converted to a cooperative apartment building, renting out the commercial storefront to offset the costs of improvements required to get a Certificate of Occupancy from the city.[50] The gallery moved to 325 Spring Street in West SoHo, reopening in February as White Columns.

In April 1980, Hovagimyan read from a work-in-progress, a novel based on remembered dialog from the 1962 film *Two for the Seesaw,* set in a New York City apartment and starring Robert Mitchum as a lawyer from Nebraska and Shirley MacLaine as a struggling dancer. Hovagimyan had seen the film as a child and reconstructed the movie from memory without looking at the script, interspersing it with street scenes from his life as an artist and things going on with him at the time. Later he got the script and compared it to his memory.

> I was trying to get to something. The movie must have made an impression on me. How a movie would influence what I was projecting about life when I was young, being an artist in New York, and the reality of being an artist in New York. Then *Bright Lights Big City* came out, and it was so similar that I gave up on it.[51]

Hovagimyan had a literary agent encouraging him to pursue the project, but as he recounted in a conversation, they were doing lots of cocaine together, and the agent's wife eventually objected to him coming over. That was the end of his short literary career.

3

Net Art

BKPC (Barbie and Ken Politically Correct), The Thing, 1993, 1995

By the early 1990s, Hovagimyan's work gravitated toward the latest computer technology. BKPC *(Barbie and Ken Politically Correct)* was composed of a series of photo vignettes playing on interracial sex and white supremacy. The work's theme is anti-racism, anti-sexism, and anti-fascism in the spirit of Situationist art, intended to challenge corporate hegemony. It presents the point of view of a little girl playing with dolls and fantasizing about sex.

Distributed as small digital files on a pre-World Wide Web bulletin board system, or BBS, it took advantage of a medium that was then in the vanguard of information technology. Users uploaded the images by a modem hooked up to the telephone line. The pixelated 34-to-72 kilobyte images, reflecting the limitations of the technology at the time, recall the primitive nature of the internet in its early years.

> That piece had a narrative, and I would upload it, one image a week for fifteen weeks, and you could download it onto your computer. That's the only way you could get the piece, because it was pre-Web.[52]

Text laid out over the photos—likely using QuarkXPress, or CorelDraw, predecessors of Photoshop—spins the story of a white Barbie Doll and Black Ken Doll who meet on a college campus. She asks him to join a punk band. They demonstrate together against racism on campus. American Nazis—figured as GI Joes with swastika armbands—show up and attack them. Black Ken Doll rescues Barbie, and they fall for each other and hop in the sack.

The images were originally offered for download in 1993 on The Thing, a pioneering internet art venue founded in 1991 by Wolfgang Staehle—an associate of Hovagimyan's going back to Colab days—with Peter von Brandenberg (aka Blackhawk). It was dedicated to online activism, media art, and cultural criticism, and was run out of the basement boiler room at 44 White Street below the Daniel Newburg Gallery. Wolfgang Staehle recalled:

> It started out, it was pre-Web time basically. There was no consumer internet to speak of at the time, there was no graphic or anything like that. What it

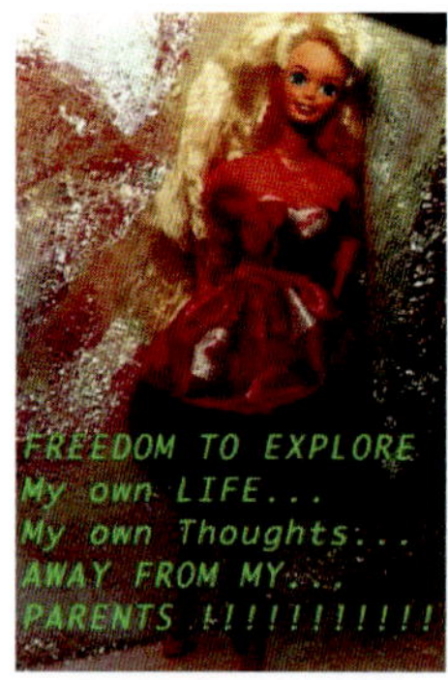

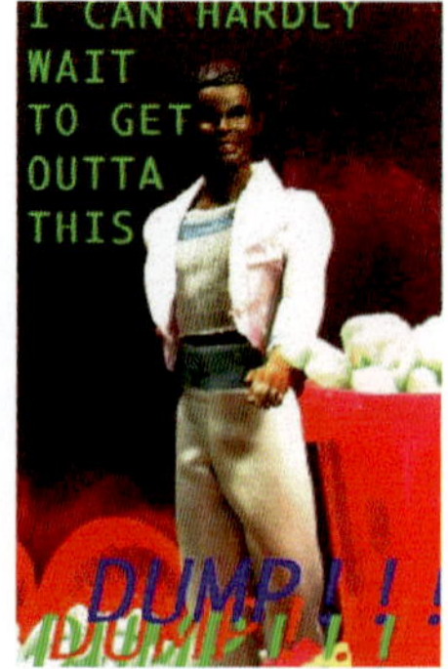

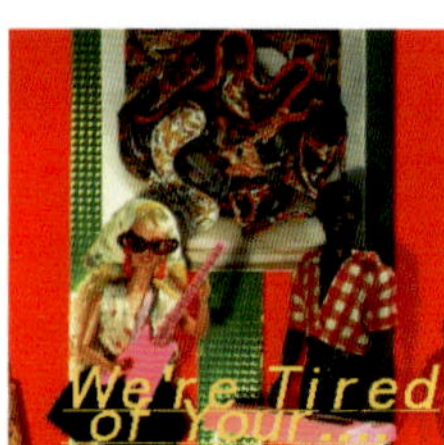

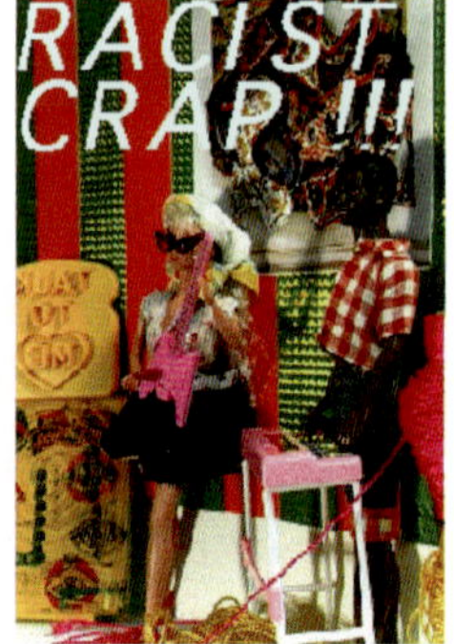

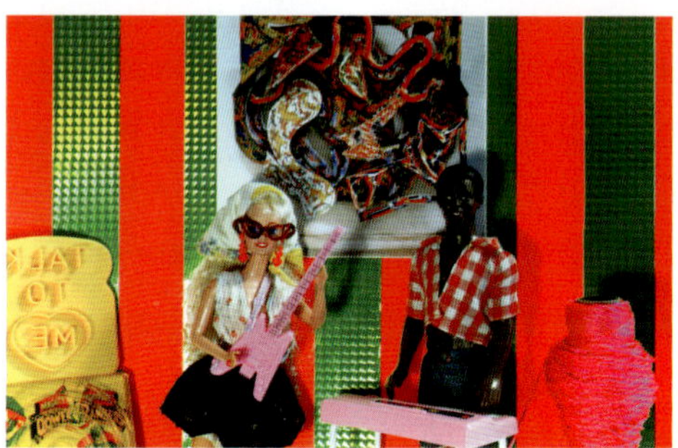

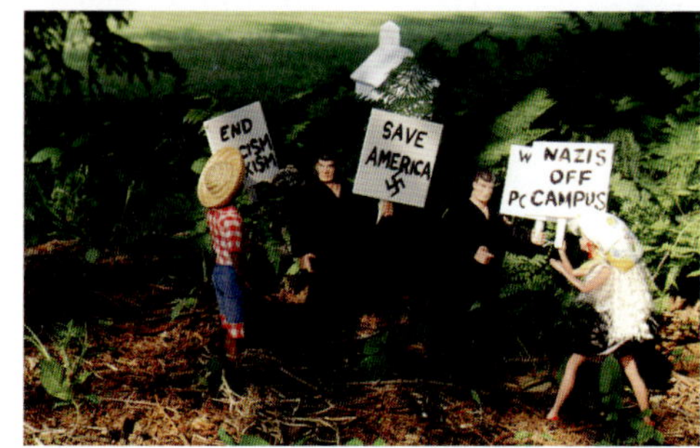

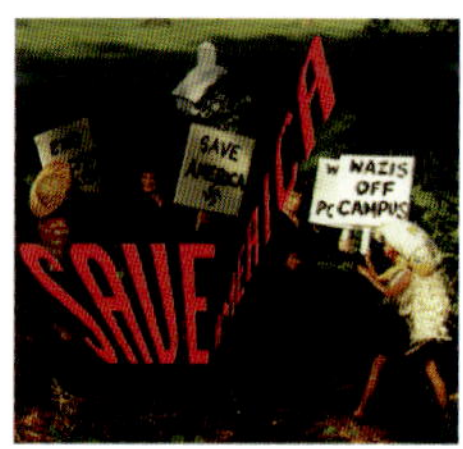

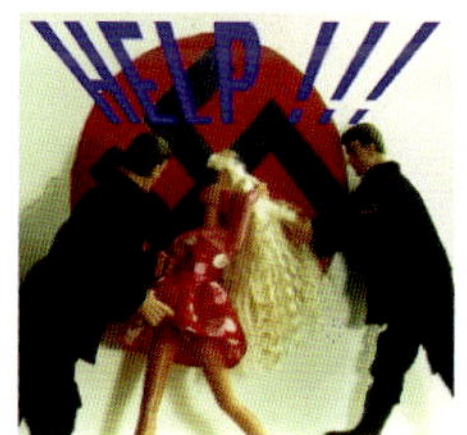

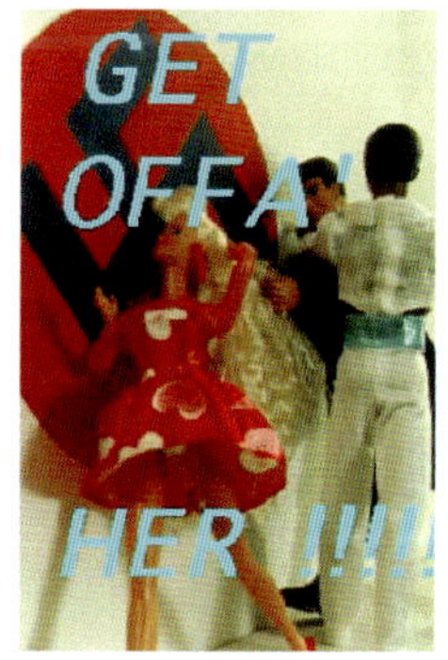

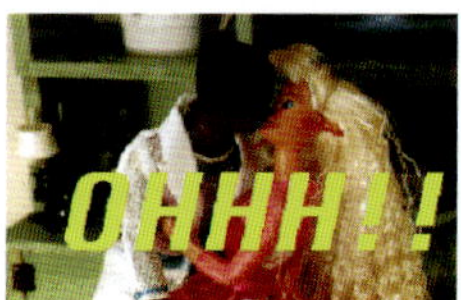

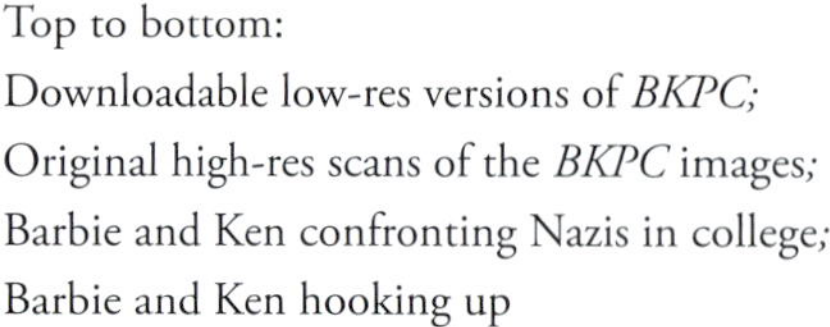

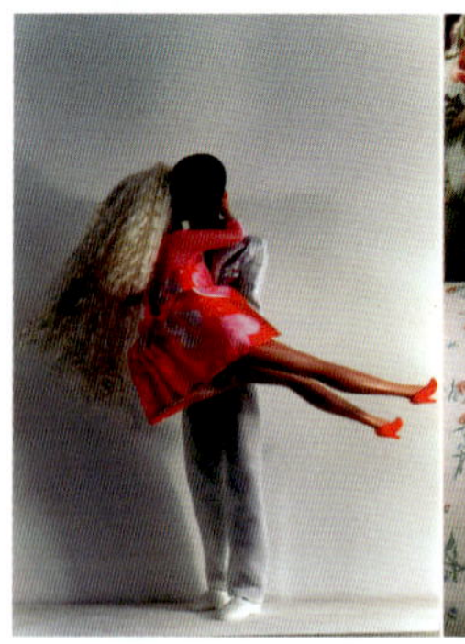

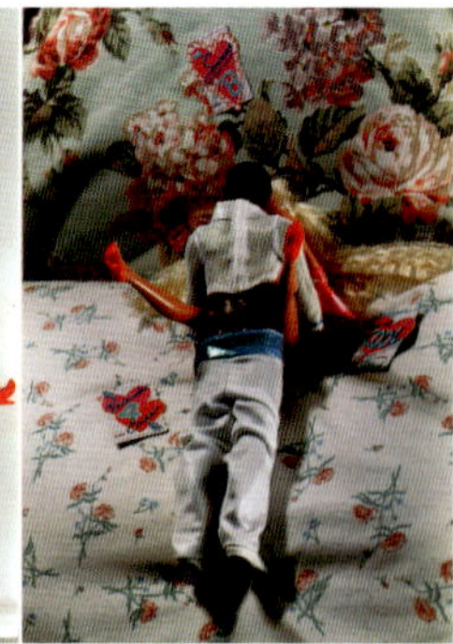

Top to bottom:
Downloadable low-res versions of *BKPC;*
Original high-res scans of the *BKPC* images*;*
Barbie and Ken confronting Nazis in college*;*
Barbie and Ken hooking up

> was, it was called BBS, bulletin board system. Electronic bulletin board systems, which were commonplace at the time with amateurs who were playing with computers and exchanging files and information over pre-Web networks, using FidoNet and things like that, which were basically storage forwarding networks, so people would connect, call up somewhere with a modem, drop something off, and maybe pick something up.[53]

"In the nineties, the first thing that happened was everybody started picking up computers," Hovagimyan says. "A lot of the people I knew from the media section of Colab were the people who were not necessarily successful, like Wolfgang Staehle, they didn't have anything plug into the market. So they basically plugged into computer systems. Wolfgang started this BBS, a bulletin board system, which was just text based, and you could upload images, but it was very slow because it was using 14.4 baud modems."[54]

During this period, Hovagimyan discovered that gallerist Thomas Zollner had downloaded BKPC and was using it as a screensaver. He realized the medium had new potential.

> At that time, I was trying to get into an art gallery in SoHo, TZ Art, run by Frederieke Taylor and Thomas Zollner. And there was no way I was going to get into this gallery. I took my slides around to all the galleries—at that point you had to print out slides and make extra sets and take them to the dealer, and they pretended to look at them and give them back to you. I was friends with them so I went to chat with Thomas Zollner. He went in the back for something, and I went and looked on—he had one of those big desktop computer monitor things. I happened to peek into the front of his computer, and the screensaver was my piece, BKPC. In other words, my work was showing in the gallery even though it was rejected by that gallery. I thought, "Ah!" This to me was a total revelation. "This is good, I like this web computer stuff."[55]

The piece was also exhibited in physical form as a photo series in the 1994 *Toys/Art/Us* show at the Castle Gallery in New Rochelle, New York.[56] It created a minor uproar when, in response to reviews in the *New York Times* and *Art in*

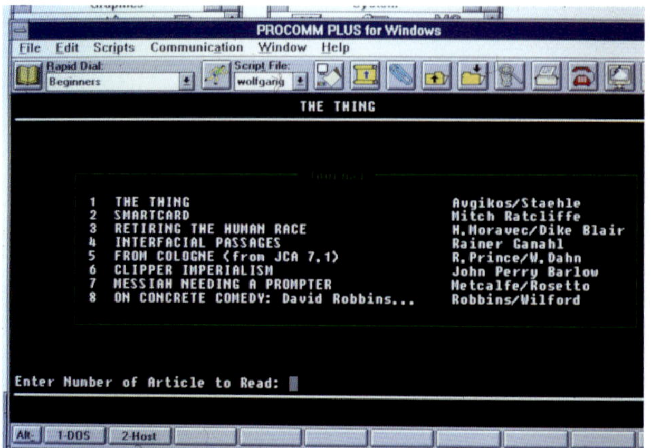

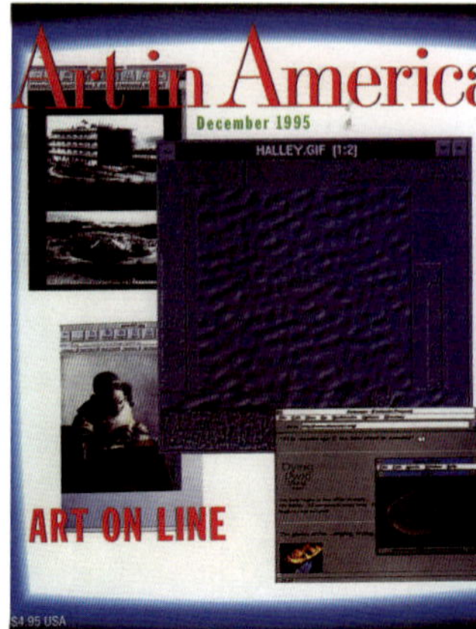

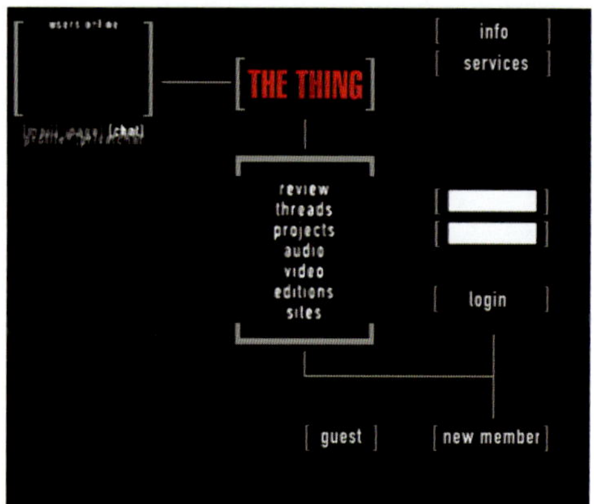

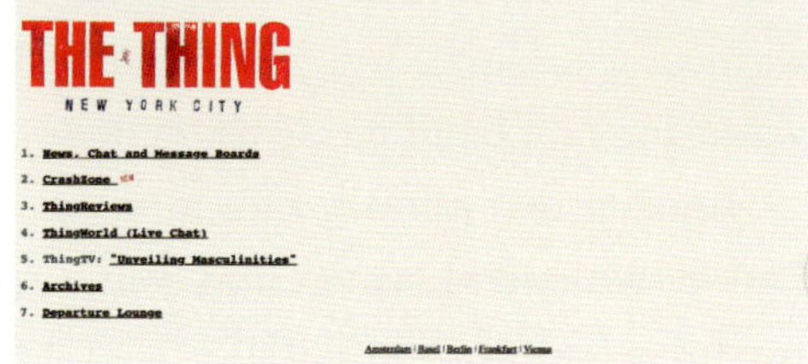

Top left: The Thing BBS interface, courtesy of The Thing
Top right: *Art in America* cover, December 1995
Above: The Thing web interfaces

America, Mattel sent a letter to The Thing accusing it of copyright dilution and demanding that the work be removed immediately.[57]

> Then around that time, all the sudden they discovered artists doing web art and browser art, and there was actually an *Art in America* article that reported all of the people doing net art. I was one of them. *Barbie and Ken Politically Correct* was cited.[58]

After the internet became more widely available in 1995, The Thing transformed into a proto-social media website and internet service provider, and *Barbie and Ken Politically Correct* reappeared as an animated gif, using JavaScript to automatically reload the page and open a new image.

"Since the early 1990s, New York-based Hovagimyan has created work in new media, including internet-based projects, video art, and multi-media performances and installations," wrote curator Jessamyn Fiore in *112 Greene Street*. "He is one of the pioneers of what is now collectively known as net art, and continues to explore the creative, collaborative, and subversive potential of emerging technologies, while also highlighting their sometimes uncanny and anthropomorphic dimension."[59]

Terrorist Advertising, Bowery & 5th Street, Sep. 23, 1993–Feb. 23, 1994

A special billboard project, *Terrorist Advertising* appeared on the northeast corner of Bowery and 5th Street in the East Village in September 1994. Hovagimyan carved into the covers of eight copies of *Artforum* to expose the inside pages. He then scanned them into high-resolution files and printed the images onto durable paper, using a four-color electrostatic printer, to create a 10-by-20-foot billboard. A manifesto accompanied the images, which he later uploaded and distributed on the internet as a hypertext piece. Users clicked through texts and photos to reveal the manifesto as a kind of narrative:

> Art magazines are the primary media to validate my work and identify me as an artist. This is one reason I decided to use an art magazine as material for

> this piece. Much in the same way as artists carve wood or work in plaster, I've carved into art magazines. When I cut into them, I expose the inside pages and accelerate the experience of reading the magazine. The result is an MTV speeded up magazine experience without ever opening it.
>
> Art magazines are specialty publications. Their readership for the most part is made up of interested professionals. Most people do not read art magazines. *Terrorist Advertising* takes specialized information from a relatively obscure source and transforms it through an art process. The final transformation brings the image to a broad-based audience and places it in a new context, "mass media billboard."
>
> We live in a media-saturated environment. Family, neighborhood, vocation, religion, and ethnic affiliation have been replaced by media-driven identities. The spectacle created by the television daytime talk shows illustrates how media attention changes people. Consider how relatively ordinary people are perceived as more important and possibly more real than they do in their daily lives, after they appear on television for any trivial or far-fetched reason.
>
> I view most advertising as an effort to manipulate peoples' opinions and desires. Advertising designed solely to increase the profits of a corporation at the expense of the individual's sense of self is just as terrible as a gun held to the head of a terrorist victim.[60]

Like *Tactics for Survival*, an underlying social criticism becomes the basis for the work, made explicit in the hypertext version. In *Terrorist Advertising*, Hovagimyan expresses a critique of consumer advertisement as equivalent to terrorism, compelling the public to act against its own interest as a society and the individual's own well-being.

Hey Bozo, Use Mass Transit, MTA Arts for Transit & Creative Time, Apr.–May, 1994

In 1994, Hovagimyan responded to a call for proposals to promote the use of public transit as part of an annual anti-pollution campaign by the New York City Metropolitan Transportation Authority's Arts for Transit program. The program was organized in collaboration with Creative Time, the downtown

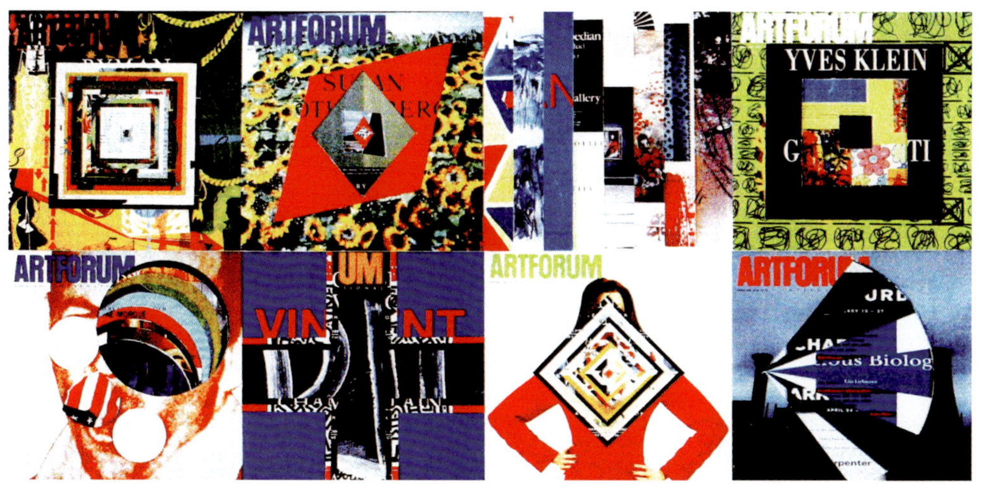

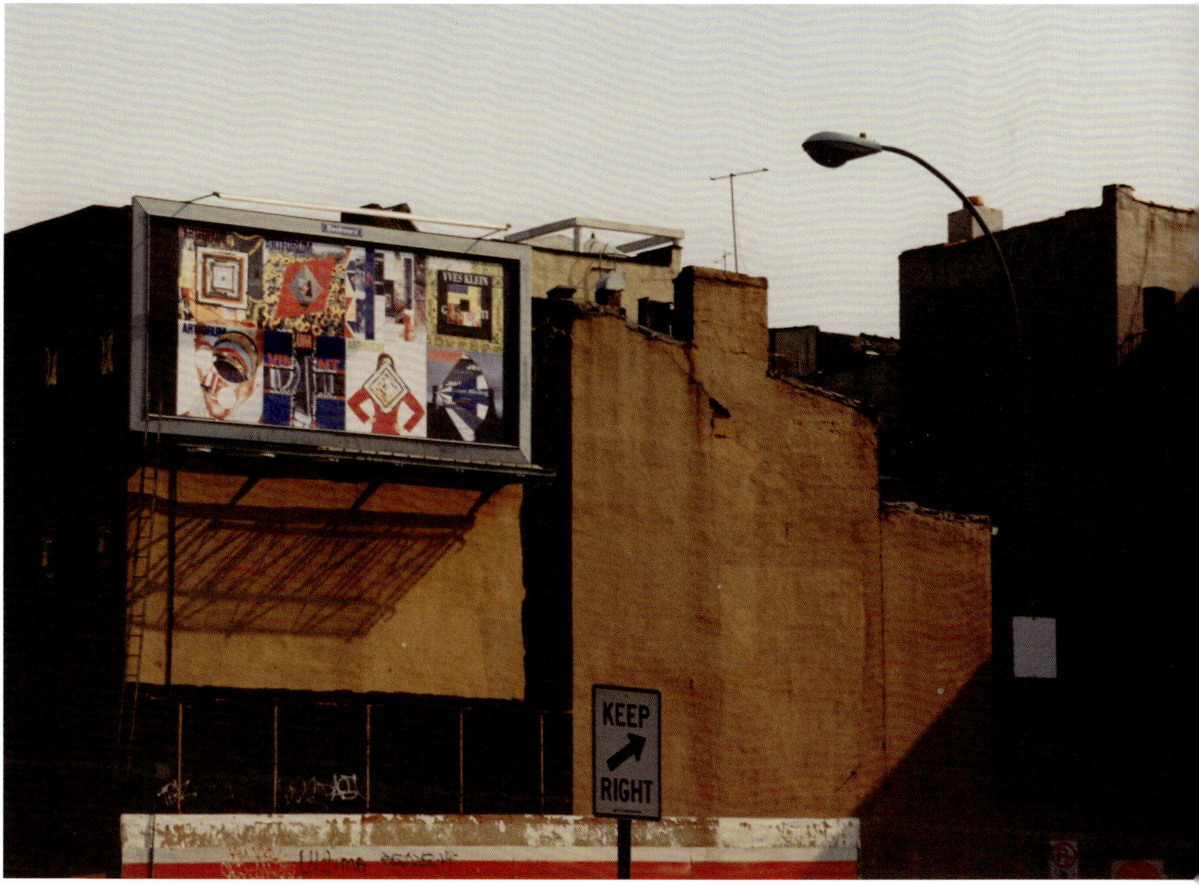

Top: *Terrorist Advertising* image

Above: *Terrorist Advertising* billboard installed at Bowery and 5th Street

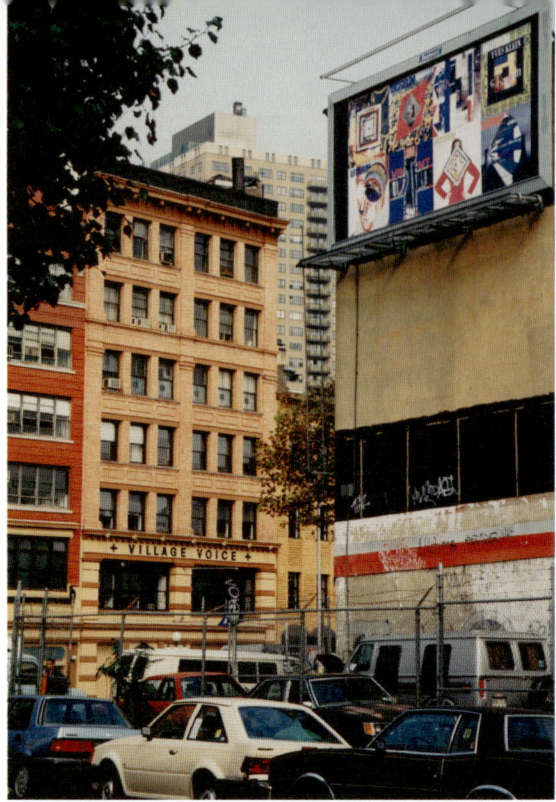

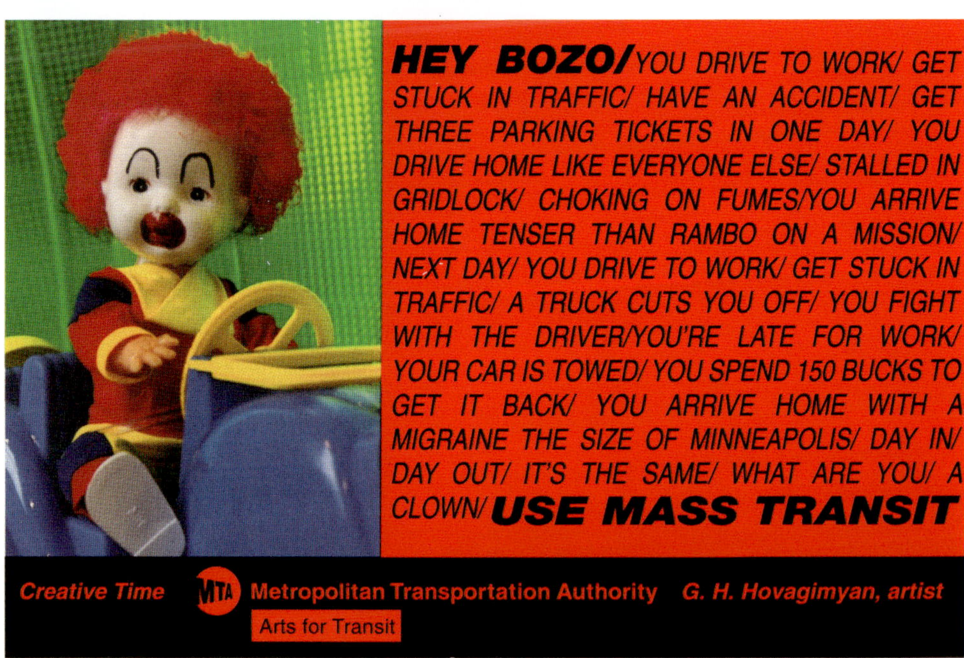

Top: *Terrorist Advertising* billboard view facing the Bowery
Above: *Hey Bozo, Use Mass Transit* postcard

public art organization founded in 1973 by Karin Bacon, Susan Henshaw Jones, and Anita Contini, which had pioneered commissioning temporary works in vacant commercial spaces in the Financial District. Five large-scale billboards announcing "Hey Bozo, Use Mass Transit" and describing in short verses the headaches of commuter traffic were installed in April and May of 1994. They were immediately controversial.

> After I did *Terrorist Advertising*, Creative Time had a call for artists to produce billboards to convince people to use mass transit. I had an idea like Ms. Subways. "Hi! This is Ms. Subways." It's one-third photo, two-thirds text. I decided I was going to do it very confrontational and punky like my *Rich Sucker Rap*. I got a girl's rainbow-colored wig, I put white clown makeup on my face, and I got an oversized tractor steering wheel, and a friend of mine took photos of me like an angry clown driving to work. Then I thought, "No, they're not going to go for it because it's the MTA Arts in Transit."
>
> I decided, "OK, what's the most inoffensive thing people see on television: a child's toy." I got a blue plastic toy car with a farm boy in it. I painted its face with clown paint, and I teased up its hair and spray-painted it fluorescent pink. Then I put it on Kodak sparkly lenticular green and blue lens paper, and I had it driving the lawn. I made a rap rant in fluorescent orange, "Hey Bozo, you drive to work, get caught in traffic, have an accident, get three parking tickets in one day. Driving home, stalled in gridlock, choking on fumes. The next day you drive to work, get cut off by a truck, get in a fight with the driver. You're late from work, your car is towed. Day in and day out, it's the same, what are you, a clown? Use mass transit."
>
> If you were driving along fast, all you saw was this clown car little thing, and then "Hey Bozo, Use Mass Transit" with a bunch of words. If you were stuck in traffic, you'd see the whole thing. I sent them both: me with the angry clown driving and one with the little clown car. They picked the clown car because it was less offensive, which was absolutely hilarious because it's sick. It's this really kind of ratty painted clown car with this angry aggressive rap. They put this up on five billboards all over the city, in front of the Holland Tunnel and the Lincoln Tunnel, and out in Staten Island.[61]

84

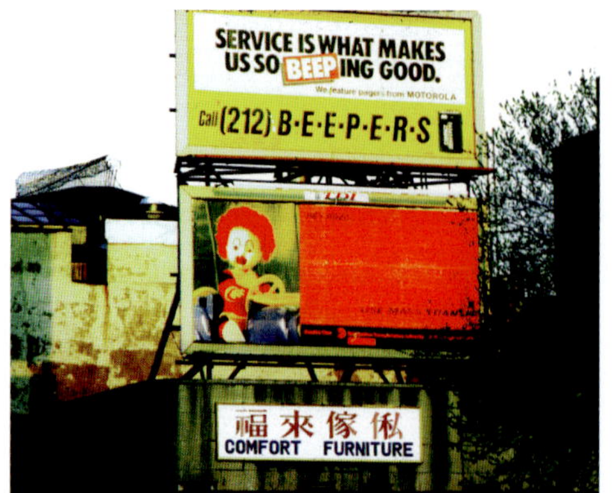

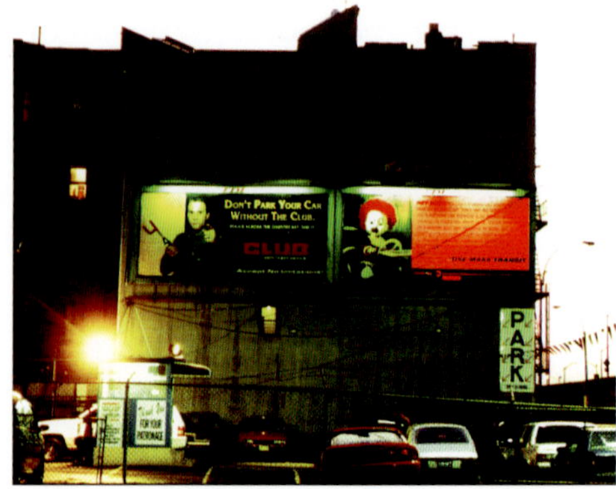

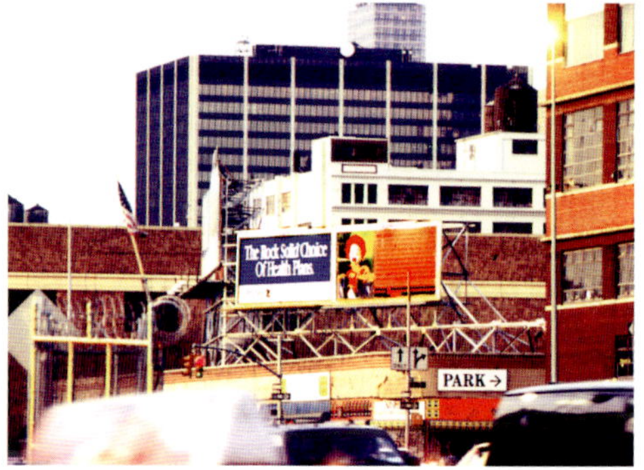

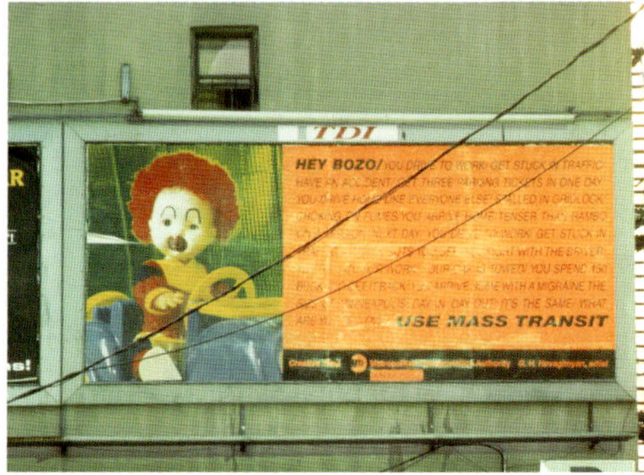

Top left: *Hey Bozo* billboard installation (approach to Holland Tunnel)
Top right: *Hey Bozo* billboard installation (38th and Lincoln Tunnel)
Above left: *Hey Bozo* billboard installation, Lincoln Tunnel (slide)
Above right: *Hey Bozo* billboard installation at Lincoln Tunnel (cropped slide)

Several network TV news shows picked up the story, such as Good Day New York and the national broadcast of NBC Nightly News with Brian Williams. It was also written up in the *New York Post*, *New York Daily News*, and the *New York Times.* The AP newswire distributed a telephone interview with Hovagimyan and a report on the controversy. "It takes a lot of *chutzpah* to call drivers Bozos," the spokesman of the Automobile Club of America was quoted saying.

> The *New York Post* picked up on it. And once it picked up on that, it went out on the Associated Press news line. And then it went viral before there was viral. I was interviewed on Good Day New York, Fox TV in front of the billboard with a right-wing representative to present the driver's side of the issue, which was absolutely ridiculous. Then I was on Good Morning America. Then NBC Nightly News nationwide. So that was a big deal.[62]

The NBC News segment reported by Megan O'Donnell interviewed drivers from their car windows. "For the artist behind the controversial Bozo billboard, provoking drivers is exactly the idea," she reported.

> "Woman: It's a little rude but . . ."
>
> "So I guess we're Bozos!"
>
> "I think it's a real funny way to try to win friends and influence people to call drivers Bozos right off the bat."

As a result of all the publicity, Larry Harmon, the "original" Bozo the Clown, filed a lawsuit claiming trademark dilution.

> The *Post,* every day, they were running a piece about outrage at the billboard. They even had a cartoon with a bunch of clowns sitting around an executive board room with another clown pointing at it saying, "Gentlemen, we have a winner!"... Apparently, Bozo the Clown saw the TV report, and the MTA received a cease-and-desist letter from Bozo the Clown. I was sued by Bozo the Clown, and not only that but Mattel went after me for *Barbie and Ken Politically Correct.* I couldn't believe it. It was absolutely hilarious. Of course,

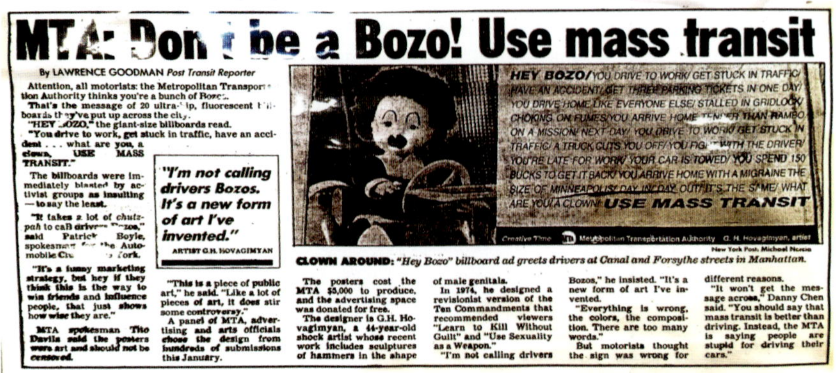

MTA: Don't be a Bozo! Use mass transit

By LAWRENCE GOODMAN *Post Transit Reporter*

Attention, all motorists: the Metropolitan Transportation Authority thinks you're a bunch of Bozos.

That's the message of 20 ultra-hip, fluorescent billboards they've put up across the city.

"HEY BOZO," the giant-size billboards read.

"You drive to work, get stuck in traffic, have an accident . . . what are you, a clown, USE MASS TRANSIT."

The billboards were immediately blasted by activist groups as insulting — to say the least.

"It takes a lot of *chutzpah* to call drivers Bozos," said Patrick Boyle, spokesman for the Automobile Club of New York.

"It's a funny marketing strategy, but hey if they think this is the way to win friends and influence people, that just shows how wise they are."

MTA spokesman Tito Davila said the posters were art and should not be censored.

"This is a piece of public art," he said. "Like a lot of pieces of art, it does stir some controversy."

A panel of MTA, advertising and arts officials chose the design from hundreds of submissions this January.

> *"I'm not calling drivers Bozos. It's a new form of art I've invented."*
> ARTIST G.H. HOVAGIMYAN

New York Post: Michael Norcia

CLOWN AROUND: *"Hey Bozo" billboard ad greets drivers at Canal and Forsythe streets in Manhattan.*

The posters cost the MTA $5,000 to produce, and the advertising space was donated for free.

The designer is G.H. Hovagimyan, a 44-year-old shock artist whose recent work includes sculptures of hammers in the shape of male genitals.

In 1974, he designed a revisionist version of the Ten Commandments that recommended viewers "Learn to Kill Without Guilt" and "Use Sexuality as a Weapon."

"I'm not calling drivers Bozos," he insisted. "It's a new form of art I've invented."

"Everything is wrong, the colors, the composition. There are too many words."

But motorists thought the sign was wrong for different reasons.

"It won't get the message across," Danny Chen said. "You should say that mass transit is better than driving. Instead, the MTA is saying people are stupid for driving their cars."

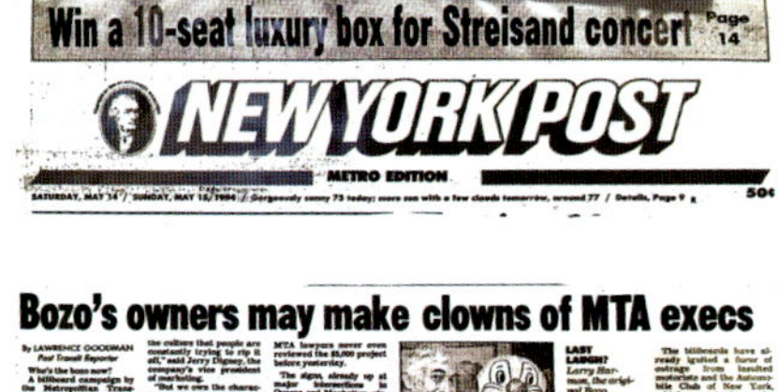

Win a 10-seat luxury box for Streisand concert Page 14

NEW YORK POST

METRO EDITION

50¢

Bozo's owners may make clowns of MTA execs

Above: *New York Post* coverage
Left: *NY Post* article, May 14, 1994
Opposite: *NY Post* cartoon on *Hey Bozo*

I had gotten one of these pro bono lawyers who argued it was fair use and only up temporarily.[63]

The project later showed at the New Museum in the *Courage* exhibition (1995), at Eastern Connecticut State University in *Meme Breeders* (1996), and at Mass MoCA's *Billboard: Art on the Road* (1999). Bozo eventually dropped the lawsuit.

Surveys & Questionnaires, Gallery 128, 1994

Later that year, Gallery 128, run by feminist minimalist Kuzuko Miyamoto, invited Hovagimyan to mount a solo exhibition. Gallery 128 had opened in 1986 at 127 Rivington Street around the time that a group of anarchistic art spaces on the Lower East Side became identified as the Rivington School. They

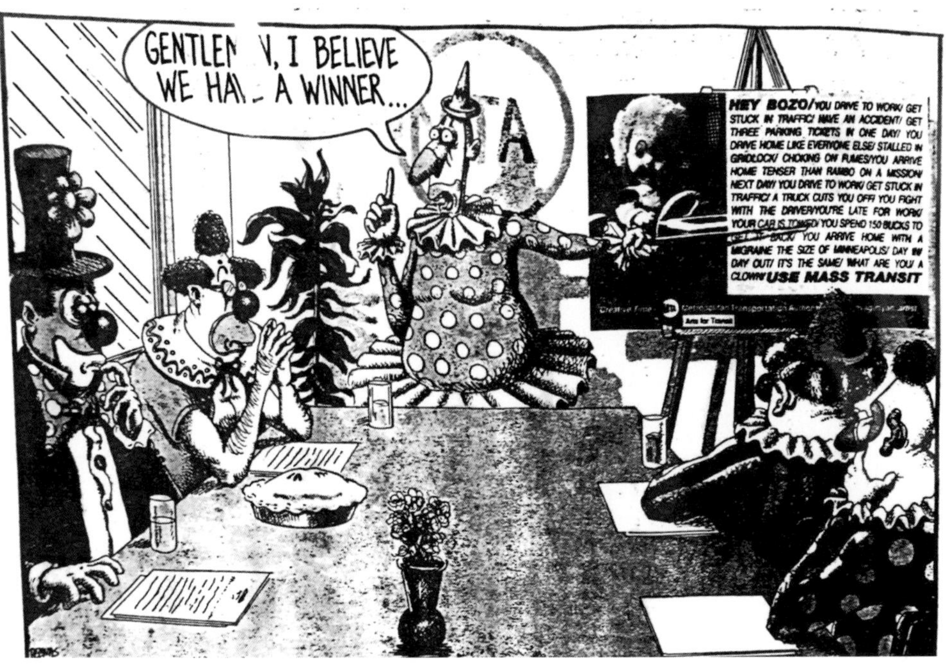

included the No Se No Social Club, the Rivington School Sculpture Garden, Kwok Gallery, Storefront for Art and Architecture, and Arleen Schoss's A's Place. On the next block, ABC No Rio opened in 1980 as an outgrowth of Colab's Real Estate Show.

Using a mashup of forms and marketing surveys paired with images of consumer products, Hovagimyan created a series of works critiquing the era's version of data mining: companies and government agencies gathering information about the population's desires and habits. The pieces in *Surveys & Questionnaires* used prevailing imaging techniques of the time, such as laser jet color prints, color photo enlargements, and large black and white Xerox prints.

> I was walking down the street, walking down Broadway, and one of these religious people, Jews for Jesus, who knows what, came up to me and said, "Can I speak to you about Jesus?" and he had this card with him. I said "OK,

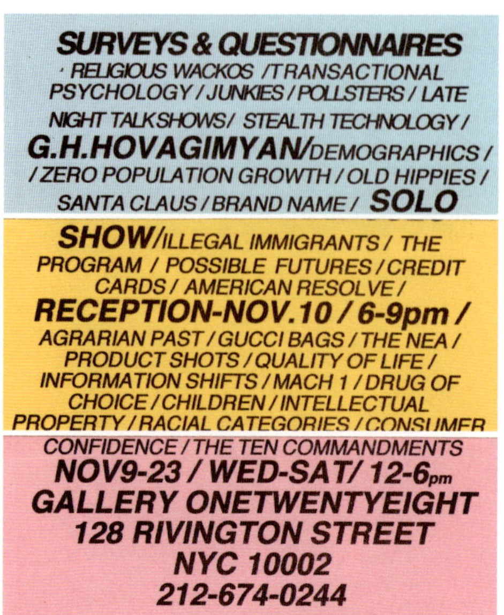

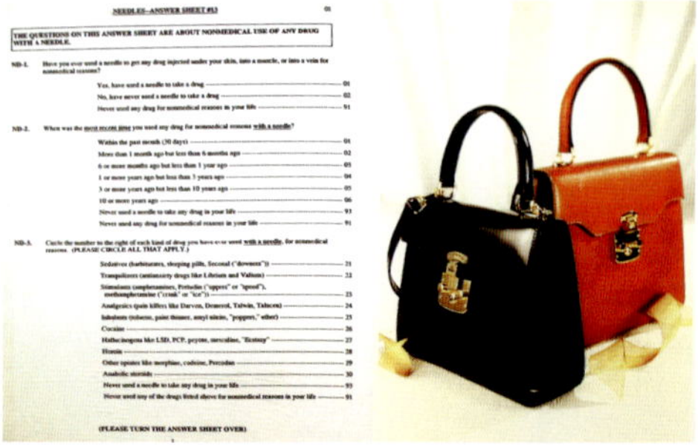

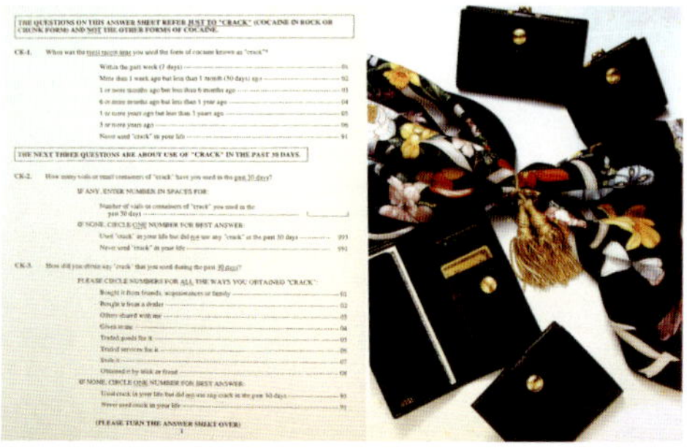

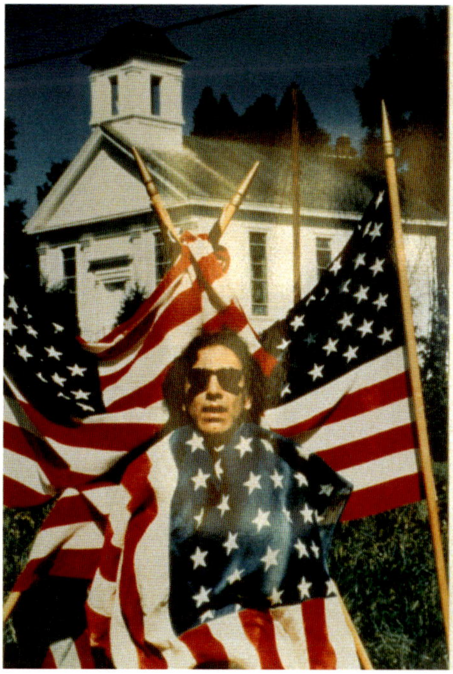

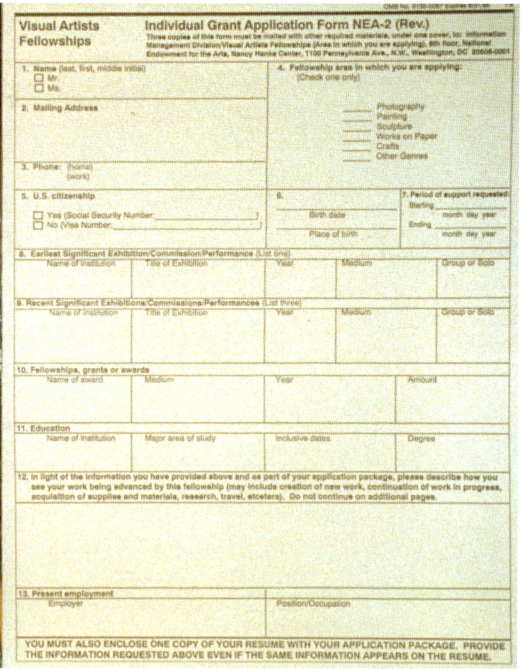

Top left: *Surveys & Questionaires* flyer. Top right: Purses and wallets paired with crack-use survey
Above: Hovagimyan in patriotic photo beside NEA fellowship application form

but only if you give me that card when you're finished." So he goes down this list of questions. And the first one was, "If you were to die in this instant, do you know that you would go to heaven?" Then there's a little check box "Yes/No." And then, "Would you like to know for sure? Yes/No." It started off, "I want you to ask questions for a survey that I'm taking." I thought it was absolutely fucking hilarious. So I take the card and blow it up in a giant Xerox. And then I had gotten a pair of praying hands at a yard sale that was made in China—a little tchotchke ceramic thing—so I painted its nails red and took a photograph of that, and blew it up the same size of the survey, like 40 inches. The pieces are all like that, a survey of marketing in Mexico City, and a survey of drug rehab stuff, they're just information, but they're information used as some sort of counterpoint to an image. So it's part text, but it's not story art or anything like that. That's what I was doing.[64]

The pieces defamiliarize the consumer images, treating them as conceptual found objects magnified in a critical context. As his press release stated:

> The subject and content of the works is the seemingly endless flow of images and information one is confronted with every day…in this series of works, he picks images and information out of the general flow, isolates and magnifies them, in order for the viewer to more readily observe and be aware of the messages being conveyed and how they shape our society. Everything from a kitschy pair of praying hands to a banal series of product shots for Gucci or the drug questionnaires for the HRA to a marketing survey are presented for our scrutiny.
>
> Since the beginning of the 20th century, as print and broadcast media began expanding to their current levels of total permeation into the fabric of modern society, traditional methods for conveying the mythic narrative function within society, that which is born by oral tradition and social function have been replaced by a media-driven mythic narrative. Traditional societies teach their mores and myths through any number of social instruments such as religious functions, songs and dance, jokes, art, theatre and so on. These tend to be static and repetitive and serve to reaffirm the commonality of the social group while upholding the groups sense of identity.

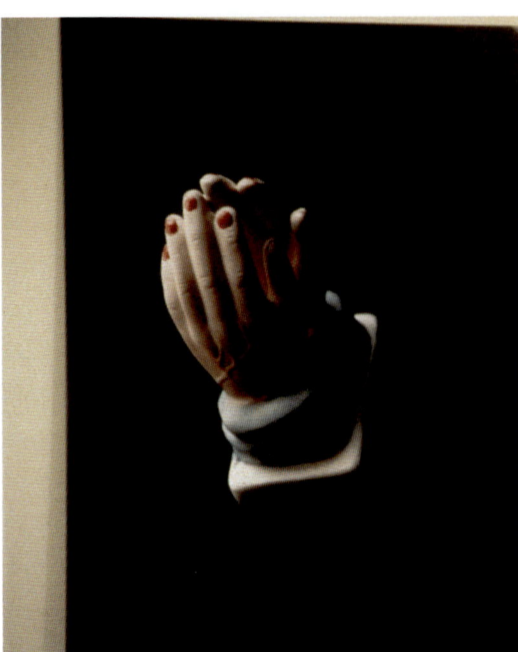

QUESTIONNAIRE ON RELIGION

1. Name ______ Street ______
   City/State/Zip ______
2. Occupation ______
3. Are you a member of a religious group?
   Yes ☐ No ☐ If so, which one? ______
4. Do you attend its functions
   weekly ☐ monthly ☐ never ☐
5. Do you believe the Bible is the Word of God?
   Yes ☐ No ☐
6. How do you think a person gets to heaven?
7. From what source did you learn this?
   ______
8. If you were to die in the next instant, do you know that you would go to heaven? Yes ☐ No ☐
9. If not, would you like to know for sure? Yes ☐ No ☐

FOR SURVEYOR ONLY

Surveyor's Name: ______ Date ______
Did you succeed in giving a complete plan of salvation? Yes ☐ No ☐
Did this person make any decision? Yes ☐ No ☐
If so, for what? ______

Here are some things you may learn about candidates running for Congress this year. After I read each one, please tell me whether it would make you more likely, less likely, or make no difference in voting for that candidate. The first is ...[ROTATE]

	MORE LIKELY	NO DIFFERENCE	LESS LIKELY	DON'T KNOW	REF.
20. Is a Republican	1	2	3	9	0
21. Is Pro-Choice on abortion	1	2	3	9	0
22. Supported U.S. involvement in the Gulf War	1	2	3	9	0
23. Voted against an extension of unemployment benefits because the bill contained no way to fund the increase	1	2	3	9	0
24. Voted for an increase in the minimum wage, but not the largest increase that was proposed	1	2	3	9	0
25. Is endorsed by the Sierra Club, a national environmental group	1	2	3	9	0
26. Supports the National Endowment for the Arts	1	2	3	9	0
27. Is a woman	1	2	3	9	0
28. Bounced 10 checks at the House Bank	1	2	3	9	0
29. Has been in Congress for 14 years	1	2	3	9	0
30. Supports gun controls	1	2	3	9	0
31. Is the only Member of Congress from New York on the House Appropriations Committee	1	2	3	9	0
32. Supports U.S. aid to foreign countries	1	2	3	9	0

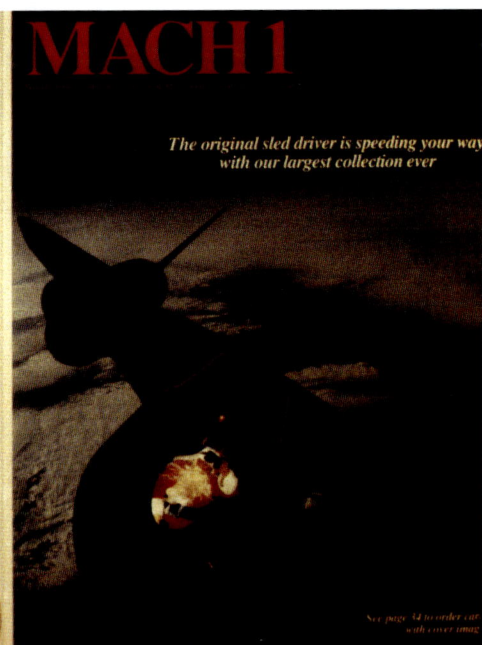

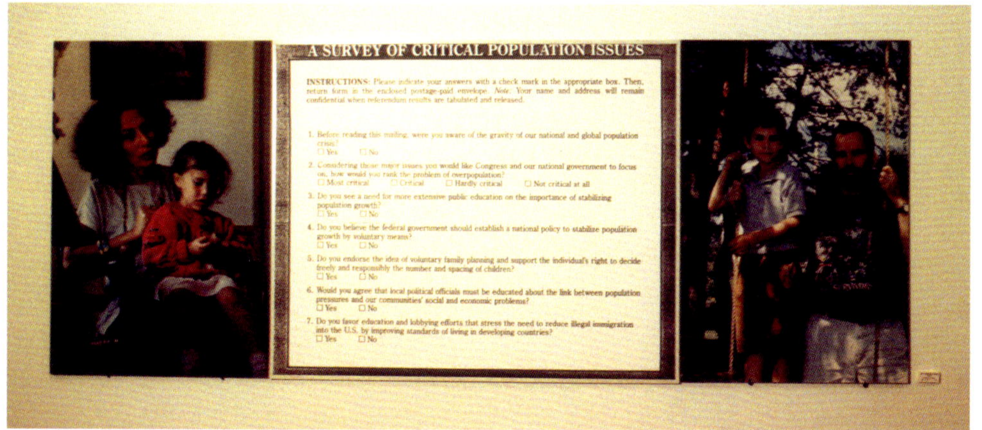

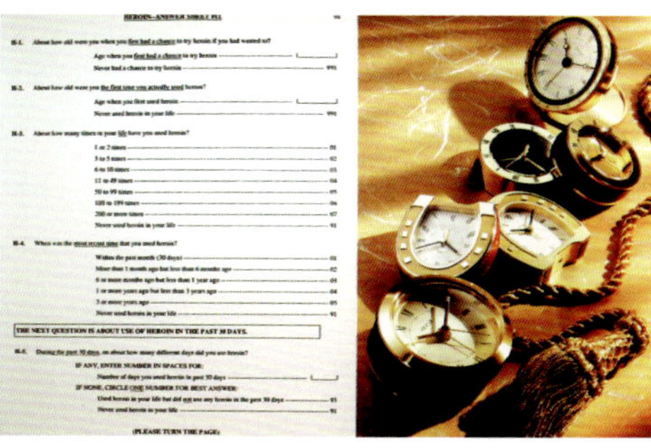

Opposite top: Botanica shop figure with religious questionnaire
Below: Political survey with military aircraft
Above: Public opinion survey and photos of families, installation
Left: Gucci watches and survey of heroin use

With television as a tool for corporate capitalism, the narrative function becomes entertainment for the sole purpose of delivering receptive consumers. New products as well as new forms of entertainment must constantly be presented to catch the attention of the public. Myth becomes an attachment to certain products from certain time periods in what Walter Benjamin terms "the commodity fetish aspect of capitalism." Since global capitalism's goal is ever-expanding markets and an ever-expanding consumer base, marketing surveys and questionnaires have been the method for determining how to best achieve those goals. These surveys are used to formulate opinions and statistics which act as the consensual basis for determining action on everything from anti-drug programs and political campaigns to sexual and religious preferences.[65]

Faux Conceptual Art, artnetweb, 1993-1995

Another New York group using the internet as a venue, artnetweb was founded in 1993 by Remo Campopiano and Robbin Murphy, initially as a bulletin board system. It established itself as an art collaborative dedicated to exploring new technologies. Hovagimyan used the platform for his *Faux Conceptual Art* series, realized simultaneously as a website and in the form of proposals and Dada objects, which deliberately copied and reappropriated works by other artists. Dating from 1993 to 1994, and appended and altered in 2007, it appeared as a website in 1995.

> It was a website I put up with artnetweb, and I also did a box set of proposal boards for an installation, and I did some 3D actual pieces. If you were to compare it to Duchamp's *Boîte-en-valise*, it's that notion of making Dada-style objects but then adding a web dimension and also doing physical pieces re-doing conceptual art works or ripping off of them. It dealt with copyright, the notion of conceptual art is an idea. It's idea art, so the question is can you copyright something that doesn't have a physical form or can you copyright words. Lawrence Weiner has a style of writing words. Anybody can make those words up, they don't have to be Lawrence Weiner's words. So I can make a fake Lawrence Weiner or a fake Dennis Oppenheim or a fake Joseph Beuys that looks like Joseph Beuys but they're not. Stylistically it would look like if I went to the museum and copied a Renoir painting.[66]

Hovagimyan made several pieces as objects in the series, including *Sit-On,* a framed color photo of a folding chair, a printed text reading "SIT ON," and a deconstructed actual folding chair protruding from the frame. He called this the fake Kossuth chair piece, imitating Kossuth's 1965 *One and Three* Chairs—an installation in the Museum of Modern Art collection with a black-and-white photo of a chair, an actual folding chair, and a printed text containing the dictionary definition of a chair. *Fibonacci Series with Calculators* was a faux Mario Merz, who had made a series of drawings based on the Fibonacci series of numbers. He later framed the piece and installed a stage light.

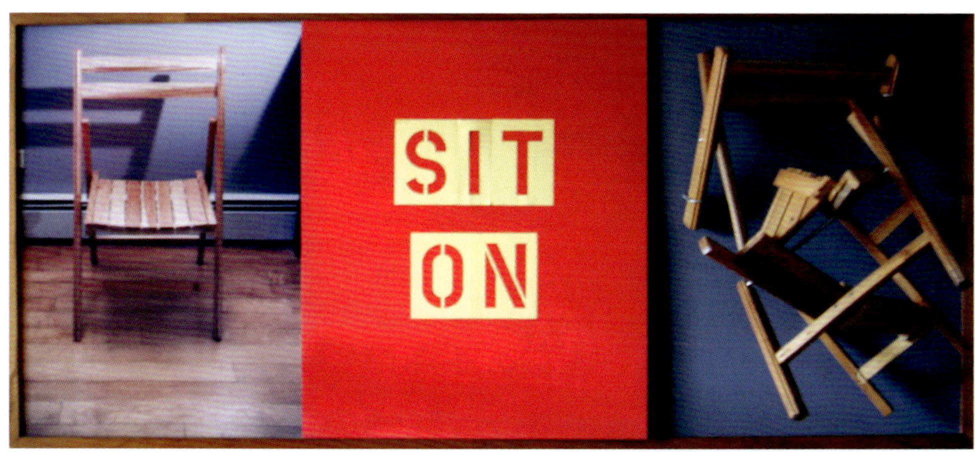

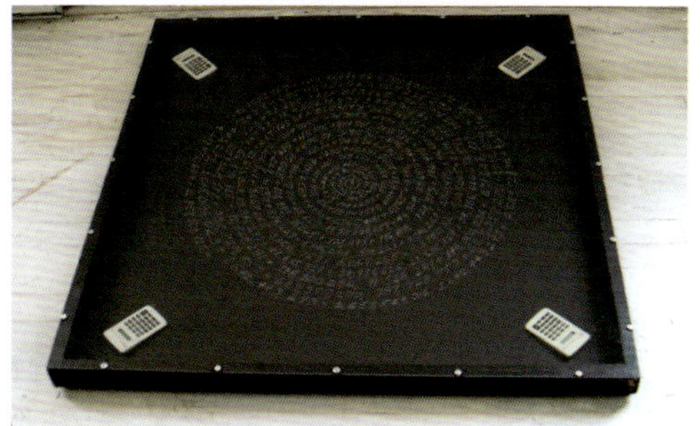

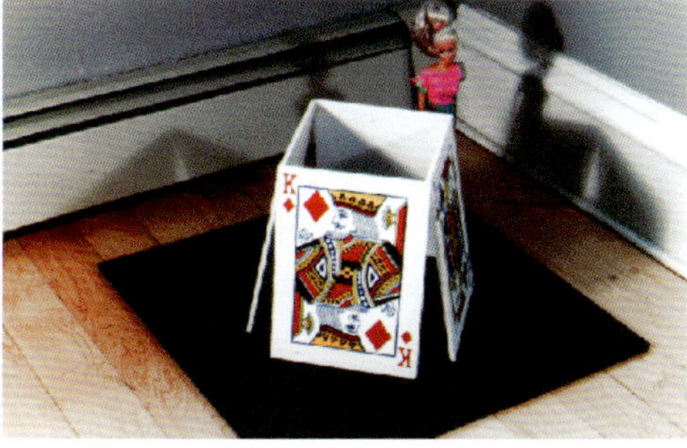

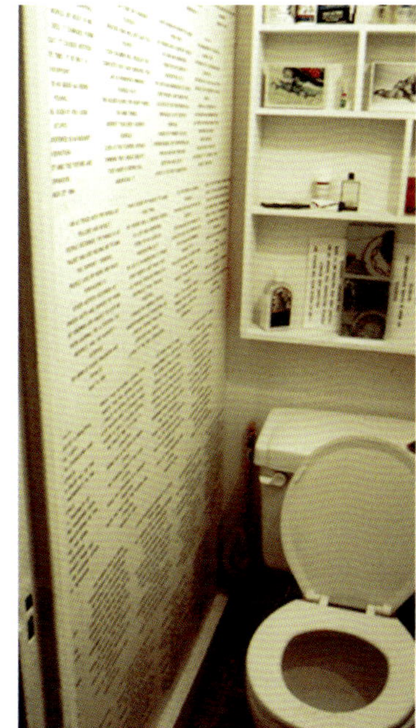

Top: *Sit-On*, 1993
Above: *Fibonacci Series with Calculators*, 1994
Above right: *Faux Richard Serra*, 1993
Right: *Toilet Conceptualism*, 1995, installed at Mimi Wheeler's loft

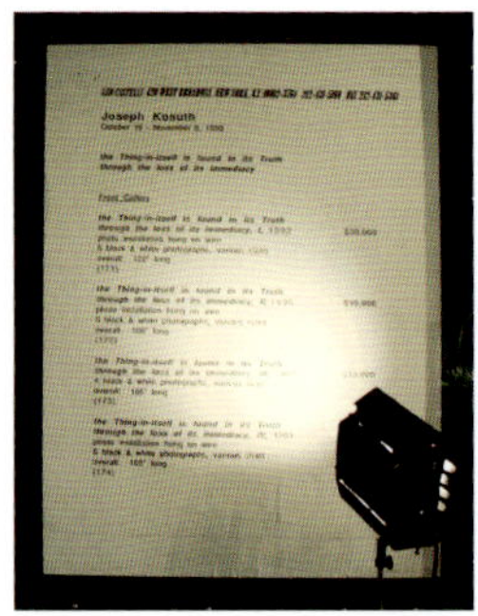

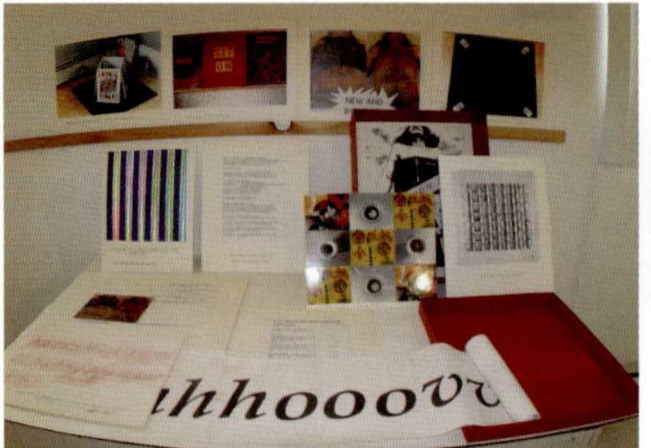

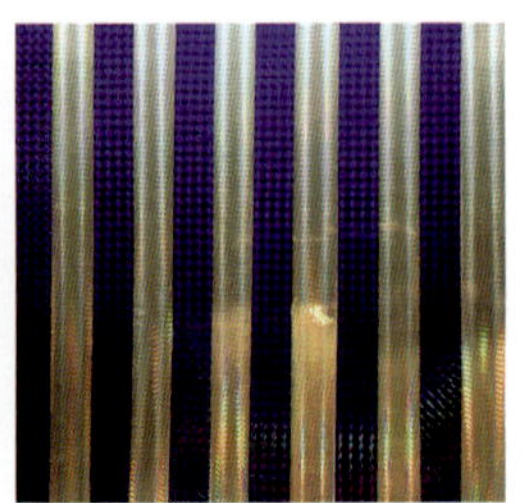

Left to right: *Giant Kosuth Price List*, 1993 & 2007 (photostatic print, framed with light); *Box of proposals*, 1995; *Faux Daniel Buren*, 1993

A series of *Video Affirmations* was also posted on artnetweb, consisting of short videos of people in clown makeup saying "Be curious, even if you look stupid." The online *Faux Conceptual Art* pieces included gifs of a faux Lawrence Weiner, composed of a series of life-affirming texts in the manner of Weiner's wall texts, displayed as text in a bathroom. A faux Daniel Buren gif had repeating colored patterns, and a faux Richard Serra showed a gif of four playing cards leaning against each other with a Barbie Doll mounted on the board for scale. Artnetweb held an opening for the works in its office at 426 Broome Street.

Art Direct/ Sex Violence Politics, Thing.net/artnetweb, 1995

By 1995, Netscape released Netscape Navigator 2.0, the first internet browser capable of running animated gifs and JavaScript, paving the way for the first interactive web pages. The Thing moved to an office in Chelsea and migrated its identity to Thing.net, a website hosting criticism, artists' projects, and webpages. Hovagimyan expanded his engagement with the web for conceptual

I AM SURROUNDED BY A BEAUTIFUL
GLOWING LIGHT.
MY HIGHER SELF IS LOVING, KIND
AND GENEROUS.
GOD WANTS ME TO ENJOY ALL OF
THE ABUNDANCE AND PROSPERITY
IN THE WORLD
I REMOVE ALL THOUGHTS OF LACK,
FAILURE AND GRASPING FEAR.
ALL PEOPLE ARE REFLECTIONS OF
THE SAME MIND,
THE SAME CONSCIOUSNESS.
I RELEASE MYSELF FROM THE
RESPONSIBILITY OF JUDGING
OTHER PEOPLE'S BEHAVIOR.
I AM AT PEACE WITH THE WORLD,
MY FELLOWS AND MYSELF.
PEOPLE RECOGNIZE THE RANGE
OF MY TALENT AND ARE HELPING
ME TO GAIN THE SUPPORT
I DESERVE.
PEOPLE LOVE MY WORK AND
ENJOY PURCHASING IT.
OTHER ARTISTS RECOGNIZE
MY UNIQUE GIFTS
AND SUPPORT MY WORK.
MY ENEMIES ARE UNABLE TO STOP ME
FROM GAINING THE ATTENTION, THE
RESPECT, AND THE SUPPORT I
DESERVE.
MY MIND IS CLEAR, BALANCED AND
INFINITE.
I NOW EXIST IN A HEIGHTENED
REALITY.
NOONE AND NOTHING CAN DISTRACT
ME.
I AM A WORTHWHILE PERSON.
WHAT I HAVE TO SHARE WITH OTHERS
IS WORTHWHILE.
MY SHYNESS MAY BE CONSTRUED AS
AS ARROGANCE.
I BELIEVE I AM WORTHWHILE SO I CAN
BE GENEROUS OF SPIRIT.
I FORGIVE MYSELF FOR NOT BEING
SUCCESSFUL.
PEOPLE ARE NO LONGER AFRAID OF
MY
POWERFUL PERSONALITY,
THEY ENCOURAGE ME TO REVEAL IT.
I CAN NO LONGER SUPPRESS MY
CREATIVE NATURE.
RATHER THAN DEVALUE WHO I AM,
I STAY AWAY FROM PEOPLE WHO ARE
JEALOUS OF ME.
I SPEAK THE TRUTH.
I SPEAK IT WITH FORCE
AND CONVICTION.
I SEE THE TRUTH, MY EYES ARE CLEAR
AND UNBIASED.
I HEAR THE TRUTH.
I LISTEN WITHOUT INTERPRETING.
I FEEL THE TRUTH.
I TRUST MY FEELINGS.
I HAVE CHOSEN MY PARENTS
TO LEARN FROM THEM.
MY FRIENDS ARE A CONSTANT SOURCE
OF LOVE AND INSPIRATION.
I FORM THE ART SCENE BY
PARTICIPATING IN IT.
MY LIFE IS AN INSPIRATION TO OTHERS
EVEN THOUGH I CAN'T KNOW THAT.
I GO INTO THE PAST AND REMOVE ALL
OBSTACLES TO MY CREATIVE
ENERGIES.
I FORGIVE MY PARENTS FOR NOT
UNDERSTANDING AND SUPPORTING
ME.
I FREE MY MOTHER FROM HER
ADDICTION
AND DEATH.
LISTEN TO THE NEXT GENERATION.
ALL MY OBSESSIONS ARE ENDING.
BREAK YOUR PATTERNS, CHANGE
YOUR
HABITS, THIS WILL INSURE SURVIVAL.
I CREATE MY WORLD, MY BODY IS ME.
LOVE NEVER DIES, IT CHANGES FORM.
DESIRE IS HEAT, IT CAUSES MOTION.
WE CREATE TIME, IT IS ONLY A
VIEWPOINT.
BEING OLD IS AS GOOD AS BEING
YOUNG.
BE CURIOUS, EVEN IF YOU LOOK
STUPID.
TODAY MY LIFE FORCE IS A RADIANT
VIBRATION.
BOTH THE PAST AND THE FUTURE
ARE OPINIONS.
THE HUMAN RACE IS BEING
TRANSFORMED
BY A DEEPER LOVE.
MY WORLD IS ONE OF MUTUAL
RESPECT
AND COOPERATION.
CEATIVITY IS MY NATURAL STATE.
AMERICA HAS CREATED THE IDEA OF
POVERTY AS WELL AS WEALTH.
REMEMBER WHEN YOU WERE A CHILD
AND ACT ACCORDINGLY.
THERE IS ENOUGH TIME TO COMPLETE
ALL THE TASKS IN MY DAY.
WAR IS NO LONGER NECESSARY
OR DESIRABLE.
TALK TO YOUR NEIGHBOR,
THEN LISTEN.
YOU CAN START BY CHANGING
YOURSELF.
CREATING FEAR WILL NOT GAIN
YOU RESPECT.
YOUR CHILDREN WILL RESOLVE THE
CONFLICTS THAT HAVE DEFEATED YOU.
LIFE IS WONDROUS, IMMERSE
YOURSELF
IN IT.
THE BLOOD FLOWS, THE HEART
PUMPS,
THE MIND THINKS.
RESPECT YOUR BODY,
RESPECT YOURSELF.
LOOK AT THE FLOWERS, WITHOUT
THINKING THEY CREATE BEAUTY.
YOUR ANGER IS WITHIN YOU,
UNDERSTAND IT.

Faux Lawrence Weiner, 1993

experiments. For the series *Art Direct/ Sex Violence Politics,* he created a new iteration of *Tactics for Survival in the New Culture* as a hypertext project. The original text from the 1974 piece is laid out on the screen, with hyperlinked words and phrases that users clicked on, forwarding to pages that provided subtexts for each statement.

> Then the next that happened was The Thing set up a website and actually had web browsers where it turned into a collaborative thing. It was still very slow, but I did my first web pieces. *Terrorist Advertising* was one of them. *Art Direct/ Sex Drugs Violence* was another one. We were just basically playing with HTML using that as a tool to make browser art.
>
> Hypertext is where you click on one thing and it jumps to the next page. *Tactics for Survival* has a list, and then if you click on the links in the list, it takes you to another subtext. It's taking you through the narrative, but there's a narrative beneath the narrative. It's about layering meaning through links, and it can be visual or it can be textual. It's about dealing with the way you think about things with layered narratives, and stringing things together.[67]

Barbie and Ken Politically Correct

Hovagimyan also reworked BKPC as a primitive HTML client-pull animation: a simple JavaScript reloaded the browser, automatically sending it to another page and another image at about 30 second intervals.

Flowers & Ecstasy

Flowers & Ecstasy plays with the dual valance of the term "wallpaper" that emerged to describe the background images on computer screens and Warhol's deliberate vulgarization of art and elevation of consumer products as culture, creating literal wallpaper out of his work. *Flowers & Ecstasy* consisted of pornographic imagery and paintings of flowers, alternating them as tiled images in the background or framed at the center.

ART DIRECT/

G.H. HOVAGIMYAN

sex, violence & politics

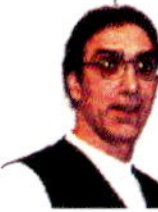

These pages contain what some may consider offensive material.
You click this link taking full responibility for your own actions

TACTICS FOR SURVIVAL IN THE NEW CULTURE

LEARN TO WITHOUT GUILT

ELIMINATE MATERIAL

RELY ON YOUR

USE AS A

NEVER YOURSELF

CHOOSE ONE :

PASSIVE-AGGRESSIVE, AGGRESSIVE-PASSIVE PASSIVE-PASSIVE, AGGRESSIVE-AGGRESSIVE

BECOME SEXUAL

CONSIDER INSTEAD OF

IN NO-ONE

DENY

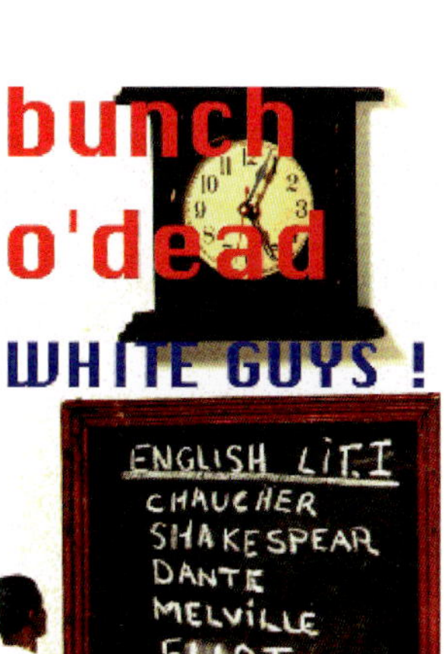

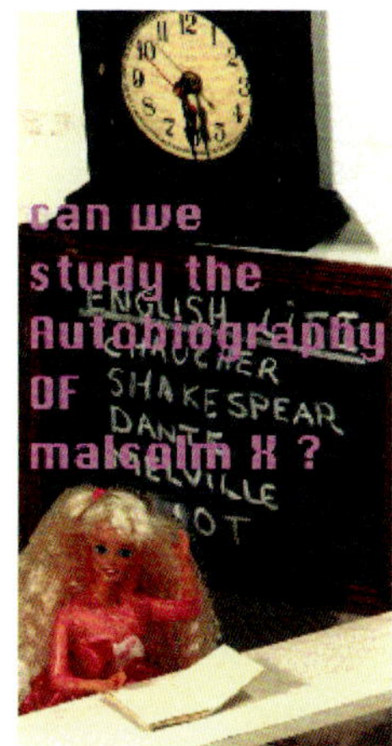

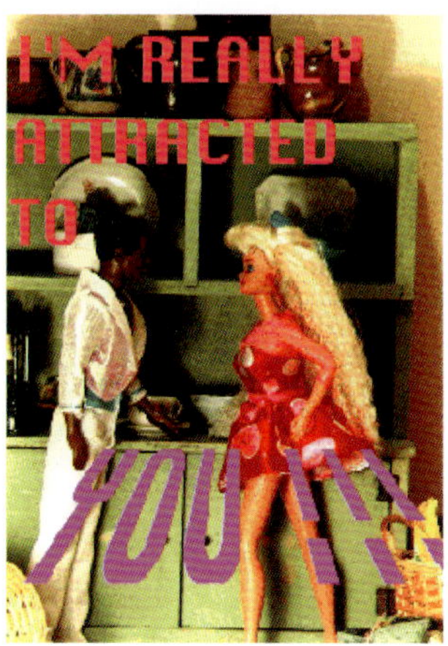

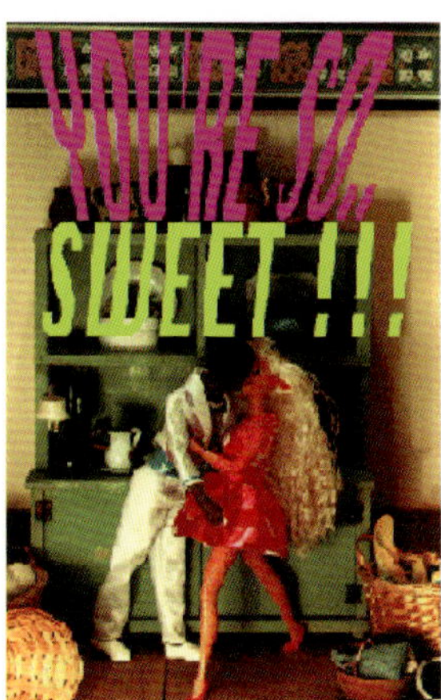

Top left: *Art Direct* page header with disclaimer

Top right: *Tactics for Survival* hypertext version, 1995

Above: *BKPC* as HTML client-pull animation

> You could print that out and make a wallpaper design out of it. That's basically what it's about if you look at Warhol wallpaper, and that's what they were calling that background tiling. They were calling it wallpaper at that point in web design. So that's what I was saying, "Sure, wallpaper! Blowjobs! Why not?" I thought it was kind of good wallpaper actually.[68]

Pray for Death

> It was all of these porno things and then National Rifle Association magazine images. Essentially that was just sex and death is what that's about. Current American imagery.[69]

Sacred & Profane

Like *Flowers & Ecstasy,* the contrasting images of *Sacred & Profane* play on the dichotomy between sets of wallpapered images, using hypertext to set up the opposition. Wallpaper of tiled dollar bills and an erect penis is paired with the repeated text "love me," while images of condoms and pornography are paired with the words "fuck me."

Opposite top: *Flowers & Ecstasy* wallpaper with flowers in foreground
Middle: *Flowers & Ecstasy* wallpaper with blowjob in foreground
Bottom: *Pray for Death*

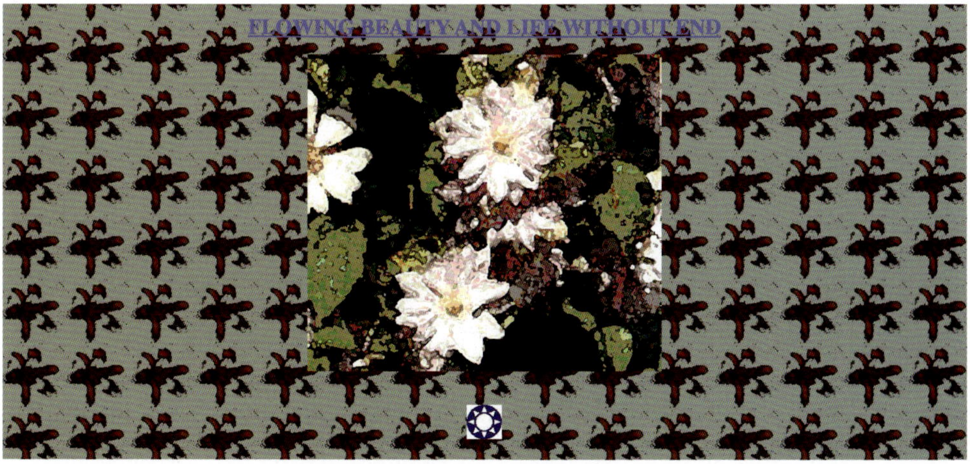

FLOWING BEAUTY AND LIFE WITHOUT END

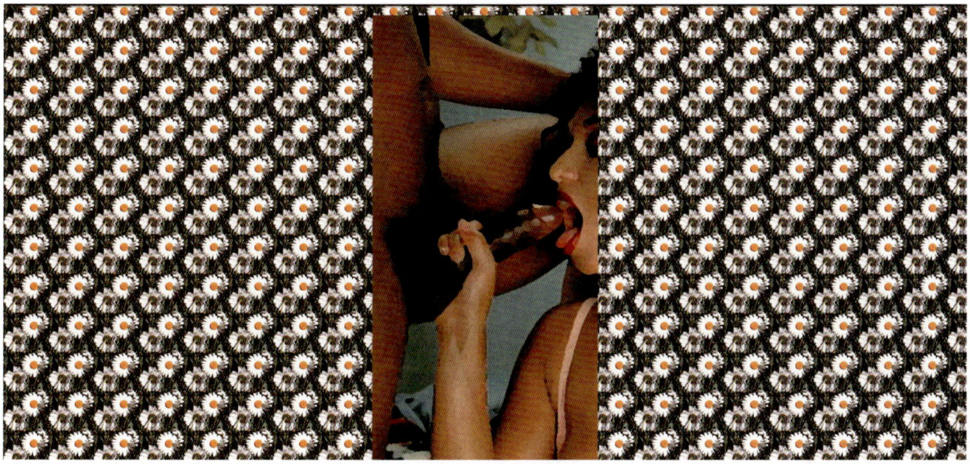

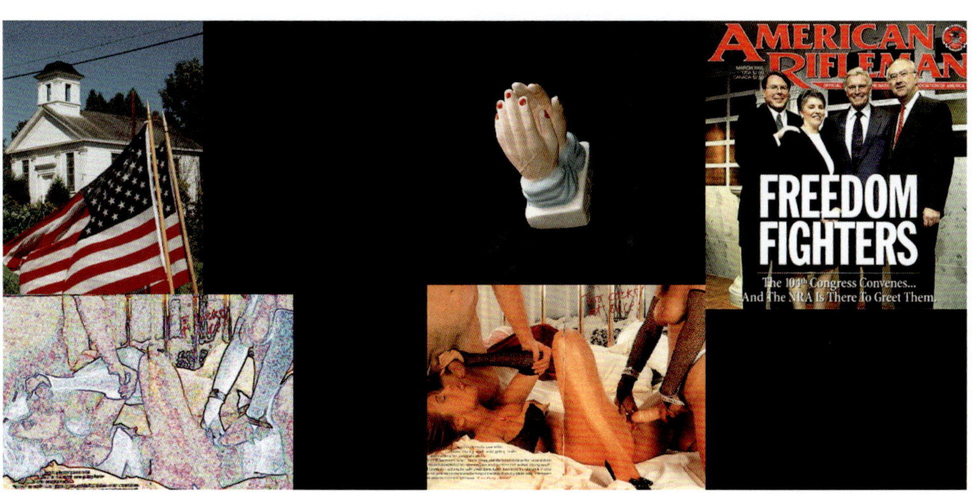

Art Dirt, Pseudo Online Radio/ Collider, The Thing, 1995–1998

Pseudo Programs, founded in 1994 by new media consultant and entrepreneur Josh Harris, belonged to the first wave of content creation of the dot-com era. It began as an outgrowth of the uncensored chat rooms Harris managed on the internet service provider (ISP) Prodigy's network, attempting to drive subscribers to the ISP by shepherding prurient interactions on sexually deviant subjects. Pseudo incorporated as a new media company conscious of the potential of the internet to "program" its listeners. They developed around 40 online radio shows by 1997 that used the newly developed RealAudio 2.0 format to "stream" audio files while they were still being downloaded. Predecessors of contemporary podcasting, the shows catered to "hip, tech-savvy young professionals" who were expected to be the cornerstone of a globally networked New Economy issuing from the creative potential of the internet.[70]

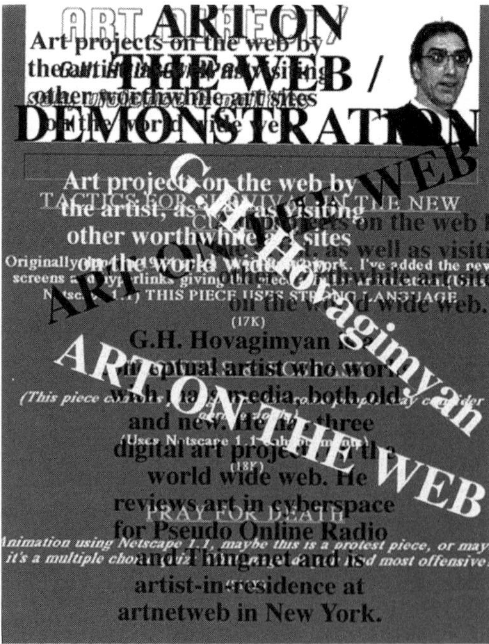

Left: Flyer for "art on the web" demonstration of *Art Direct* at artnetweb
Opposite top: *Sacred & Profane,* condoms
Middle: *Sacred & Profane,* sex
Bottom: Article in special issue of *artpress*[71]

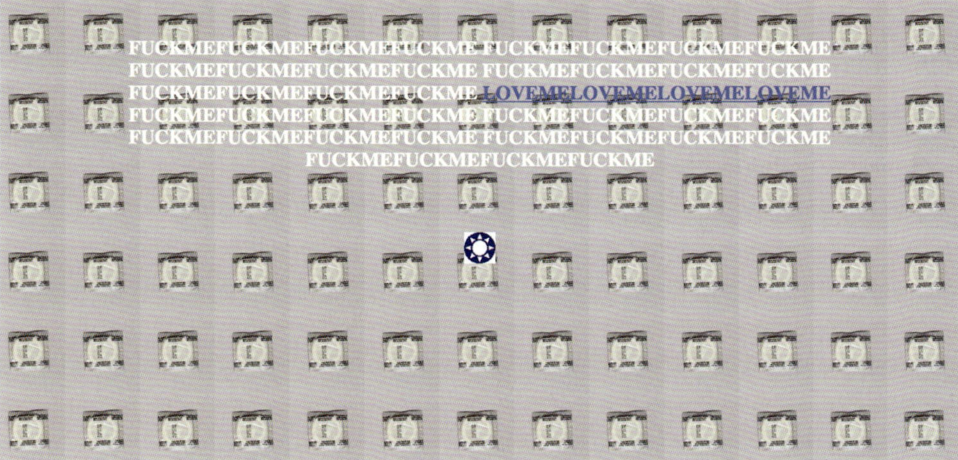

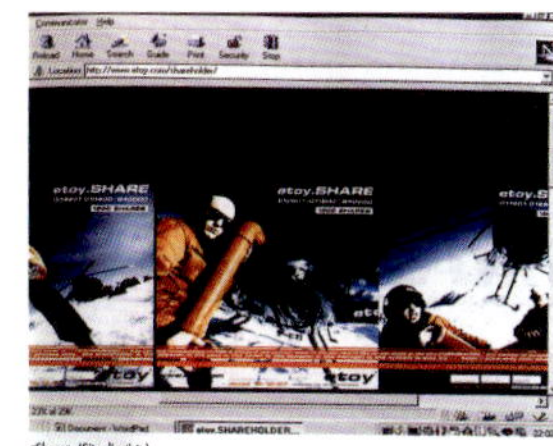

«Shore». (Site d'artiste)

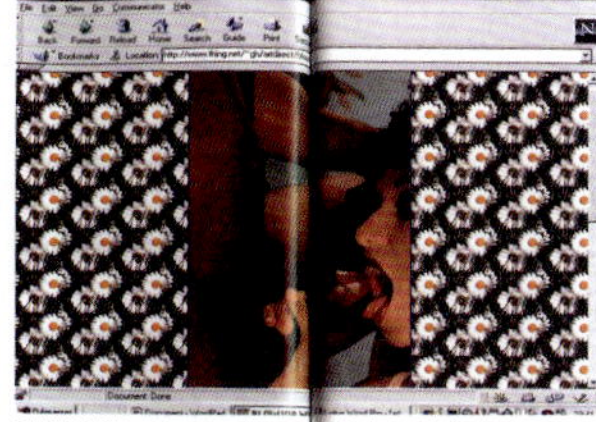

G.H. HOVAGIMYAN. «ArtDirect». New York.

(Site d'artiste). «Blowjob with Daisies»

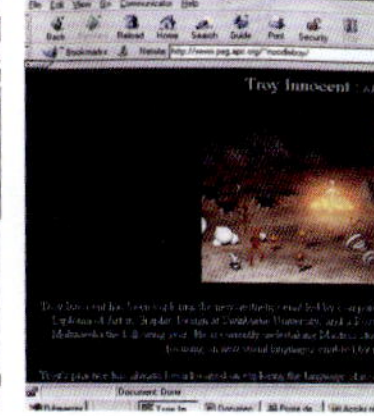

TROY INNOCENT. «Noodle boy». (Site d'artiste)

(réseaux, Internet), un grand nombre de plasticiens ont bénéficié de l'avènement des premiers browsers (logiciels de navigation) sur le world wild web (le web est un des réseaux parmi le très grand nombre de réseaux constituant Internet) permettant la constitution de pages écrans faits de textes et d'images, pour investir ce nouvel environnement médiatique. L'aubaine était trop belle : un média puissant, international, devenait accessible. L'information n'était plus verrouillée. Le web est alors devenu une fenêtre, la faille d'un système toujours plus puissant. Le hacking devint une culture, l'Unix (langage de programmation utilisé sur les servers) le langage dominant.

Pratique pirate et culture paranoïaque

Des artistes simulent des erreurs systèmes, déboussolant les internautes dans des dédales de données erronées. Le web devient un miroir aux alouettes. Plus de liberté, notre

écrans rappellent ceux des servers Unix à fond noir avec une typo verte ou jaune et simulent des erreurs systèmes provoquant la panique chez les internautes. Leur site, par son côté décalé, a été l'un des plus influents et des plus cités. D'autres plasticiens ont une démarche comparable, utilisant une syntaxe et un langage très proches des codes informatiques, réfléchissant ainsi sur la mutation permanente de ces métalangages. Comment échapper à cette tentation, quand on est confronté pour la première fois dans l'Histoire au fait que l'homme invente des langages toujours plus consommables ?

=cw4t7abs (1998) est parfaitement anonyme, et sous cet acronyme susceptible d'évoluer sans fin au travers des citations de chacun réalise des «funny machine art» provoquant des navigations dans des écrans déstabilisants faits d'images, de graphismes et de méta-codes constituant des textes vindicatifs et violents.
D2B (1998) s'amuse à dilater des signes

réseaux, déclenchent des *infowars* (guerres informationnlelles) pour mieux révéler la désinformation. Ils n'hésitent pas à provoquer des *spamings* (encombrements des messageries électroniques) en série pour congestionner les flux d'e-mails, etc.
Heath Bunting, originaire de Londres, a participé à la Documenta X (1997), et a utilisé tous les méta-codes de l'Unix pour faire entendre ses critiques politiques. Au départ grapher de rue, puis hacker, il a organisé différents events évoquant des performances en ligne, qui consistaient à détourner les images les plus fortes du web (images de grosses sociétés telles que American Express, 7-11, Mark and Spencer, Yahoo...) pour réaliser de vrais-faux websites (forum virtuels) où les clients de ces compagnies trouvent leurs messages mêlés à des débats esthétiques ou politiques. Le travail de Heath Bunting repose sur la création de situations ambiguës, paradoxales. Les utilisateurs, complices de la supercherie, sont agacés de recevoir des messages dans leur email box (boîte pour les

l'occasion du projet *Arctic Circle* (1996), ont mené une réflexion sur ces espaces en comparant un topos sur les réseaux et le cercle polaire. Ils ont cheminé sur cette ligne géographique avec un van (avec une antenne parabolique) et ont envoyé chaque jour des messages, des textes et des clips vidéo sur leur site. Au-delà de la réflexion écologique qui est ici menée, une nouvelle idée de la géographie se dégage. Celle-ci est plus basée sur les expériences subjectives et individuelles réalisées par des artistes au cours de ce déplacement sans finalité objective. Au travers des récits, un nouvel espace mythologique appelé «cercle polaire» se met en place, s'opposant à un territoire aux enjeux écologiques et stratégiques importants. Une poésie se crée, générant une prise de conscience planétaire.

Le web facilite la formation de collectifs d'artistes. Dans ce contexte, des compétences multiples sont nécessaires et expliquent cette nécessité de se réunir. Des plasticiens ont su

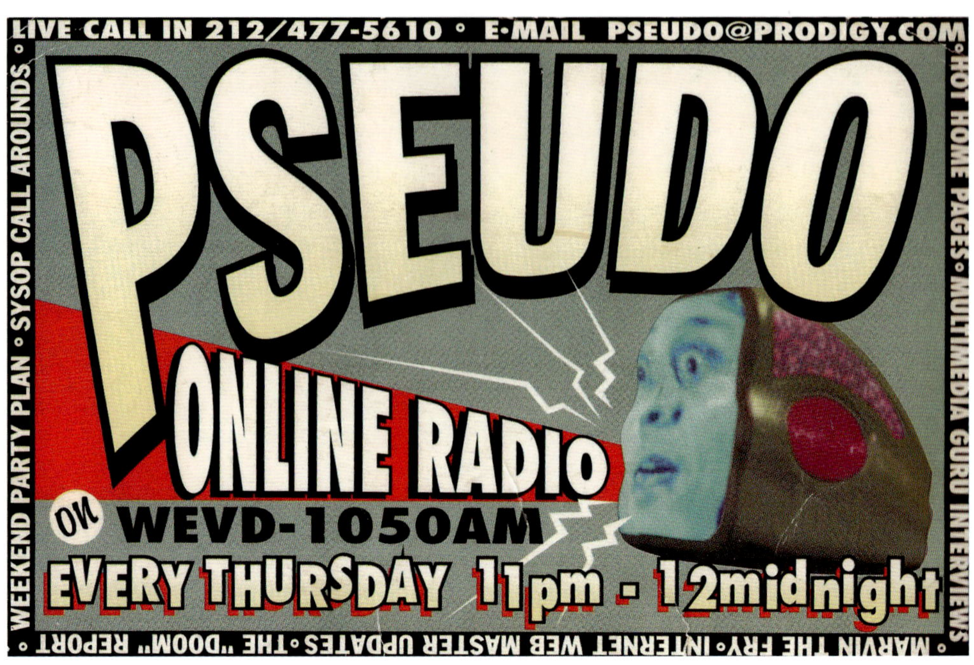

Above: Pseudo postcard, c. 1995–1997
Opposite: *Art Dirt* ad on Pseudo network

Art Dirt:

An online radio show broadcasting on
The Pseudo Online Network
hosted by **G.H. Hovagimyan, Robbin Murphy** and **Adrianne Wortzel.**

The show features round table discussions with the artists, curators, writers and dealers who are powering the digital art scene.

Listen/Watch the live show every Tuesday at 5pm EST time or check out the past shows, available on demand, in the show archives.

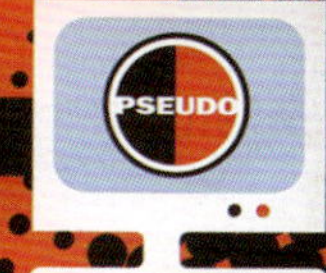

the pseudo online network **http://pseudo.com**

In 1995, downtown artist/impresario Robert Galinsky, a Pseudo co-founder and producer, invited Hovagimyan to host an online radio talk show about art. Hovagimyan invited artists Robbin Murphy and Adrianne Wortzel to co-host *Art Dirt* as a roundtable discussion, streamed live on Fridays from 1 to 2 pm. They interviewed other artists about their work—especially about work available on the internet—reviewed shows and held a "no-holds-barred dissing segment" called Art Trash.[72] In his notations on past work, Hovagimyan frames *Art Dirt* as an extension of his early punk performance pieces and media deconstructions, using hybrids of new forms as a counterpoint to mass media.[73]

> I was asked by Galinsky to do a streaming video talk show about art for Pseudo, because he had all these different things like comedy shows and game shows. He set up this chat radio video thing. So I came up with *Art Dirt*. I invited Adrianne Wortzel and Robben Murphy, and then we invited a bunch of digital artists and musicians on to talk about what they were doing.[74]

Among the guests were *Wild Style* director Charlie Ahearn; an editor from *Wired*; sculptors Bruce Beasley, Rob Fisher, and Robert Michael Smith; performance artist and Franklin Furnace director Martha Wilson; Christina Rees and Rainey Knudson of Texas online art magazine Glasstire; the cyberartist Flash Light; digital media artist Bruce Wands; technology-based installation artist Adam Brown; immersive artist Ebon Fisher; Yael Kanarek; Antoinette LaFarge; semiotics-based website Jodi; installation artist kHyal; artist Hans Breder; Victor Acevedo; the net art and installation collaborative MTAA (M. River & T. Whid Art Associates); Australian media artist John Hopkins; and the Polar Circuit Media Art Workshop from Tornio, Finland.

Events would periodically stage live broadcasts of *Art Dirt*, such as a Location One November 1996 party in the loft of Pseudo on the corner of Broadway and Houston, which became an early aspirational model of the internet startup lifestyle. A *New York Times* story in late 1996 captures the moment's novelty, skepticism, and improbable dreams:

The art world, never allergic to a social trend and recovering from the bust that followed the market boom of the 1980's, has been quietly but intently gravitating to that gravityless, giddy boom town in cyberspace called the World Wide Web, where text and pictures are easily displayed on what are known as sites or pages. How big is this virtual-art boom? From July through November last year, 4,850 artists, museums, galleries and other arts organizations around the globe opened visual-arts sites in the Yahoo! Directory….

Yet things on the Thing may be viewed differently by generations growing up in front of video games and computer monitors. "We may perceive the real object as the valid object," says Markus Kruse, who founded World Wide Arts Resources. "But down the line, younger people who grew up on digital delivery systems for all kinds of entertainment and education will have another view. Virtual art will be just as much a visceral art form for them as painting and sculpture. Maybe more so."

…Nicholas Negroponte, founder of the Media Lab at the Massachusetts Institute of Technology and the best-selling author of *Being Digital*, replied to an E-mail query with the prediction that the web would give artists new access to the public, enabling them to short-circuit the gallery system. "Sell direct!" he said. "The bad news for consumers and buyers," Mr. Negroponte continued, "is that the-signal-to-noise ratio will skyrocket in the absence of profession and collective judgments."[75]

Art Dirt Im-Port, Port MIT: Navigating Digital Culture, MIT List Visual Arts Center, Jan. 25–Mar. 29, 1997

Art Dirt's high point may have come in the first half of 1997, when its live-streaming capacity became incorporated into an exhibition at the MIT List Visual Arts Center from January 25 to March 29. Organized by Remo Campopiano of artnetweb in collaboration with Hovagimyan, Robbin Murphy, Adrianne Wortzel, and Ebon Fisher, *Port MIT: Navigating Digital Culture* may have been the first internet art show in history, credited as ground-breaking by *Art in America*.[76] It exhibited what they described as the flux of "networked visual worlds on the internet," projected onto four large rear-projection screens in the

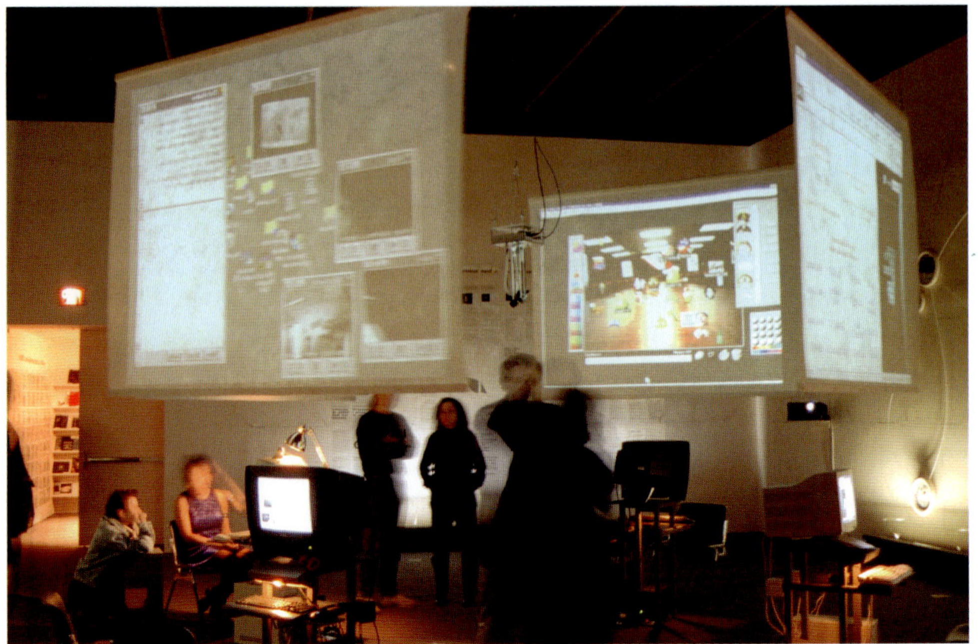

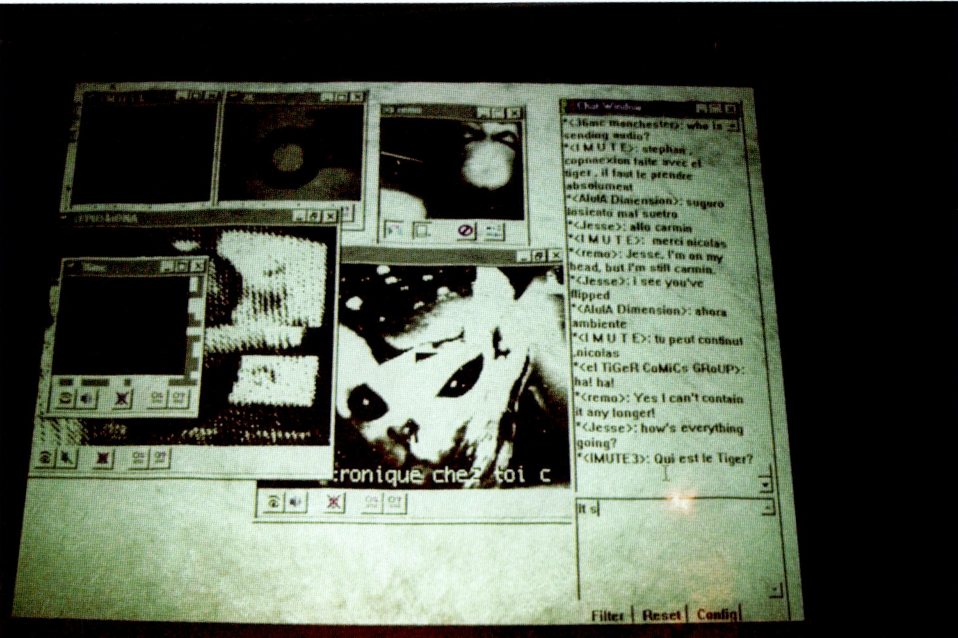

Top: *Art Dirt Im-Port* at MIT List Center
Above: International chat in live-streamed event at MIT

gallery and also accessible online. Architect and digital artist Marek Walczak visualized the screen installation using VRML (virtual reality modeling language), which he also performed live during the show, based on extensive discussions between the group and List curators about how to realize an internet art show. Hovagimyan wrote:

> The ground rules for the digital art of the next century are being worked out now. One of the stickier points, how to do an internet show that goes beyond a row of computers with links to people's homepages. This presentation is what one usually encounters in art galleries trying to accommodate the new form. It works to a degree, but somehow the viewer is still trapped in the box. Furthermore, the metaphor doesn't begin to explore the flexibility of the internet.[77]

For the opening, Hovagimyan organized live-streaming video performances and music from Aix-en-Provence to MIT, in which both live events were connected by RealMedia and CUSeeMe, an early videoconferencing client. These types of live-streaming events were an avant-garde novelty at the time and depended on high-speed servers that tended to only be possessed by institutions and corporations.

The *Art Dirt Im-Port* contribution became a platform within the exhibition for hosts and guests of the radio show to stream projects to the List Center. It included Ricardo Dominguez and Ron Rocco presenting a Zapatista performance, and Adrianne Wortzel and Heather Wagner showing their online interactive multimedia project *Starboard.*

Art Dirt also broadcast live during the SoHo Arts Festival that March, and Hovagimyan taught a class that spring at Cooper Union, Hybrid Art v. Web. He lectured later that year about online art at the University of Tennessee and the United Nations Forum. The Thing relaunched in the fall with a new design and interactive components, featuring a radio show of Hovagimyan with another collaborator, Peter Sinclair. But by June 1998, Pseudo ended the *Art Dirt* program. Hovagimyan posted the announcement in an email on Rhizome.

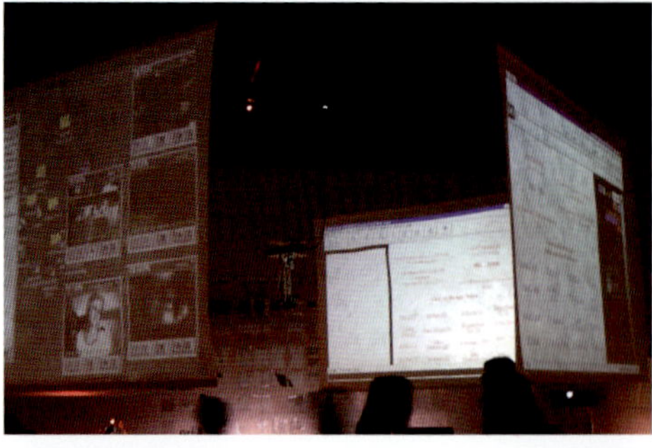

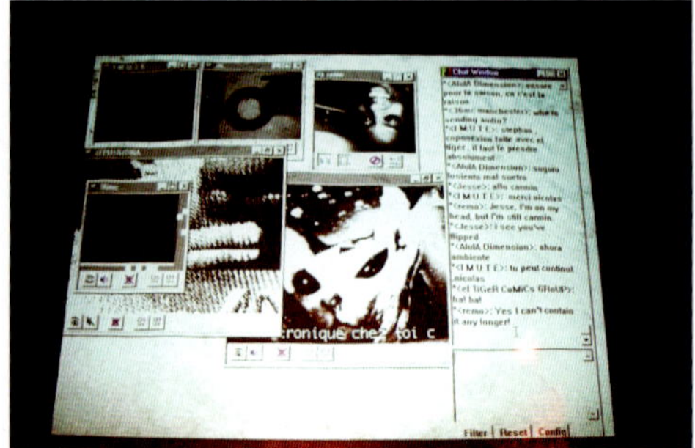

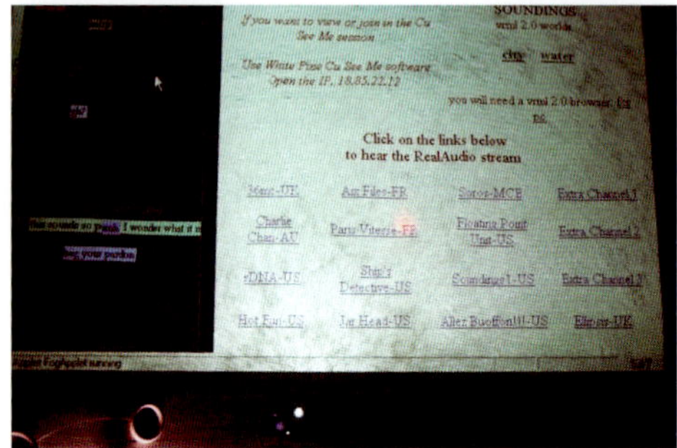

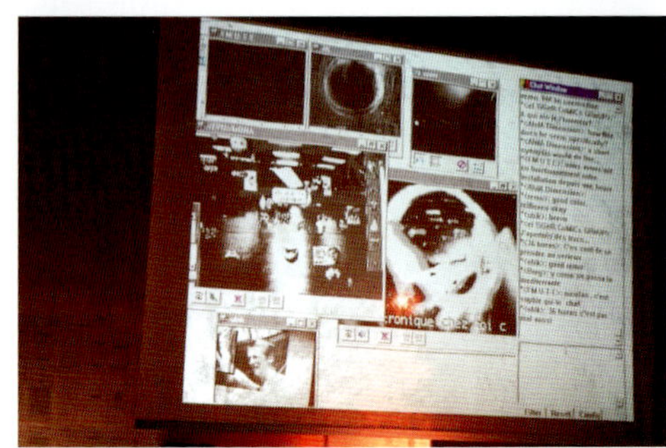

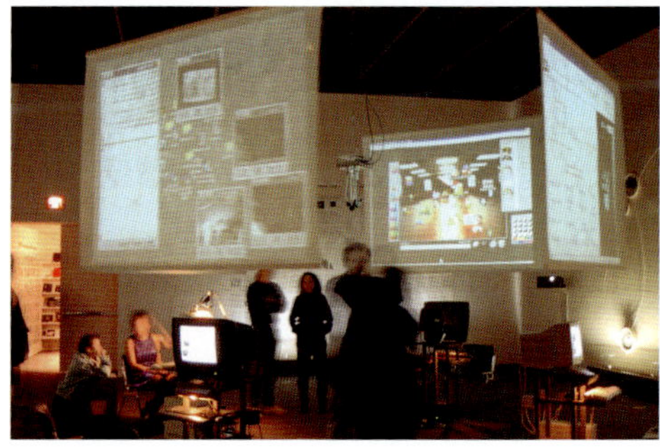

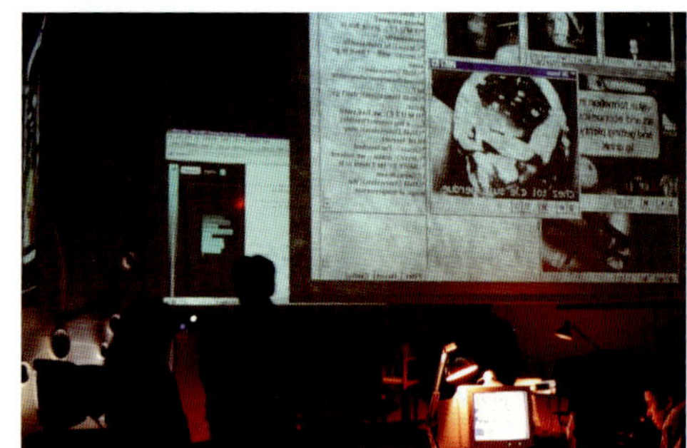

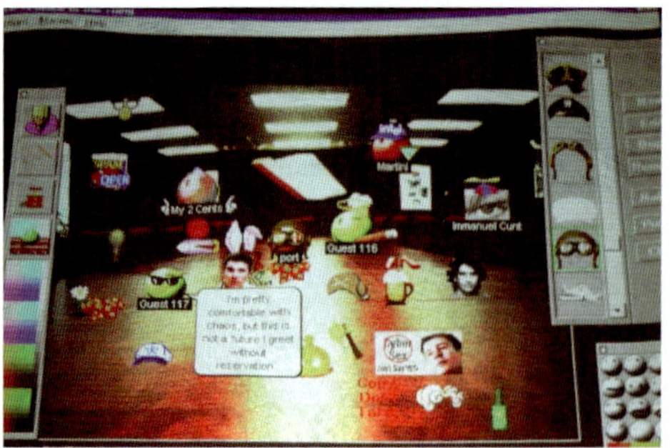

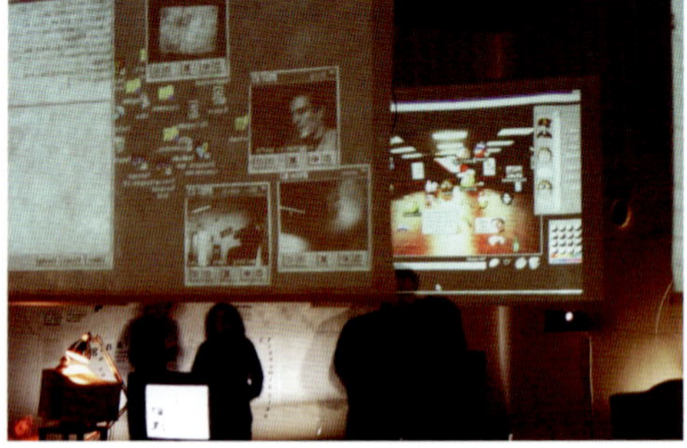

Assemblage of images from *Art Dirt Im-Port*

> I'm sorry to announce that *Art Dirt* is no longer streaming from Pseudo studios. The heads of Pseudo decided it wasn't commercial enough to continue support. In a rather aggressive move, they have also removed the *Art Dirt* archives from the web. This is probably all to the good. The people at Pseudo admit they know nothing about art and are more interested in mainstream media. I have kept copies of the audio programs and some of the video programs of *Art Dirt*. I assume at some future point they will be of historical interest. Galinsky, who is the senior producer for Pseudo's performance channel (channelp.com), has said that this is just a hiatus for *Art Dirt* and perhaps they will bring back the program. I seriously doubt it... The best part of *Art Dirt* was the social aspect of meeting people in a forum setting. This functioned in a similar manner to the idea of "social sculpture" that Joseph Beuys had put forth in many of his "Aktions." Indeed, I view *Art Dirt* as a collaboration between Robbin Murphy, Adrianne Wortzel, myself, and all the people who were our guests. You cannot put a price tag on that type of energy. Sadly, that is the problem.[78]

By October 1997, *Art Dirt* had begun broadcasting in streaming video. Two of the final episodes feature a new art project by Hovagimyan and Sinclair, *A Soa(p Op)era for Laptops*, with low-resolution videos from SoHo and Marseille. A new iteration of the *Art Dirt* show, *Collider*, resurfaced on The Thing the following year. In 2000, Pseudo collapsed in a blaze of glory during the implosion of the dot-com bubble, burning through $25 million in private and institutional capital in seven years. Harris later claimed it was a fake company and piece of conceptual art from the beginning. Walker Art Center archived all of the *Art Dirt* programs in its Digital Arts Study Collection, which it was in the process of preserving in collaboration with Rhizome in 2020.

Art Dirt show list[79]

Feb. 9, 1996 (guests include Simon Biggs and Stuart Jones)
Feb. 16, 1996 (guests include Blast/X Art Foundation, Jordan Crandall, Shawn Vonsel, and Heather Wagner)
Mar. 29, 1996 (guests include Ricardo Dominguez and Martha Wilson; PORT: Webjam_01)
Apr. 19, 1996 (guests include Andrea Troygel)
Jun. 6, 1996 (guests include Matthew Drutt)
Jun. 27, 1996 (guests include Sandra Gering and John Simon Jr.)
Jul. 8, 1996 (guests include Wolfgang Staehle)
Jul. 11, 1996 (guests include Margaret Morton and Doris Vila)
Aug. 15, 1996 (guests include Plaintext Players, Heather Wagner, and Antoinette LaFarge)
Aug. 22, 1996 (guests include Lara Lee)
Aug. 29, 1996 (guests include Richard Leeds)
Sep. 5, 1996 (guests include Martha Wilson, Thomas Lanigan-Schmidt, Julia Heyward, Barbara R. Rusin, and Grace Roselli)
Sep. 20, 1996 (special edition with CuSeeMe hookup)
Sep. 23, 1996 (guests include Susan Hoeltzl and Robert Atkins)
Sep. 26, 1996 (guests include Richard Leeds and Christiane Paul)
Oct. 3, 1996 (guests include Antonio Muntadas)
Oct. 24, 1996 (guests include Martha Wilson and Daniel Ostrow Georges)
Nov. 7, 1996 (guests include Alex Melamid)
Nov. 12, 1996 (guests include Joseph Nechvatal, Akke Wagenaar, Arno Coenen and Rene Bosma)
Nov. 14, 1996 (guests include Matthew Yokobosky and Danny Hobart)
Nov. 14, 1996 (guests include Carol Stakenas, CB Cooke, Kendall Queer Morrison, Corey Sica, and Nick Debbs)
Dec. 5, 1996 (guests include Eric Rosner, Paul Garrin, and Andreas Troeger)
Dec. 12, 1996 (guests include Walter Robinson)
Dec. 19, 1996 (guests include Peter Fend)
Jan. 2, 1997 (guests include Jerelyn Hanrahan)
Jan. 9, 1997 (guests include Remo Campopiano and Marek Walczak)
Jan. 30, 1997 (guests include Christiane Paul)
Feb. 18, 1997 (PORT: Webjam_02, M. River, T. Whid, and Ricardo Dominguez)
Feb. 20, 1997 (guests include ISIS Conceptual Laboratory)
Feb. 25, 1997 (guests include Ricardo Dominguez; PORT: Webjam_03)
Mar. 4, 1997 (PORT: Webjam_04, Joachim Batista, and Ricardo Dominguez)
Mar. 11, 1997 (guests include Jennifer and Kevin McCoy; Ricardo Dominguez)
Mar. 13, 1997 (PORT-MIT)
Mar. 20, 1997 (guests include Janet Abrams)
Apr. 17, 1997 (guests include Danae and Alexandre Stratou, D.A.S.T.)
Apr. 22, 1997 (guests include Hakim Bey)
Apr. 29, 1997 (guests include Christiane Paul and Bob Dobbs)
Jul. 22, 1997 (guests include Lapland simulcast and Charlie Morrow)
Aug. 5, 1997 (guests include Yael Kanarek)
Aug. 12, 1997
Aug. 19, 1997 (guests include Alex Galloway)
Aug. 26, 1997 (guests include Benton Bainbridge)
Oct. 7, 1997 (guests include Elise Barna and Leo Fernekes)
Oct. 14, 1997 (guests include Vivian Selbo and Paivi Jukla)
Oct. 21, 1997 (guests include Kathy Brew, Helen Thorington, and Andrea Wollensack)
Oct. 28, 1997 (guests include Roz Dimon, Valery and Natalie Cheraskin)
Nov. 4, 1997 (guests include Mark Amerika, Danny Hobart, and Wolfgang Staehle)
Nov. 18, 1997 (guests include Cary Peppermint)

Nov. 25, 1997 (guests include Hans Breder and Christiane Paul)
Dec. 2, 1997 (guests include William and Kathleen Lazizza)
Dec. 9, 1997 (guests include Tivo)
Dec. 23, 1997 (guests include Peter Sinclair)
Dec. 30, 1997 (guests include Arno Coenen and René Bosma)
Jan. 20, 1998 (guests include Victor Acevedo)
Jan. 29, 1998 (guests include Lauren Amazeen and Ken Butler)
Mar. 2, 1998 (guests include Eungie McMaster)
Apr. 9, 1998 (*A SoaPOPera for Laptops*, SoHo)
Apr. 23, 1998 (guests include Victor Acevedo, Cynthia Pannucci, and Lynn Pokog)
May 14, 1998 (*A SoaPOPera for Laptops*, Marseilles)

Complete *Art Dirt Im-Port* Lineup

Robert Galinsky, word artist
Rabinal Achi/ZapatistaPortAcion by Ricardo Dominguez & Ron Rocco
BUYING TIME: The Nostalgia-Free History Sale by M. River and T. Whid Art Associates
THE FRENCH CONNECTION: Boston, Aix-en-Provence, NY interface with Emmanuelle Baron, Guillaume Stagnaro, Pascal Silondi, Guillaume Blanchard, Celine Bellanger, Francoise Parra, Yann Goulm, Djamel Achour, Renaud Courvoisier, Stephen Lassis, Eddy Godeberge, Christiane Soucaret, Peter Sinclair, COSY DISCO, Alexandre Pazmandy, Bougie Manu, Estelle Vautaret, Cecile Brouard, Elodie Brouillard, François Lejault, Climax production, Natalie Andrei and "OX," Julien Hokim, "MOKI"

Single-Event Performance Interfaces

Jan. 24, 1997 COSY DISCO, Peter Sinclair, France
Jan. 28, 1997 Rose Stasuk/MR Petit/Echonyc Arts Conference, U.S.
Feb. 4, 1997 Rose Stasuk/MR Petit/Echonyc Arts Conference, U.S.
Feb. 11, 1997 Martha Wilson, U.S.
Feb. 18, 1997 Melantie Pandilovski, Welcome to Empire, Macedonia
Feb. 25, 1997 Charlie Chan, Australian Mardi Gras, Australia
Mar. 11, 1997 Intermedia Workshop, Hans Breder-Steven Strait, guests, U.S.
Mar. 18, 1997 Julia Scher, Intermedia Workshop, U.S.
Mar. 25, 1997 Arleen Schloss, U.S.

4

Multimedia Performances

A Soa(p Op)era for Laptops, 1997–1999

In late 1996, Hovagimyan met the Aix-en-Provence-based French artist Peter Sinclair at the office of artnetweb. He invited Sinclair onto the Art Dirt radio show in December, and they began collaborating on a series of multimedia performances and installations.

> At that point Peter Sinclair, who's this sculpture/sound artist who was teaching at the École d'Art d'Aix-en-Provence, he walked into artnetweb because we had this storefront. Remo didn't know quite what to do. He was trying to figure out whether to do design/web design stuff and this and that; he was trying to make money obviously. But anyway, Peter walked in, and he showed me his work, he said he was teaching in Aix-en-Provence. I invited him onto my *Art Dirt* talk show, right? At this point, everybody had websites. The Thing went from a BBS to a website. Artnetweb went to a website. Those are the two main starts of website art group collaboration.[80]

A Soa(p Op)era for Laptops used Apple's MacinTalk text-to-speech and speech recognition, and Opcode's Max object-oriented graphical interface programs to stage a play based on the interactions of computers. They mounted four Apple Power Mac laptops on top of radio-controlled cars, accompanied by mouth animations on the computer screens and polyurethane wigs on top.

> Subsequently I started collaborating with Peter and came up with this idea—MacIntosh had this text-to-speech and speech recognition within MacIntosh operating system. So then we decided we're going to do this thing called *Soa(p Op)era for Laptops*. And what we did essentially was create these primitive fake robots where we took laptops, put them on radio-controlled cars, and then I hand-coded the voices so they would sing, and I wrote all the text. It was four characters singing and having these kind of stupid conversations, like chitchat, [animating] the four characters of the Apple voices—two men, two women. Then we had this whole opera.[81]

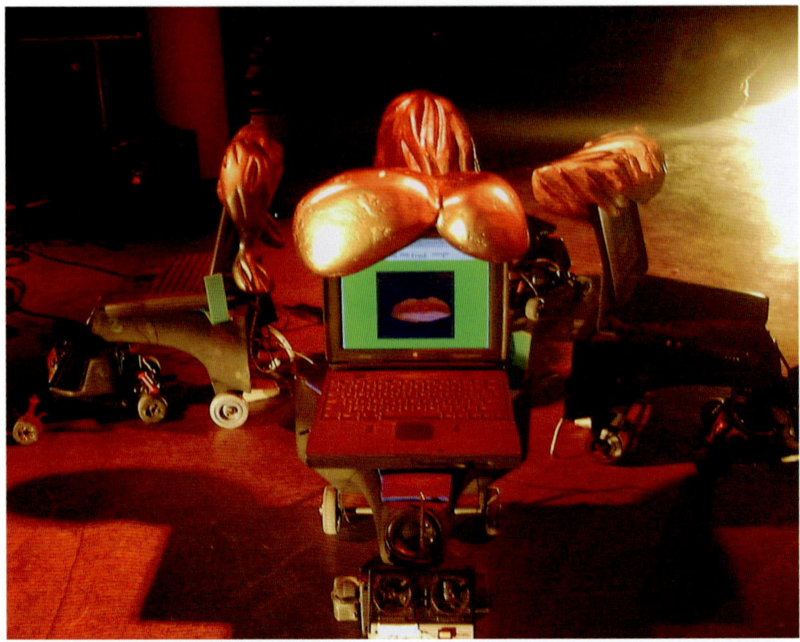

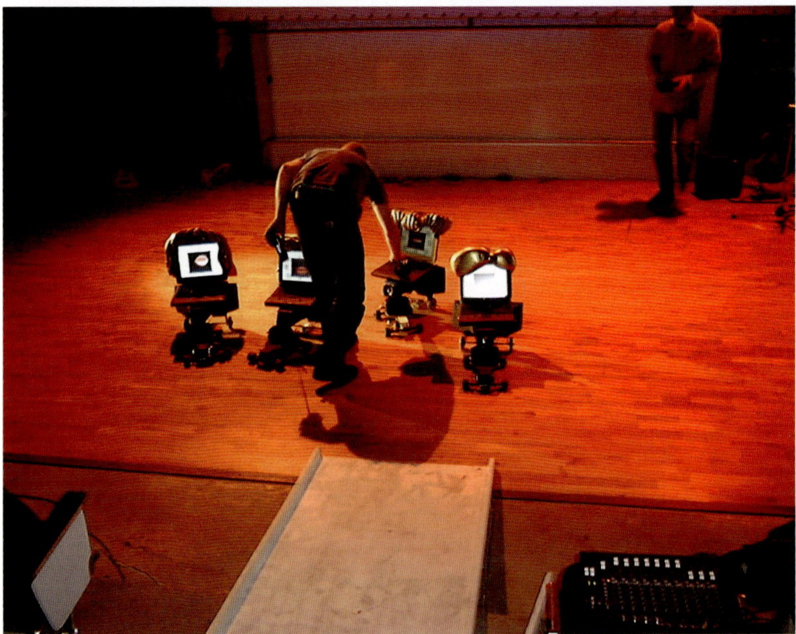

Top: *A Soa(p Op)era for Laptops* at École Supérieure d'Art d'Aix-en-Provence
Above: *A Soa(p Op)era for Laptops* at Musée d'Art Contemporain, Marseille

Developed by the artists through email "file exchanges" between New York and France, as the *Village Voice* reported, it combined a characteristically playful spirit with an urge to experiment with new technologies that made it good fun for audiences, overlaid with enough conceptual rigor and intellectual seriousness to appeal to the art world. Hovagimyan hand-coded the text to make the computer voices "sing," and Sinclair used a pitch tracker to compose a techno-influenced background soundtrack accompanying the voices. The artists' statement read:

> The intention of *A Soa(p Op)era for Laptops* is to create a society in action. The action/speaking/singing dialogue is triggered in several ways. One way is through a proximity sensor that will set off a scripted dialogue whenever two laptops come within range of each other. Another triggering action is a laptop pecking order. A location on the stage will also trigger a certain type of talking/singing. For example, if a laptop moves to the front or main area, this will indicate a solo performance. A Dolby surround sound stereo system will create a 3D immersive sound environment. *A Soa(p Op)era for Laptops* is part musical comedy, part soap opera and part pop media discourse.[82]

The project launched Hovagimyan and Sinclair into a mini tour of emerging venues for new media art, including a January 1998 preview at *Wired*'s fifth anniversary party in San Francisco and a performance in February at Postmasters gallery in New York. Austin Bunn previewed the Postmasters performance in the *Village Voice*:

> GH. Hovagimyan's *Soa(p Op)era for Laptops* is melodrama distilled down to its elemental truth: no lingering stares or gauzy sex scenes, just noisy overacting at its finest. Except that nobody moves. For Thursday's performance at Postmasters Gallery, four PowerBook 5300s—what the artist calls 'synthespians'—speak, shout, and scat like Meredith Monk, from perches splayed out on stage.
>
> The show relies on one of the oddest and most underused Apple features, the MacInTalk text-to-speech application that makes the computers "speak" text. According to Hovagimyan, the 17 pre-set voices on the PowerBook, such

as "Victoria" and "Ralph," create "society in miniature"—"Victoria is a voice that is prim, but she's a bitch, and Ralph is a doofus-y American guy," he says. "There's already a relationship there." By adjusting the tone and pitch on the MIDI sound files, he makes the computers "sing blues riffs, slur, speak in Jamaican patois—things that they're not supposed to do at all."

The performance runs through five dramatic segments, including an a capella rap, a rant at 300 words a minute, computer karaoke, and a "kitchen combat" between husband and wife while washing the dishes (scored to the sound of knives chopping and plates crashing). The blisteringly fast scat, called *Communicatin' Frenzy*, is about a "Lolita type" seducing an older man, says Hovagimyan. "It's like a DoubleMint commercial with seagulls and motorcycle sounds."

...Though the work might mystify some, Hovagimyan, who started as a "no wave" performance artist in the '70s and now produces and hosts the *Art Dirt* show on Pseudo.com, enjoys the deliberate confusion. After the *Wired* anniversary party, where the opera debuted, "people were coming up to me and saying, 'What language is that?'" he says. "I said, 'New York English,' and then they said, 'Oh, now we understand.'"[83]

They performed *A Soa(p Op)era* that April at the Musée d'Art Contemporain, Marseille.[84] Later in 1998, the project won an honorable mention from Ars Electronica in Linz, Austria. An iteration of it reappeared at Postmasters at the end of the year under the title *Les Jaseurs*. In January 1999, it was performed in the *Sound Artists of North America* exhibition at the Musée d'Art Contemporain, Lyon, alongside works by La Monte Young and Marian Zazeela, Charlemagne Palestine, Doug and Mike Starn, and Christian Marclay. In May, they performed in the show *Art et Technique: Emergence d'un Dialogue* at Espace-Exposition in Toulon. In November and December 1999, SVA's Visual Arts Museum hosted a New York Digital Salon, where they performed another iteration of *Les Jaseurs*.[85]

G.H. HOVAGIMYAN
& PETER SINCLAIR

postmasters gallery

november 20 - december 18

reception saturday 6 - 8

POSTMASTERS

459 w 19 street nyc 10011

212 727 3323

postmasters@thing.net

"Jaseur–Kathy" 1998–1999 mobile talking laptop performe

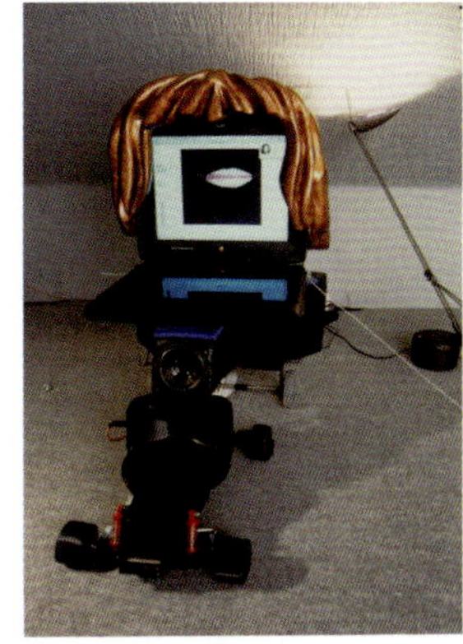

Les Jaseurs - ASoaPoPera for Laptop:

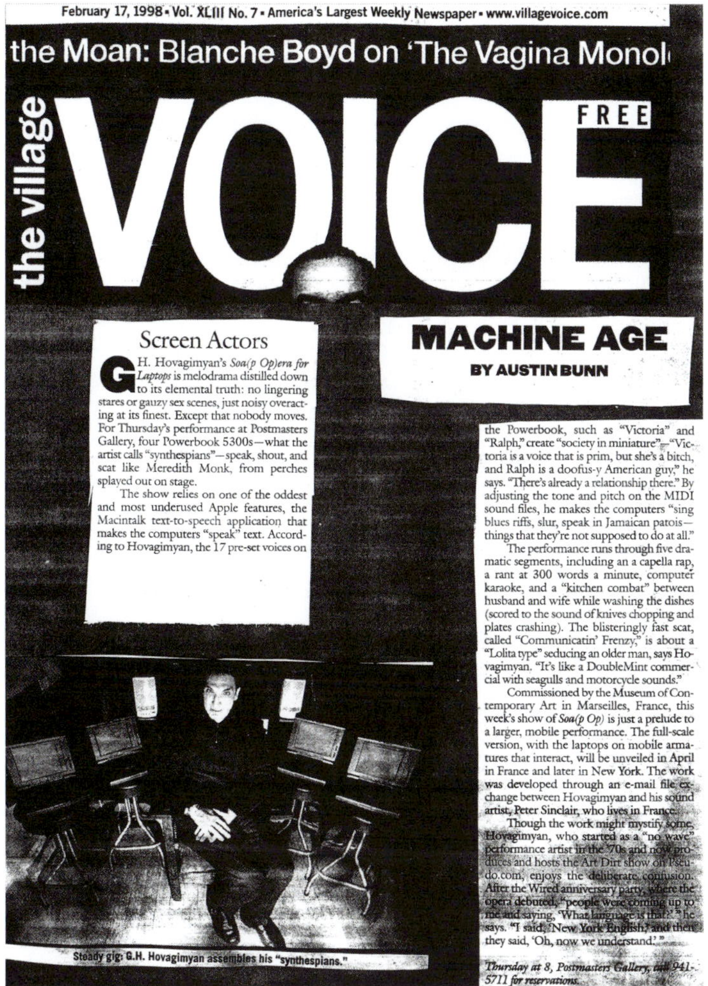

February 17, 1998 • Vol. XLIII No. 7 • America's Largest Weekly Newspaper • www.villagevoice.com

the Moan: Blanche Boyd on 'The Vagina Monol

the village **VOICE** FREE

Screen Actors

G.H. Hovagimyan's *Soa(p Op)era for Laptops* is melodrama distilled down to its elemental truth: no lingering stares or gauzy sex scenes, just noisy overacting at its finest. Except that nobody moves. For Thursday's performance at Postmasters Gallery, four Powerbook 5300s—what the artist calls "synthespians"—speak, shout, and scat like Meredith Monk, from perches splayed out on stage.

The show relies on one of the oddest and most underused Apple features, the Macintalk text-to-speech application that makes the computers "speak" text. According to Hovagimyan, the 17 pre-set voices on the Powerbook, such as "Victoria" and "Ralph," create "society in miniature"—"Victoria is a voice that is prim, but she's a bitch, and Ralph is a doofus-y American guy," he says. "There's already a relationship there." By adjusting the tone and pitch on the MIDI sound files, he makes the computers "sing blues riffs, slur, speak in Jamaican patois—things that they're not supposed to do at all."

The performance runs through five dramatic segments, including an a capella rap, a rant at 300 words a minute, computer karaoke, and a "kitchen combat" between husband and wife while washing the dishes (scored to the sound of knives chopping and plates crashing). The blisteringly fast scat, called "Communicatin' Frenzy," is about a "Lolita type" seducing an older man, says Hovagimyan. "It's like a DoubleMint commercial with seagulls and motorcycle sounds."

Commissioned by the Museum of Contemporary Art in Marseilles, France, this week's show of *Soa(p Op)* is just a prelude to a larger, mobile performance. The full-scale version, with the laptops on mobile armatures that interact, will be unveiled in April in France and later in New York. The work was developed through an e-mail file exchange between Hovagimyan and his sound artist, Peter Sinclair, who lives in France.

Though the work might mystify some, Hovagimyan, who started as a "no wave" performance artist in the '70s and now produces and hosts the Art Dirt show on Pseudo.com, enjoys the deliberate confusion. After the Wired anniversary party, where the opera debuted, "people were coming up to me and saying, 'What language is that?' " he says. "I said, 'New York English,' and then they said, 'Oh, now we understand.' "

Thursday at 8, Postmasters Gallery, call 941-5711 for reservations.

MACHINE AGE

BY AUSTIN BUNN

Steady gig: G.H. Hovagimyan assembles his "synthespians."

Above: *Les Jaseurs: A SoaPOPera for Laptops* postcard, Postmasters, Nov. 20, 1998–Dec. 18, 1999
Left: Preview of *A Soa(p Op)era* in the *Voice*

A Soa(p Op)era for iMacs (with Peter Sinclair), 1999–2005

After the release of the iMac in 1998, Hovagimyan and Sinclair installed a number of iterations of *Soa(p Op)era* using the watershed all-in-one computer, combining the screen and hard drive in a brightly colored translucent plastic enclosure. The set-up was similar to the laptops, with lips on the screen animating the speech, wigs on top, but instead of remote-controlled cars the computers sat on neoclassical pink sofas and lounge chairs arranged around a decorative area rug, illuminated by a floor lamp.

> There was also a demand for static installations. We solved this by using iMacs sitting on living room furniture. It was sort of like a computer tea social. Once we turned on the computers, they would talk to each other and recognize words to continue the conversation. Of course, they misunderstood words so the conversation would go off in bizarre directions.[86]

Among other places, it appeared in the first International Electronic Art Festival at Belfort, France (1999); the *Avignon Numérique* exhibition in Avignon, France (2001); Split Festival of New Film in Croatia (2002); and the *Burlesques Contemporains* exhibition at the Jeu de Paume in Paris (2005), alongside people like Dennis Oppenheim, an associate from 112 Greene Street.

> Then we turned that into soap opera for iMacs where we had these four iMacs, then Peter made these polyurethane wigs to go over the iMacs, and he had lip animations. What they'd do is, they would be talking and singing and doing whatever, and if they heard a phrase which was recognized in the dictation text-to-speech voice-to-text, it would then trigger a conversation. And we were using cycling 74 Max MSP as the programming language. We showed that at the Jeu de Paume—it was artists who were somehow inspired by burlesque, and they had Dennis Oppenheim's bell piece where he's got that bronze puppet that bangs his head on the bell.[87]

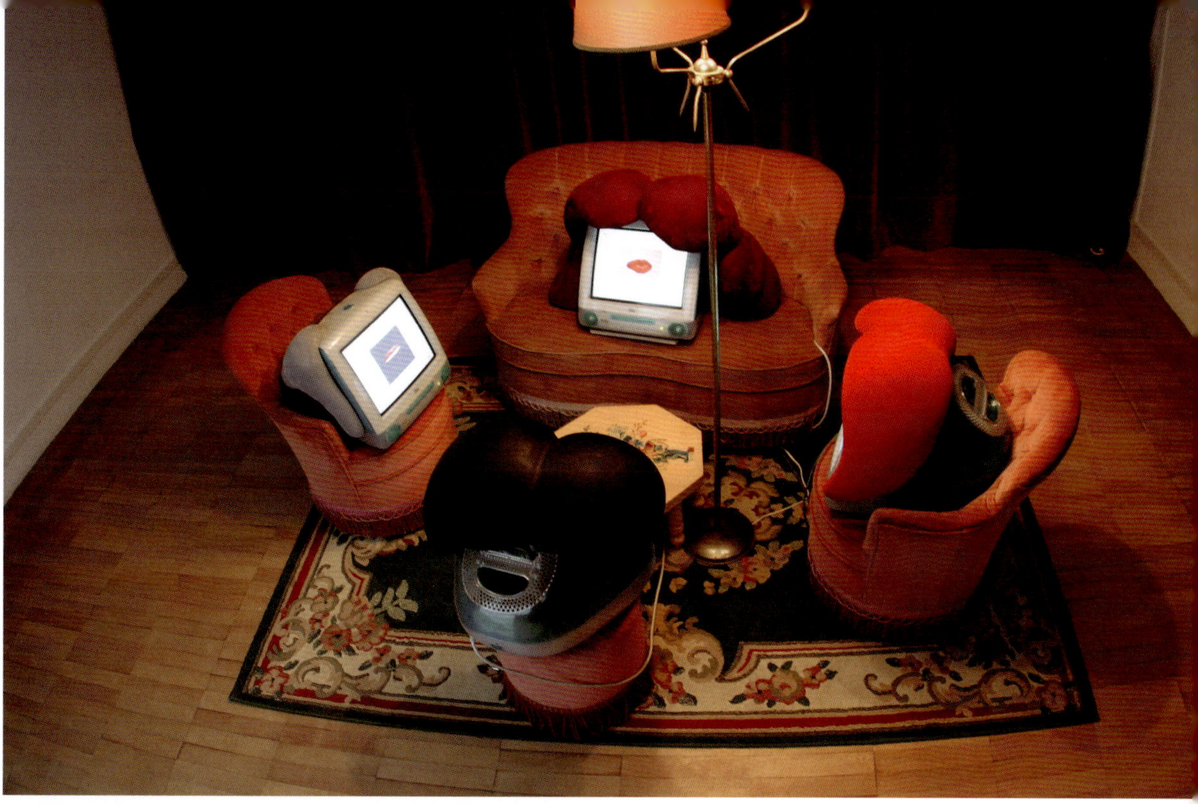

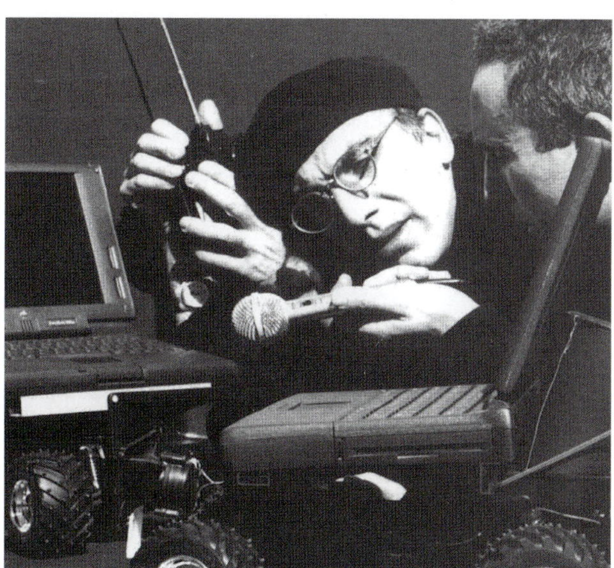

Top: *A Soa(p Op)era* for iMacs at Jeu de Paume, Paris
Above: *A Soa(p Op)era* photo in Musée d'Art Contemporain Lyon catalogue

The online and print magazine *Neural* reviewed the project on its site in 2003:

> *A SoaPOPera for Imacs* is the installation of the duo formed by G.H. Hovagimyan and Peter Sinclair, who [make] four independent...Mac[s] in[to] a performance in its own right. Placed on a couch and two chairs, computers (called Fred, Kathy, Ralph, and Princess) communicate using speech synthesis software ("text to speech") to "talk," and voice recognition software to "listen." There are four topics in this synthetic conversation: sex, cars, politics, and sing songs. With the animation of a fleshy mouth at the center of the screen, this performance represents the culture of the people as expressed by the media and inspired by movies, rock music, and, of course, soap operas. The gaming functioning, however, represents both the creative short-circuit that can be created among machines, [and] is a working model of systems that interact autonomously, leaving to Dexterity programmers the level of realism and unpredictability implemented.[88]

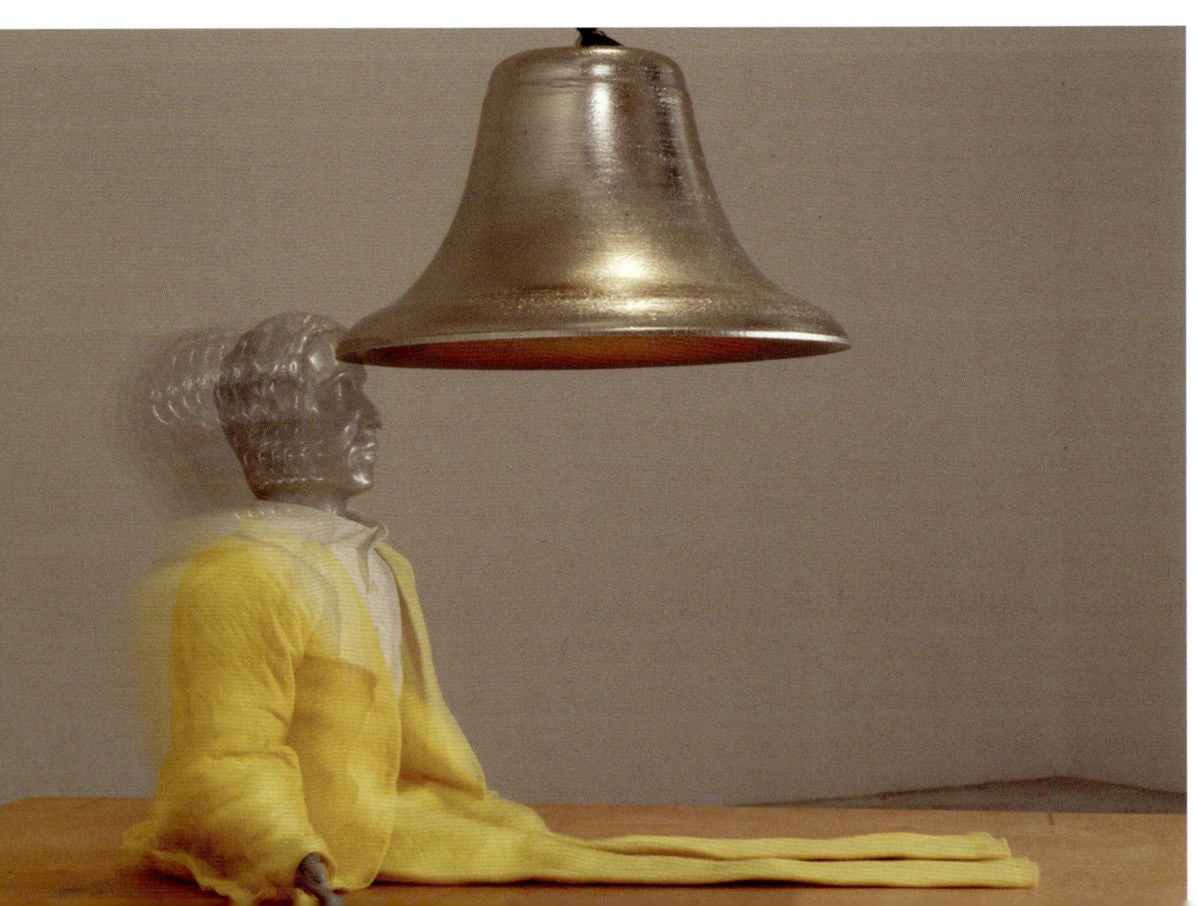

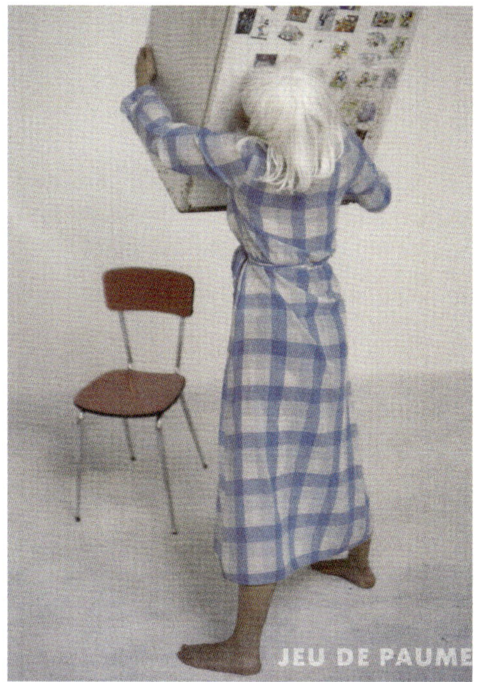

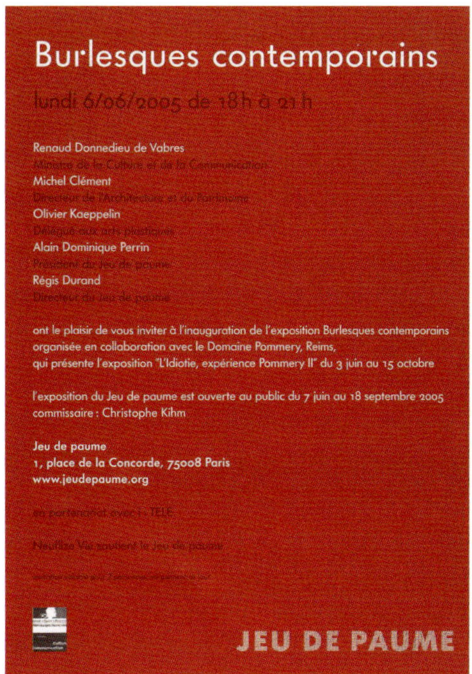

Burlesques contemporains

lundi 6/06/2005 de 18h à 21 h

Renaud Donnedieu de Vabres
Ministre de la Culture et de la Communication
Michel Clément
Directeur de l'Architecture et du Patrimoine
Olivier Kaeppelin
Délégué aux arts plastiques
Alain Dominique Perrin
Président du Jeu de paume
Régis Durand
Directeur du Jeu de paume

ont le plaisir de vous inviter à l'inauguration de l'exposition Burlesques contemporains
organisée en collaboration avec le Domaine Pommery, Reims,
qui présente l'exposition "L'Idiotie, expérience Pommery II" du 3 juin au 15 octobre

l'exposition du Jeu de paume est ouverte au public du 7 juin au 18 septembre 2005
commissaire : Christophe Kihm

Jeu de paume
1, place de la Concorde, 75008 Paris
www.jeudepaume.org

en partenariat avec i-TELE

Neuflize Vie soutient le jeu de paume

JEU DE PAUME

Opposite: Dennis Oppenheim, *Attempt to Raise Hell,* 1974. A magnet forces the seated figure to clash the cast iron bell, producing an echo that fills the room: "as well as the mind." D. O. Collection: Radchofsky House, Dallas Photo: Ace Gallery, New York
Above: Program for *Burlesques Contemporains* at Jeu de Paume

Heartbreak Hotel (with Peter Sinclair), 2000

For the next several years, Hovagimyan and Sinclair pursued a string of collaborative experiments and commissions that put them at the forefront of the emerging field of new media installation and performance.

> A lot of the process of what I've been doing since the 90s I consider to be aesthetic research rather than art per se. In digital new media art work, you set up a system of problems, and then you kind of deal with it. You come to some sort of aesthetic realization, which you might call an accentuation point, and then you go back to doing the research. So it's almost as if you're presenting a research paper, but in the form, it's an artwork or an installation. So I've been doing residencies to do that, going around the art gallery/museum/market system, because I just find that to be really kind of restrictive and boring.[89]

Heartbreak Hotel continued their play with computer-generated voicings and sound scripted by programming, this time triggered by a video camera fed to an Apple G4 computer running the visual processing program Max/MSP Cycling '74. A glass table lit from the below had figures on top to be moved by the audience. Each figure had dots on the bottom that the program used to identify the distinct figures, triggering snippets of scripts voiced synthetically. They downloaded free text generators from the internet for English (Janus) and French (Corvophraseur), and used two different voice synthesizers, Mbrola for the French and VocalWriter for the English. It brought them closer to a rudimentary form of artificial intelligence.

Developed in conjunction with residencies by Sinclair that year at Centre National de Création Musicale, Marseille (also known as Group Musique Experimental de Marseille) and Studio for Electro-Instrumental Music, Amsterdam and jointly at Centre International de Création Vidéo, Pierre Schaeffer, in Hérimoncourt, France, *Heartbreak Hotel* debuted in Belfort, France at Interferences, the International Festival of Multimedia Urban Arts, from December 14 to 20, 2000.[90] For the piece, they built a six-chambered immersive spatialized sound environment designed with the help of architect

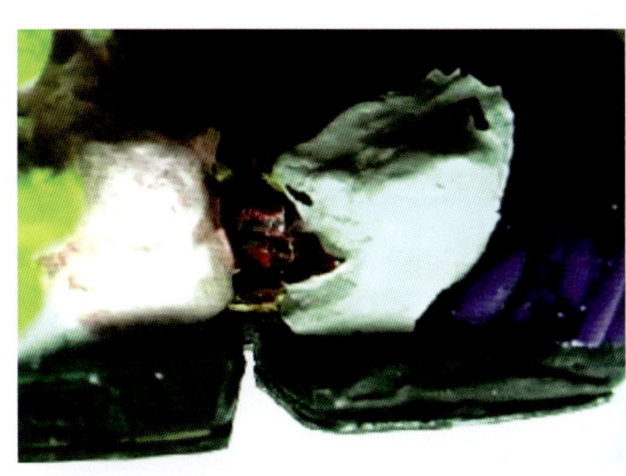

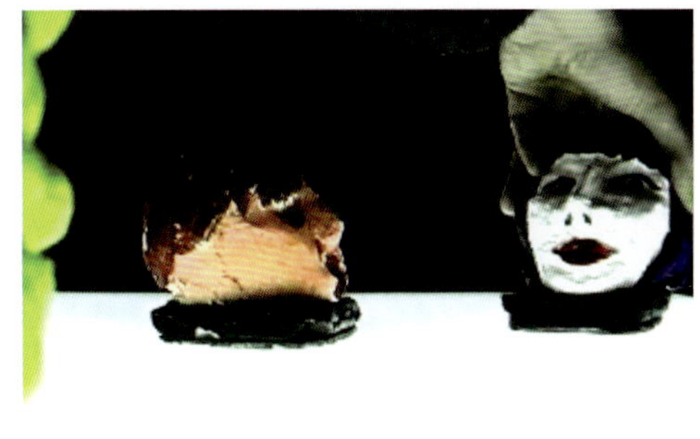

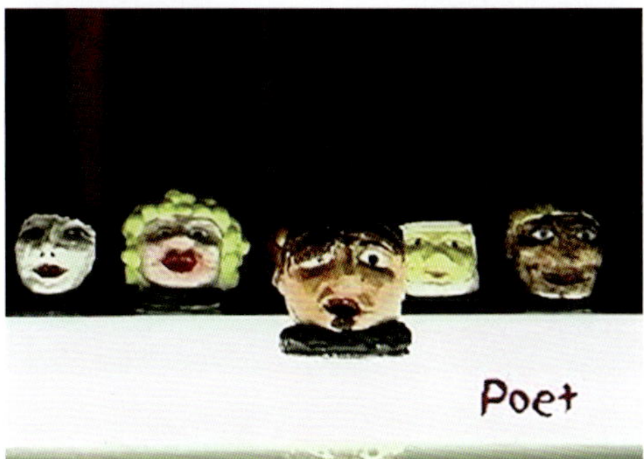

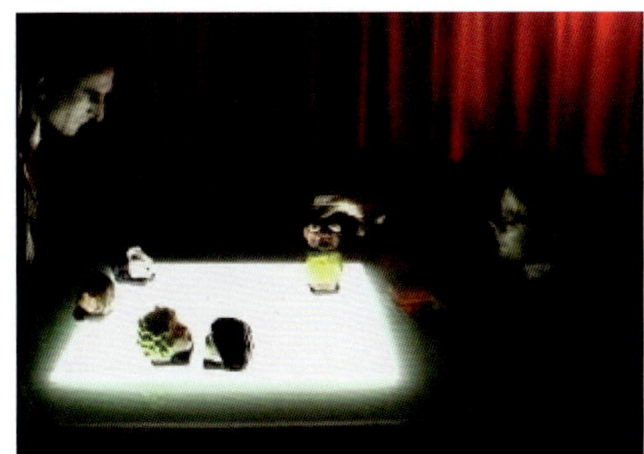

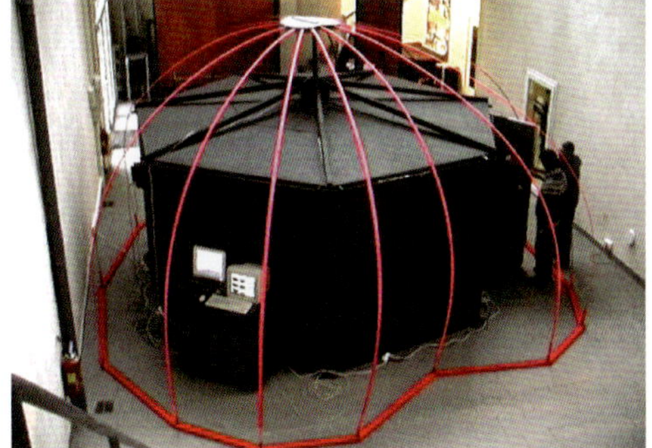

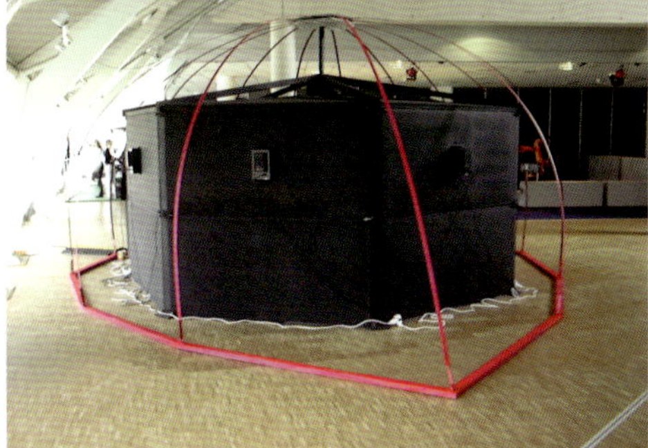

Heartbreak Hotel at Centre National de Création Musicale, Marseille

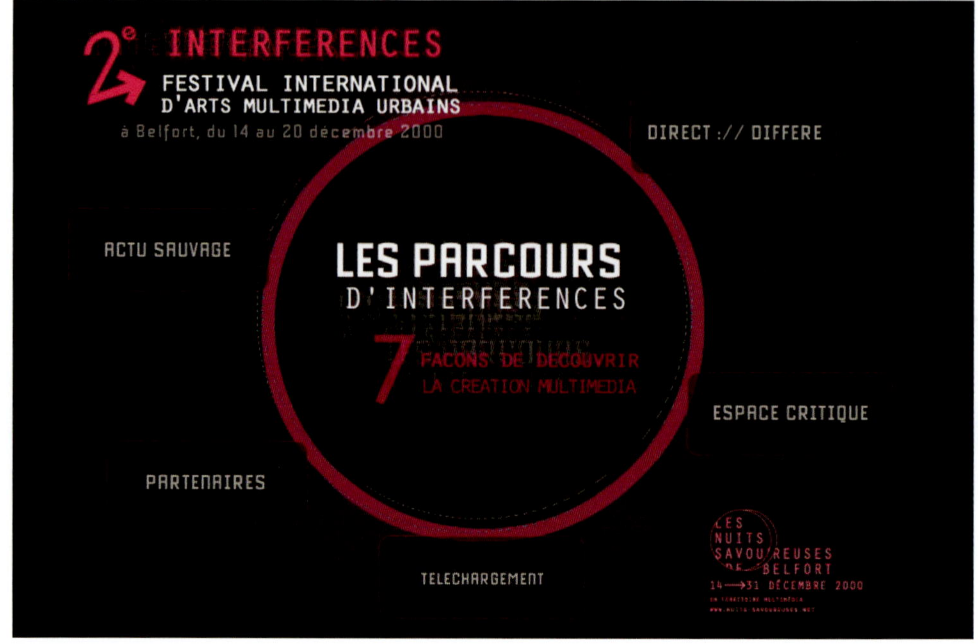

Program for the Interferences festival in Belfort, 2000

Tilman Reichert. On the table in the room, six sculptural figures personified the archetypes of a male yuppie "dot-commer," a "dumb blond," a female rock-and-roll goth, a cowboy/survivalist, a male poet, and a nun. Eight speakers—four above, in each corner, and four below—spatialized movement of the figures in relation to their location.

> We took text from, for instance, a Catholic catechism to make that. The little sculpture pieces were heads of characters on a table, and you could move them around, and as you move the head around, the voice of that character would move around the space. If you put two characters together, they would start talking to each other facing each other, so it was kind of a game.[91]

As Hovagimyan would later note, the use of AI demonstrated just how difficult it is for a computer to descend to the level of a typical bar-room conversation.[92]

"When a group of two or more figurines…come within a certain distance of one another[,] they start to converse with each other, exchanging comments in a pattern which although not predefined tends to 'make sense . . .'"[93] Their notes accompanying the piece placed the work in the context of sociological and media critique:

> So much of modern society and an individual's identity is filtered through media images that often a person shapes their identity to fit the flattened icons of media. *Heartbreak* points out this flattening. In a process of removing the author, Peter and I sought to utilize computer programs to generate text. In this way we could write dictionaries of words and expressions specific to each character, input these into the programs, and generate the script.[94]

They referenced Guy Debord and Antonin Artaud in explaining their intention to use electronic media to break apart the structure of performance, making it audience-generated and automated, turning visitors and machines into co-creators of the work.[95]

Shooter (with Peter Sinclair), Eyebeam, 2001–2002

In 2001–2002, Hovagimyan and Sinclair received a fellowship from Eyebeam, the New York-based arts organization founded in 1998 to support electronic and technology-based art. In the fall of 2002, they joined a group including Cory Arcangel, Yael Kanarek, and MTAA in *Beta-Launch*, Eyebeam's first exhibition of artists-in-residence at its Chelsea space.

Their project, *Shooter*, reacted in part to the aftermath of the terrorist attacks on the World Trade Center the previous September 11th, which had overwhelmed the life of New York City, especially in Hovagimyan's Tribeca neighborhood, and launched the U.S. into wars in Afghanistan and Iraq. Much of the combat was conducted on video screens, both from on high in warplanes that dropped bombs from a distance using precision-guided missiles and by drones that could be directed to kill targets—often mistakenly massacring civilians—from a suburban office in the United States.

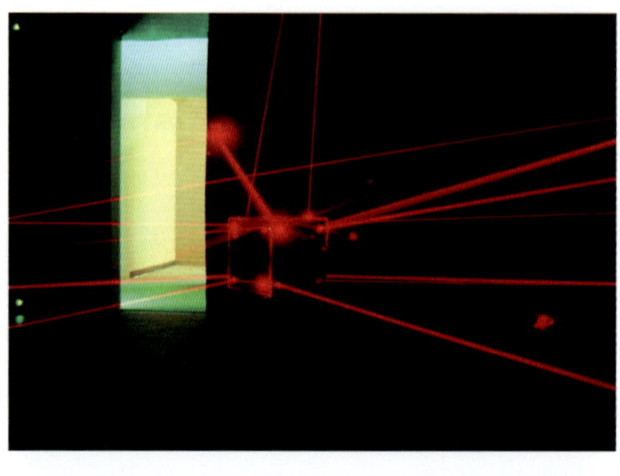

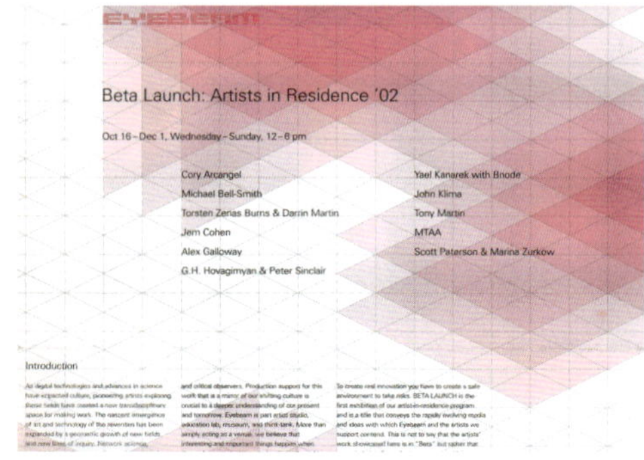

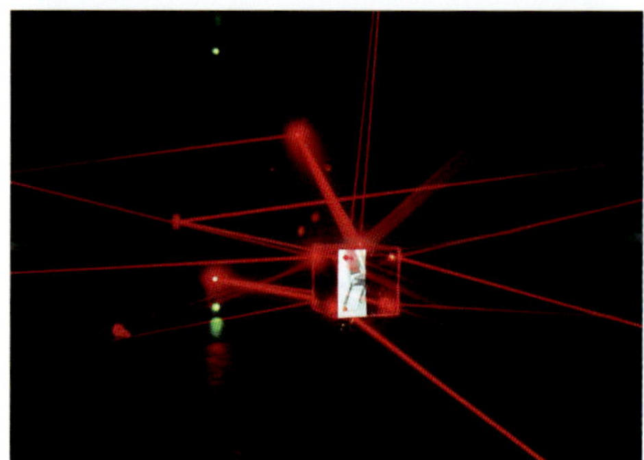

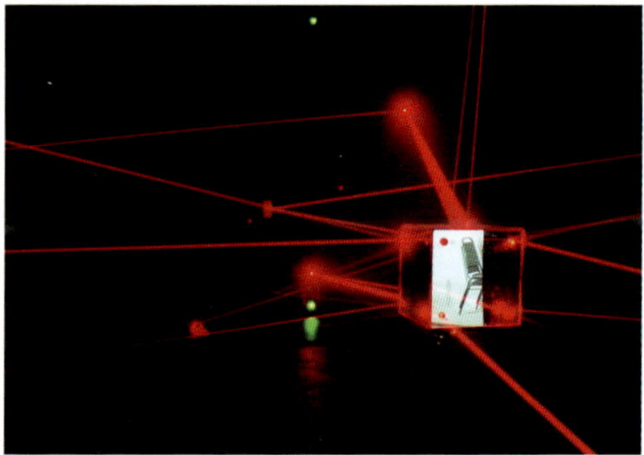

Top left: *Shooter* at Eyebeam, 2002
Top right: Program for *Beta Launch* artists in residence exhibition at Eyebeam
Above: *Shooter* installation at Eyebeam, 2002

The *Shooter* installation placed a two-square-foot mirrored cube at the center of a 16-square-foot room. A web of red lasers pointed at the mirrors and reflecting mirrors around the room tripped sound files when interrupted. A smoke machine made the lasers visible in the air. Eight loudspeakers, four on the ceiling and four on the floor, used Holophon 3D sound-spacialization software to play the menacing barks of a dog circling around, rockets, explosions, xenophobic rants, and a hellfire-and-damnation sermon by Sinclair in his British accent, along with recordings of game sounds on 42nd Street from an interactive boxing machine. The piece reflected on the technology of war through a lens of media critique and video games:

> I wanted to create the Hollywood cliché of a room protected by lasers. I first saw this in a 1960s movie *Topkapi*. It was also used in *Mission Impossible*. Peter and I decided on the theme of a first-person shooter game...We were up to a Times Square arcade and did sound recordings of all the video games...We then created a sound mix that included me doing xenophobic rants, Peter reading a hellfire-and-brimstone religious sermon, war sounds, guns firing, bombs, and the recordings from the arcade...When a person stands outside the room they hear the arcade sounds and Peter's sermon. When they enter, as they trip a laser, sound is fed into the space. They become the target of the box.[96]

Hovagimyan described the Eyebeam installation: "It was called *Shooter*, but you were the target," he said. "You were in the game immersed in the sound environment, which was this blackened room, and then we had this smoke machine which would periodically emit smoke so you could see the laser beams. Aside from that, there were no lights...Dennis Oppenheim was afraid to go into the piece. This was showing at Eyebeam, but he wouldn't go in. We kept on saying, 'C'mon Dennis, go in!'"[97]

After the Eyebeam exhibition, they showed it again the following year during *Open Source 3* at La Gaîté Lyrique, a 19th century Paris theater reopened in 2002 as a venue for digital culture and contemporary music.[98]

> The texture and psychology of war and violence is becoming yet another abstracted set of meta-linguistic parameters fed into the media machine of

global information. There is an increasingly fuzzy borderline between gaming violence, television violence and the internalized human will to power cited by Friedrich Nietzsche. Instead of teaching a person to discipline and control their base urges, the thrust is to indulge and act out these urges in a digitized virtual world, to experience brutality without the physical consequences. Yet there is but one step from virtual to real. Scratch the surface of any civilized human and the savage lurks just beneath . . .

At the moment of this writing, the George W. Bush White House has set up an incredible information juggernaut to convince the U.S. population and the world that the U.S. should attack Iraq. What is astounding is the level of discussion, precipitated by that political information machine, among the expanded cable and broadcast TV news shows. It is in some measure the extension of mass media as propaganda weapon, but more chillingly as a way to convince the world of the inevitability of a war with Iraq. This type of heightened anticipation keeps people watching the news, and while they are at it, all the commercial sponsors' advertising that surrounds the news reports. In the new monetary climate of war profiteering, the TV news programs are the winners…War fever creates anxiety. Anxiety translates into a need for information. Advertising foots the bill. We are moving into a virtual world of mediated violence that is enacted in order to be interpreted. The perpetrators are not only the men who go to war and the generals and politicians who promote, nay, relish, such actions, but also the media vehicles that present violence as an hourly dose on the screens of televisions and gaming terminals.[99]

Cocktail Party, Whitney Art Port: Portal to Net Art, Nov. 2001

In March 2001, Whitney Museum digital art curator Christiane Paul launched *Art Port: The Whitney Museum Portal to Net Art* as her first project to bring net art into the museum and showcase it. Paul commissioned Hovagimyan to create *Cocktail Party*, a Flash animation that converted a typical conversation you might have at an art opening into Mac voices, using VocalWriter for Mac and MIDI instruments, presented as the voices of computers pretending to be

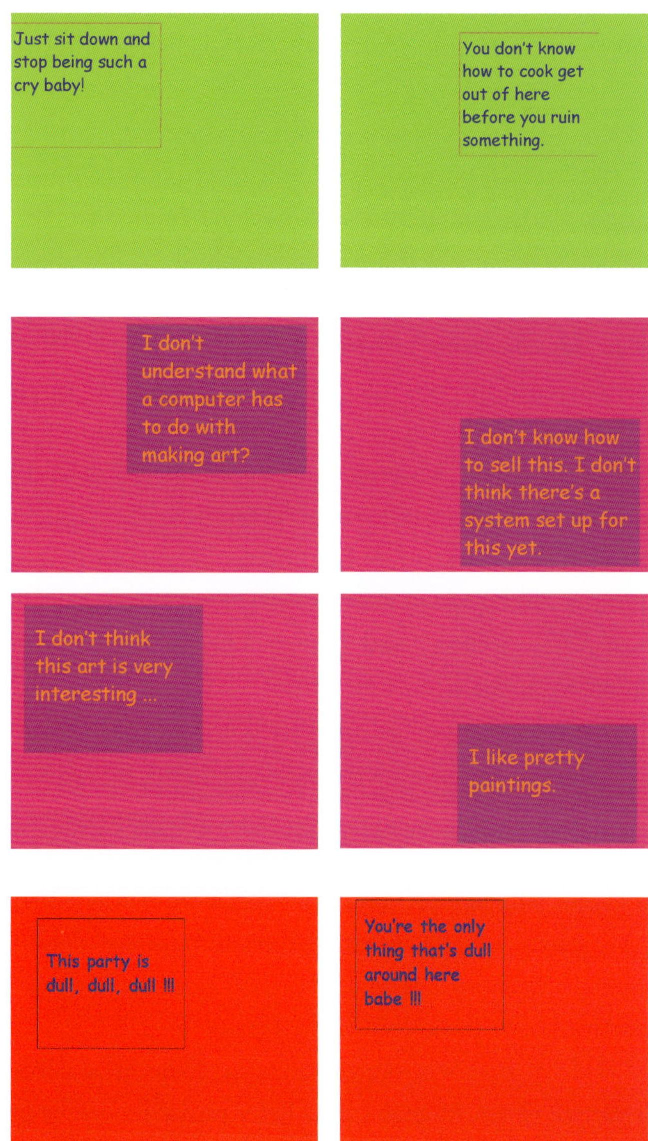

Top: Slides from *Cocktail Party,* kitchen
Middle: Slides from *Cocktail Party,* garage
Above: Slides from *Cocktail Party,* studio

human who "may have spent too much time socializing with bohemian types, mistaking intoxicated ramblings for small talk."[100] Each of four conversations takes place in a nominal room—a den, garage, studio, or kitchen—and is selected to play randomly. The screen expresses the voices as texts popping up and floating over a brightly colored magenta, red, orange, or neon green background. It's a fun and musical piece given a rough edge by Hovagimyan's biting, punk humor.

In the March 2001 issue of *Artforum*, Rhizome founder Mark Tribe mentioned one of Hovagimyan's computer songs, which had appeared in an online exhibition of Takuji Kogo's Candy Factory.[101] That May, Hovagimyan participated in the *net.ephemera* show at Moving Image Gallery curated by Tribe. Later that year, he performed *Lovers, Swingers & Shooters* at Postmasters, singing text-to-speech songs with four computers in chorus.

On September 30, 2001, in the aftermath of the World Trade Center attacks, Postmasters included *Cocktail Party*, *Shooter*, and *End of America* (from *Palm Rants*) in a series of digital performances alongside works by Takuji Kogo and the team Torino: Margolis. The Whitney posted *Cocktail Party* on its website in November.

> It's supposed cocktail conversation at an art opening. There's also an affinity for the work of Richard Prince who is a contemporary of mine, but he chose painting as a medium. My play is on the "great" American painters such as Barnett Newman or Robert Motherwell. The text doesn't sync up with the voices. It makes it disjunctive, as do the colors of the text vs. field.
>
> This piece is a sort of aside or maybe a sketch for my collaborative piece with Peter Sinclair, *Heartbreak Hotel*. In that work, Peter posited a group of people sitting at a bar talking. In a certain sense this is a "deconstruction" or a re-enactment of the art world as I've experienced it. It resembles a Bertolt Brecht play, albeit much more facetious. There's also a reference to Sunday morning cartoons on TV in the voices. Of course, this is all a personal narrative that has to do with my own obsessions about art.[102]

Palm Rants, (re)distributions, 2001

PalmPilots launched in 1997, becoming the first consumer handheld device to be able to upload and download video over the internet. *Palm Rants* returned to Hovagimyan's early punk performance roots: spoken-word pieces distributed as audio and video files, which were downloadable on PalmPilots using TealMovie software and viewable online as texts and animations. Originally created for the *(re)distributions* exhibition of artist and curator Patrick Lichty, they became among the first artworks for mobile devices, exploring the "expressive potential of handheld computing (PDAs), information appliances like pagers and cellular phones, as well as nomadic technologies like embedded processing and distributed systems.[103]

The *Palm Rants* pieces include *Entertain Me—Entertain Me* (first presented at the Warhol Hijack), *Who Pays? Who's Paying for This? Big Cars Are Not Cool Anymore*; *Who Turned Off the Lights and Air Conditioning! (California energy lament)*; *My Food is Poisoned*; *Foreplay*; *Love Songs from My Computer (synth voices put you in the mood)*; *Dot Com Today, Dot Gone Tomorrow*; *You Have Been Replaced by a Machine*; *The First One's on Me. The Second One's on You*; *Ever Feel That You Are Fooling Yourself*; *What Will It Take? The First Blackout*; *Big Medicine Killed My Father*; *Video Art Is Not the Next Big Thing. DUH*; *Buy and Sell and Buy and Sell and…*; *And You Thought You Were Famous*; *Several Ways to Brush Off Telemarketers*; and *The End of America*.

It received a mention at the time on Rhizome's Net Art News email newsletter: "What has experimental Net artist G.H. Hovagimyan been up to lately? Check out *Palm Rants*, a series of Web and PDA-based performances. The pieces will be delivered in either a short animation, an audio file, or a text. New performances will be available weekly for four months. Each performance (with titles such as *Love Songs from My Computer*) is a meditation on the ways we disperse information in a networked environment."[104]

> This piece was an early attempt to send video over the web onto a handheld platform. I had the idea of going back to my early video performance from the late 70s and sending them to handheld devices…I like the idea of having a "miniature" performance you can keep on a handheld device. In the 1970s,

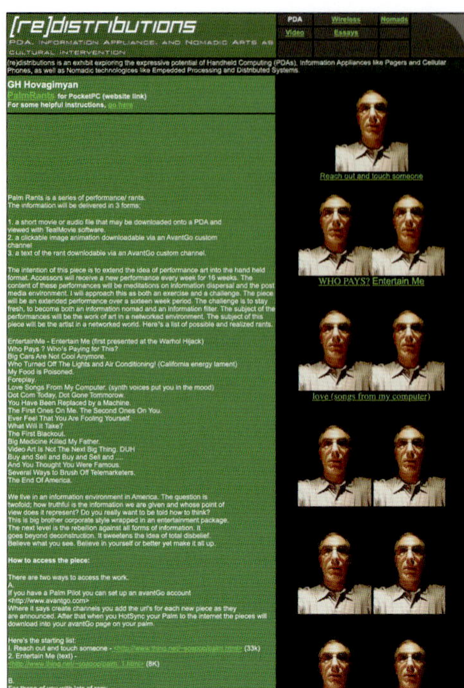

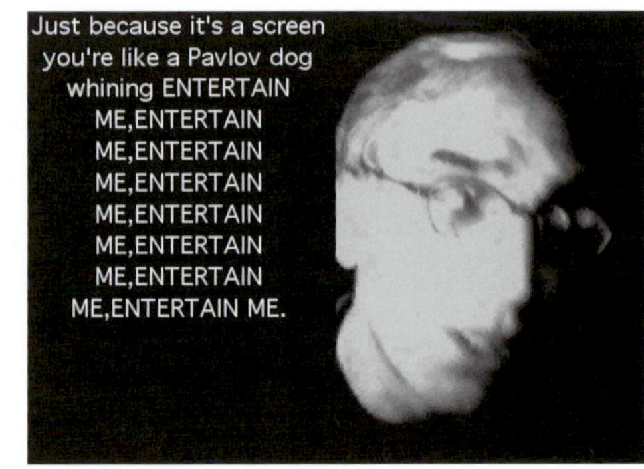

Left: Screen from *(re)distributions* exhibition
Above: Still from *Palm Rants*
Below: Images from *Palm Rants*

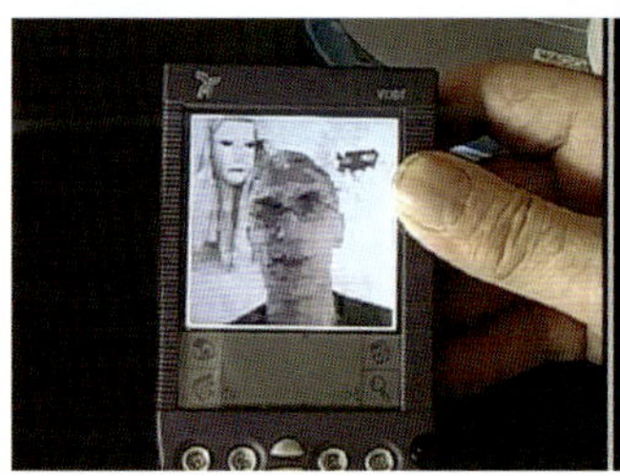

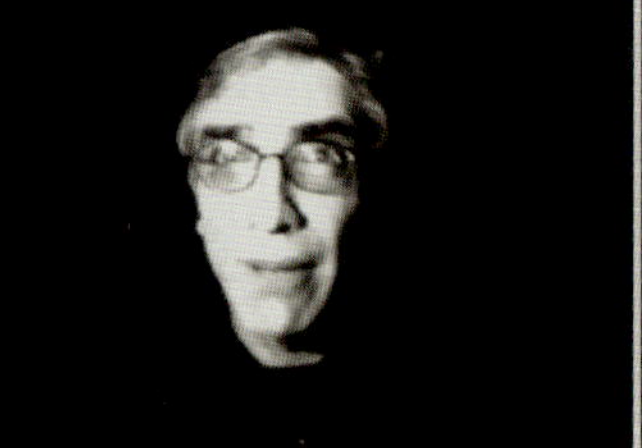

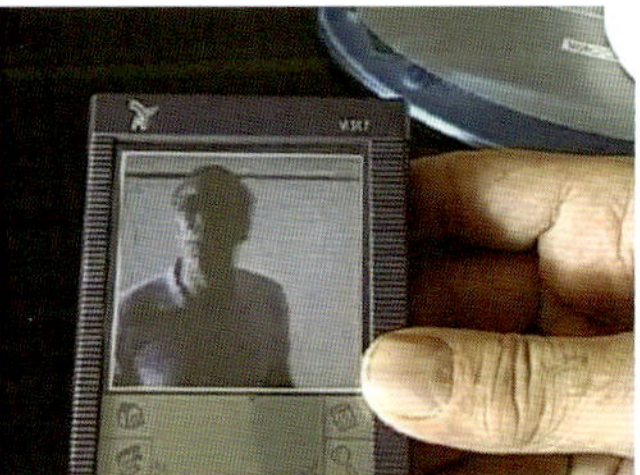

when I was doing video-performance, the equipment was very primitive. People would do performance that was a "talking to oneself." The idea of the video camera and monitor was a closed system, and if you viewed yourself on the monitor, it was considered "reflexive" performance. I thought that with the internet and handheld devices I could do a series of performance/rants that used the new video system of production, distribution and viewing. This started with the rant titled *Entertain Me*. I noticed when I was teaching that the students were always trying to get the highest quality video they could to stream on the web. I took a punk position, basically stripping out the color and dropping the frame rate. I then added the text window, which was a feature of QuickTime movies. Of course, it also harkens back to silent film. *Entertain Me* is especially effective in large outdoor projections on buildings because it doesn't need sound. It's actually a silent video performance work. I tend to incorporate words and language into my pieces. Sometimes performing myself, other times using synth voices. The subjects are usually topical current events. I see that as part of the fabric of media.

> The content of these performances will be meditations on information dispersal and the post-media environment. I will approach this as both an exercise and a challenge. The piece will be an extended performance over a sixteen-week period. The challenge is to stay fresh, to become both an information nomad and an information filter. The subject of the performances will be the work of art in a networked environment. The subject of this piece will be the artist in a networked world.[105]

He described his intentions on the *(re)distributions* site: "We live in an information environment in America. The question is twofold; how truthful is the information we are given and whose point of view does it represent? Do you really want to be told how to think? This is Big Brother corporate style wrapped in an entertainment package. The next level is the rebellion against all forms of information. It goes beyond deconstruction. It sweetens the idea of total disbelief. Believe what you see. Believe in yourself or better yet make it all up."[106]

Brecht Machine, Franklin Furnace, Sep. 2002

In 2002, along with talks in the spring at Hunter College as featured speaker in the *Untamed Signals: Cutting-Edge Media Creators* program and in the *Electronic Intersections* panel on net art at the Alfred University School of Art & Design, Hovagimyan received a $5,000 grant from Franklin Furnace for that year's *Future of the Present* artist residency program.

He was working on *Brecht Machine*, which used patched together dictation-and-translation as well as text-to-speech software for a live two-way web conference and performance. Hovagimyan wrote an app in which speech-to-text translated into another language and was spoken with synthetic voice. Since the planned performance was taking place in Split, Croatia, but there was no Croatian translation program, their English was translated to French, badly, creating a nonsense word salad like a poetry machine. He used off-the-shelf software and wrote a script to tie all the various bits together.

During the September 26 event corresponding to that year's Split Festival of Film & New Media, the remote hookup featured two performers, one in New York and one in Split, Croatia. At each location, the translation was automatically spoken by a synthetic voice. Since the dictation and translation systems are imperfect, it produced poetic mayhem and unexpected translation errors. "The whole piece was an exercise in the absurdity of technological claims and the difficulty of communication," he said.[107]

Nujus.net, 2003

In 2003, Hovagimayan and Sinclair set up an experimental web server to solve the problems they had experienced with university and commercial ones. They made it available to other artists for projects, especially Locus Sonus, a sound art collective and post-graduate workshop in France set up by Sinclair and Jerome Joy. Most of Hovagimyan's work remains documented on the site.

Smart House/Dumb Interactivity, 2003

In the early 2000s, Hovagimyan went to graduate school at NYU, taking classes over a period of several years to get a master of arts degree. For his thesis project, he created *Smart House*, a video using synthetic voices that looks at how a person might interact with the interactive homes and appliances of the future. In a video of himself in an orange jumpsuit with his initials in front

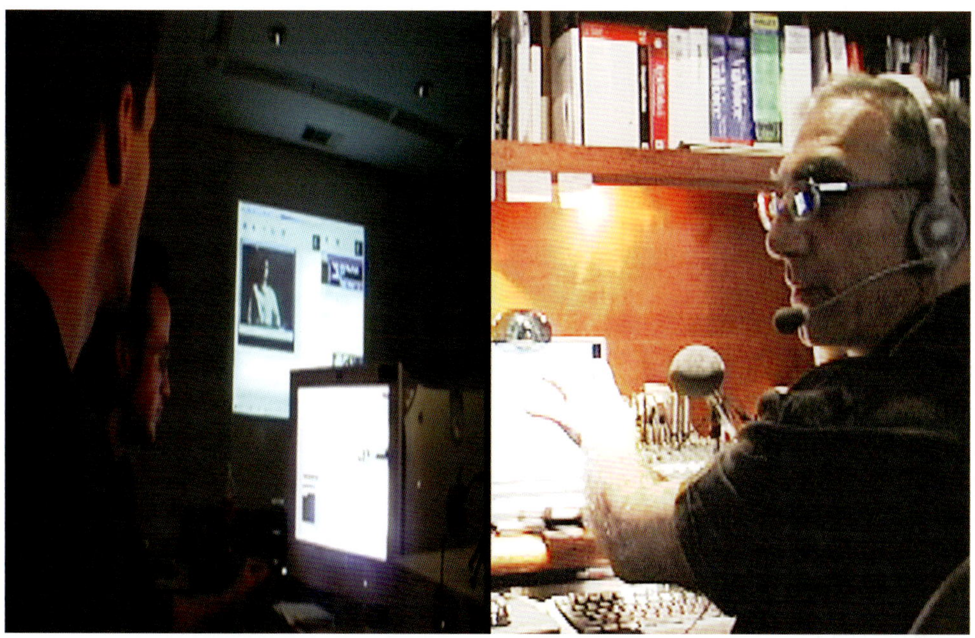

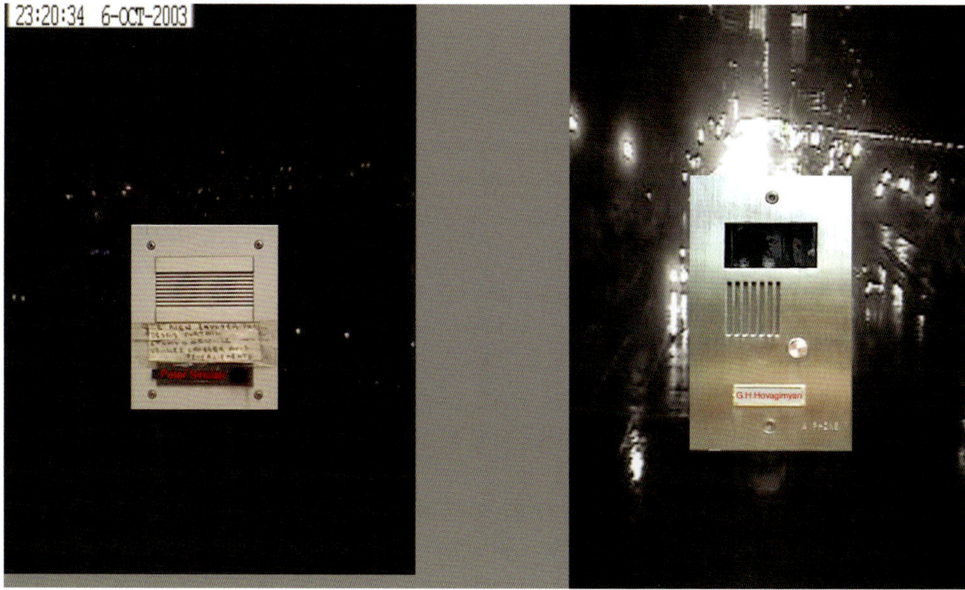

Top: *Brecht Machine* production
Above: Original landing page of Nujus.net

and the word "THEORY" in back, a synthetic female voice directs him as he goes about his daily routines, with an upbeat techno background track:

> "Good morning, time to wake up. I have made you a nice breakfast."
> "*Thank you*, House."
> "You are very welcome."

He described the project's context:

> I went back to school to get a master's degree at NYU. This video was part of my thesis, which was about housing and how it reflects a society's aspirations and technological advances. America in particular has organized many different communities and housing styles that reflect a period, a political doctrine, or a social movement. This includes industrialization and the digital revolution.
>
> The video itself is another video-performance work. It actually questions whether the information we are getting through digital systems does anything other than become another distraction, at least on the consumer level. It's a techno-utopian nightmare in my opinion. The structure of programming is a series of commands to be executed. If you extrapolate to an interactive house, or indeed any interactive computer application, you will see that it's actually very rigid. There's quite a bit of discussion around the idea of analog as being wave-forms while digital is on/off binary logic. A techno-utopia which is being heralded may not be as good as we envision it. The deeper meaning of the piece is the daily static in one's mind about chores, tasks, etc. These thoughts are not creative, although they are what is necessary to live. Often there's a struggle to make enough mental space to allow your creativity to emerge. Some people are swallowed up by their daily tasks and become prisoners. So the essence of a techno-utopia in which everyone is freed from the drudgery of labor and is able to engage in creative activities seems to me to be impossible, if not contradictory to creativity.
>
> In fact, I see the multiplication of information and data as crushing the creative spirit. As an artist, working in New Media (a contradiction in itself), I try to find ways to humanize data and programming. It's often bad or sloppy programming that gets me to a creative place. Or restructuring the interactive

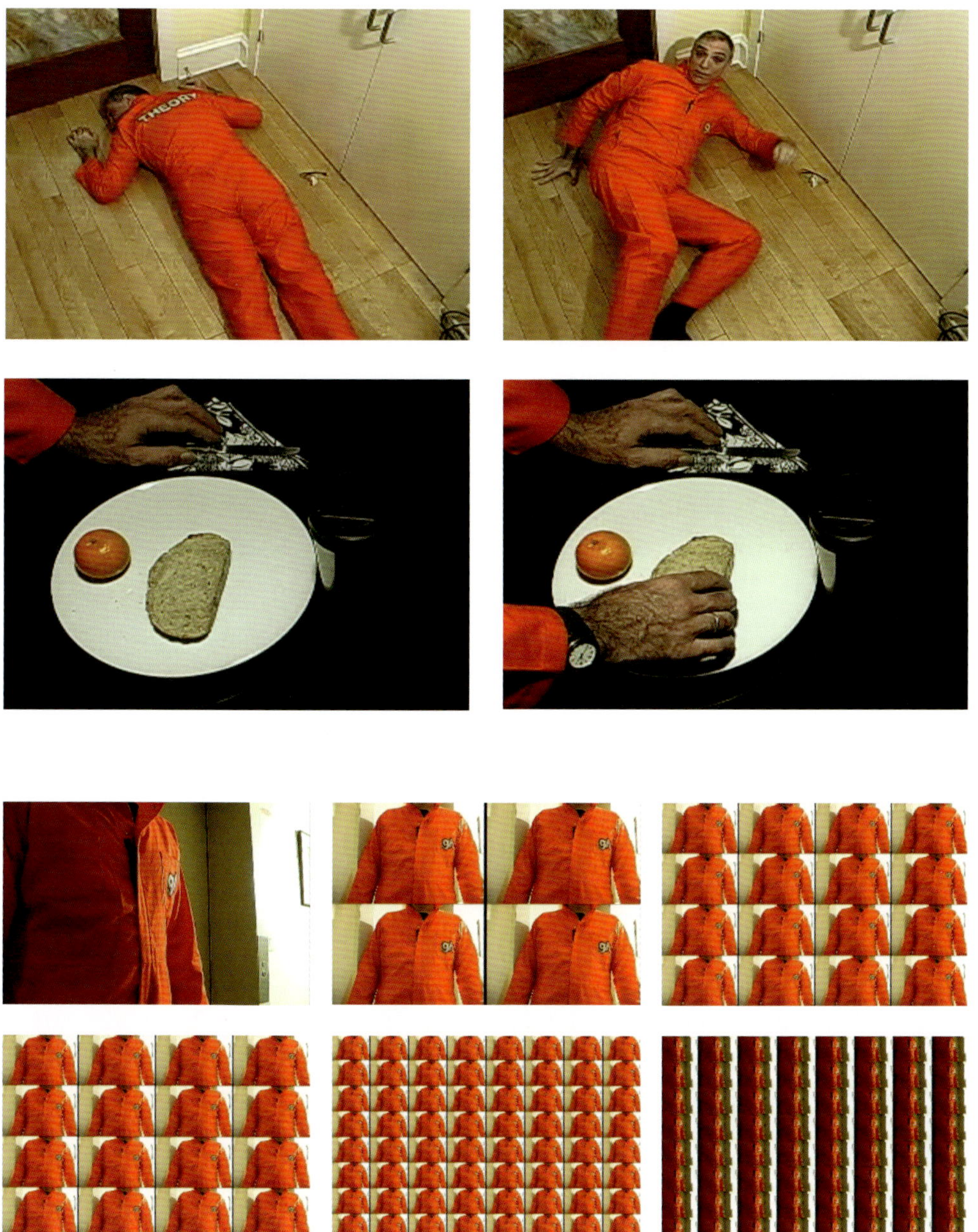

Stills from *Smart House/Dumb Interactivity*

> paths to do unexpected or illogical things. It reminds me of the Nabokov novel *Ada* in which the plumbing is connected to the telephone system in the house. Every time someone flushes a toilet the phones lose power.[108]

The Royal Ontario Museum's Institute for Contemporary Culture presented *Smart House* in May 2003, and it received a 2003 Award for New Media and Intermedia Performance from mediaThe foundation Inc. It screened again in April 2004 at the *Digit: Digital Media Exposition*, showing at the Tusten Theatre in Narrowsburg, New York.

Rant/Rant Back/Back Rant, performance (with Peter Sinclair), 2003

The setup for *Rant/Rant Back* involved Hovagimyan and Sinclair face-to-face on either end of a long table, with a video projection screen on the wall behind showing a time clock. Hovagimyan performed into a microphone, adopting the persona of a borderline/schizophrenic personality unable to distinguish between news, gossip, and paranoid rumors. Accompanied by a laptop and sound board, Sinclair used a custom patch designed in Pure Data (PD) visual programming language to capture audio snippets and feed them back into the sound mixer, loop them, or speed them up. They first performed it at La Gaîte Lyrique in Paris in September 2003 as part of the exhibition Open Source 3.

> I fashioned a performance based on a crazy person you see on the street. Often they are ranting about the headlines. It's as if they've lost the separation between information and real life or the information world has overwhelmed them. I created a script based on newspaper articles that have a particular writing style and media catch phrases or hooks. I mixed that with odd ways to string information together to make a coherent narrative that is nonsense. At the time, Bush was engaged in Afghanistan and Iraq. There were such phrases as "Ghost Detainees" or the fact that the Israelis manufacture the chips in cellphones and have location tracking capacity. These are all ranted and repeated. Peter also grabs my voice and throws that back into the mix creating the potential for live improvisation and "jamming."

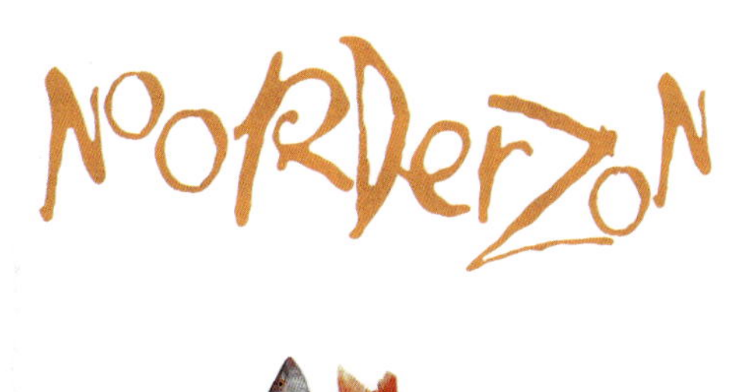

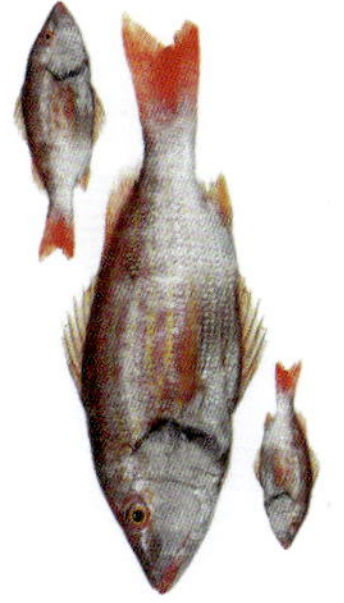

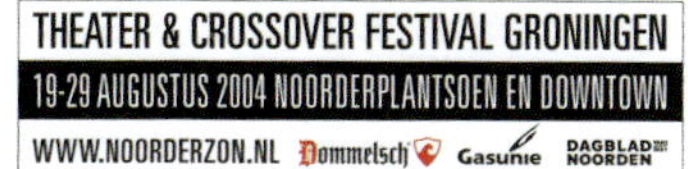

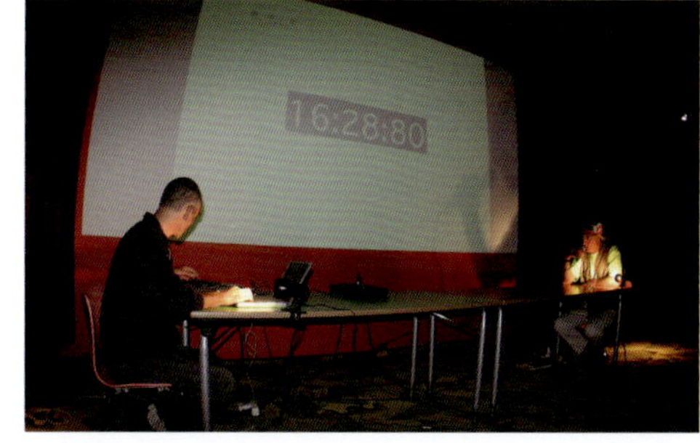

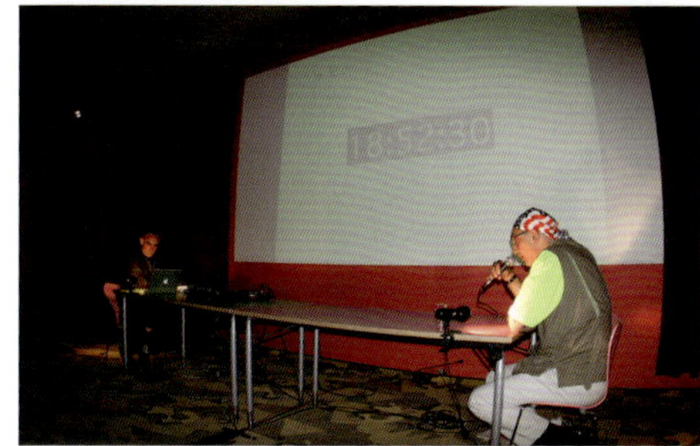

Above: Program of Noordezon Festival at Groninger Museum
Above right: *Rant/Rant Back* performance

> My reference is to Wittgenstein's idea of specialized language. It also deals with the global information system. Peter for his part created a digital tool that allows him to perform with my voice. It's a dialog that is cut up and remixed. This piece was performed in two places in the Netherlands and by remote video conference from New York City to Aix-en-Provence and back. For the French performance I was in my studio and Peter was in an auditorium with an audience. I liked the idea of telematic performance. I could hear Peter's sound mix in my headphones albeit with a slight delay.[109]

They performed again that September at the Split New Media Festival and the following August 2004 in the Netherlands at the Groninger Museum during the Noordezon Festival and at STEIM Institute in Amsterdam, as well as by live performance and via internet link at Postmasters. In September 2004, another live internet video performance took place between New York and Aix-en-Provence for *Les Rencontres Place Publique* in Marseille.

5

Videos and Hacked Interfaces

Vanity Search, 2004

In the early 2000s, when Yahoo!, AltaVista, and Lycos were top search engines and Microsoft's Internet Explorer was still the dominant consumer browser platform, Hovagimyan returned to his net art roots in a couple of playful hacks of search algorithms. *Vanity Search* is a joke on how during the early internet years, people used to be self-conscious about searching their own name, but it was presumed that everyone did it. Hovagimyan created an automated search tool, setting up a client-pull animation to repeatedly search his own name and using JavaScript to open the searches in new windows and renew the result each time the program refreshed the browser windows.

Created for the online Computer Fine Arts Collection, founded by digital, video, and computer artist Doron Golan, it was essentially a Fluxus-influenced conceptual art work that used a script to expose online information. "Vanity Search creates an instant web collage using search engines doing a vanity search on the name G.H. Hovagimyan. One might call this Neo-Fluxus information art. The interesting part is that the piece changes as more information is added to the web."[110]

Artist and curator Marisa Olson reviewed *Vanity Search* for Rhizome that year:

> We've all done it, haven't we? What is often referred to as the "vanity search" can take many forms. Whether you're just curious how many MySpace users share your name or you're obsessed with the number of people citing your blog, the internet search for one's self has become a common, if private pastime. American performance artist G.H. Hovagimyan makes the process public in his "instant web collage" aptly titled *Vanity Search*...The site automatically flashes through the real-time results of the queries, raising questions about the eventual entropy of both the information sought and the corporations in place to track it. The artist categorizes the project as "Neo-Fluxus information art," and the "Neo-" might arguably refer to the new conditions of life in search engine culture—including constant surveillance, imbalanced attention spans, the blurred distinction between public and private, and the bittersweet possibility of being "internet famous."[111]

Like much of Hovagimyan's computer-based work, the stability of *Vanity Search* depended on keeping the programming updated on new versions of the browsers and the search engines themselves staying in business. Yahoo! purchased AltaVista in 2003, and by the end of 2004, Google quickly overtook Yahoo! and rose to the top of the search food chain with its ranked choice results and contextual advertising.

> This is a very fragile piece. It depends on all the search engines now in existence to continue to function...How many search engines will be in existence in ten years? Will the web become censored like in China or "privatized" and made the domain of commercial culture only?[112]

Vanity Search is now preserved in Cornell University's Rose Goldsen Archive of New Media Art, along with the entire Computer Fine Arts Collection.

Opposite: *Vanity Search* screenshots

LYCOS
altavista
altavista
amazon.com

YAHOO! SEARCH
Google
metacrawler
Ask.com
altavista

Google Images
altavista
alltheweb
YAHOO! SEARCH
Ask.com
WebCrawler

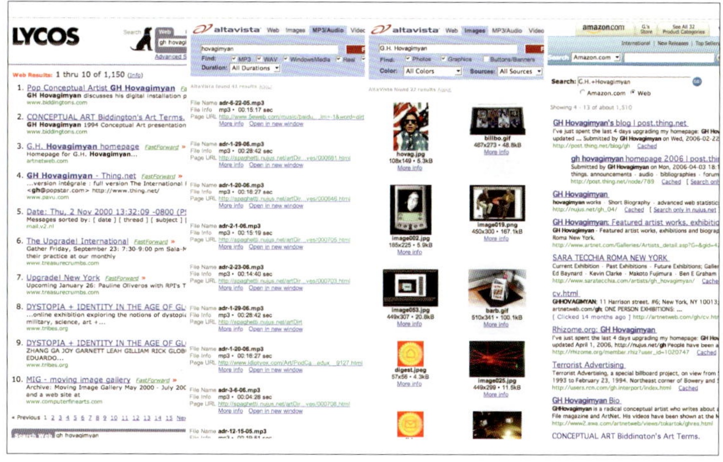

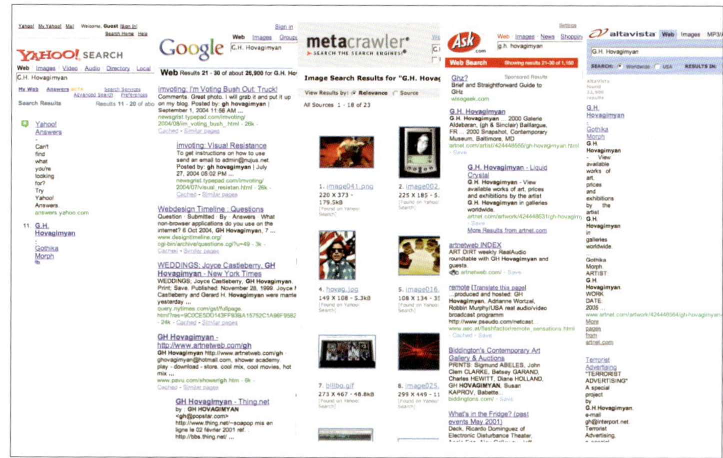

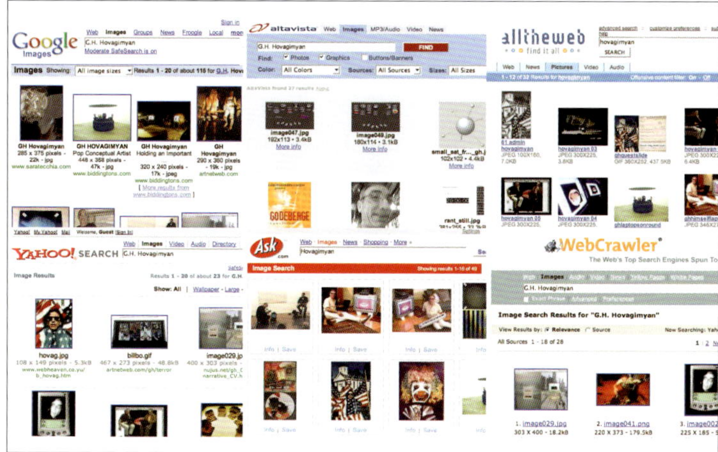

143

IFC Hack, 2004

Around the same time as *Vanity Search*, Hovagimyan's *IFC Hack* played with the easily manipulated platforms cropping up on the internet for user participation. The Independent Film Channel allowed filmmakers to upload films for users to vote on. He used his nujus.net server to create multiple email addresses to game the system.

> The IFC channel set up a web 2.0 site where people could upload their short films and vote on which were the best. You could vote if you joined the site with your email address. I looked at the site and saw it was mostly commercial filmmaker wannabes. I thought it would be amusing to add my rant videos and see what happened. When I first put up my videos I, of course, voted for myself. This sent them briefly to number one, but they quickly shot down to the bottom of the list. This happens if someone gives you a negative rating. I became suspicious because I noticed after a week that the same five films were always on top. I started to search the site for people who had just uploaded their videos and were so honest they hadn't even voted for themselves. I gave them all five-star ratings, knocking the top five off the list. But sure enough, the same films were back on top in a matter of hours. I realized that some film marketers were rigging the contest either with a robot or a crowd swarm. I decided this was like a game battle. Since I have my own server, I gave myself a lot of email addresses and started to vote for myself and any new uploads to keep knocking off the top five crappy films (they were really horrible!). Of course, they kept on being reset to the top after a time. This went on for two weeks when I finally got an email from their sysadmin saying my IP address was banned from using the site. I wrote back and told them their voting system was flawed and the site was being rigged to put the same five movies on top. They tried to fix the problem by limiting votes, but that limited traffic to the site. They did that for a couple of days and then went back to their original format. It's a cautionary tale about the supposed "democracy" of the internet and the idea of a popularity contest for art.[113]

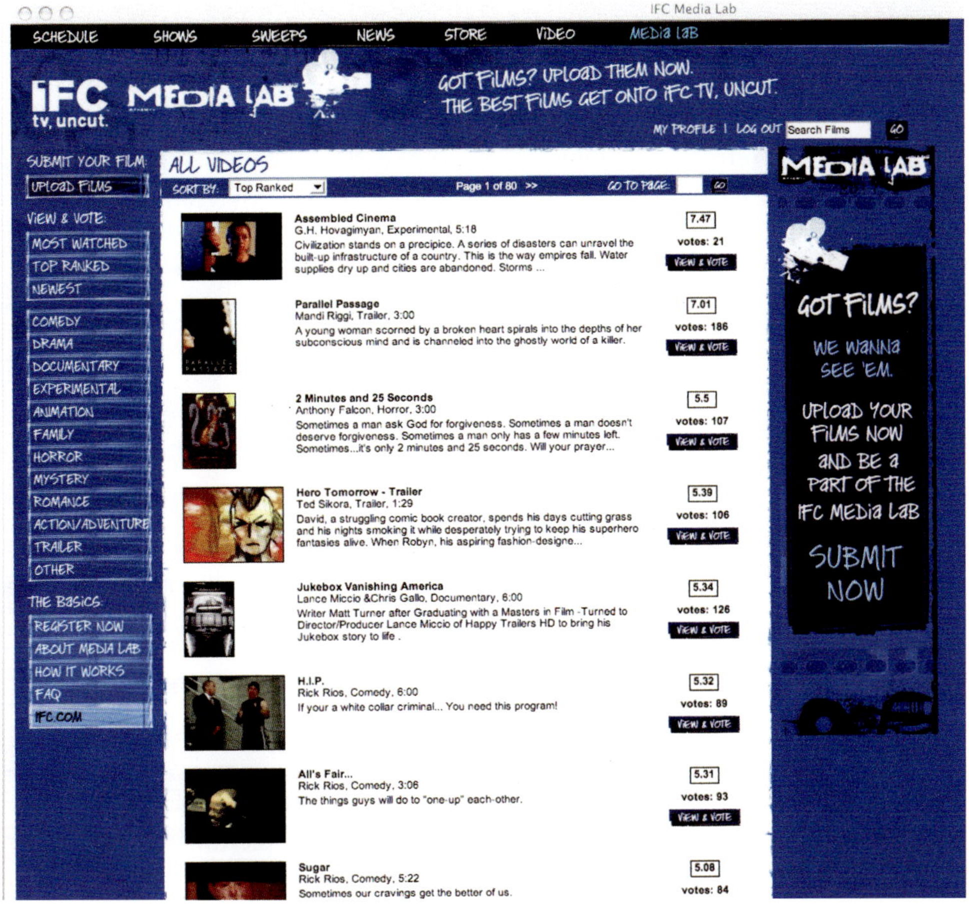

IFC Media Lab

SCHEDULE SHOWS SWEEPS NEWS STORE VIDEO MEDIA LAB

IFC tv, uncut. MEDIA LAB

GOT FILMS? UPLOAD THEM NOW.
THE BEST FILMS GET ONTO IFC TV, UNCUT.

MY PROFILE | LOG OUT Search Films GO

SUBMIT YOUR FILM: UPLOAD FILMS

VIEW & VOTE: MOST WATCHED, TOP RANKED, NEWEST

COMEDY, DRAMA, DOCUMENTARY, EXPERIMENTAL, ANIMATION, FAMILY, HORROR, MYSTERY, ROMANCE, ACTION/ADVENTURE, TRAILER, OTHER

THE BASICS: REGISTER NOW, ABOUT MEDIA LAB, HOW IT WORKS, FAQ, IFC.COM

ALL VIDEOS

SORT BY: Top Ranked — Page 1 of 80 >> — GO TO PAGE: GO

Assembled Cinema
G.H. Hovagimyan, Experimental, 5:18
Civilization stands on a precipice. A series of disasters can unravel the built-up infrastructure of a country. This is the way empires fall. Water supplies dry up and cities are abandoned. Storms ...
7.47 — votes: 21 — VIEW & VOTE

Parallel Passage
Mandi Riggi, Trailer, 3:00
A young woman scorned by a broken heart spirals into the depths of her subconscious mind and is channeled into the ghostly world of a killer.
7.01 — votes: 186 — VIEW & VOTE

2 Minutes and 25 Seconds
Anthony Falcon, Horror, 3:00
Sometimes a man ask God for forgiveness. Sometimes a man doesn't deserve forgiveness. Sometimes a man only has a few minutes left. Sometimes...it's only 2 minutes and 25 seconds. Will your prayer...
5.5 — votes: 107 — VIEW & VOTE

Hero Tomorrow - Trailer
Ted Sikora, Trailer, 1:29
David, a struggling comic book creator, spends his days cutting grass and his nights smoking it while desperately trying to keep his superhero fantasies alive. When Robyn, his aspiring fashion-designe...
5.39 — votes: 106 — VIEW & VOTE

Jukebox Vanishing America
Lance Miccio &Chris Gallo, Documentary, 6:00
Writer Matt Turner after Graduating with a Masters in Film -Turned to Director/Producer Lance Miccio of Happy Trailers HD to bring his Jukebox story to life .
5.34 — votes: 126 — VIEW & VOTE

H.I.P.
Rick Rios, Comedy, 6:00
If your a white collar criminal... You need this program!
5.32 — votes: 89 — VIEW & VOTE

All's Fair...
Rick Rios, Comedy, 3:06
The things guys will do to "one-up" each-other.
5.31 — votes: 93 — VIEW & VOTE

Sugar
Rick Rios, Comedy, 5:22
Sometimes our cravings get the better of us.
5.08 — votes: 84

MEDIA LAB

GOT FILMS? WE WANNA SEE 'EM. UPLOAD YOUR FILMS NOW AND BE A PART OF THE IFC MEDIA LAB SUBMIT NOW

IFC Hack screenshot

Assembled Cinema, 2005

Composed of a series of short video segments of actors uttering phrases like "There's nothing left; it's all gone," "This is the end of me," "Hang on tight," "The roads are jammed; this is a nightmare," "The police are saying we have to evacuate," "They've released water from the dams," "I've never seen clouds like that," and "Let's stay put," *Assembled Cinema* created a playlist programmed to randomly organize the scenes without pretext or other narrative, relying on the viewer's mind to retroactively make sense of it. Kate McCamy shot the footage, and Hovagimyan, Lindsey Roberts, and Randy Noojin performed the dialogue in their apartments, by the Hudson River, and on the street in TriBeCa.

> You walk into a room and a film/video is projected on a wall. The scenes played are not in any particular order yet they make sense. What occurs is that a computer is picking sequences in a random order and playing them. Your mind and your imagination fill in the story.[114]

Hovagimyan described his motivation for the project:

> I wanted to do a "movie" about the feelings of people during and after a disaster. This script is distilled from reports about hurricanes Katrina and Irene as well as my own sense of things and my feelings about 9/11 and more recent storms and floods. It was shot on the Hudson River during a very windy day. Since 9/11, whenever I return to the city I fill my tank with gas. I remember being stuck in Holland Tunnel traffic for three hours during a blackout. All I could think was that I would run out of gas. I keep thinking that we are really living in a disaster America, and like the Roman empire, our hold on civilization is fragile…You don't need a literary theme to understand what's happening.[115]

It's an observation that continues to be documented in behavioral research and reiterated by the tilt of history toward increasing complexity. "Cognitive scientists are researching how the brain assembles meaning and narrative," Hovagimyan said. "There's a lot more that can be done to understand what's

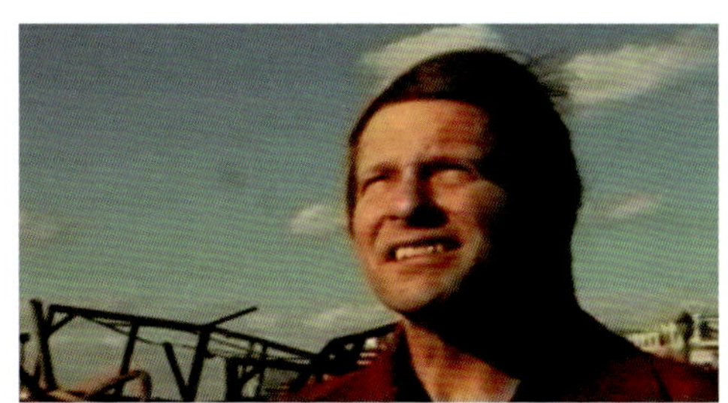
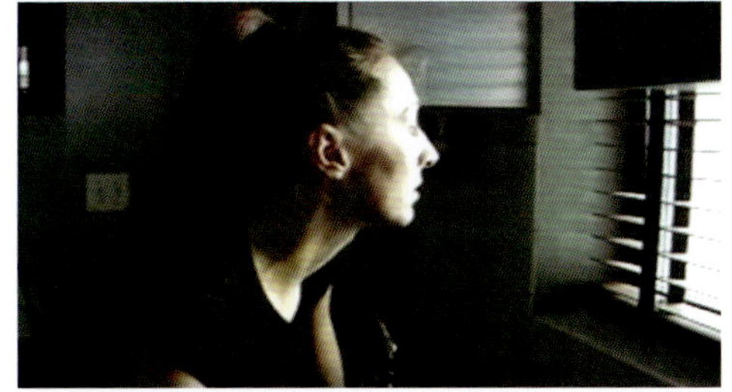
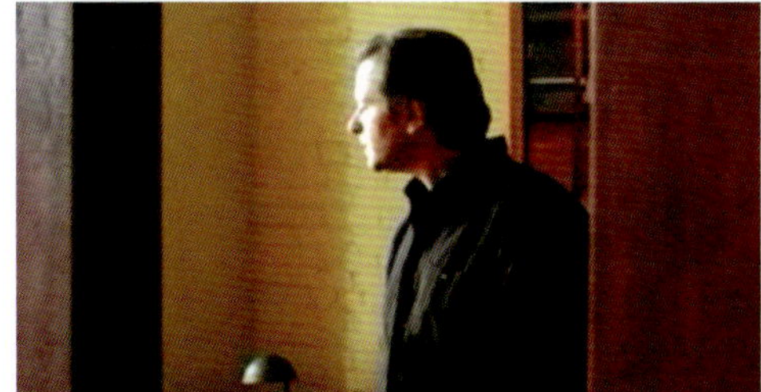
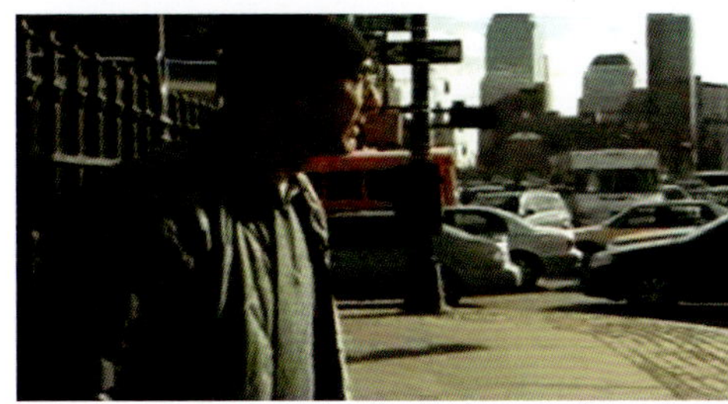

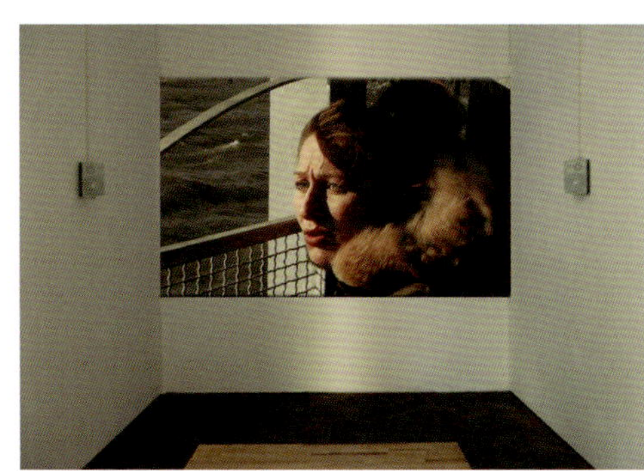
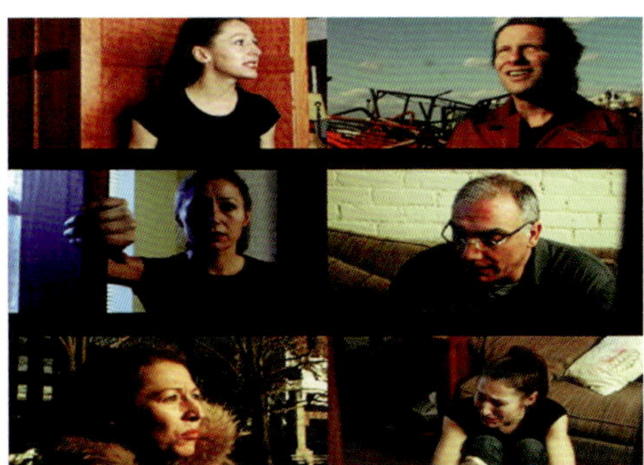

Top: Stills from *Assembled Cinema*
Above: Installation shots of *Assembled Cinema*

not apparent through language or formal structure. It's where we're at, at the moment, politically and sociologically: narratives are happening without any kind of logic or any reason. It's like when they talk about people trying to quantify the stock market or other human behavior but they can't quantify it. It doesn't make sense."[116]

HD Morphs/Fluid Dynamics, 2005

In 2005, Hovagimyan used a free app called MorphX, developed to transform one image into another, to make *HD Morphs*, a series of constantly changing digital paintings on high-definition video. Distributed in some exhibitions as *Fluid Dynamics* (Seoul Net Festival), and *Glass Morphs* (Cinema-Scope: Environment-Object-Inhabitant), the source images were steel and glass shown in a continuous loop on a high-definition monitor or projector.

> Hovagimyan's morphs are essentially moving paintings. The objects in and of themselves create a language, where a suprastructural meaning is created by stringing a series of objects together. Because a software program randomly assembles and constantly reorders the videos, Hovagimyan emphasizes the constant separation between signifier and signified, where no signifier ever rests on any particular signified.[117]

The Seoul Net Festival catalogue described the results: "With [its] morphing steel digital image and roof, *Fluid Dynamics* gives body to [an inquiry of the] processing of organic transformation. The advanced digital abstraction and disposition of the digital image [shows] modern physics chasing order within unfixed chaos. . ."[118]

Opposite: *HD Morphs*

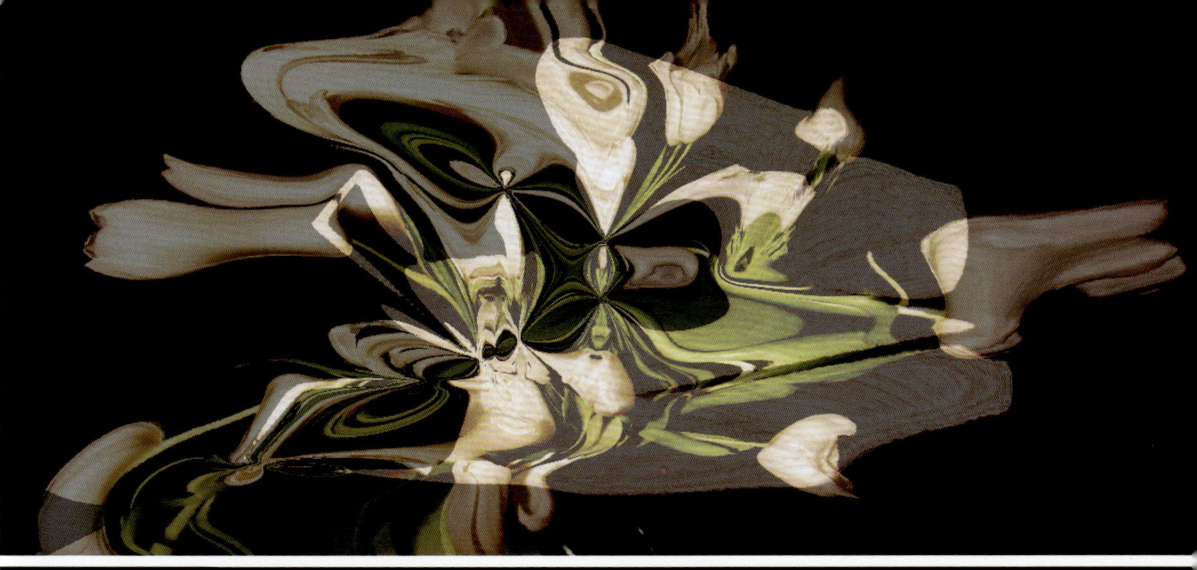

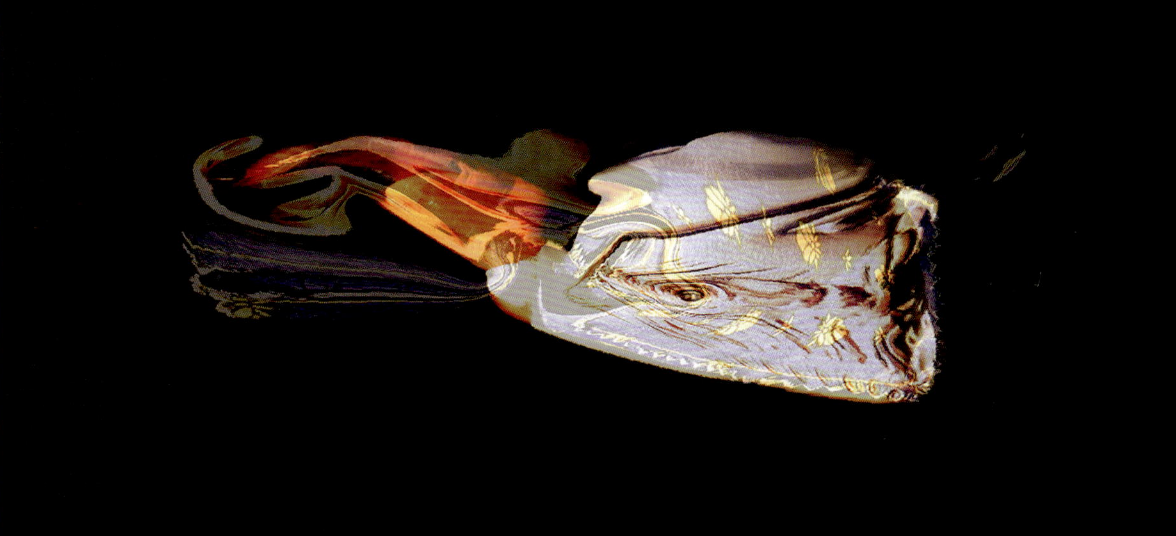

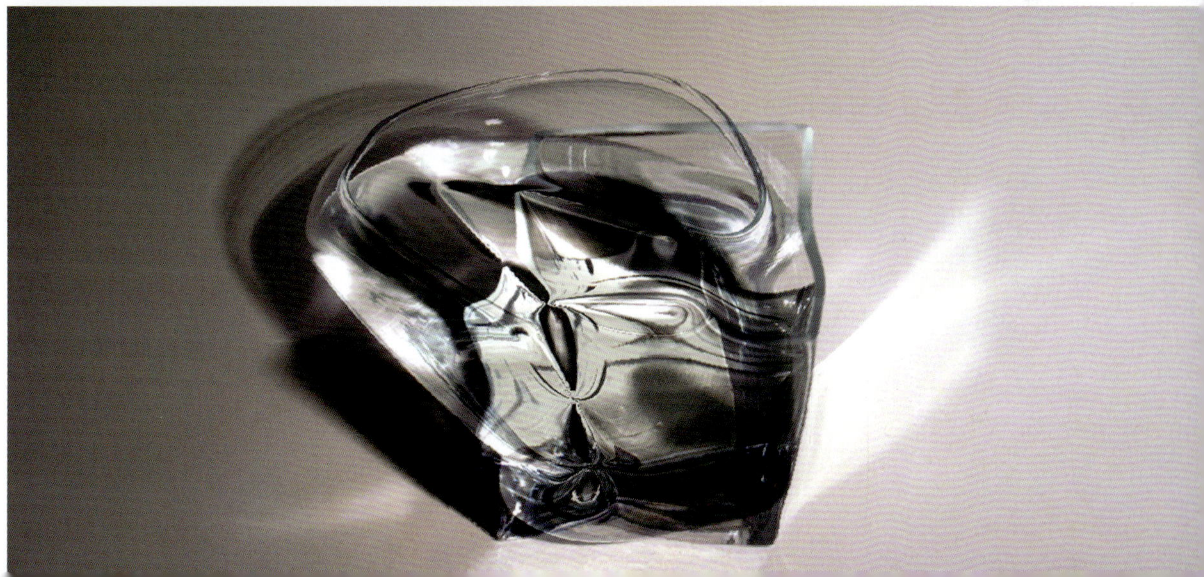

Hovagimyan hand-manipulated the transformations using MorphX to abstract the shapes—in what he described as a painterly process—and assemble a video database. He asked media artist Hans-Christophe Steiner to write a program to randomly choose from the database and match the last frame of the morph to the first of the next morph and create an endless movie.

> I got the idea from a Philip K. Dick book that talks about people going to see the same movie but it being slightly different each time. The deeper question is about the idea of recognition and cognition. How we see and how we remember.[119]

Rantapod, 2006

In his continual exploration of emerging media platforms and technologies, Hovagimyan returned to his punk performance roots to list his catalog of confrontational rants critiquing media and culture on iTunes. Apple had launched iTunes in 2002 and added video and a podcast directory in 2005, opening up a space for new media. He stripped down the rant videos to the lowest-quality format to be easily downloadable on iPods.

> I decided to go back to the initial premise of video-performance, using the camera in a reflexive manner. The rants are actually rhetorical discourses based on current political thinking. I decided to continue with the idea of video-performance distributed over the internet. This first came to me with *Palm Rants*. I set up a podcasting site but obviously it wasn't a commercial site. I was able to get it listed on Apples iTunes for two years. As I experimented with post production, I started to take visible ticks, stutters, and mistakes and multiply them rather than take them out. This set up a percussive rhythm. I began to cut sections of the video-rant and rearrange them, realizing that one would still understand the message even if it was jumbled up. Finally, I began to copy the repetitive ticks created by the program, in essence training my performance based on what a machine can do.

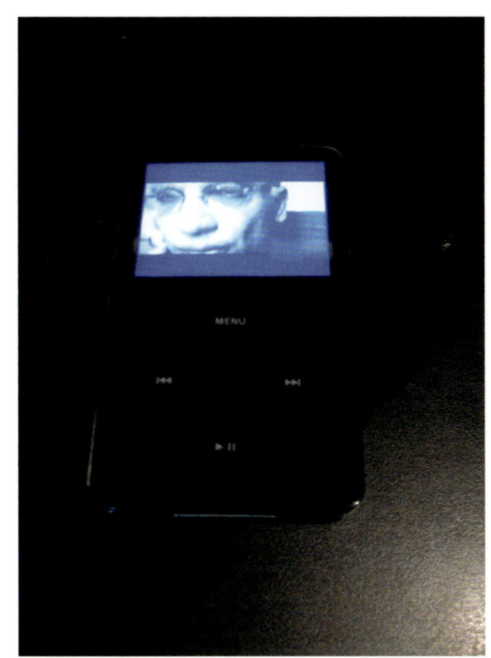

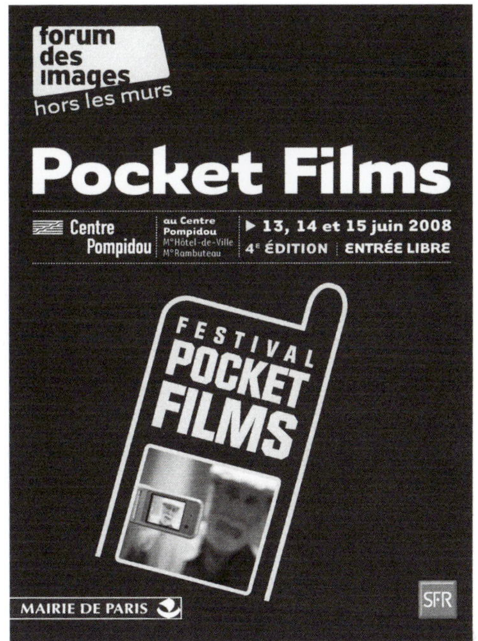

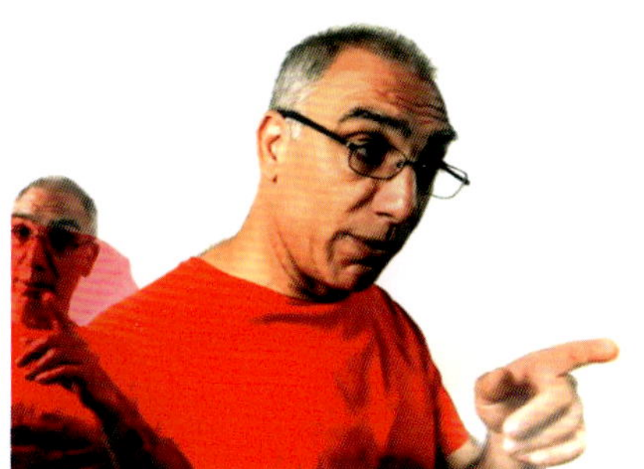

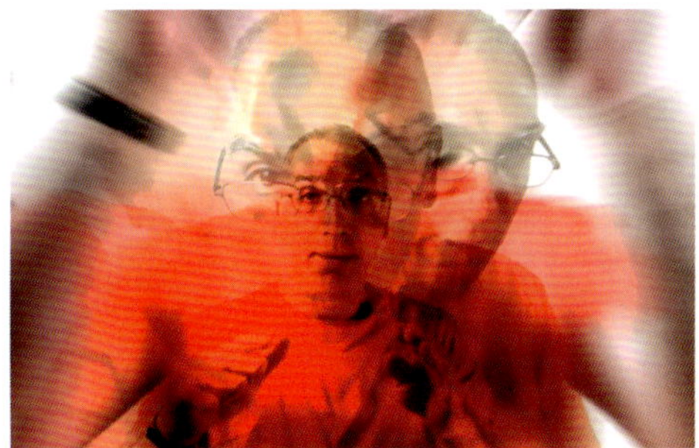

Top left: *Rantpod*
Top right: Program of Pocket Film Festival
Above: *H_D Rants* stills

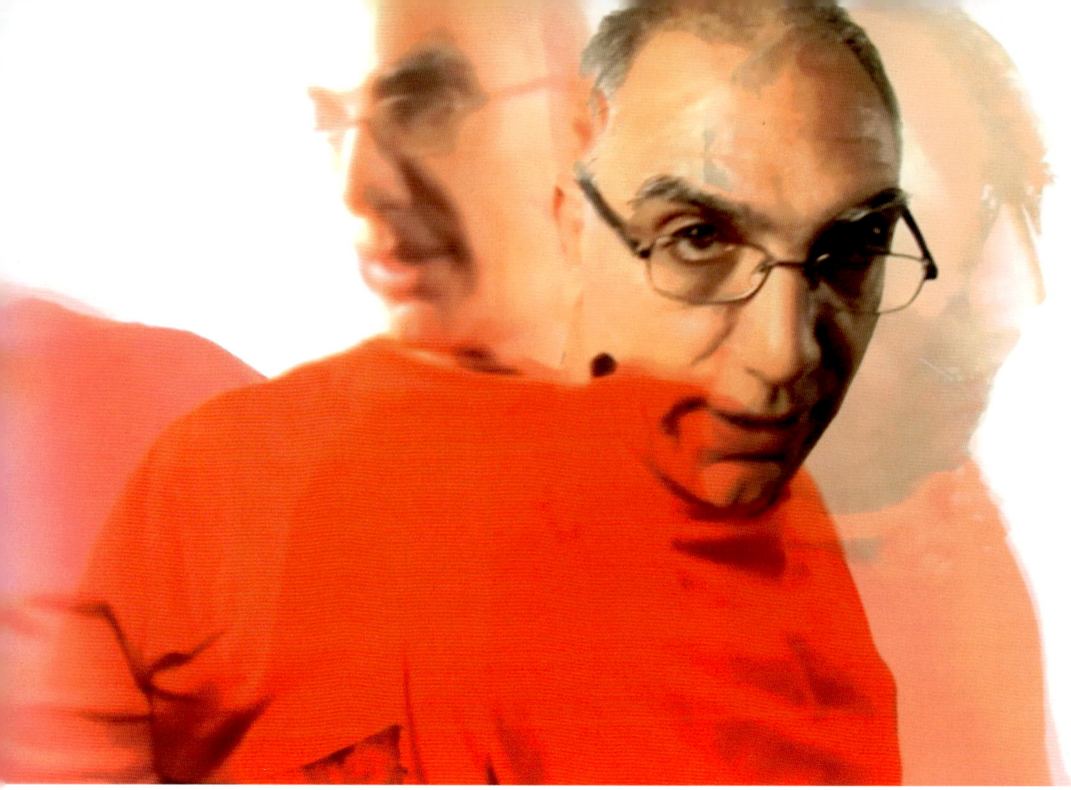

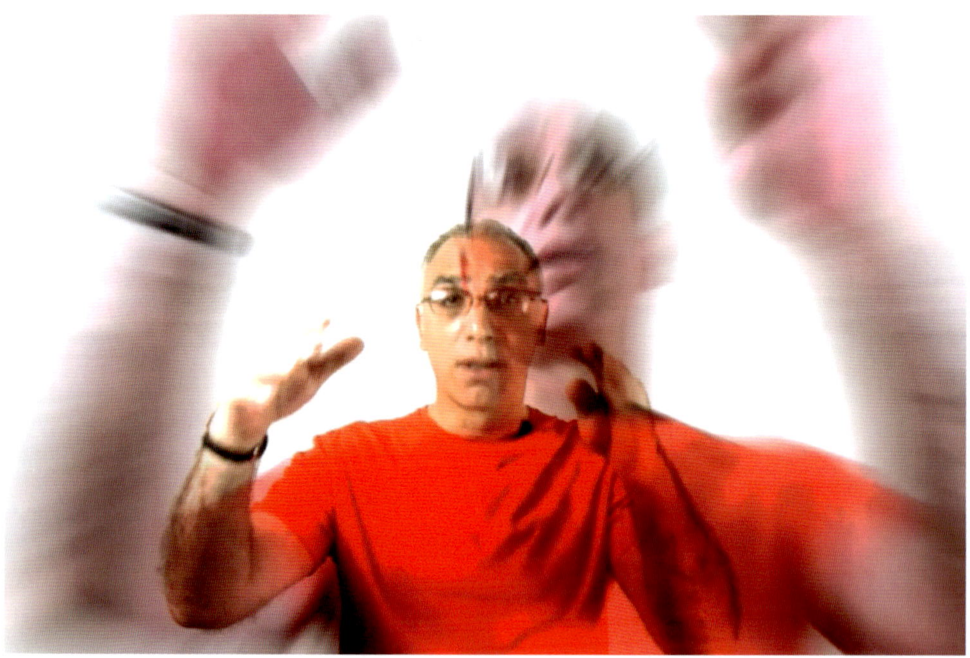

H_D Rants stills

> I set up a web playlist that uses a specific type of coding. They're lists of videos with reference pointers, text codes that say whenever it's updated, used for newsfeeders and push announcements. Once you set up the list, you put a link onto a website, and if the link has been updated, you get the updated playlist. It's a way to stream mpeg files or the latest video. I was interested in that as a distribution system, because you can use the corporate structure—Apple's podcast system—so I presented them on iTunes. You make this list, they approve it, then all of the sudden you're on iTunes, which is absolutely hilarious because it's this artwork in the middle whatever people are listening to.[120]

Videos from *Rantapod* screened widely, including at the Fourth Screen Festival organized by Postmasters's Tamas Banovich at Lincoln Center's New York Video festival in July 2006, the Festival of Pocket Films at Centre Pompidou in 2007 and 2008, Digit festival in Lackawaxen, Pennsylvania, Split Film Festival in Croatia, and Pixel Pops in Prague. "We are at a moment when the heads of media companies, Vietnamese peasants, artists, hackers, activists, governments, and private corporations are trying to grab us through mobile phenomena," Banovich wrote in the program. "Lots of space remains for big ideas, dream creations, and addressing real needs."[121]

H_D Rants (with Brian Caiazza), 2006

For *H_D Rants*, Hovagimyan got access to three high-definition video cameras and shot himself riffing on his confrontational rant pieces from right, left, and center, simultaneously. Working with video editor, animator, and producer Brian Caiazza, he layered the videos over each other and synchronized them using Adobe After Effects. The rants on subjects like how people are getting brainwashed by media, religion, and politics combine with broadcast-quality video, disjunctive effects, and his presence wearing a brightly colored T-shirt to increase the audio-visual impact of the pieces.

> Each piece is a short rant meditation. Caiazza's brilliant post production editing in After Effects and the HD video puts these works in a realm of their

> own…*HD_Rants* uses words as repetitive percussive elements. Caiazza picks up on the ideas of sampling but in this case it's self-sampling and repetition.[122]

H_D Rants circulated widely through Perpetual Art Machine (PAM), an archive of video created in December 2005 as a collaboration between Lee Wells, Raphaele Shirley, Chris Borkowski, and Aaron Miller, which at one time featured more than 5,000 videos and 2,000 artists from 80 countries. Wells showcased some of them at Art Basel Miami Beach from December 6–10, 2006 as part of the *Guerrilla Media Vehicle*.

> Lee Wells, he got one of those video trucks, the video screen advertising projector trucks, and he went down to the Miami art fair and drove around the streets with this truck with the video projecting with my rants on it, which was unbelievable…the *Rich Sucker Rap* (*laughs*). Lee liked that.[123]

Another installation appeared as *For Love & Money*, a two-part radio show broadcast on Resonance FM at Frieze Art Fair in the same year. Other screenings and appearances occurred at the Dumbo Arts Festival, Art Frames at Pioneer Theater, CIRCA in San Juan, Puerto Rico, PAM at Coachella, as well as online on VernissageTV and in Doran Golan's Computer Fine Arts Collection. Museum exhibitions included M21—The Museum of 21st Century, Fundacio Clovis Salgado/Palacio des Artes in Belo Horizonte, Brazil, and Museum of Modern Art Linz in the exhibition *Video as Urban Condition* in April 2007. In 2007, Natacha Roussel curated it in Atlanta at Eyedrum in *Furious: The Angry Show*, an "exploration of the dark side" whose publicity offering that "Those offended by the word 'fuck' are invited not to attend."[124]

Video Projections, Artists Meeting, Art Under the Bridge Festival, Dumbo, Sep. 28–30, 2007

Beginning in 2006, Hovagimyan and fellow artist and photographer Daniel Blochwitz initiated a group that gathered under the name Artists Meeting. They discussed ways of collaborating, framing it as "an open dialogue and discussion

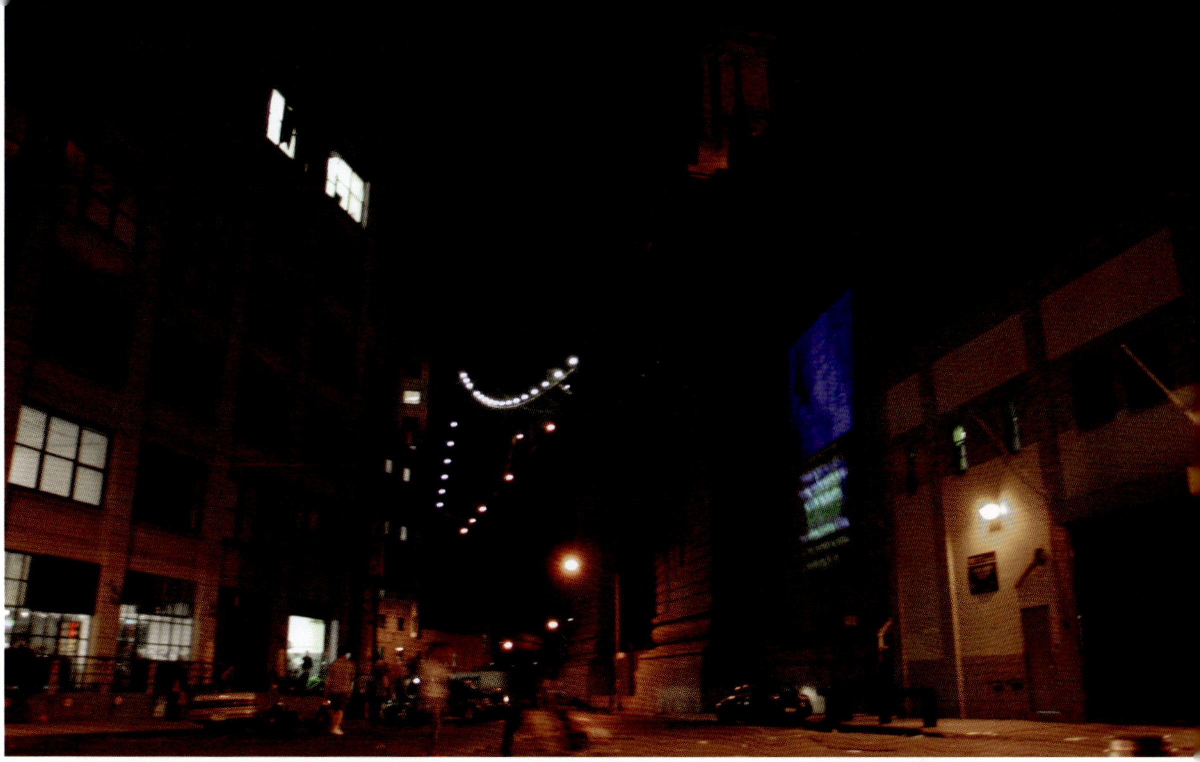

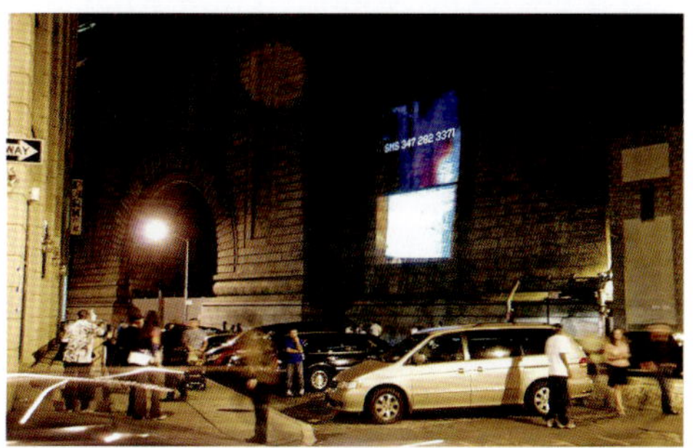

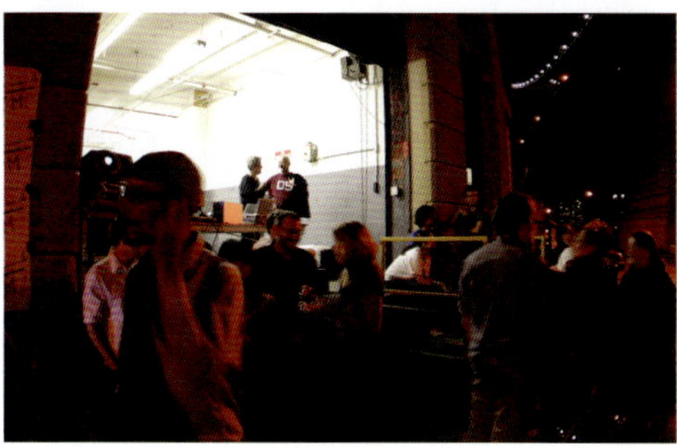

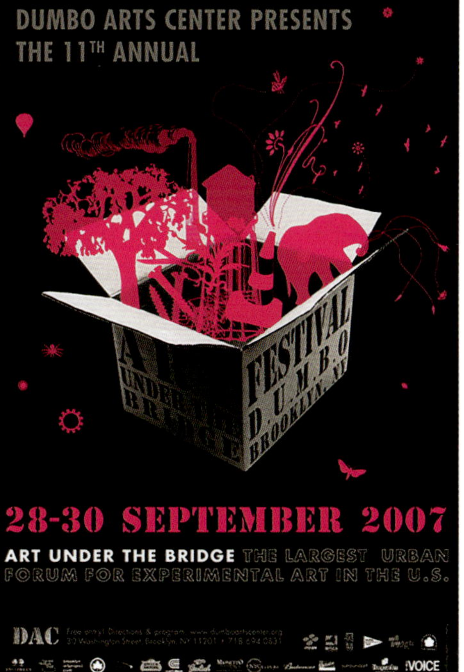

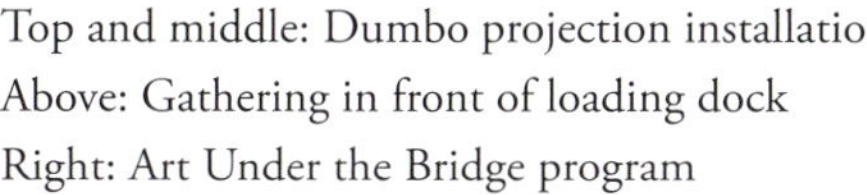

Top and middle: Dumbo projection installation
Above: Gathering in front of loading dock
Right: Art Under the Bridge program

about art and group praxis." In September 2007, they presented a collaborative video installation at the Art Under the Bridge Festival in Dumbo, Brooklyn. Sharing two large-scale projectors, they displayed videos, text, still photos, and ephemera of their meeting notes on the south side of the Manhattan Bridge anchorage, stationing themselves on a loading dock at Front and Adams streets.

> We were basically jamming video projections of what everybody was doing. We just had a playlist of separate things that each of the artists did, and also text phrases that would flash up, or notes from a meeting or conversations, because we had a lot of conversations back and forth on internet text servers, stills of videos, still photographs, or anything that we felt like putting in. It's more like a Fluxus jam. I got these text-to-speech apps, and I had the soundtrack to the video on little chips that were plugged into personal loudspeakers that four members wore, so it would be like a four-channel, quadrophonic sound system, then they'd walk around in the crowd randomly with the soundtrack that was up there on the screen. Nobody knew what was going on but *we* did (*laughs*). It was very Dada or Fluxus.[125]

"The result is an energetic display of sound and image can be seen in the tradition of Guy Debord's, *The Society of the Spectacle*," read the press release. The participating artists included Leesa Abahuni, Nicole Abahuni, James Andrews, Daniel Blochwitz, Chris Borkowski, Ursula Endlicher, G.H. Hovagimyan, Thomas Hutchison, Lara Star Martini, Nsumi Group, Perpetual Art Machine, João Salema, Raphaele Shirley, Jason Wee, Lee Wells, and Edita Zulic.

Love Songs from My Computer, 2007

Love Songs from my Computer originated as a 2001 *Palm Rant* conceived as a sound piece for Palm Pilots, but in 2007 he revisited it in a web-based sound installation hosted by the Alternative Museum, co-founded by Robert Browning, Geno Rodriguez, and Janice Rooney in 1975 to present sound and visual art that addressed pressing socio-political issues.[126]

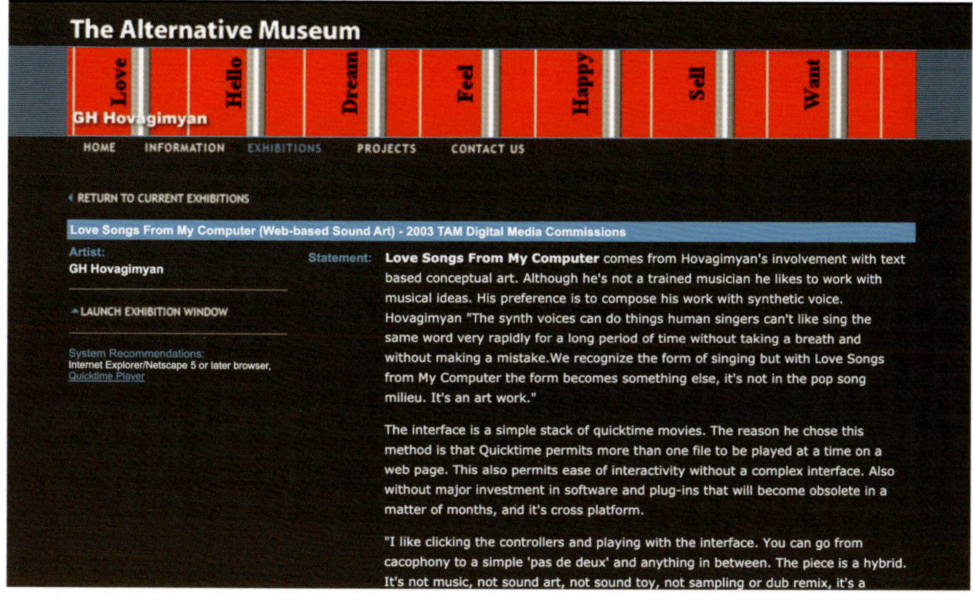

157

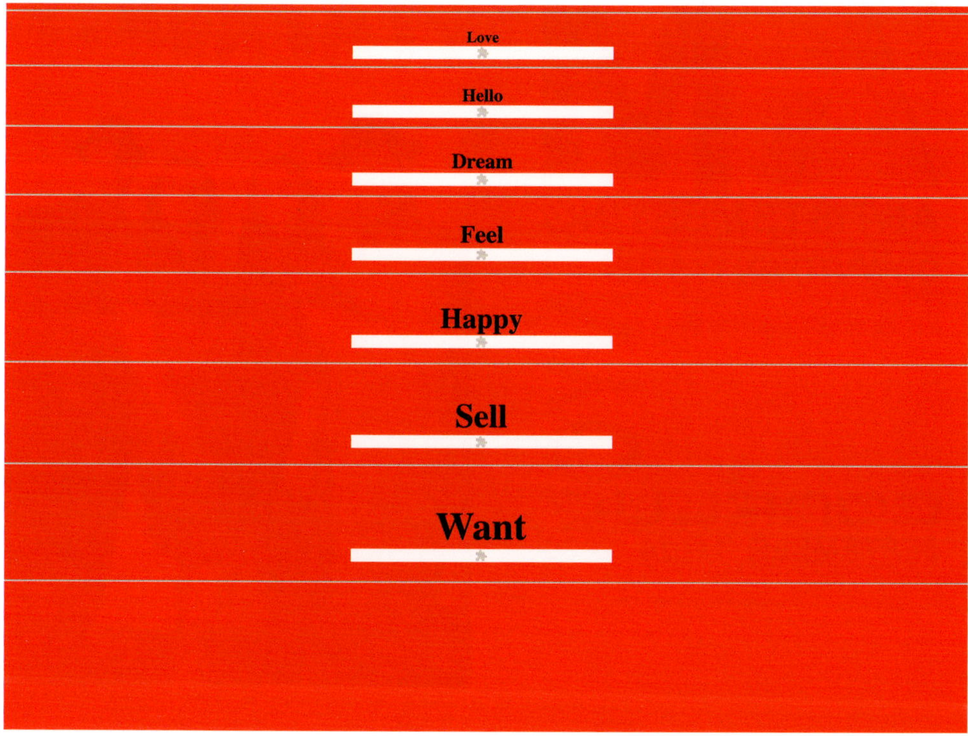

Landing pages of *Love Songs from My Computer*

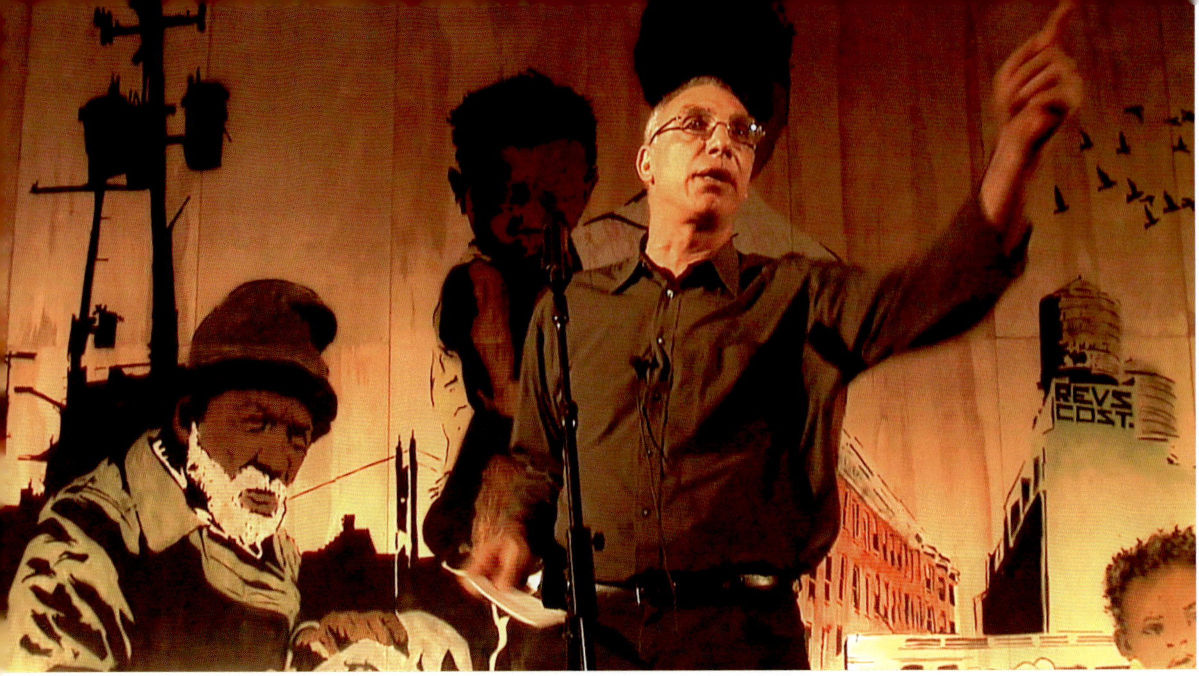

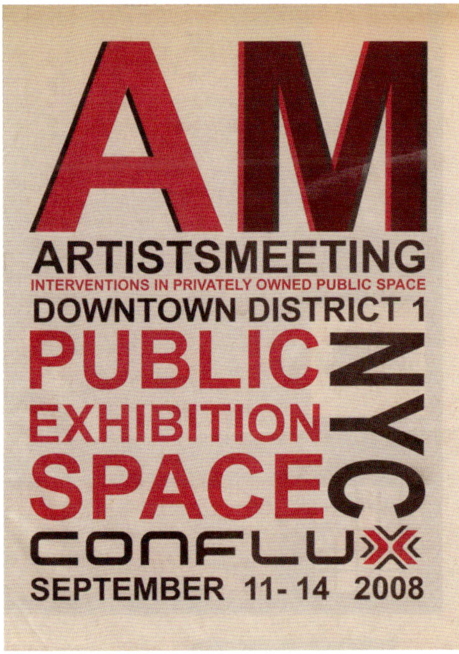

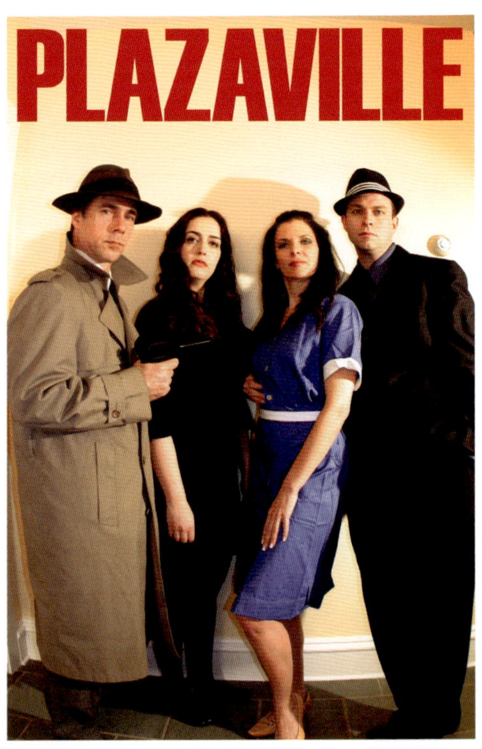

Top: *Smart Money* performance
Above: *Public Exhibition Space* pamphlet

Above: *Plazaville* postcard

> I started to do small compositions seeing if I could make the voices do things no human voice could, such as singing faster than humanly possible with a large range or without taking a breath. I then put these compositions up on the web. One could choose to play them one at a time or all at once.[127]

Using the text-to-speech VocalWriter app that synthesizes a computer voice from texts, he tried to push the limits of what a human voice could sing, assembling them as individual QuickTime files that could be played simultaneously on the web page without a complex interface.

> The synth voices can do things human singers can't, like sing the same word very rapidly for a long period of time without taking a breath and without making a mistake. We recognize the form of singing but with *Love Songs from My Computer*, the form becomes something else. It's not in the pop song milieu. It's an art work.[128]

"I like clicking the controllers and playing with the interface," Rodriguez said of the piece. "You can go from cacophony to a simple 'pas de deux' and anything in between. The piece is a hybrid. It's not music, not sound art, not sound toy, not sampling or dub remix, it's a combination of all of them."[129]

Smart Money, Democracy in America, Creative Time, Sep. 2008

In September 2008, Hovagimyan performed one of his punk rants, *Smart Money*, for Creative Time's *Democracy in America: The National Campaign*, a year-long traveling public art-and-performance project leading up to the 2008 U.S. presidential election "to glean perspectives from artists and activists on the state of democracy." Performances and commissions took place on the street and in public spaces, and at the Democratic and Republican conventions. It included an activist ice cream truck and *A Guide to Democracy in America* publication in which artists reflected on American democracy.[130]

Public Exhibition Space, Artists Meeting, Conflux Festival, Sep. 11–14, 2008

Artists Meeting participated in the 2009 Conflux Festival, founded by Christina Ray and David Mandl in 2003, based on the Situationist-influenced idea of psychogeography, "the investigation of everyday urban life through emerging artistic, technological and social practice."

The participants' projects were a loosely associated collection of actions and performances called *Public Exhibition Space: Interventions in Privately Owned Public Space*. They included *Pillows for (POPS)* by Noah Apple, Mayuko Nakatsuka, and Abigail Weg; a sound piece using metal benches called *Public Experiment #2* by Leesa and Nicole Abahuni; a performance by Daniel Blochwitz, *Not Public!*; distribution of pillows by the group; *Rushing to Your Death?* billboard and stickers by Eliza Fernbach; barrier tape installations; *Pleasant Places* postcards by Maria João Salema; a *Melted City* installation by Raphaele Shirley; and happiness warning stickers by Lee Wells. Other participants included James Andrews, Thomas Hutchison, Christina McPhee, Lara Star Martini, and Edita Zulic. Hovagimyan screened *Plazaville,* a video remake of Jean Luc Godard's *Alphaville*.[131]

Plazaville, 2009

For *Plazaville*, Hovagimyan used Jean Luc Godard's classic 1965 film *Alphaville* as a premise, downloading the script and re-enacting, interpreting, and improvising on it based on Godard's original notion of a dystopian science fiction scenario set in then-contemporary Paris. *Plazaville* is set in the 21st century New York of the Chelsea's morphing architectural spectacles, Times Square billboards, cell phone towers, corporate banks, and lifestyle advertising, mixed with modern, Art Deco, and neo-classical details, edited with video effects.

The scenes are broken up into two-to-eight-minute segments, distributed as short clips in January 2009 on YouTube, which had been founded four years earlier as a platform for user-generated video content. Viral videos quickly propelled YouTube to market dominance: by 2006 it was sold to Google for $1.65 billion, and by 2008 it was distributing Hollywood film content. *Plazaville*

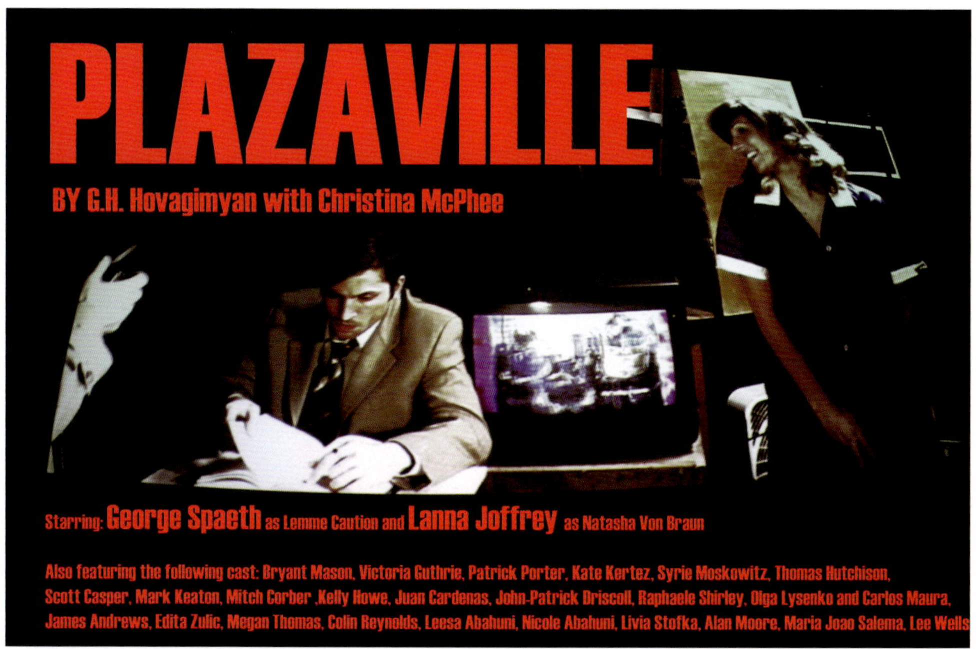

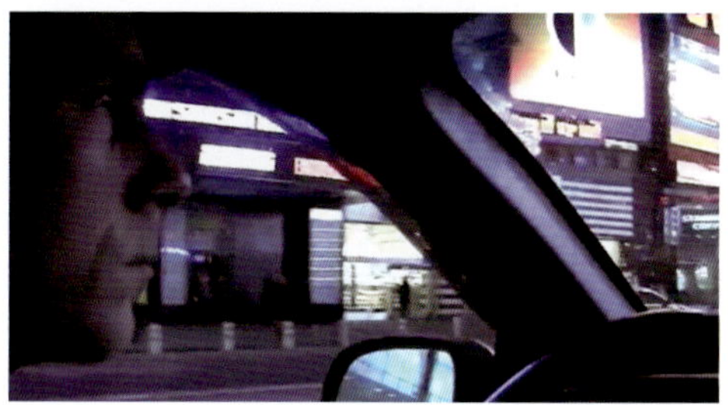

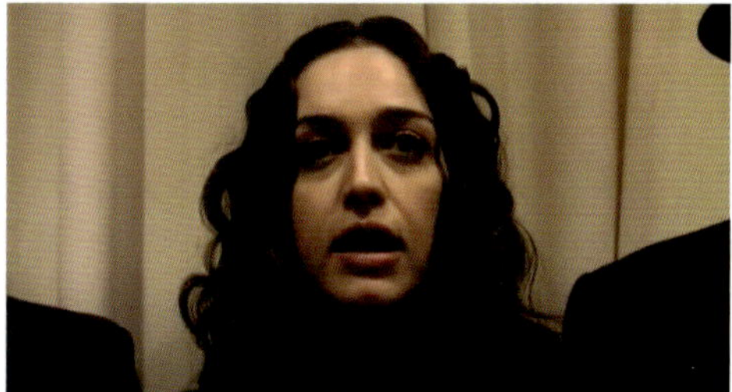

Top: *Plazaville* postcard
Above: Still of George Spaeth from *Plazaville*
Above right: Still of Lanna Joffrey from *Plazaville*

screened at the Pace Digital gallery on April 7, 2009 as a randomly stitched together movie and in a VernissageTV program at Art Cologne.[132]

> This is a remake of Godard's *Alphaville*. I was inspired by a Philip K. Dick book *VALIS*. In the book, three guys go to a movie, and then they go back and see the same picture, but it's different each time. I wanted to do a shuffled narrative film that would play endlessly and not be a loop and yet still make sense. I am irked by walking into galleries and museums and viewing "movies" that are more appropriately shown in theater settings. I wanted to make a filmic work that allows you to dip in at any point and grab the narrative threads then piece together the story in your mind.[133]

Hovagimyan and Christina McPhee shot the video, and members of Artists Meeting acted and produced, with support from New Radio and Performing Arts, Inc. for its Turbulence web site and the New York City Department of Cultural Affairs.

> I was also reading various tracts on cognition. It appears that the mind receives information and then filters it and organizes it for meaning. The simplest example is switching letters in a word and still being able to ascertain the word. I assume that film is a language form [with] a series of understood narrative conventions. My premise was similar to if you watched a film on TV and saw the last 15 minutes, and then a few weeks later the first hour, and then maybe a week later the middle hour. You would pick up the narrative each time and complete the story in your mind.[134]

Shot at night in New York City to avoid the cost of locations, it also used free music downloaded from the internet. The entire project cost $2,000. "I shot the scenes individually and then had a grad student write a Max patch that randomly selected the separate scenes and fed them to a projector. The film plays continuously but is not a loop. People are fascinated by the disjunctive narrative and enjoy trying to piece the story together."[135]

Art Machine, Artists Meeting, 2009

In another Artists Meetings collaboration, Hovagimyan fabricated a mechanized vending machine with a corrugated plastic facade and a clean modern appearance that delivered silkscreens and 3D artwork, which scrolled through a slot or dropped into a compartment.

> For Art Machine, we started by having a discussion about the Japanese mania for vending machines. We decided to build an art vending machine that could be put into art fairs. This adds a rather wry critique of the art market as a whole.[136]

Behind the 4x12-foot facade, functional mechanized controllers made of an automatic paper towel dispenser, Arduinos, a control module, and an object dispenser operated when coins were inserted. Two artists at NYU's Interactive Telecommunications Program helped with the programming.

> The machine dispenses objects in clear plastic envelopes. These are DVDs, T-shirts, small sculptures, and other Dada-style objects. When installed in an art fair, the machine is manned by a person who sells tokens for a certain amount. The customer then puts the coin in a slot and gets either a length of drawing or an object. The piece breaks down to three suitcases and can be transported on a plane as baggage. This was shown at the Pulse Art Fair in Miami and the Verge Art Fair in New York.[137]

Triptych Party, Artists Meeting, Postmasters, 2008–2009

Appropriating an Eyebeam project called You3b by Jeff Crouse and Andrew Mahon that allowed users to make triptychs out of YouTube videos, Artists Meeting organized two YouTube events at Postmasters, a *YouTube Slam* in November 2008 and a *Triptych Party* in 2009, announced as "an evening of video curiosities: found, outsider and accidental video art, culled from YouTube."[138]

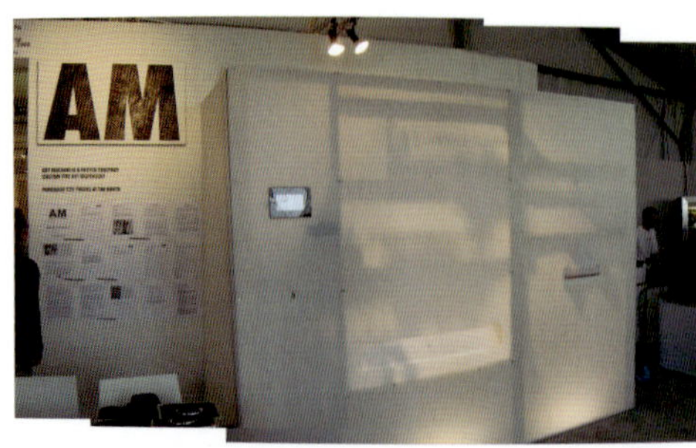

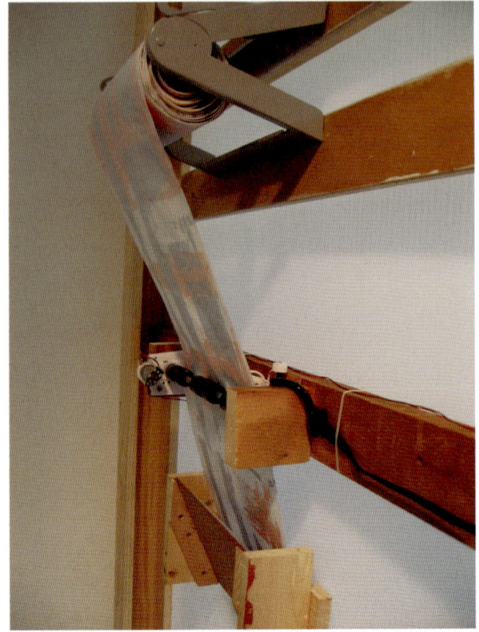

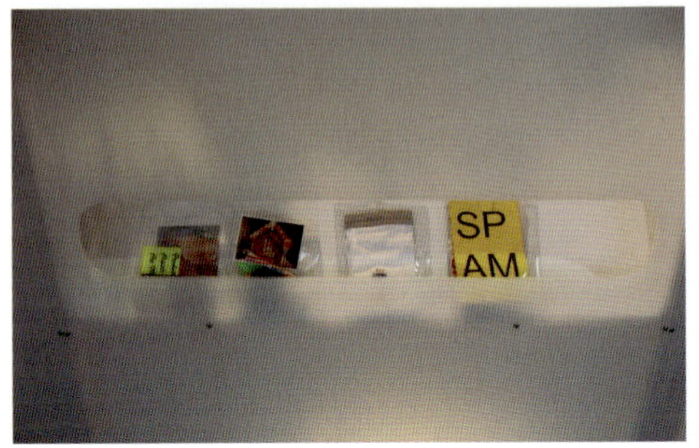

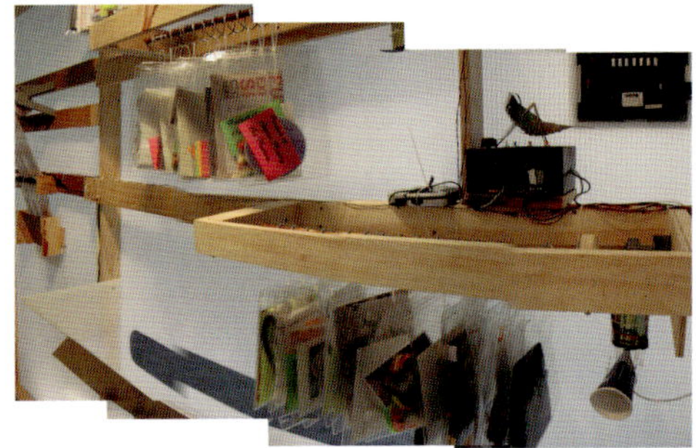

Top: *Art Machine*
Above: *Art Machine* slot
Right: *Art Machine* feeder
Below: Artists Meeting *Triptych Party*
Bottom: YouTube Triptych screenshot

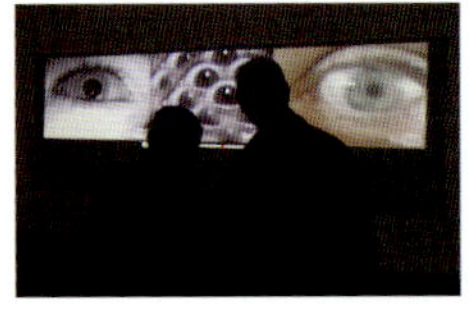

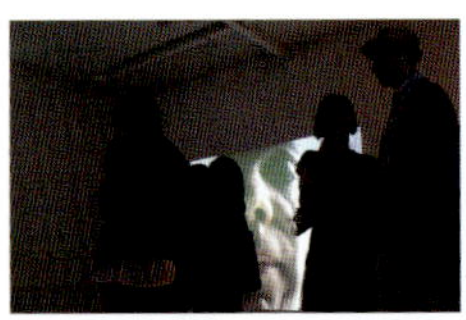

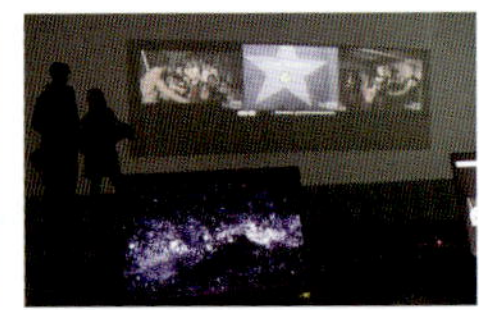

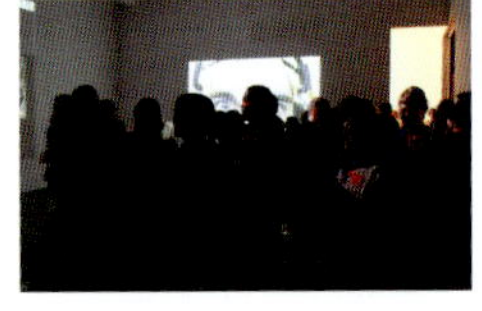

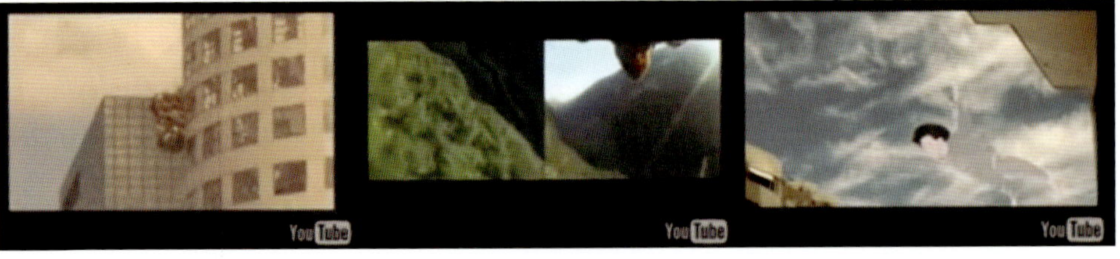

> Today anyone can be a star. The famous, the infamous and the everyday Vlog [video blog] web stars are here today and possibly gone tomorrow. Andy's 15 minutes of fame now barely last 30 seconds, and the YouTube phenomena creates instant fame to be quickly replaced by the next lunchtime sensation or overnight international viral hit by a five-year-old kid from Nebraska named Fred. Through a process of performative appropriation and the over-sized projection of three simultaneous video streams on the gallery wall, Artists Meeting spins YouTube videos into triptychs using the unique features of You3b.com and the process of "digital wandering" or "drifting" through the parallel universe of public online video.[139]

The You3b programming was conceived by Crouse, produced by Crouse and Mahon, and designed and coded by Mahon. During the events, three simultaneous video loops projected side by side on the gallery wall, assembled from YouTube videos curated by Artists Meeting members Thomas Hutchison, Maria João Salema, and James Andrews for their thematic resonances. "While formally simple, the effect of the looping sequences, overlapping sounds and awkward juxtapositions is uncanny and unsettling," they wrote in the press release. "This is due to the slippery dis-harmonization of clip lengths, and the conceptual layering of the elements within the videos."[140]

See/Saw, Floating World, Building 110, Governors Island, 2010

Installed for the first time in Building 110—the Lower Manhattan Cultural Council's Arts Center on Governors Island—during *Floating World*, curated by Erin Donnelly and Melissa Levin, an exhibition of the inaugural 2010 LMCC Swing Space residency on the island, *See/Saw* integrated Hovagimyan's programming of mechanical devices and hacked video software into an interactive sculpture. A sensor embedded in *See/Saw* relays up-and-down movements of riders to a computer that plays the 1962 Shirley MacLaine and Robert Mitchum movie *Two for the Seesaw*. Hovagimyan cut the film into 112 segments based on the original edits and fed them into a specially coded Pure Data program. Movements of the seesaw trigger a horizontal split-screen projection of scenes.

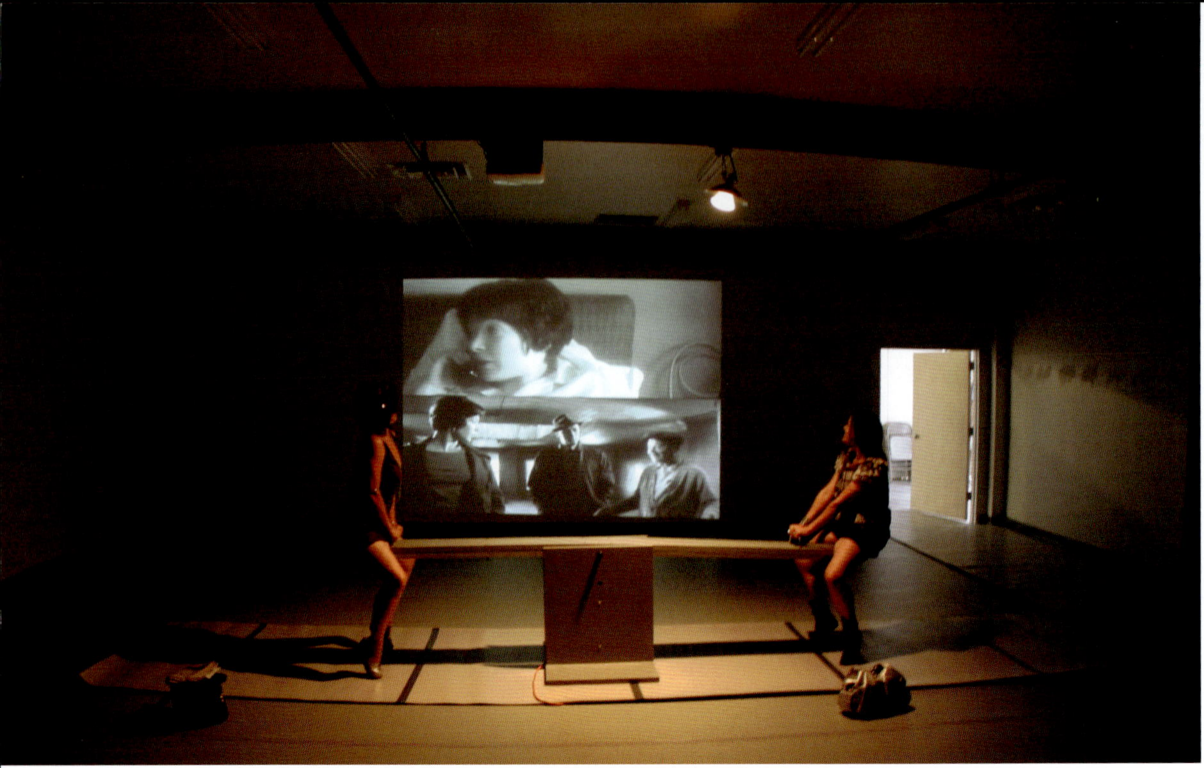

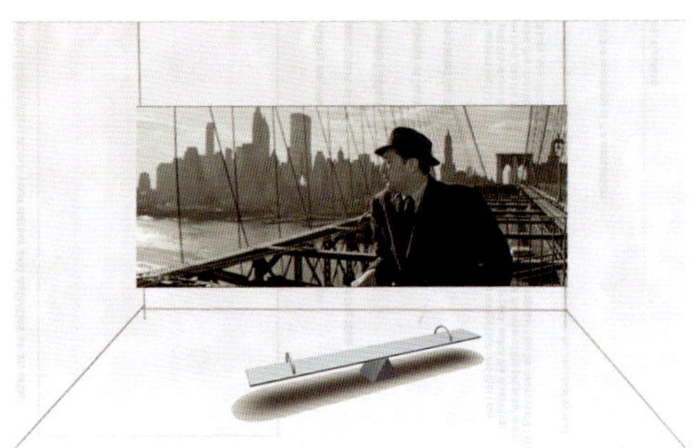

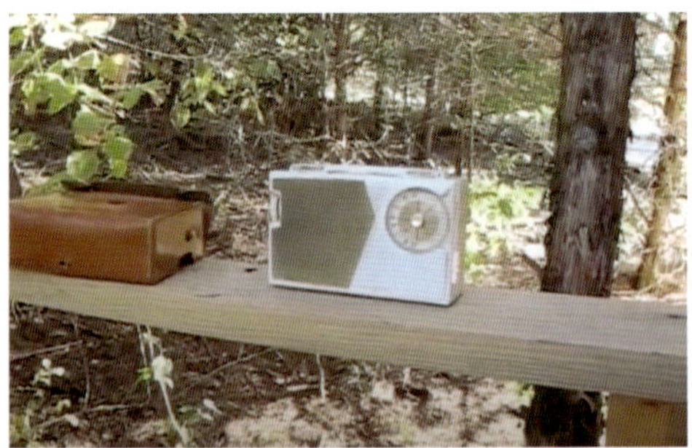

Top: *See/Saw* installation in use
Above: *See/Saw* rendering
Right: View of *Radios* installation

Hovagimyan associated the film with his earliest memories of New York City, and it became a text he continually referred back to, consciously and unconsciously in his work.

> When I was in my 20s, I started writing a novel. It was a view of the downtown art scene and club scene interspersed with scenes from the 1962 movie *Two for the Seesaw*. I never finished the novel and lost the manuscript but revisited the movie 30 years later. That movie and *Alphaville* sat in the corner of my subconscious as a media dream or a theme. I sometimes think of it as peripheral consciousness, and I believe that's where my art comes from. It is when I seize these notions floating around on the periphery and explore them that I engage my creative processes. I've been thinking a lot about generational narrative. My generation and that of my parents are intertwined in a narrative. The movie deals with my parents' generations ideas of changing mores and bohemianism à la 1962. It also has a film noir vision of New York City that is very evocative. These create the idea of photography as memory...This is an alternative type of interactivity. When you are on the seesaw, you have a visceral dialog with the person opposite. You also have the kinesthetic sensations of the seesaw. Along with that, you notice you are controlling the projected windows. You try to assemble the jumbled narrative of the scenes you are viewing. This is immersion and deconstruction at the same time. The piece refers to any number of dance performances from the 1960s and 70s, as well as pieces done by Robert Morris. My sculptural references are from Arte Povera and 90s cyber-punk DIY installation.[141]

Radios, 2010

Music and sound played a role in Hovagimyan's art going back to his spoken-word rants and drumming for the Communists in the 1970s. The changing media of production and transmission remained a current throughout his early net art and online radio shows up to the multimedia pieces of the 2000s and AR installations in the 2010s. *Radios* adds the anachronistic component of mp3 chips embedded in old transistor radios playing period music, tapping into a strain of nostalgia also present in *See/Saw*.

I did a series of hacked radios, where I took portable radios, and I put in these mini-player chips, so they would play specific playlists over the radios. One of them was music that you would hear coming out of a radio of that era. If it was a 60s radio, you hear all 60s music. It was playing with the notion of media, image, memory, and nostalgia.[142]

The mp3 players are programmed with playlists from music of the late 50s/ early 60s; classic blues; Japanese pop garage bands and Pacific Rim surf music from the 1960s that might have been broadcast on an American Naval Base in Okinawa, Japan; rock & roll that would have played in juke joints along Highway 67 in northeast Arkansas; and songs about loneliness.

This is a bit of steam punk iconography. It's also circuit bending and hacking but for the specific idea of tying the sound one hears to an object...The radios play in the background in a room. You tend to ignore them. It's just ambient sound. It's also directional sound that is tied to a location. After a while you might ask what radio station is playing. This is one of those incidental references to a movie scene in which a camera pans across an interior showing a radio or a television playing. It sets the time frame based on the type of radio or TV and the music playing.[143]

Originally created in 2010, he would later install them in his 2014 TRANSFER gallery exhibition *((ANA)Chronisms++)*, in East Williamsburg, Brooklyn.

These are really odd and evocative works that are part sound art, part circuit bending, and also very personal...The art historical references can be tied to Ed Keinholz as well as the Neo-Geo style and recent installation work. My father was an electrical engineer, and for him radio was the entry point to technology. I struggled trying to emulate him but turned to music and art later in my youth. These pieces reflect specific times in my life such as my first Motorola portable radio that my mother gave me in 1960.[144]

Boxing Rants, Being & Event, Postmasters, 2011

Originally developed in 2010 for use with Microsoft's Xbox video game systems, Kinect cameras possess motion sensors and depth-mapping capabilities, which Hovagimyan began adapting for artistic purposes in 2011 with *Boxing Rants.* The Kinect has an infra-red camera that assigns precise x, y, z point coordinates, creating a three-dimensional point cloud, as well as an RGB camera that maps video onto the point cloud.

Hovagimyan wrote Pure Data programs to superimpose the 3D video onto a wireframe puppet and 3D cubes to animate the piece. In the piece, he wears boxing gloves and works out in front of the Kinect camera, which superimposes him over the 3D forms.

> I've been exploring using the Kinect Camera as a controller. I decided to revisit my rants, but this time use clichés from boxing movies as the performance vehicle. I had taken boxing training at the gym, and what interested me was the idea of precise placement of punches.[145]

He performed *Boxing Rants* at Postmasters in June 2011 as a part of an Artists Meeting performance night, *Being and Event.* The live video appears on a screen as he works out to the audio track playing in the background.

> The rants use the clichés of speedbag punching, jumping rope, shadow boxing, and punching the hard bag, competition in the art scene, and getting old. The difference between performance art and acting is very simple. In performance art, you find an emotion or narrative within yourself and bring it out into the open. Acting is presenting someone else's emotions. Performance art is exposing one's own emotions...In this case, there was a mix of types of space: the physical space, the virtual space and a video-performance space. The work...extends the ideas of classic performance art into new media space.[146]

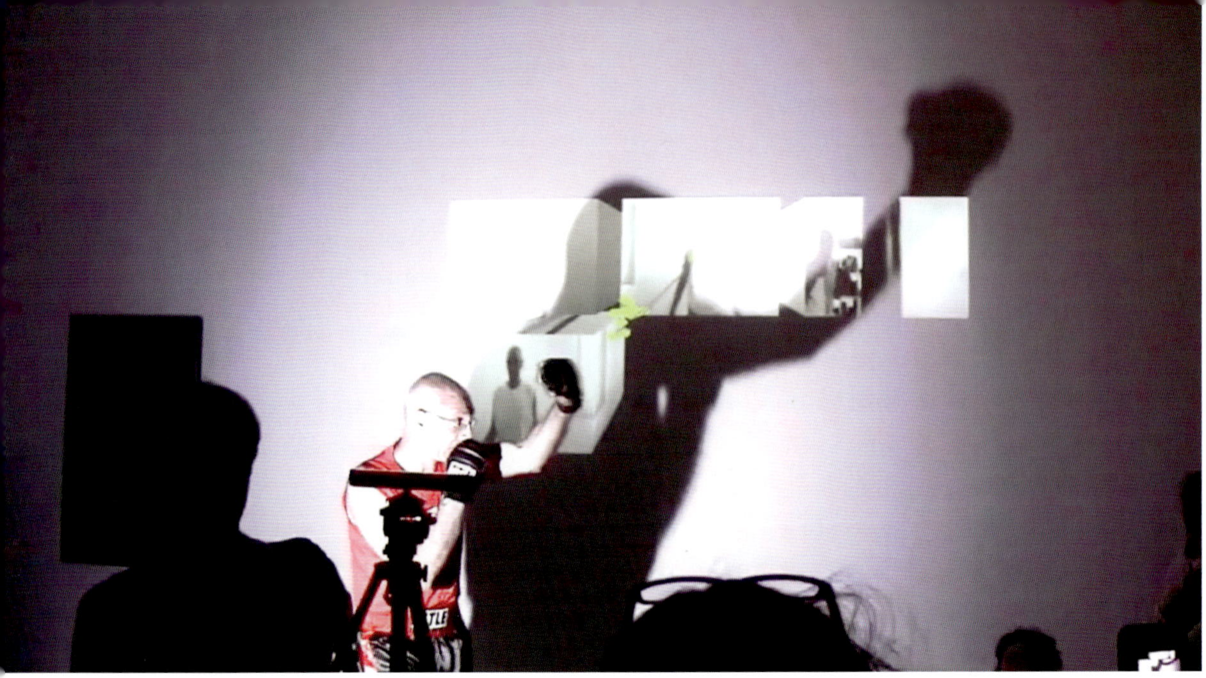

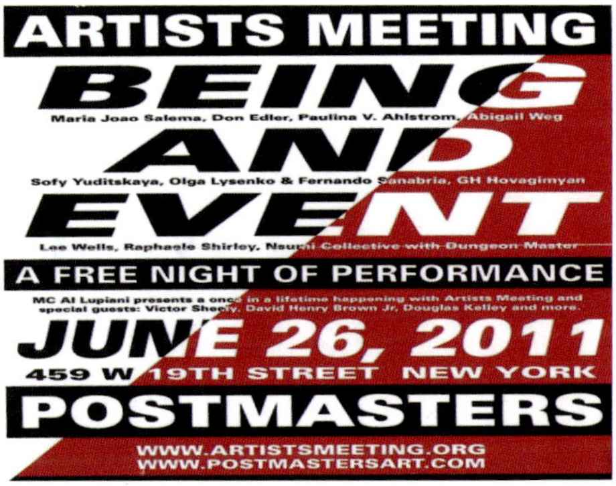

Above: Still from video of *Boxing Rants* performance at Postmasters
Left: *Being Event* flyer
Opposite, right, top to bottom: *Boxing Rants; Boxing Rants* performance at Postmasters; *Mapped Morphs* at Postmasters; *Mapped Morphs* 3D objects

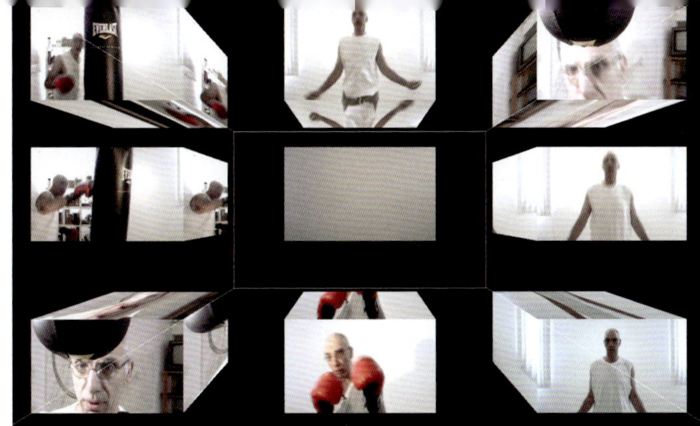
EVERLAST

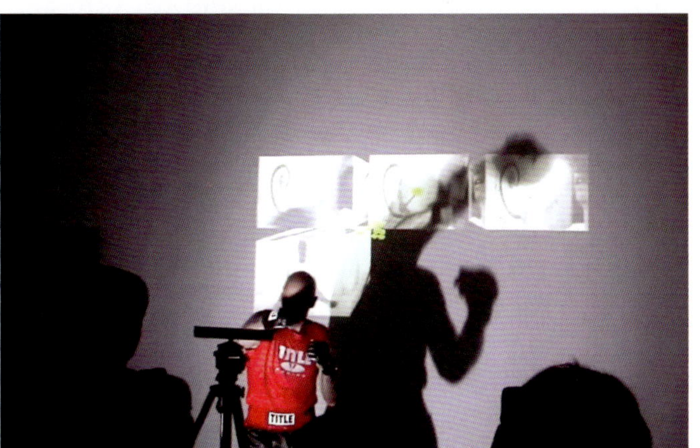
TITLE

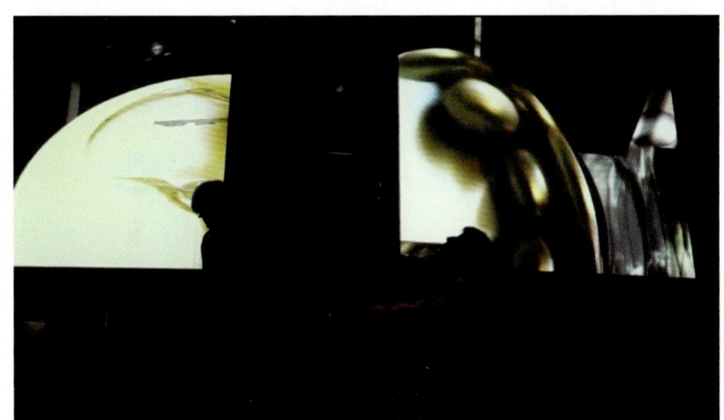

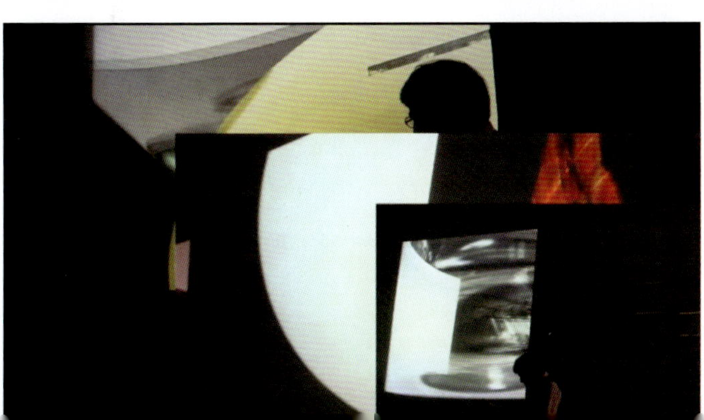

Mapped Morphs, performance (with Rhys Chatham), 2012

Hovagimyan continued experimenting with the Kinect camera and Pure Data (PD) programming in 2012. On June 14th 2012, he performed with Rhys Chatham at Postmasters, using a purpose-built projection-mapping program. The PD program feeds cubes, spheres, cylinders, and pyramids into the projection space, rotating and moving the objects, and simulating different camera movements. "I listen to his music and perform animations using the Kinect camera. The morphs come from an earlier work *HD Morphs*, but in this case, I've mapped them onto 3D virtual objects."[147]

As Chatham loops trumpet, guitar, and percussion sounds, the Kinect camera captures Hovagimyan's gestures to control live video projections and manipulate their composition, morphing the video into irregular shapes. In the gallery at the time hung abstract photo collages by Holly Zausner.

> Mapped Morphs brings together world-renowned minimalist composer Rhys Chatham and internationally acclaimed new media artist G.H. Hovagimyan for a special collaborative performance. Mr. Chatham will premiere four short works, two for trumpet and two for electric guitar, and Mr. Hovagimyan will perform a series of 3D virtual animations using a custom-designed NI (Natural Interface) that reacts to his gestures as well as responds to Mr. Chatham's music.[148]

The idea of a natural user interface in the tech world is an interaction design term for how users of devices intuitively learn their functions, enabling them to seamlessly control their operation. In that sense, Hovagimyan's performance aimed to manifest these back-end systems as a real-time embodied experience visible to the audience.

> The program responds to Rhys's music. The objects have the morph video mapped onto them. The projection space also shows the live infrared 3D scan of my body and the virtual 3D controllers to trigger the animations. My gestures are very minimal, but I am responding to Rhys's music as well, changing the projections as we go along. There are several levels to this piece

> that present a multimedia, multi-spatial, and auditory environment. It's not really theatrical but more of an immersive performance space.[149]

The D6 residency he would attend in 2013 explained: "The data world has moved into our real lives via smart phones and tablets. The 'natural interface' attempts to integrate the real world and the data world in a more seamless manner. Hovagimyan challenges himself to work within and humanize the data world…By adapting a Kinect camera, Hovagimyan created a real time virtual experience in which the whole body was engaged and immersed in the data, allowing the audience to physically interact with the data while viewing their virtual body in the dataspace.[150]

3D Karaoke, 2012–2013

In a characteristically playful project for an audience outside of the traditional art world, Hovagimyan adapted the motion-sensor-and-depth-mapping capabilities of Kinect cameras to produce entertaining public events. For *3D Karaoke*, he faced two Kinect cameras toward each other to capture 360-degree images of karaoke performers. He programmed open-source MeshLab software to process the information and export the pixels and point cloud into a 3D environment. Then Hovagimyan selected the most popular karaoke songs and input the lyrics to stream as captions alongside the music. A live video projection shows the performer's faces on the screen in 3D, so they and the audience can view themselves performing as a kind of abstracted 3D video-animation.

> Basically, I took two Kinect cameras, because they'll scan your body and create a point cloud, then you can map the live video stream onto the point cloud. You've got 180 degrees for each camera. If you put them opposite each other you're creating a stage where you can take the two separate images and map them together into a live 360-degree video of a person. I thought that's kind of interesting, but you know, that's interesting for about 15 seconds when you wave your hands around. But then I thought, "Ah! Karaoke! Now we're talking."[151]

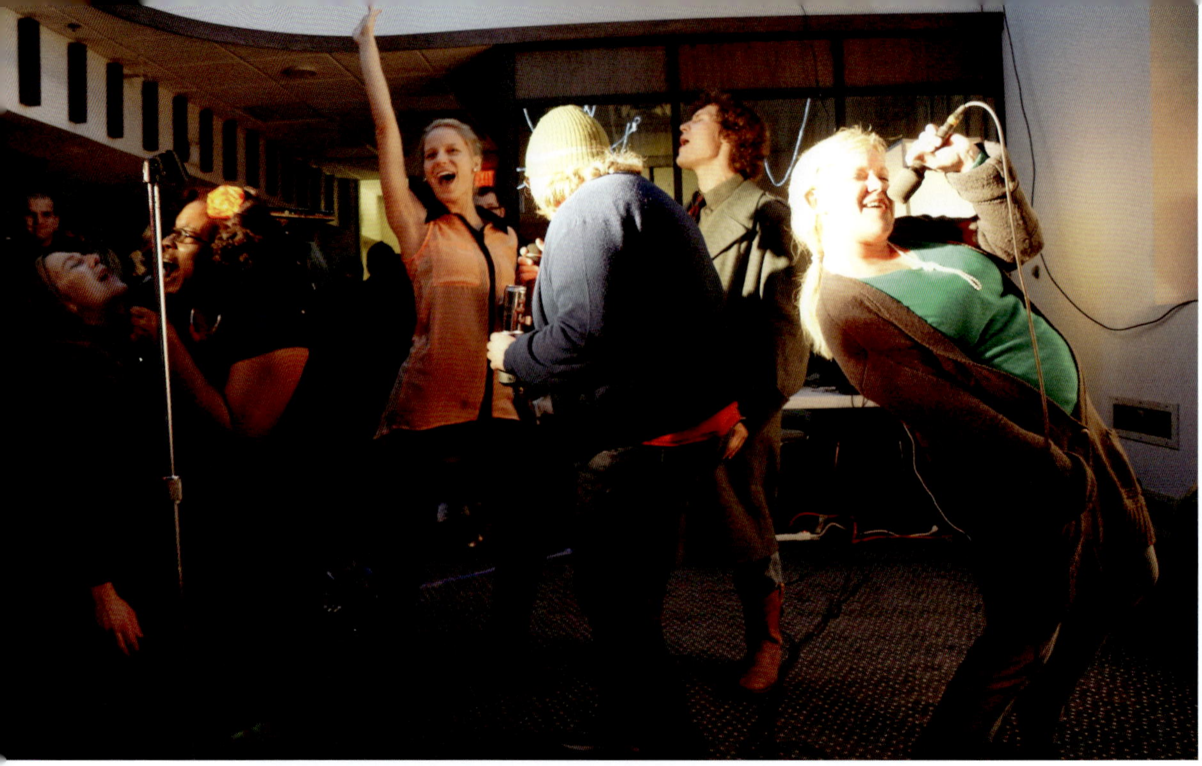

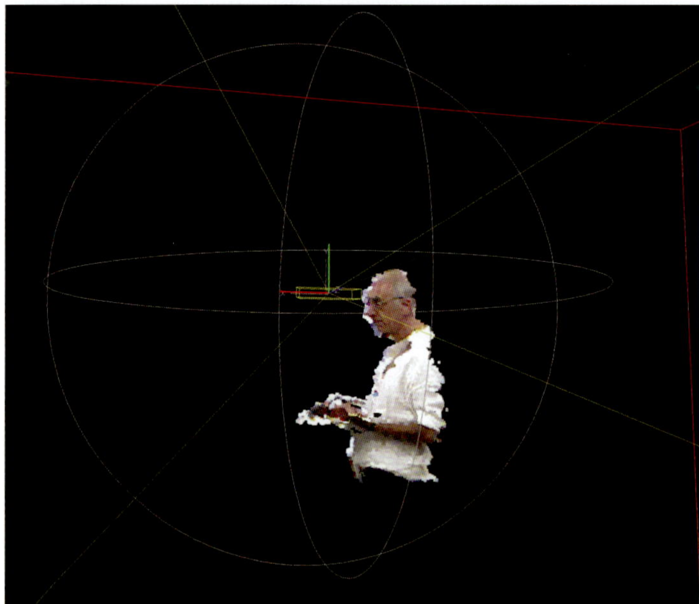

Top: *3D Karaoke* installation at a temporary space in Flint, Michigan
Above and opposite, top: Screen capture of a *3D Karaoke* processed video
Opposite, below: Postcard from 2012 Pixel Palace residency

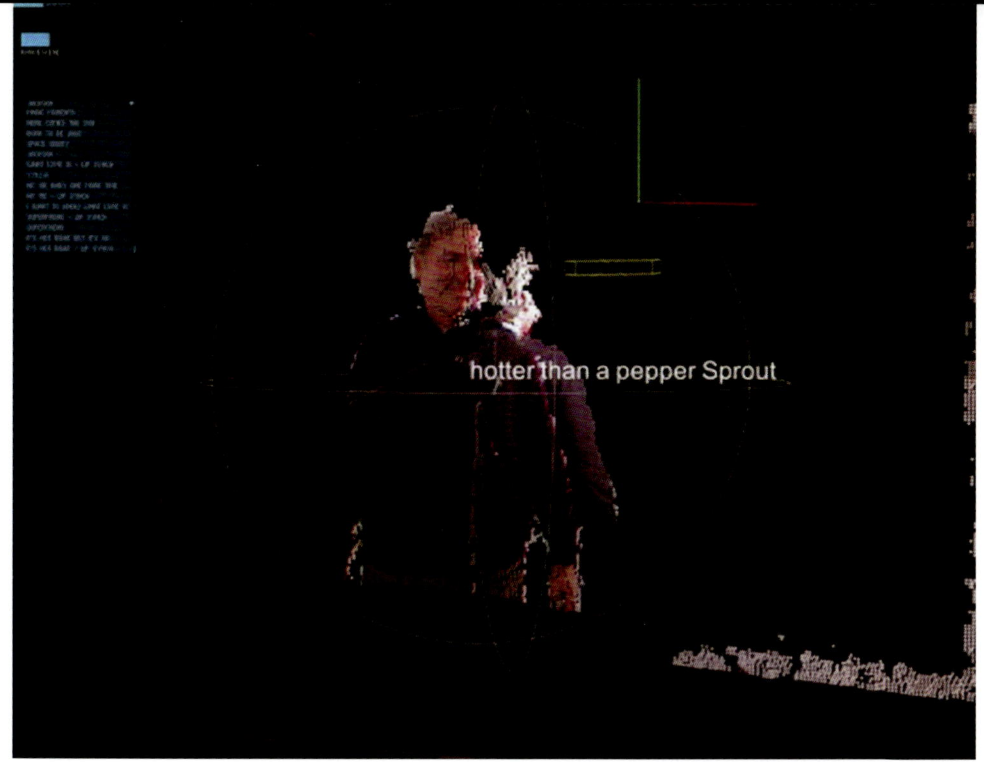

pixel.palace

artists in residence 2012
Max Hattler
G.H. Hovagimyan
Lucy Pawlak

www.thepixelpalace.org

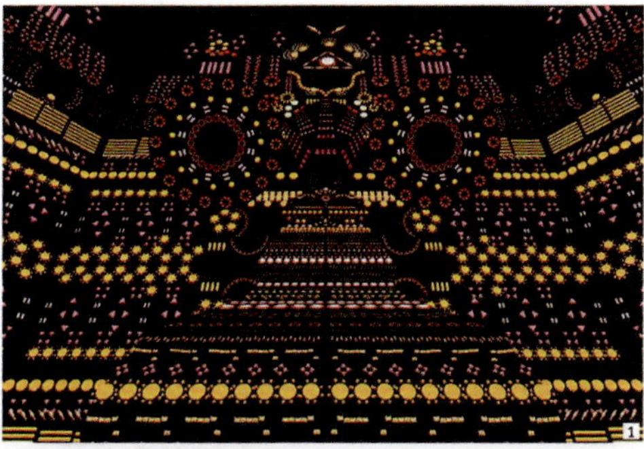
1

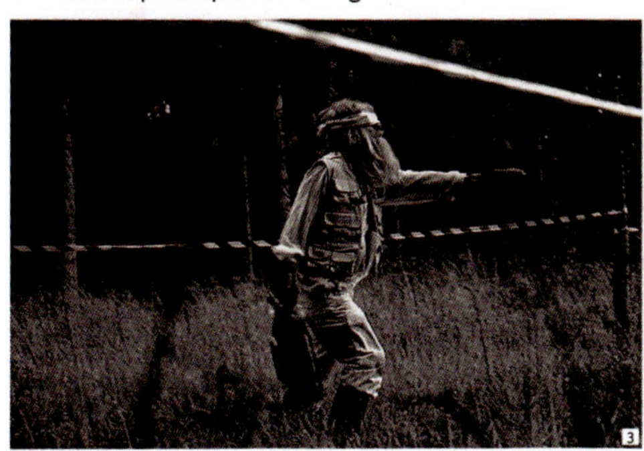
3

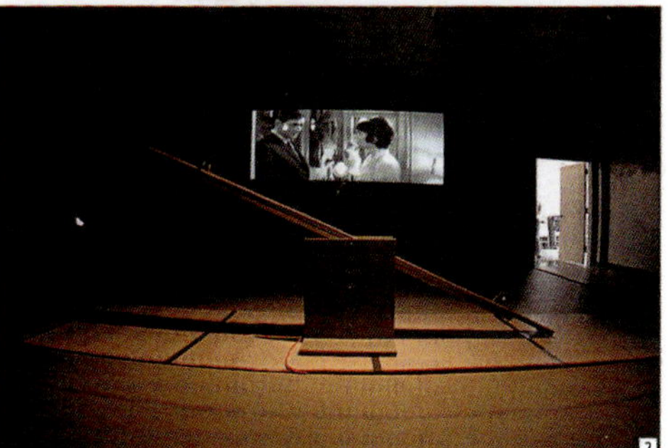
2

Because of the limited computer-processing power of consumer laptops, even with advanced graphics cards, the 3D video was rudimentary and pixelated, but the concept turned everyday karaoke into a new media performance vehicle.

> This is fairly low-res, but it has a DIY hacker aesthetic that I favor. By itself, the 3D video is a gee-whiz moment, but adding karaoke bumps it up to a different level. The singers see themselves in 3D. They choose a song from a pull-down menu, and the lyrics stream across the screen as the music plays. It's an immersive environment that also engages a social aspect and mass media memory of the song.[152]

The idea emerged during an Artists Meeting group workshop on augmented reality in July 2012. Hovagimyan further developed the project during a residency in August at the Pixel Palace in Newcastle, England, adding the mp3 files and streaming text to create a *3D Karaoke* program. He used Processing, an open-source coding language and environment developed in 2001 for graphics and electronic arts purposes, as well as open-source libraries, to access the Kinect camera data stream. Later, he added a pull-down menu to play the songs easily, as well as a virtual camera frustum to simulate the rotation of the 3D image on the screen. "During the residency, Hovagimyan worked on developing a 'natural interface' tool, which he described as 'a sequence in the movie *Minority Report* that has Tom Cruise grabbing digital images floating in the air and manipulating them," the publicity read. "This is the natural interface . . ."[153]

In November 2012, Hovagimyan presented it for the first time in a temporary space in downtown Flint as part of Flint Public Art Project's programming of new genres during the city's monthly Art Walk.[154] On March 1, 2013, he performed it at Harvestworks, the new-technology art space founded in 1977 and run by Carol Parkinson since 1987 in downtown New York, and he presented it again that April at NewBridge Project Space during a residency with D6: Culture in Transit in Newcastle, U.K.

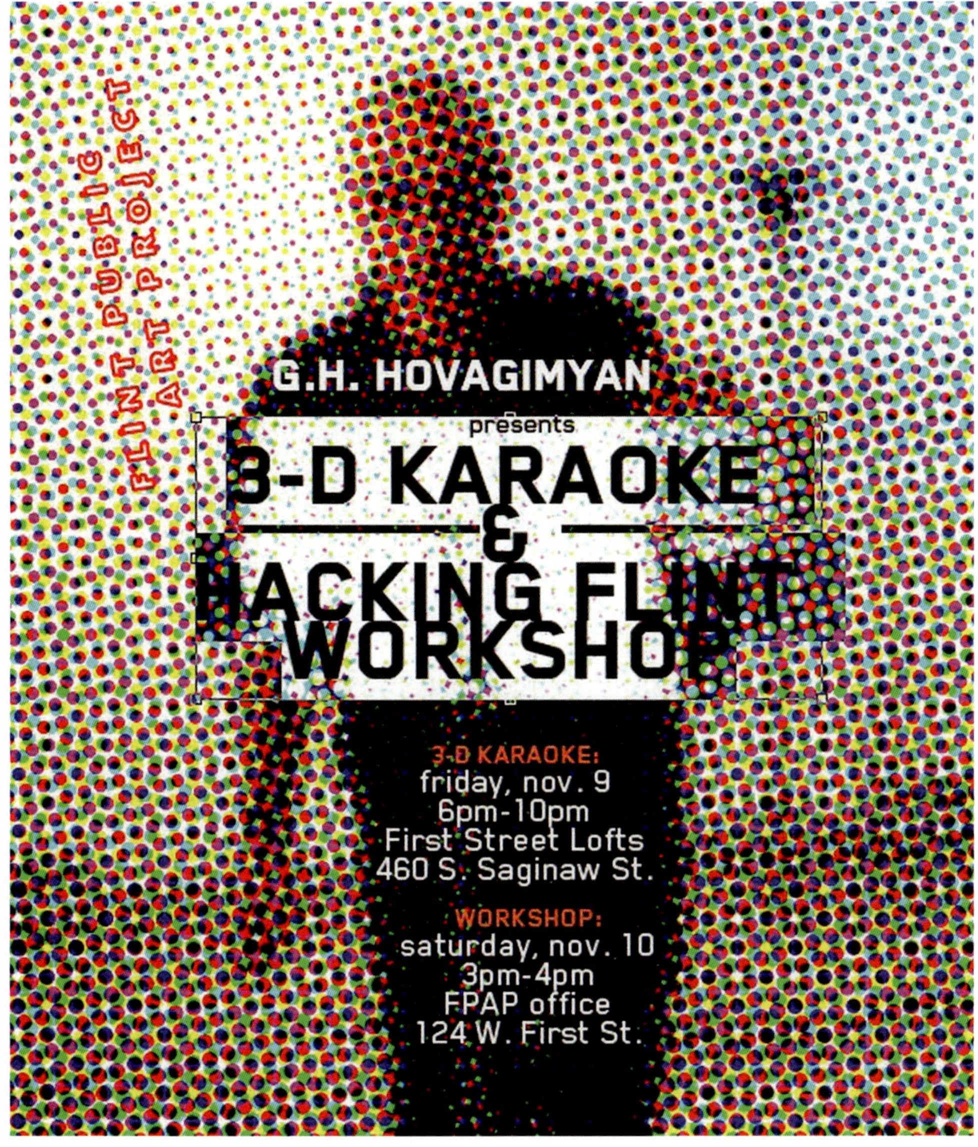

Publicity for *3D Karaoke* in Flint at First Street Lofts, November 9, 2012. Design by Cedomir Kovacev

6

Augmented Reality

AR Paintings, ((ANA)chronisms++), TRANSFER, 2014

In 2014, Hovagimyan exhibited in a one-person show at TRANSFER, a gallery in Brooklyn launched a year earlier by curator Kelani Nichole to exhibit computer-based experimental art focused around "a critical encounter with software." The title *((ANA)chronisms++)* mimicked coding language to express the idea of going backward and forward in time: the show included his 2010 transistor *Radios* embedded with mp3 chips, a projection-mapping piece that incorporated his 2006 *HD_Rants*, a new work called *Post Browser* projecting a 3D information environment, and a wall of his *AR Paintings*. The *AR Paintings* are exact copies of Josef Albers color-theory works with sawtooth augmented reality (AR) markers embedded in the black center square. The AR markers were copied from icons of Pokemon, the viral game phenomenon of the moment. An iPad attached to a rolling tripod captured the AR markers, displaying the tiers of colored squares in 3D and inserting clown cars and other virtual objects floating above.

> Painting tends to work within the visual context of any period. Although quite recently I feel that painting has not caught up with or understood virtual space. In particular, virtual space uses isometric geometry rather than a fixed point of view, planar perspective. I decided to make paintings that would function as augmented reality markers. These define the space and allow a fixed point for walking around the augmentation. Simply putting AR markers on the wall leaves the virtual space in its own domain. By making paintings the AR markers, there is a real dialog with both physical space and painterly space.[155]

He enlisted painter Maria João Salema to realize the Albers works as oil paintings on canvas and used Vuforia, an AR software development kit for computer vision edge detection, to identify and trigger augmentations for each one. The augmentations were an image of himself; a dictionary definition of a painting, referencing Joseph Kosuth; 3D extrusions of the Albers squares; and a toy clown car, citing his earlier *Hey Bozo* billboards.[156]

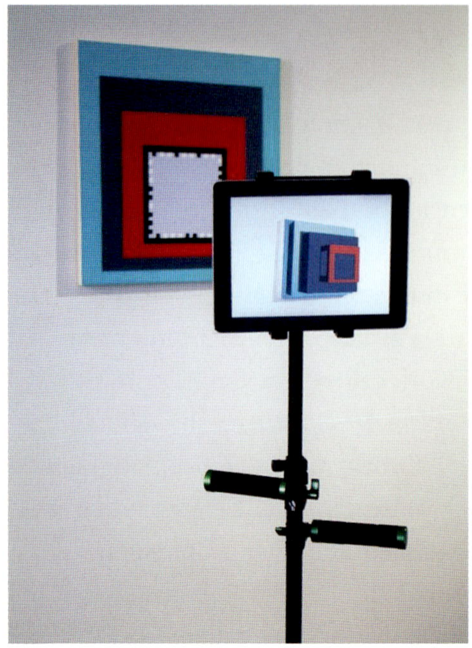

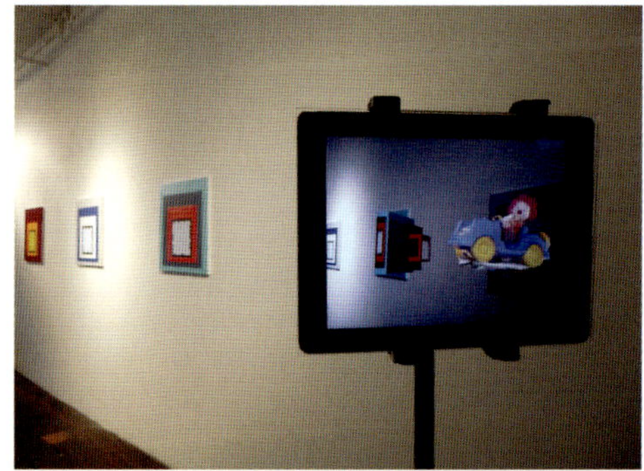

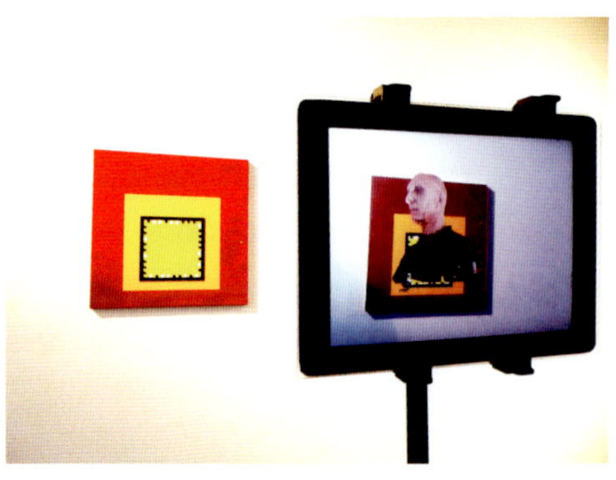

Top: *Augmented Reality Painting (Albers Boxes)*, 2014. Acrylic on panels (24×24 inches), iPad on rolling armature, AR Software
Middle: *AR Paintings* at TRANSFER gallery
Left: *AR* self-portrait at TRANSFER

> In new media all information is utilized because it is flattened out into rhizomatic linkage. By adding the AR markers onto the paintings, they become truly net art. I enlisted Maria João Salema because she is an excellent painter and we collaborate well together. The augmentations give four variations on types of art. There is realism in the self-portrait, conceptual art with the text, minimalism with the extension of the painting into 3D, and pop art with the toy clown car. The car and the self-portrait are 3D scans that make good use of isometric geometry. The physical interface is an iPad on a rolling stand that has handles. The viewer rolls this "device for viewing paintings" around, thus creating a physical interactivity as well as a virtual one that is viewed through the iPad.[157]

Exhibited February 1–22, 2014 at TRANSFER, the show brought together his combination of conceptualism, performance, culture jamming, and technology hacking. The press release pitched at as being "united by a single overarching concern—the interrogation of systems, whether they be systems of communication, systems of consumption, or (especially) systems of power…In an art world that has typically aligned itself with the capitalist notions of innovation and stylistic obsolescence, Hovagimyan's work functions to both celebrate and repurpose existing forms and techniques, while still keeping an eye on future potentialities."[158]

In February 2015, *((Ana)chronisms++)* traveled to Philadelphia's CRUXspace, a new media art space curated by Kim Brickley, in conjunction with a lecture at his alma mater, Philadelphia College of Art (renamed University of the Arts in 1985). He explained the coding language of the title in the CRUXspace press release: "I was struggling with a title for the show and came up with 'anachronisms.' After reading the dictionary definition, I decided to turn the title into a pseudo-algorithm to reflect the implicit coding structure. ANA means before, chronos means 'time' in Greek, and ++ in code means stepping forward. So the title means backward and forward in time."

Both shows included performances of *3D Karaoke* at the opening, which Benoit Palop promoted in *Vice*:

> There might actually be David Bowie singalongs at TRANSFER Gallery tomorrow, though we're not sure if there's free booze. Regardless, the Brooklyn art space is keeping its roots in the digital arts exhibition game by highlighting renowned net artist G.H. Hovagimyan in an exhibition with the amazing title, *((ANA)chronisms++)*. The opening reception will be followed by a *3D Karaoke* party, so if you're not in it for the art, you can be in it for the duets (maybe Hovagimyan will join in).[159]

Pile O' Rants, ((ANA)chronisms++), TRANSFER, Feb. 2014

Pile O' Rants epitomizes Hovagimyan's continual readaptation of work to new media contexts. For *((ANA)chronisms++)*, he reappropriated *HD_Rants*—itself based on iterations of *Palm Rants* and *Rantapod*—for a projection-mapping installation onto the surfaces of six pieces of country furniture. Using the free software program Little Projection Mapping Tool (LPMT), an outline of the shape of each object is drawn in the application. A different rant projects simultaneously on each piece of furniture, loosely arranged in an assemblage that indirectly references Robert Rauschenberg's *Combines* (1954–1964).

> The trajectory of that whole series of rants goes…back to the original black-and-white video things I was doing in the 70s, where you take a video camera and do reflexive video performance on it, and then from there to my rants in the 90s, using the notion of digital video, and then streaming on the web, then doing podcasts but having these miniature artworks you can get on your cell phone or handheld devices, to video projection mapping where it's mapping onto these objects in an installation.[160]

The tops of the furniture are painted white for better projection, and individual speakers link the sound to locations within the piece, so that as viewers walk around and lean in, they hear the separate soundtracks. The use of furniture and checkerboard carpet tiles root the piece in a normalized physical space, breaking down a linear theatrical presentation format. "The videos and sound are used as textures rather than discreet presentations," read

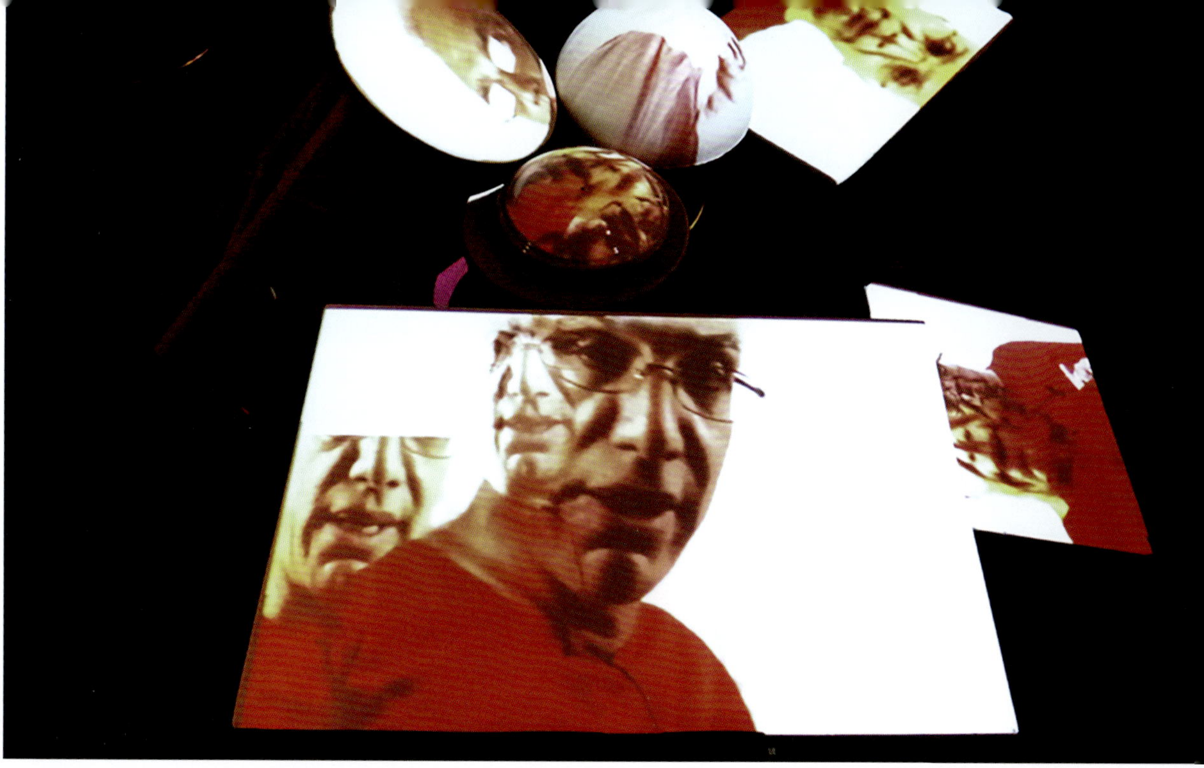

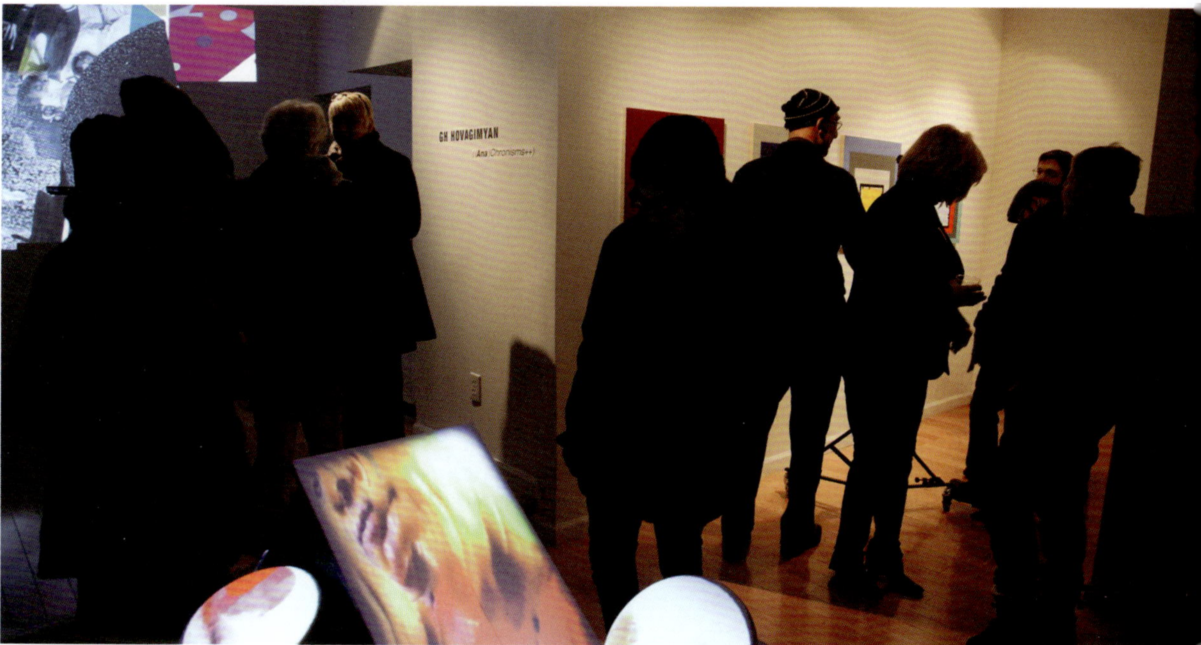

Top: *Pile O' Rants* installation
Above: *Pile O' Rants* at TRANSFER

the press release. "The emotion and the feel of the works comes through while the storyline is de-accentuated."[161]

Post Browser, ((ANA)chronisms++), TRANSFER Gallery, 2014

Post Browser draws from Hovagimyan's research on data visualization and the programming language Processing during his residency in Newcastle, England. He described the piece as an alternative approach to information access, a physical browser/net art piece that incorporates live information from the internet and exports it into in a geometric 3D space. A Kinect camera allows the viewer to move the data objects around within the video projection using hand gestures. He drew images from the Museum of Modern Art's website as the source of data. "I wrote an html parser to get around the MoMA's web page layout and grab the current exhibitions images. These are made public on the internet. I wanted to lay them out in my own design."[162]

As in *Vanity Search* and *IFC Hack*, Hovagimyan saw it as a kind of detournement and re-embodiment of information that had been instrumentalized and corporatized on the internet, manipulating its framing and layout to abstract and aestheticize it. He also appropriated content from a live weather feed as a text circle around the ring of images from MoMA. For audio, he flowed an RSS feed from the art blog *Hyperallergic,* read by a synthetic computer-generated voice.

> The other question is the browser and web page metaphor in general. It's a hangover from print media, and it's the importing of a static media form into a dynamic information space. I chose to allow viewers to immerse themselves in the information space and interact with the information through their body movement and eyes…I feel that data visualization and immersive browsing is the future.[163]

Sofy Yuditskaya collaborated with him on the code, but like the instability of his other net art work, once MoMA changed the JavaScript on its site, the piece stopped working and had to be recoded.

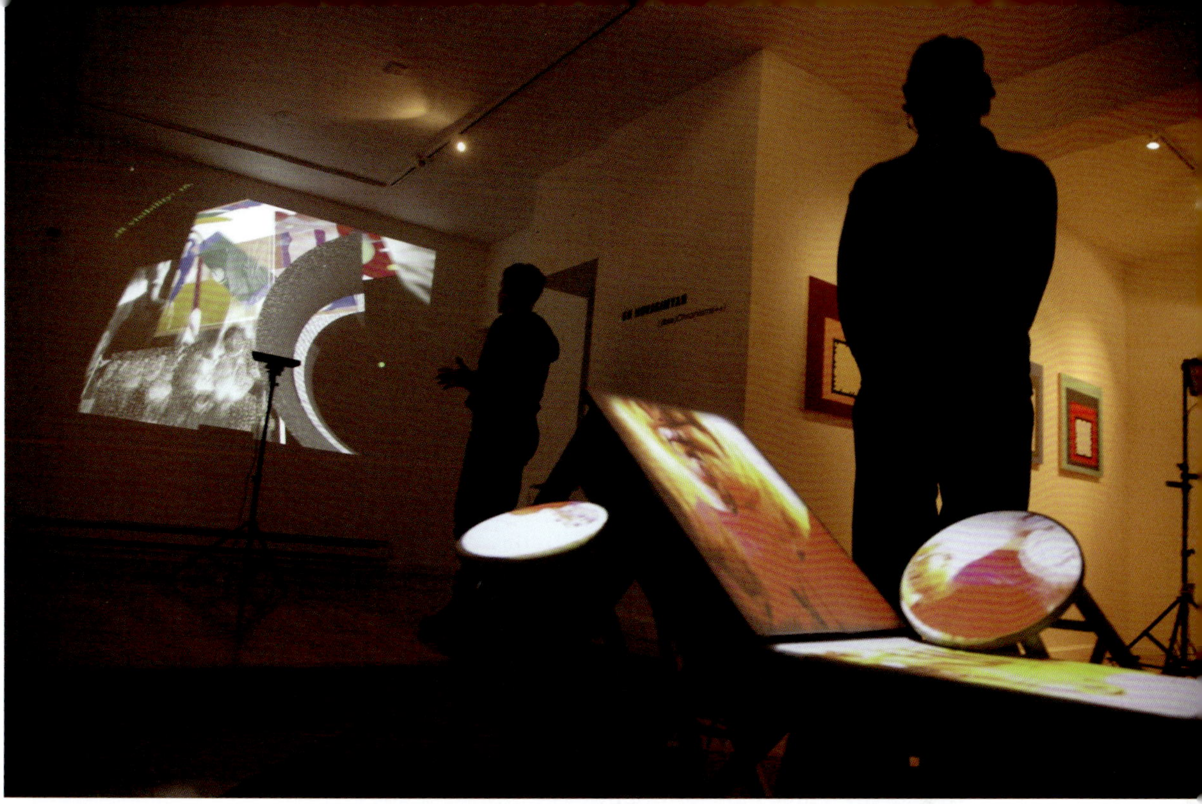

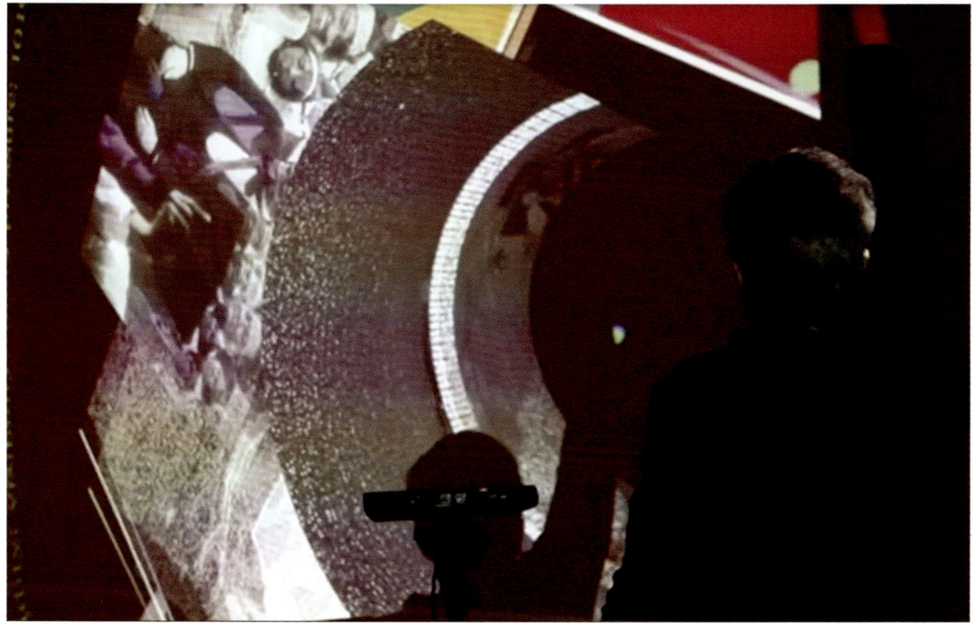

Post Browser installation at TRANSFER

Fibonacci Spiral, Galilee, Pennsylvania, 2014

The *Fibonacci Spiral* is a sculptural slide and video projection surface based on the Fibonacci series of numbers. Observed as a principle of growth in nature and the cosmos and analyzed as a geometrical form in the Western tradition since the time of Euclid, the Fibonacci series is composed of a sequence in which every number comes from adding the two preceding ones (0, 1, 1, 2, 3, 5, 8, 13, 21, 34, 55, 89, 144 . . .). Hovagimyan used it to calculate the curve and ascent of the sculpture's form.

In the 1980s, Hovagimayan purchased an old house and barn on the edge of the Western Catskills in Galilee, Pennsylvania, just across the Delaware River from Callicoon, New York. Over the course of the next 30 years, he restored the house and converted the barn into a working studio and exhibition space for his work. In 2014, outside his studio in Galilee, he built the first installation of the *Spiral,* conceived as an interactive sculpture and projection surface displaying videos about the golden ratio.

> The Fibonacci series is the golden section, and the spiral is the spiral of growth. Things like seashells make a spiral…I thought it would be fantastic to make a spiral ramp. I wanted to combine the notion of luge, so I made this 20-foot spiral that has a 40-by-60-foot footprint.[164]

He built the first installation 20-feet tall, using repurposed two-by-fours from a demolished house next door for the structure, corrugated plastic sheets for the cladding, and 55-gallon drums for the slide. He described it as a community building project, enlisting the help of friends to assemble it.

The sources for projections were downloaded YouTube videos explaining the wonder of the Fibonacci series as an expression of natural form. "They call it the God number, and it turns out that galaxies actually form in the same spiral, so it goes all the way from an embryo to a galaxy," Hovagimyan said.[165]

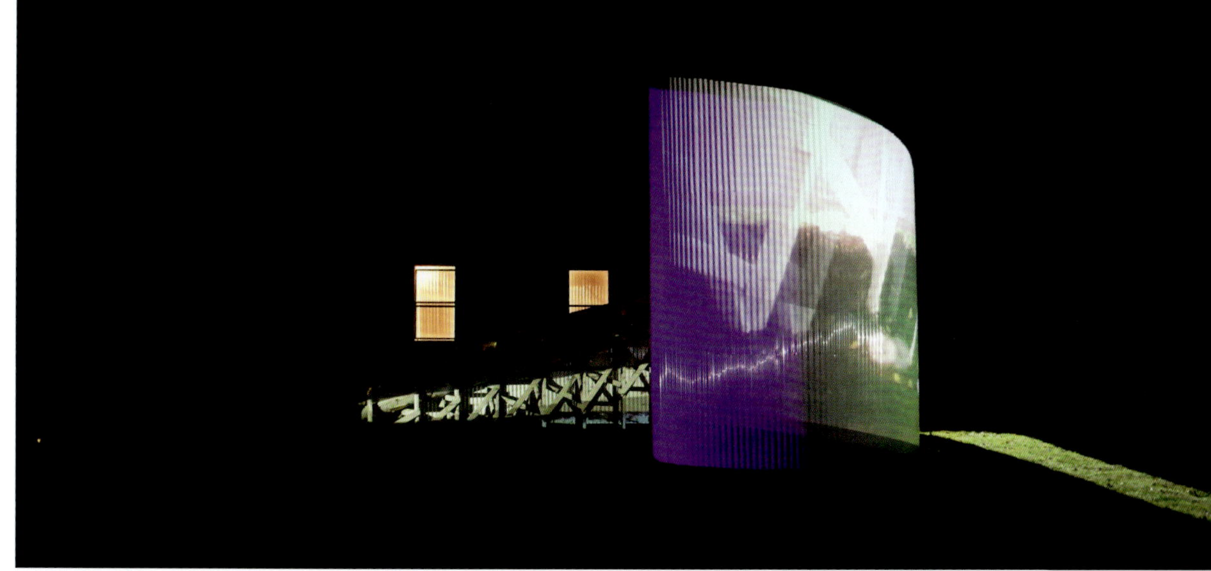

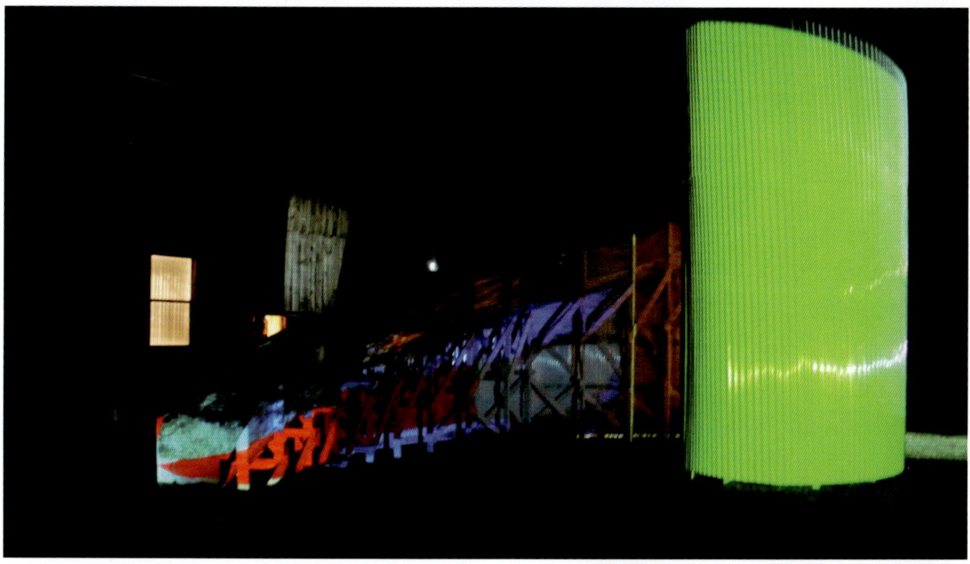

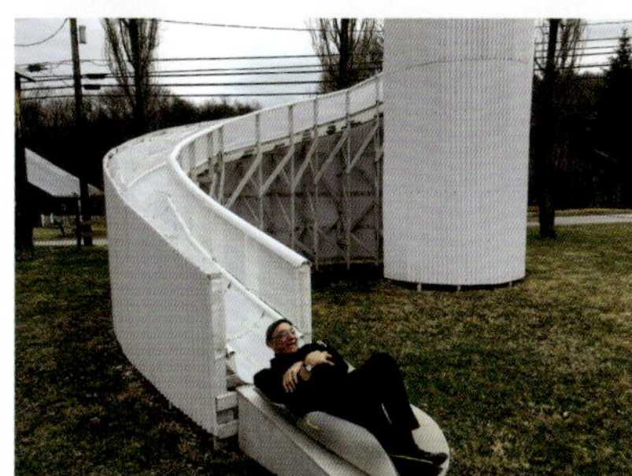

Above: Projections on *Fibonacci Spiral*, Gallilee, 2014
Right: Hovagimyan used *Fibonacci Spiral* as a slide

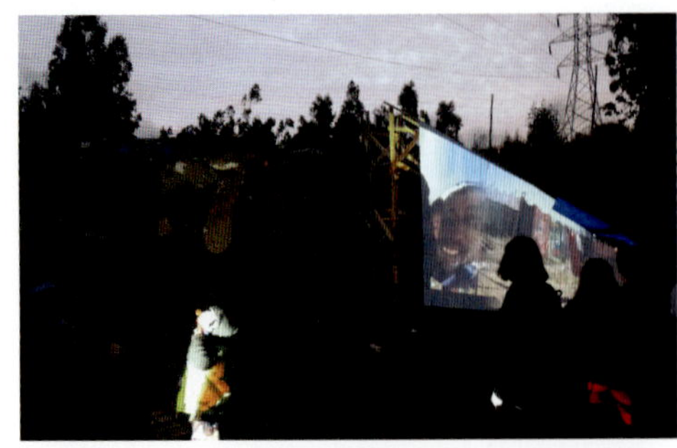

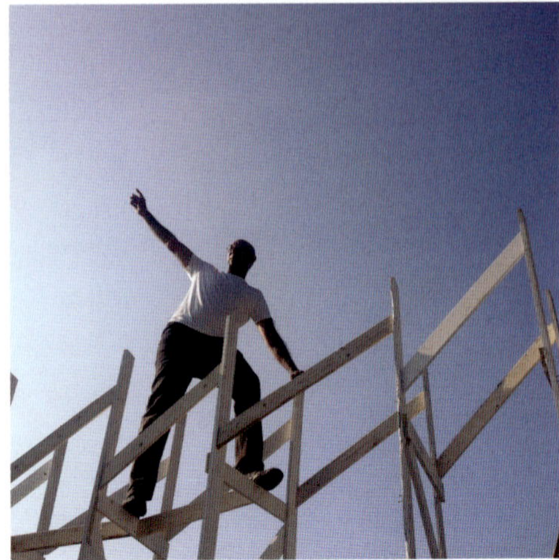

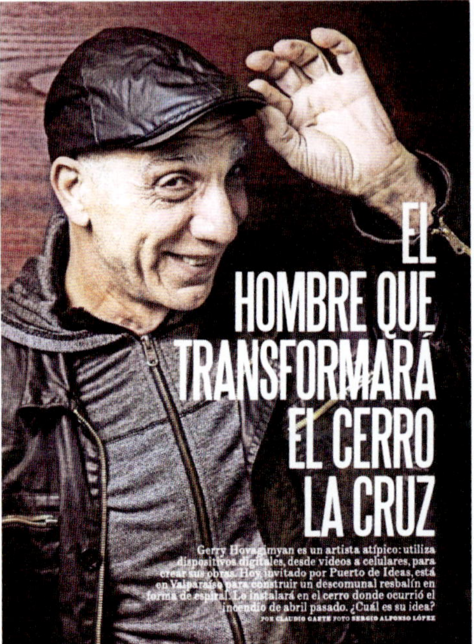

EL HOMBRE QUE TRANSFORMARÁ EL CERRO LA CRUZ

Gerry Hovagimyan es un artista atípico: utiliza dispositivos digitales, desde videos a celulares, para crear sus obras. Hoy, invitado por Puerto de Ideas, está en Valparaíso para construir un descomunal resbalín en forma de espiral. Lo instalará en el cerro donde ocurrió el incendio de abril pasado. ¿Cuál es su idea?

POR CLAUDIO GAETE FOTO SERGIO ALFONSO LÓPEZ

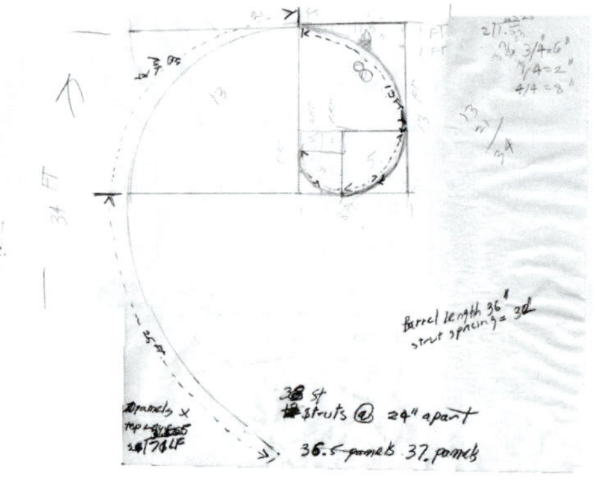

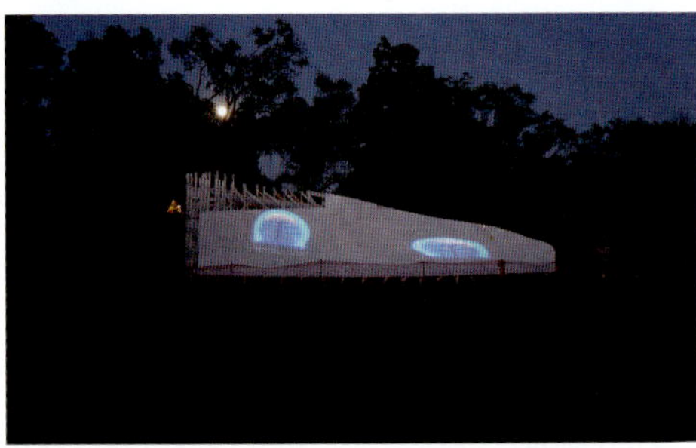

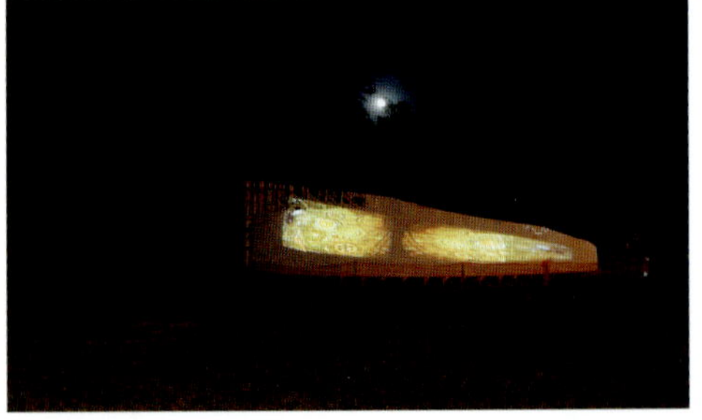

Clockwise from top: *Fibonacci Spiral*, Valparaíso; *Fibonacci Spiral* construction, Flint, 2015; aerial site plan calculating height and span in Flint; projections onto the structure in Flint; press coverage of Valparaíso Fibonacci Spiral, 2014

Fibonacci Spiral, Puerto de Ideas, Valparaiso, Chile, 2014

In November 2014, Hovagimyan was invited to Valparaíso, Chile for a lecture and installation as a part of "Encounter with Digital Culture," a program of Puerto de Ideas Valparaíso, an annual festival of writers, thinkers, artists, and scientists to reflect on possibilities for the world of tomorrow.

On the hillside of La Cruz, the epicenter of a devastating fire that April, he installed a second *Fibonacci Spiral,* constructing the piece with young people from the El Vergel Alto area most seriously affected. The installation culminated in an event in which he projection-mapped their stories through collected audio, photos, and videos onto the sculpture.[166]

Fibonacci Spiral, Flint Public Art Project, Flint, Michigan, 2015

In the summer of 2015, Flint Public Art Project hosted Hovagimyan for a third installation of *Fibonacci Spiral* on a vacant lot on Flint's East Side for a community art event. They employed youth community-service volunteers in the building process, which attracted attention from locals and passersby, creating traffic jams of drivers gawking at the 16-foot structure taking shape. Neighbors stopped to find out what was going on, remarking that it was the first time anyone had paid any attention to the area. As the project neared completion, a city building inspector passed by and demanded the structure be removed. While lobbying to get it permitted, they kept it in place for a community art parade the following week. Video projection-mapped at night showed the Fibonacci sequence of natural forms from embryos to galaxies. Ultimately, it had to be dismantled.

Teenage Zombie Avatars, Ensign Sgr A,* Radiator Arts, 2015

Exhibited at Radiator Arts in the show *Ensign Sgr A** about artists using notions of absence as a banner for exploration and loss, *Teenage Zombie Avatars* followed the trajectory of *AR Paintings*, using an iPad to add live video augmentations to a two-dimensional image.

> This is an interactive work created using 3D scans of young people as avatars and placing them in a gaming environment…The viewer holds an AR marker up to an iPad, and the avatars appear in virtual 3D space. The viewer can twist and turn the markers to view the various sides of the virtual sculptures. The avatars are moving through space, creating a kinetic art world in a virtual gaming space.[167]

Zipline, Chance Ecologies, Radiator Arts, 2015

In 2015, artist Catherine Grau toured the author through a vacant postindustrial site along the East River in Long Island City, Queens, Hunters Point South overtaken by nature, with remnants of a pier half-sunken in the water. For a guerrilla exhibition called *Chance Ecologies*—reminiscent of Creative Time's *Art on the Beach* (1978–1985) on the grounds of the World Trade City landfill that became Battery Park City—they invited Hovagimyan to install a zipline between the trees and the abandoned pier.

Hovagimyan and the curators decided it was impracticable to install without permissions in the two days before construction of a waterfront park was set to begin on the site. For the subsequent Radiator gallery exhibition, Hovagimyan created a model of the *Zipline* concept. He hung a line diagonally from the top corner of the gallery to a shelf attached to the wall and attached a mountain climber action figure to the line. When the figure reached the end of the line, it triggered an Arduino chip with a motion sensor, signaling an applause file to play on a speaker. Young children ran around playing with it at the opening. "I don't know if it's art or not," said one visitor, "but I like it."[168]

3by3by3 (with Rhys Chatham & Raphaele Shirley), 2016

During a second Harvestworks residency in 2016, Hovagimyan collaborated with musician Rhys Chatham and sculptor Raphaele Shirley on *3b3by3*, an interactive immersive performance. Hovagimyan created another custom natural interface that recognized live gestures to modulate light sculptures and

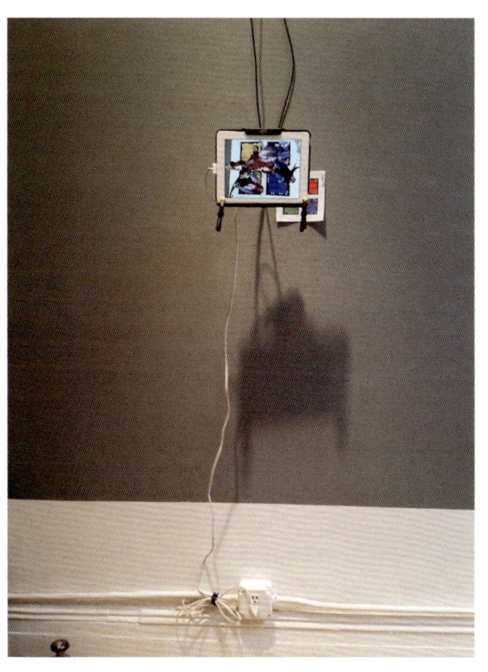

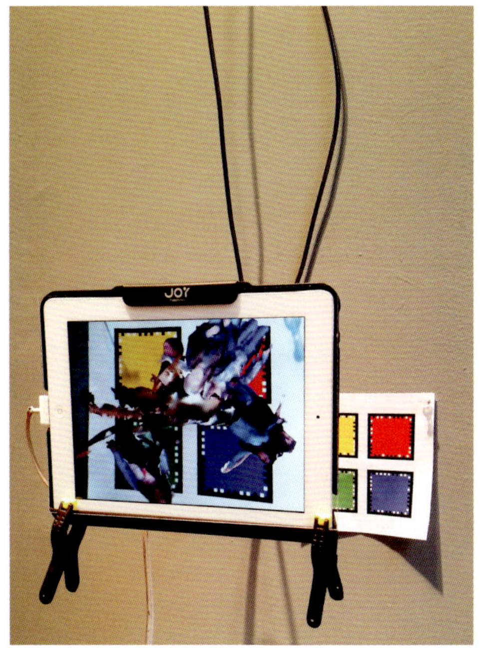

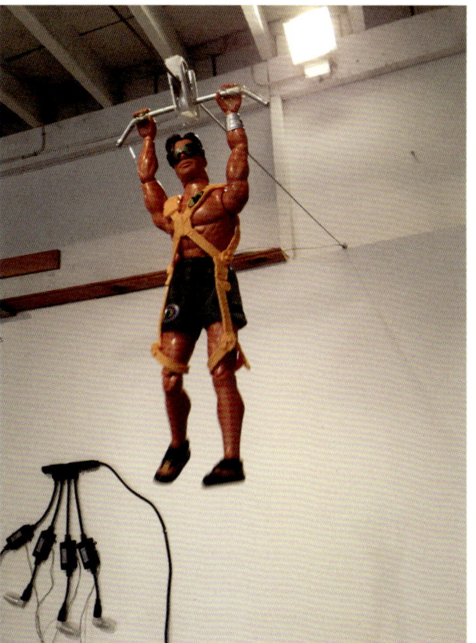

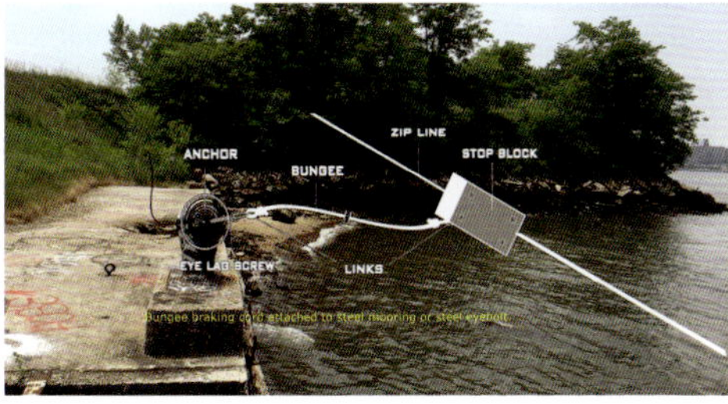

Top: *Teenage Zombie Avatars* at Radiator. Photos: Michael Sarff
Above: *Zipline* rendering for Hunters Point South
Left: *Zipline* installation at Radiator

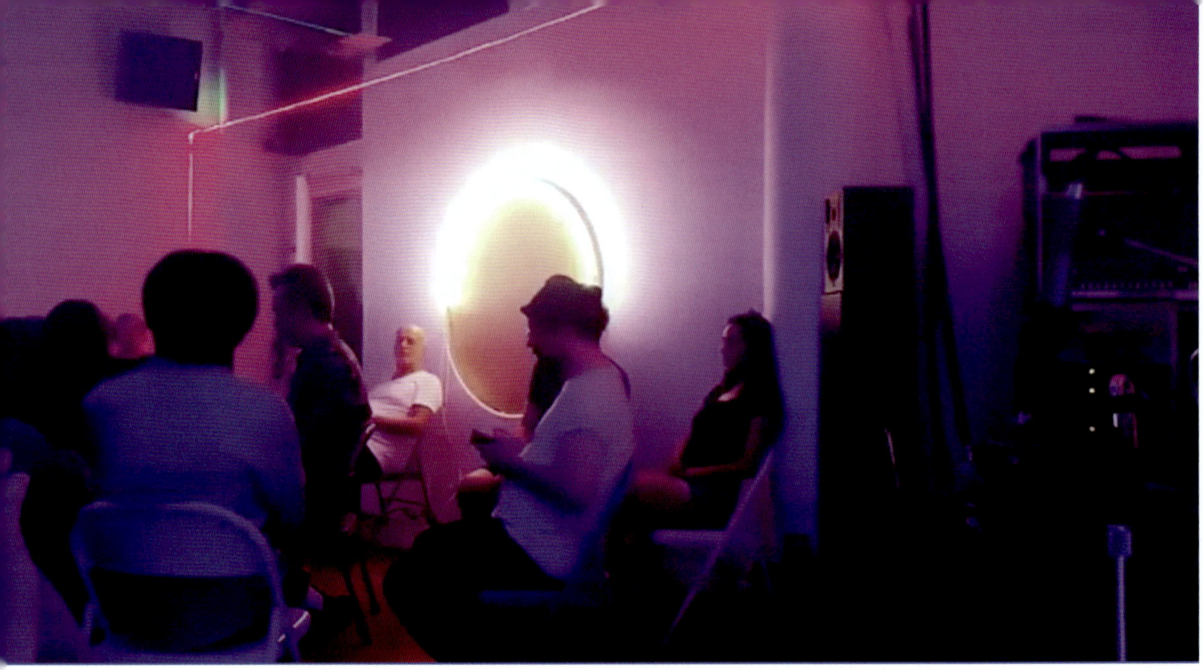

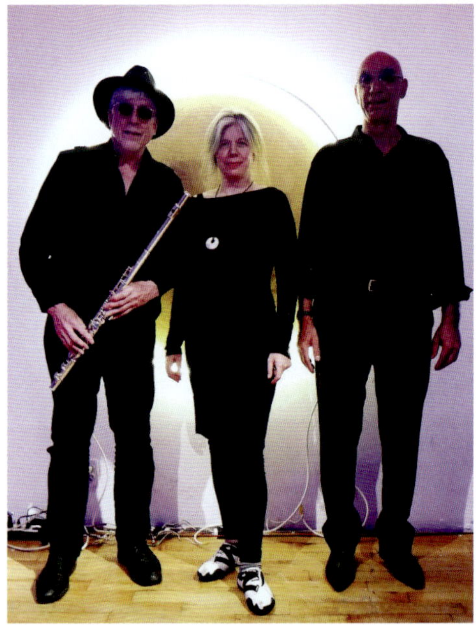

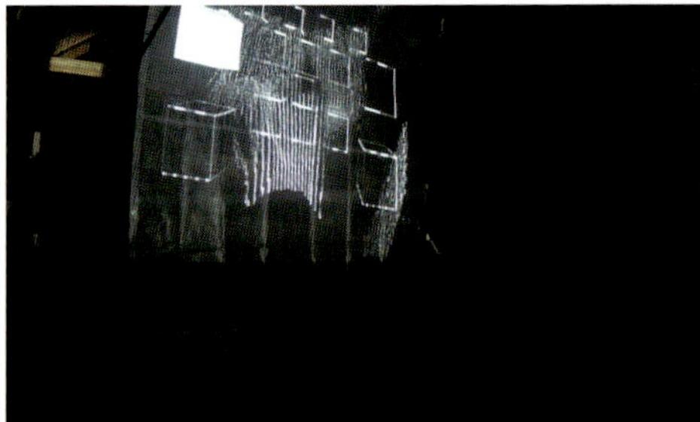

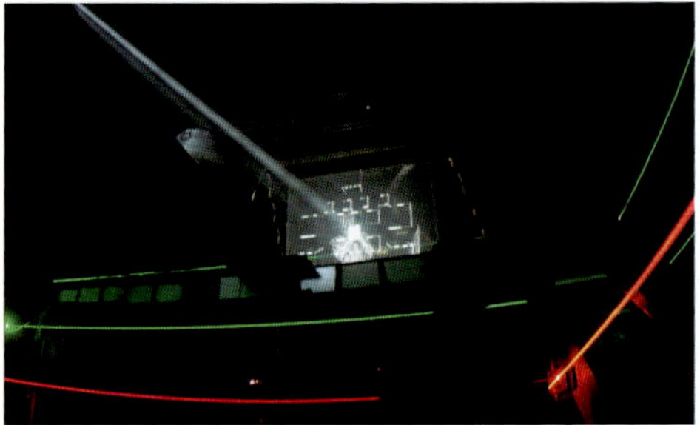

Top: Performance at *3by3by3* at Harvest works.
Above: Chatham, Shirley, and Hovagimyan. Photos: Michael Sarff
Above right: *3by3by3* workshop rehearsal in Galilee

environments by Shirley. As Chatham played minimalist compositions, solo or with a combo, Hovagimyan responded with hand and arm gestures and movements altering the lights.

The audience viewed the work from around and within the environment as a multisensory experience of light, sound, performance, and spatial volumes. The group performed *3by3by3* in workshop presentations at Shirley's loft, Hovagimyan's studio, and Harvestworks.

AR-VR, Split Festival for New Film, 2017

In 2017, Hovagimyan made a series of AR-VR prints that used Vuforia software to trigger 3D virtual reality animations from two-dimensional images. Visitors accessed the animations by means of a wearable iPhone viewer. The program recognized the flat image—an assemblage of figurative and abstract forms—and augmented it with three-dimensional animations that Hovagimyan composed in the program. Shown as an installation at the Split Festival for New Film, it was the beginning of an exploration that would continue for the next two years in several new works shown at a 2019 one-person show at the Delaware Valley Arts Alliance in Narrowsburg, New York.

> It goes back to Dziga Vertov, who did all of those silent films with machines; it's very Constructivist in what it does with the animations. It hearkens back to German Dadaist, Constructivist era, World War I silent film. That's what I was thinking of when I did the animations.[169]

As opposed to the Albers-based *AR Paintings*, in which the iPad showed stationary 3D images, the *AR-VR* pieces morphed dynamically as you moved around in relation to the two-dimensional surfaces. The animations drew from architectural and engineering drawings and stock game objects like a generator and a jetfighter, reminiscent of Dada and Futurist artists manipulating watches, train engines, and mechanistic objects to create altered-reality effects.

> Once you decontextualize these objects, they're no longer game objects. They become another 'word' in visual language, so you can put it in a larger context of filmic and animation and art language. I may use the tools of game engines, but they're subverted in a way that frees them in a kind of liberation soup.[170]

Applause Please, Algorithmic Landscapes, Callicoon, New York, 2018

During the Radiator gallery installation of *Zipline*, Hovagimyan observed people's enjoyment when triggering applause as they entered the room while the motion sensor was still pointed out into the open gallery. As part of *Algorithmic Landscapes of the Western Catskills,* a series of special installations and performances in conjunction with the Callicoon Art Walk, Hovagimyan hung an Arduino with a sensor, amplifier, and speaker in the alleyway between from River Road and Callicoon Creek Park.

Passersby needed no explanation of *Applause Please* as they walked through the alley, laughing and waving as if being cheered by a crowd. Workers in the adjacent coffee shop got annoyed by the repeated cheers, however, and turned down the speakers after several hours. "I'm always getting censored by someone," Hovagimyan laughed.[171]

At Home in Space, Loft Gallery, Delaware Valley Art Alliance, 2019

In 2017, Hovagimyan sold his TriBeCa loft with Castleberry and moved year-round to his country house in Galilee, Pennsylvania. Fellow ex-pat New York artist Forrest "Frosty" Myers owned property nearby and had moved there full-time as well. Myers was best known for his 1960s geometric sculptures as a founding member of Park Place cooperative gallery with Dean Fleming, Peter Forakis, Marc di Suvero, and Leo Villeador; for *The Wall* (1973), his teal blue wall at Houston Street and Broadway mounted with cuts of I-beams, which serves as a portal to SoHo; and for his *Moon Museum* (1969), a wafer with tiny, engraved paintings sent up to space on Apollo 12.

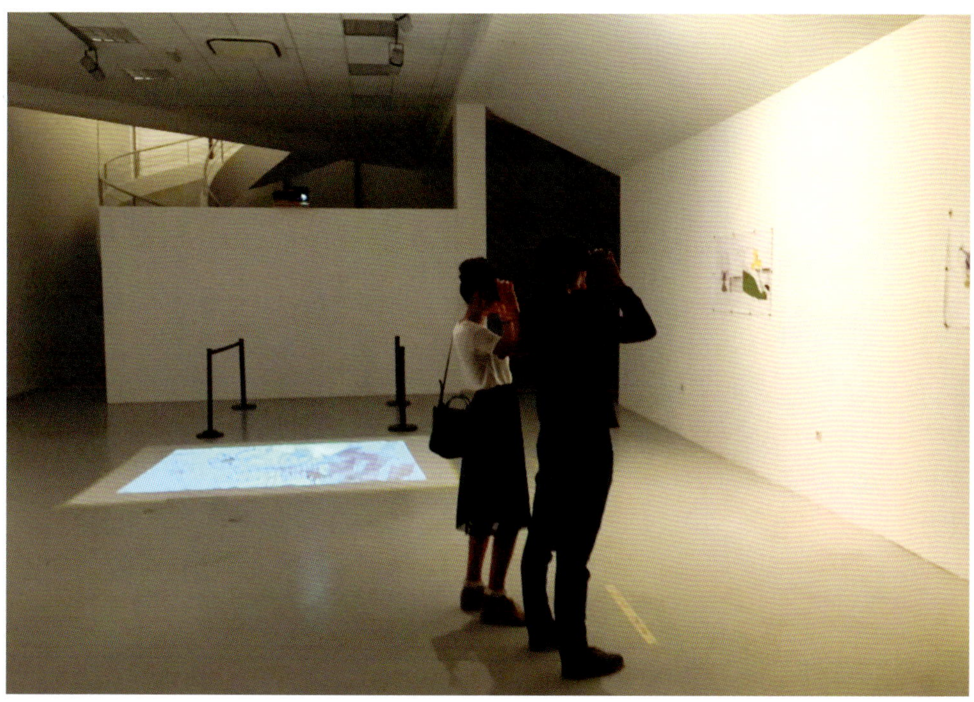

195

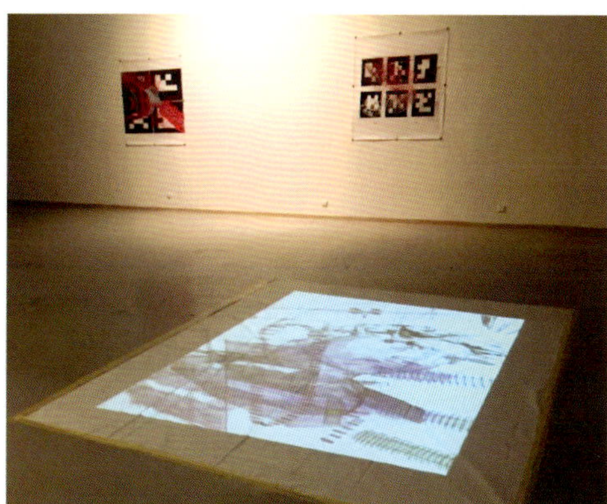

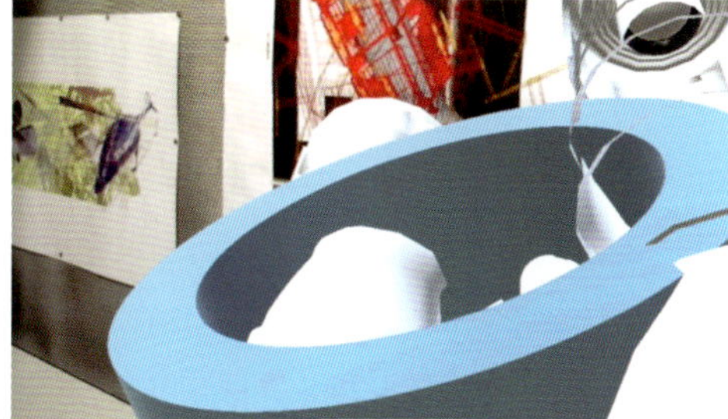

Top to bottom, clockwise: *AR-VR* in Split; screenshot of *AR-VR* animation in Galilee studio; concept drawing for *AR-VR; AR-VR* projection

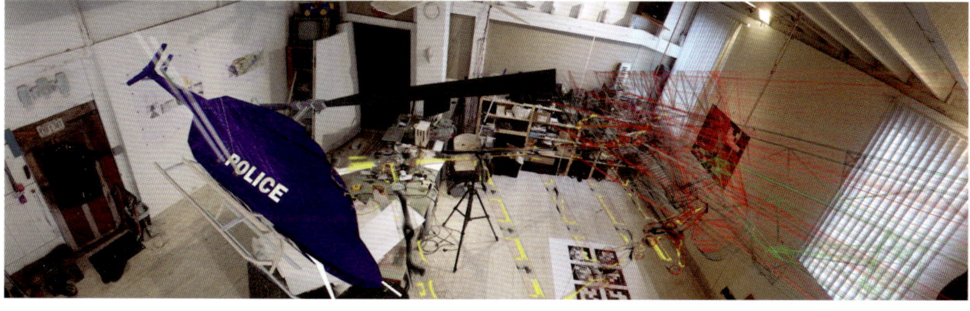

In 2019, the Delaware Valley Art Alliance (DVAA), the Arts Council for Sullivan County, 20 miles downriver from Galilee in Narrowsburg, New York, invited Hovagimyan and Myers to exhibit dual space-themed one-person shows in its gallery. Myers took the ground floor for a show entitled *Spaced Out at Home*, and Hovagimyan the second-floor loft gallery for *At Home in Space*. He included eight new AR pieces created for the exhibition, which ran from August 10 to September 14, 2019.

Six of the works were ink-jet printed assemblages on canvas, four mounted on stretcher bars and hanging on walls, the other two draped over a table and laying on the floor. When viewed through an iPad, they triggered 3D animations that rotated and changed orientation as you moved through the space and activated other pieces.

Space Painting 1

> I was going through this period of inspiration by American Precisionists like Charles Sheeler and Joseph Stella. I took all of these 3D objects and architectural forms, put them into a 3D program and made virtual assemblages, and then I would take a screenshot of that and export it. It looked like one of these Precisionist paintings, and then I would take all of the objects I used to make the piece and put them into the augmented reality game engine program and had them trigger separately and rotate in animation.[172]

Space Painting 2

The paintings included wire frames of structures, a Soviet constructivist sign, medical equipment to measure blood pressure, a fire extinguisher, and various furniture, augmented using Vuforia game engine software to activate the animations. The movement from flat wall-hung and horizontally laid-out prints to 3D animations situated viewers within the mediated virtual space of the iPad as well as the physical space of the gallery, producing a complex interactivity between the digital and the object, and re-orienting people in relation to one another and the environment.

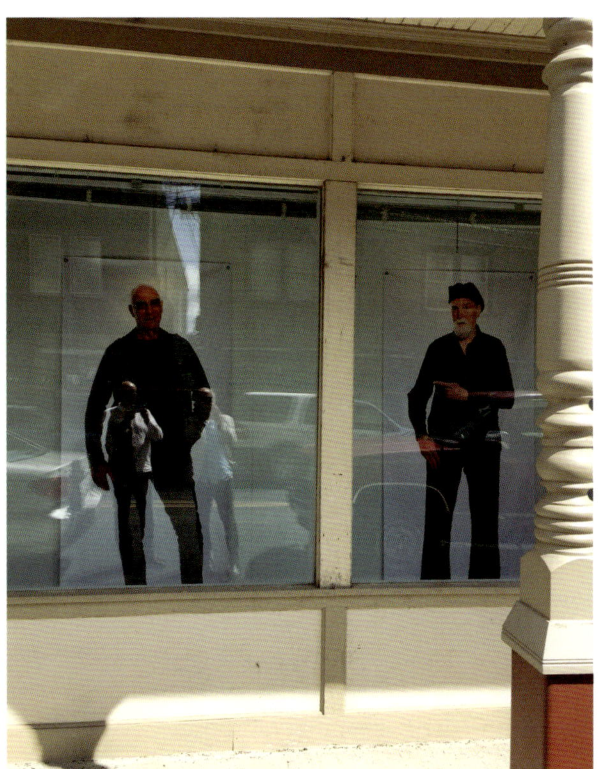

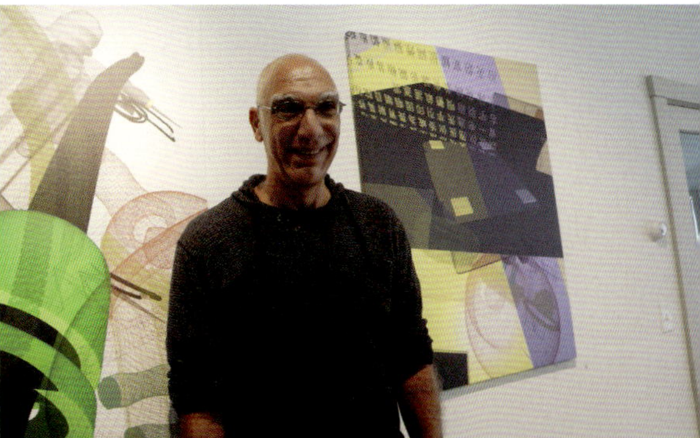

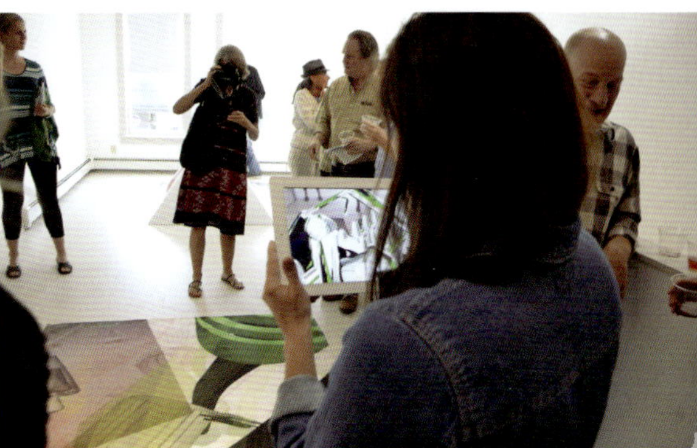

Above: Posters of Hovagimyan and Frosty Myers at DVAA in Narrowsburg, New York
Above right: Hovagimyan in front of *Space Painting 3* and *4*
Bottom right: *At Home in Space* opening

Space Painting 3

> I realized that we're going into space, so we've got this different type of consciousness, which is the virtual world's consciousness, where there's no up or down, there's no gravity, there's no anything…That means that everything—machines, architecture, all object forms, become subjects as well, because they're now free from their functionality.[173]

Space Painting 4

> In *At Home in Space,* the theme is objects that you would have in the home, but when you're out in space, they're all exploded and blown apart and floating. There's no up or down or anything, because all of these objects are freed from the post-and-lintel constraints of architecture. So, again, it's a liberation and a recombination, deconstruction, reconstruction, or decontextualization, loosening them from their intended purposes…it creates a whole other place.[174]

Space Rug

> That goes back to the origination of net culture and computer culture, which flattens everything, because they're all equal…in other words, the President of the United States is equal to a punk hacker on the web. All words have equal weight; there's no such thing as media hegemony. By the same token, architecture loses its authority in a certain sense.[175]

Space Table

Space Table is composed of a printed canvas on a table with representations of things like spoons, a glass, and furniture in assemblage form, and a coiled object placed on the table.

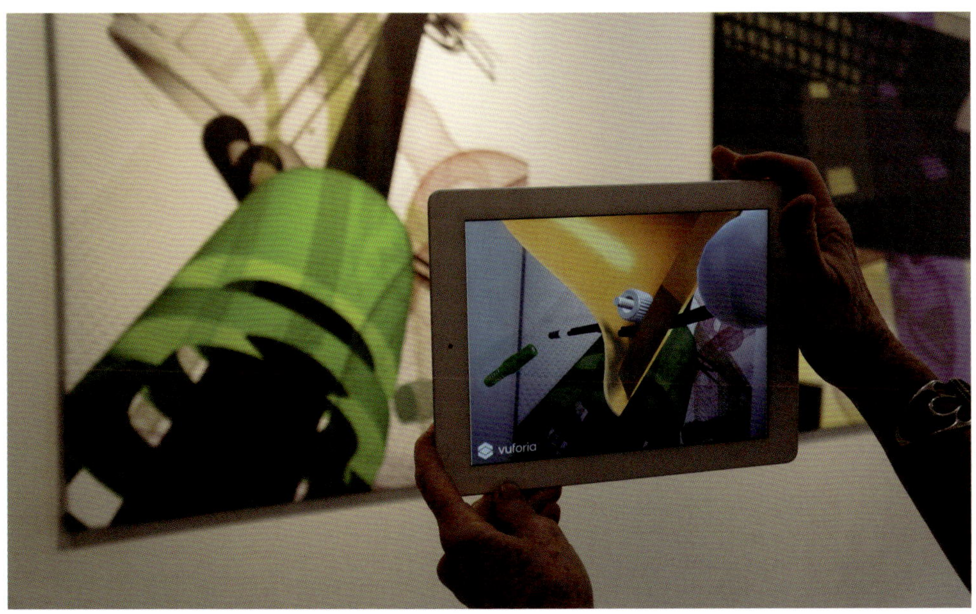

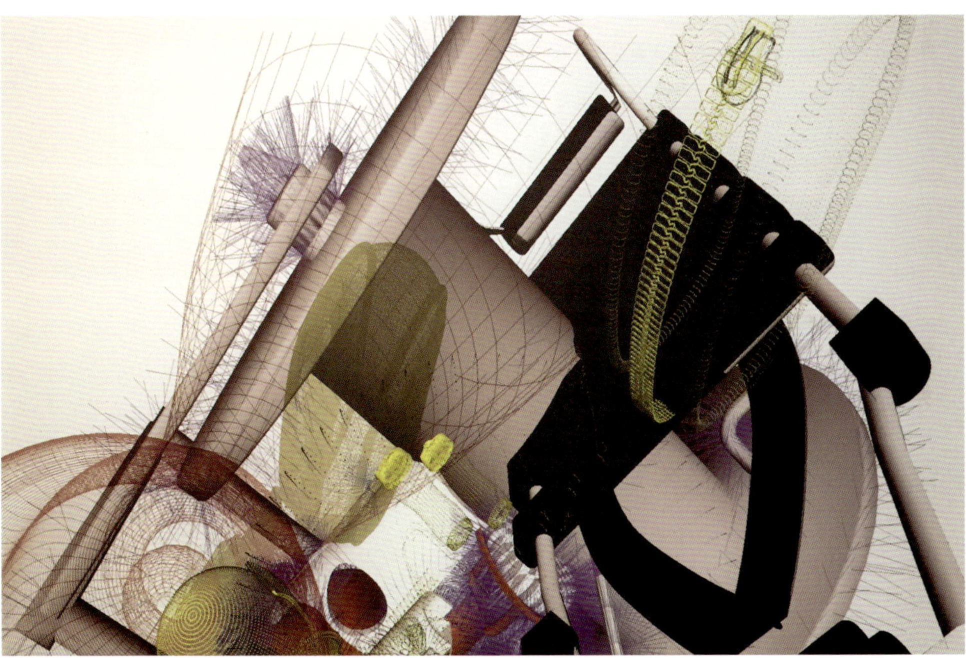

Top: *Space Painting 3* viewed through iPad at DVAA
Above: *Space Painting 1* at DVAA

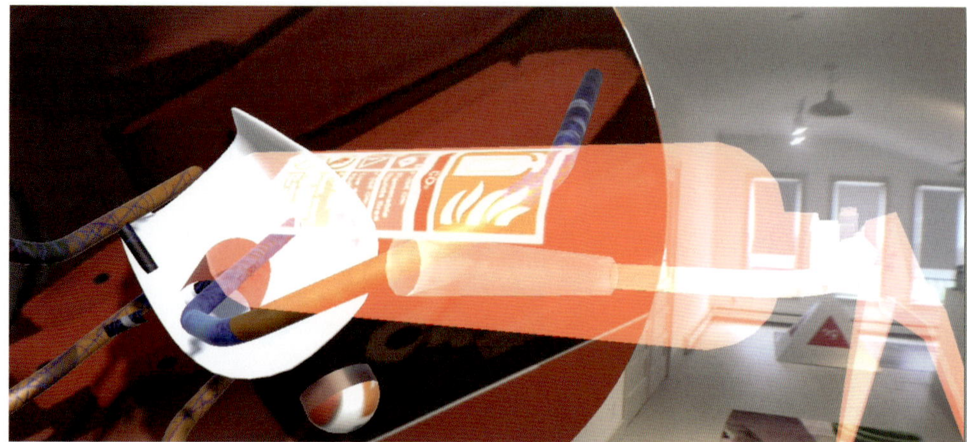

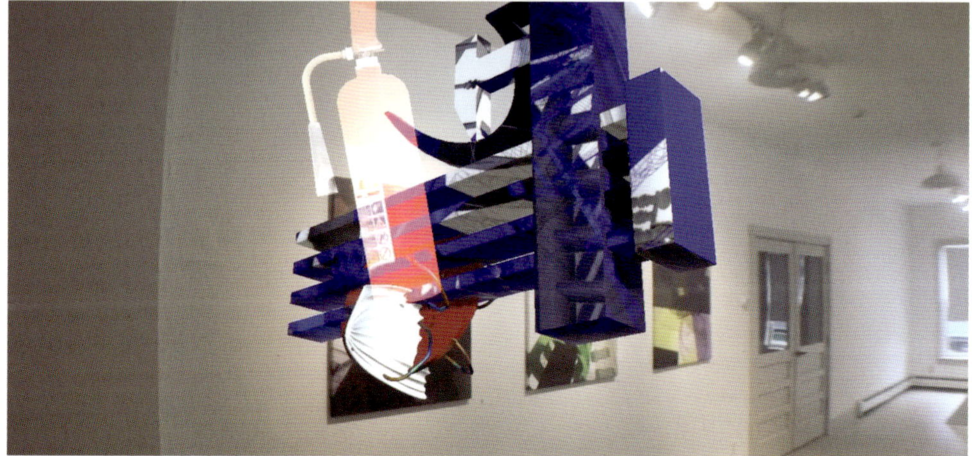

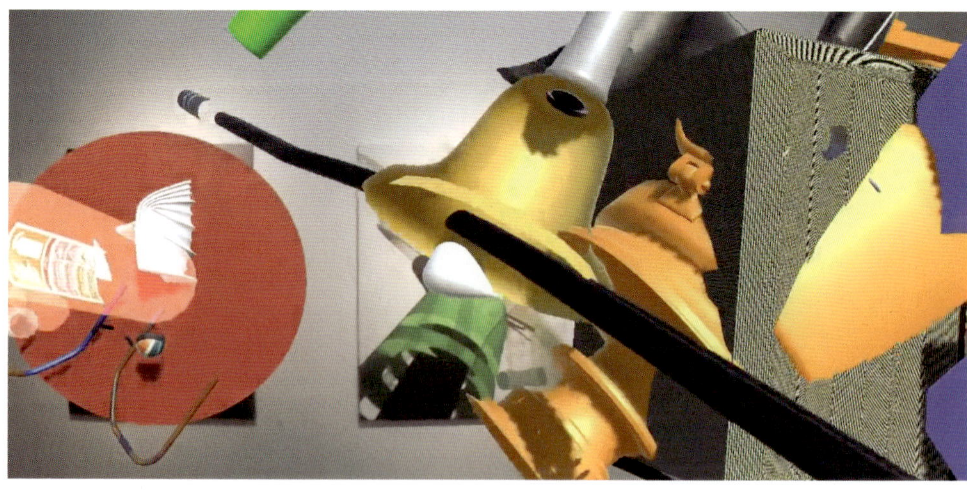

> I very much wanted to deal with what the virtual world/augmented world is going to be, freed from the commercial applications, because what happens—the same thing with the web—is that the web was great when no one knew anything about it. It was all chaotic and people were exploring it, and it was anarchy. But the minute the corporate interests got in, it was "we're going to build a business, we're going to do printing, and advertising," which is really very narrow. The same thing with the game industry and the cell phone. You've got this whole social media network, which is about selling cell phones and subscriptions to cell phone services. The whole notion of augmented reality, they don't know quite what to do.[176]

Quantum Steps

On the steps leading to the second-floor gallery, Hovagimyan printed another installation for the stair risers. A print on the wall triggered 3D animations mirroring the pattern on the stairs.

> I had an icon so these risers animated as you were going up the steps. They were coming at you. I had a rough time triggering the animation because I had two colors, blue and black. When it was separated into the risers on the steps, the camera didn't recognize the 3D, so I had to put the image on a flat digital print on the wall, and that would trigger out on the stairs. I thought that was OK because the stairs had the same image referenced as well, and that's animated so that it makes it into this odd...you're disoriented going upstairs but then have these abstract digital prints, and the prints also have images coming at you from the viewers. It made a kind of *in situ* piece.[177]

Top: Screen capture of *Space Painting 2* and *3* installation

Middle: Screen capture of *Space Painting 2 and 3* at DVAA

Above: Screen Capture of *Space Painting 1, 2,* and *3* installation

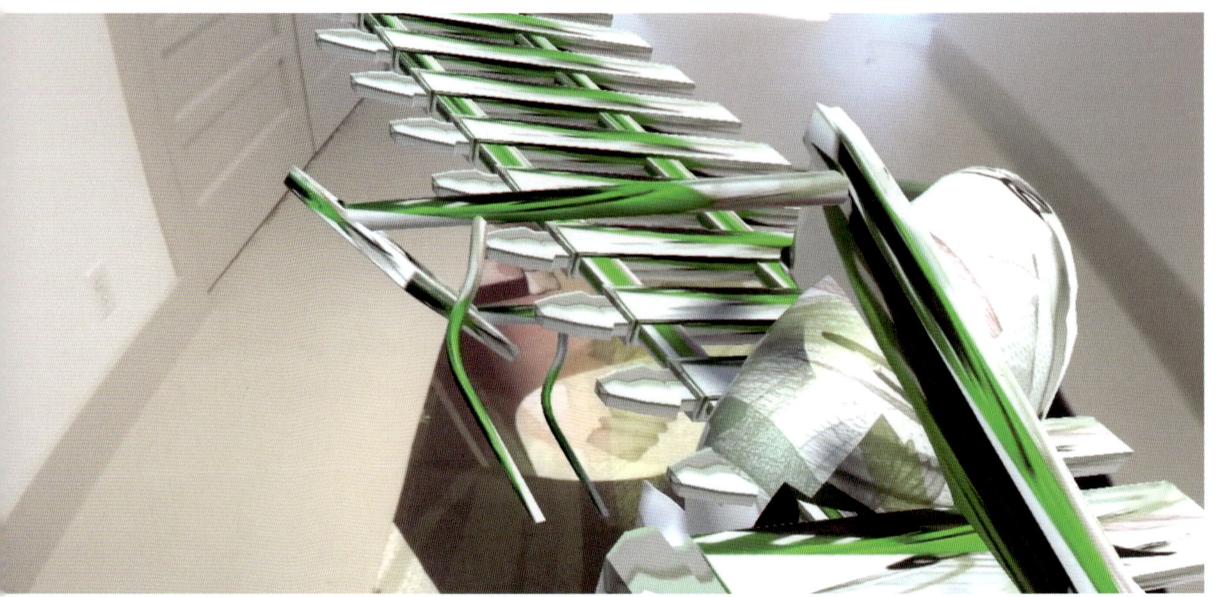

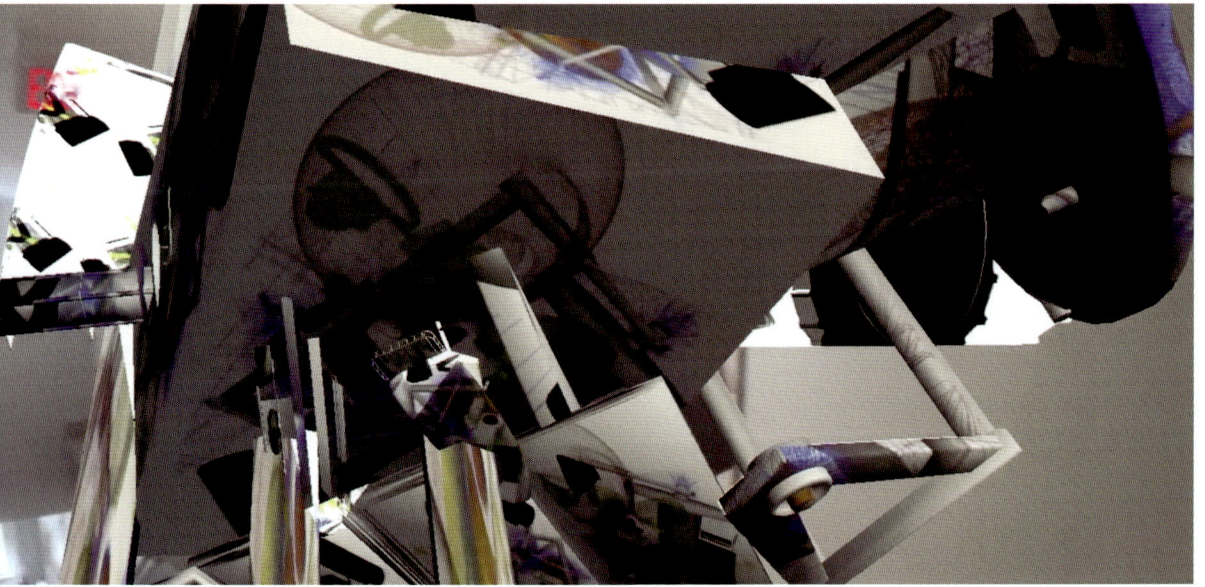

Top: Screen capture of *Space Rug*
Above: Screen capture of *Space Table* at DVAA

Superman's Pyramid

For *Superman's Pyramid*, he created an immersive sci-fi city triggered by a sculptural pyramid and graphic decals on its surface, which used a made-up computer language referencing Roswell Air Force base. He fabricated the pyramid from cuts of stainless steel mounted on foam panel, glued together to make an equilateral-triangle structure.

> I put this digital print decal on it to trigger the augmentation so the camera had something to recognize apart from the object…Again, it has a 360-degree viewpoint rather than flat planar. In this case, it's a sculptural object that has a 360-degree immersive augmentation on it…It triggered a whole sci-fi city that you were immersed in, and you could rotate all the way around to see the city.[178]

AR Column, 2019

Hovagimyan continued his aesthetic research on the interaction of 2D and 3D images and objects with physical space, and virtual and augmented representations later that year with *AR Column*. He composed assemblages of 3D representations, printed them as 2D images, then pasted them onto a columnar sculpture. Then he used Vuforio to explode the images into augmented reality objects, which hover, rotate, and move around in live video of the space as you view them through an iPad.

> Now what I've done is after constructing these kind of assemblage montages of 3D objects, then taking a still of them, I digital print them back to painting. So they basically start as virtual objects and then they become paintings—digital print paintings—or rugs or tablecloths. Then I create virtual animations augmentations that you see by holding up a viewer or a stereo viewer or an iPad.[179]

He described the trajectory of research in *At Home in Space*, which continues in ongoing projects like *AR Column* and *Satellites*:

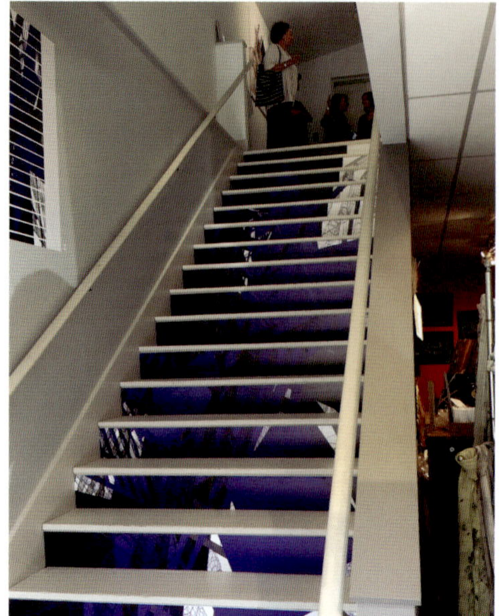

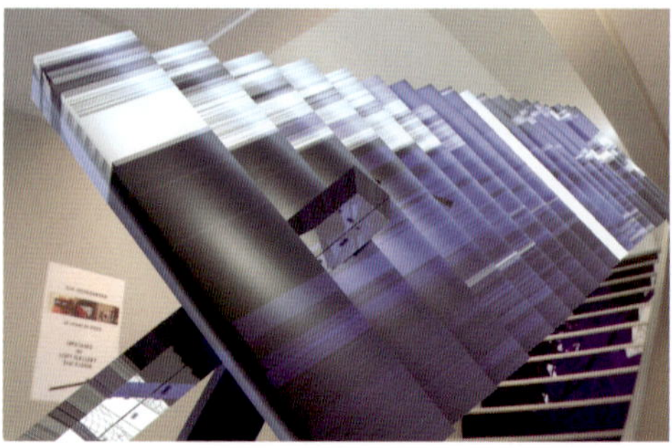

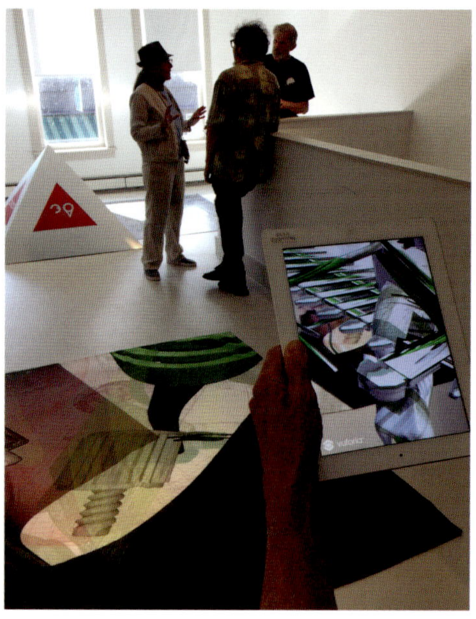

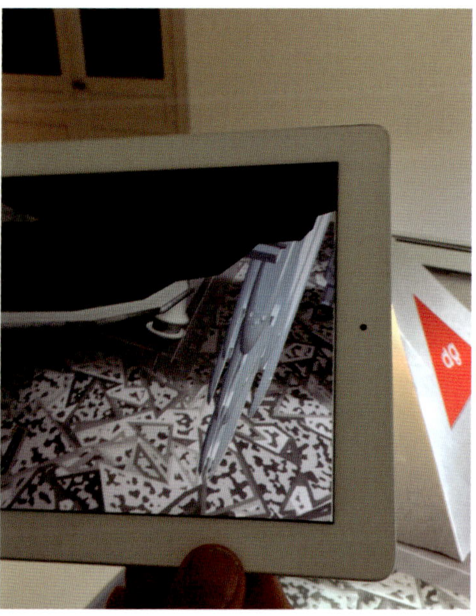

Top left: *Quantum Steps* installed at DVAA
Top right: Screenshot of *Quantum Steps* installation
Above: *Superman's Pyramid* installed at DVAA

> You can access the virtual space, so you are physically in the real space, and you are physically confronting physical objects, but then you're also in a virtual space and linguistic space, because it's all these objects like a vase, a gym exercise machine, a scratch awl, a gear, a bell, a couch, a Rietveld chair, batteries, on and on and on it goes…a fan. Then I also reveal the wireframes, which is the structure below the 3D object. It's all kind of stripping away, moving them out of their language, moving into a different space.[180]

Satellites, installation, Galilee, Pennsylvania, 2020

Satellites takes the real-world physical and AR dimensions even further, situating eight cubes with printed icons and Zapf Dingbats text pasted on their surfaces in an outdoor environment that makes the natural scenery, trees, grass, barns, other people, and everything visible and audible in the area a part of the experience. Through the Vuforia app, the cubes and scenery are augmented with hovering and rotating satellites downloaded from NASA, sci-fi sounds, and explosions geo-located to be activated and get louder or softer as you move through the space.

> I like the reference of satellites, but my whole starting point for it was there's something like 30,000 objects up in space now—satellites and this and that. Some of them are dead, and some of them have split apart, had collisions with micro-meteors, so you've actually got a satellite belt. There's a guy who's writing programs to locate each one of them, so when you're plotting a trajectory for launching a rocket, you avoid these things. That's part of my original inspiration is the notion of space junk and satellites surrounding the earth. Then you take the notion of explosions and games. I'm using those references, but I'm not making a game, and I'm not making satellites, and I'm not a space buff in particular…I'm more interested in stepping back as an artist and looking at the total environment…it's about contemplating the various languages assembled together. It becomes a virtual digital augmented reality assemblage.[181]

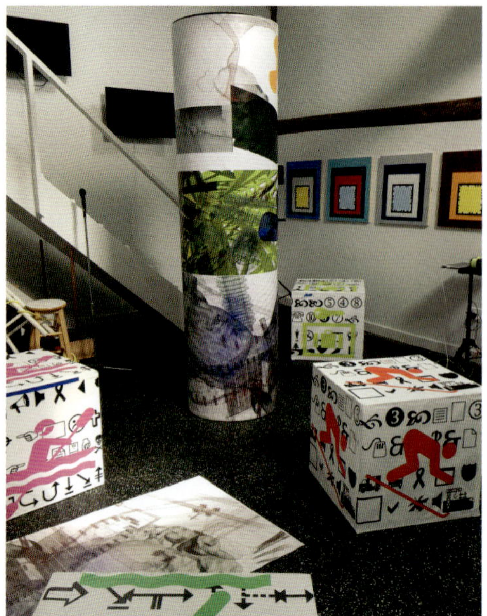

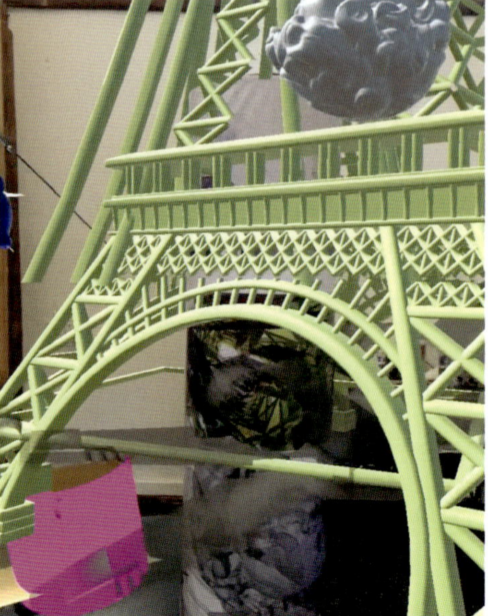

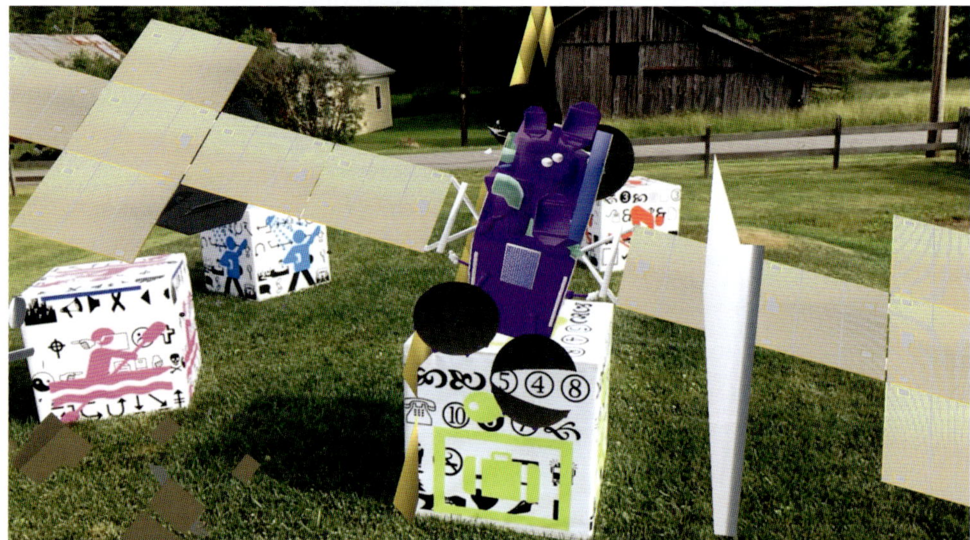

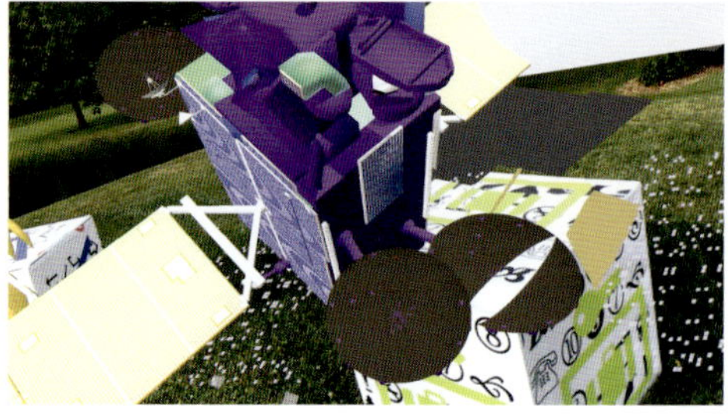

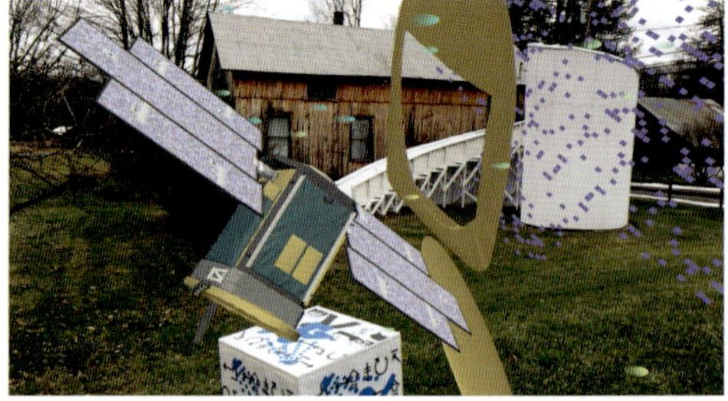

In the end, *Satellites* returns to Hovagimyan's critique of media's appropriation for commercial purposes, forecasting alternate uses and an awakening of sensibilities through their aesthetic liberation.

> Hollywood wants immersive VR movies. They want you to go to a theater, sit down, and have these VR goggles on, then you're immersed in the movie. It's a commercial model. What it does is it narrows the sense of wonder other than some kind of cheap thrill. Within a game, it's simple: either you shoot or you get shot, and make points. You win or you lose. In movies, you're basically in the narrative: the filmmaker or producer or director has a narrative, he's telling a story. It's restricted to the proscenium arch. It doesn't deal with perception in terms of how humans perceive the world. It doesn't even deal with the way in which our perception of the world is changing based on having this new kind of mediasphere in the way we deal with information and the physical world. That's what I'm exploring: language, media world, game, virtual world, physical environment, information environment.[182]

Top: *AR Column* in studio
Top right: *AR Column* animation in studio
Middle: Video still from screen capture of *Satellites* installation in Galilee
Above: Screen captures from video of *Satellites* installation

Notes

1. G.H. Hovagimyan interview with author in Galilee, PA, Jun. 25–26, 2019
2. Interview, Jun. 25–26, 2019.
3. Interview, Jun. 25–26, 2019.
4. Interview, Jun. 25–26, 2019.
5. Interview, Jun. 25–26, 2019.
6. Interview, Jun. 25–26, 2019.
7. Jessamyn Fiore, *112 Greene Street*, David Zwirner Books: New York, 2012. Note: Fiore incorrectly states that Hovagimyan worked at Food restaurant. He never did.
8. Interview, June 25–26, 2019.
9. "Richard Serra & Robert Bell . . . Prisoner's Dilemma," *Avalanche Newspaper*, May/Jun. 1974. See also Roberta Smith, "Video, in Its Infancy, Had to Crawl Before It Could Walk," *New York Times*, Jan. 24, 2003. [Name misspelled as Hovagymyan.]
10. Interview, June 25–26, 2019.
11. G.H. Hovagimyan interview with author at 11 Harrison Street Apt. 6, Apr. 20, 2012.
12. Interview, Apr. 20, 2012. See also Michael Kimmelman, "Matta-Clark's Cross Sections of Yesterday," *New York Times*, Feb. 23, 2007.
13. Interview, Apr. 20, 2012.
14. Interview, Apr. 20, 2012.
15. Interview with Scott Billingsley by author, Jan. 2, 2021.
16. Interview, Jun. 25–26, 2019.
17. Alan Moore, "Loft Show at 597 Broadway," *Artforum* 19, No. 10, Summer 1975.
18. Interview with Billingsley, Jan. 2, 2021.
19. Interview, Apr. 20, 2012.
20. "Beth B and Scott B." Section 2—Punk Magazine & School of Visual Arts. 98bowery.com. Excerpted from *Punk Art Catalogue*, Washington Project for the Arts, Washington D.C., 1978.
21. Dieter Runge, Festival of Patience site, https://dieterrunge.wordpress.com/.
22. Interview, Jun. 25–26, 2019.
23. Dieter Runge, emails with author, Aug. 20, 2020.
24. Robert Christgau, "Choices," *Village Voice*, May 8, 1978.
25. Email to author from Julia Gorton, Jan. 20, 2021. "BTW, it was a real fight, not a fake fight! James had insulted Cristgau's [sic] wife, and he wasn't having it. Christgau pounded him."
26. Thurston Moore and Byron Coley, *No Wave: Post-Punk. Underground. New York. 1976– 1980*, New York: Abrams, 2008. See also James Wolcott, "A Conservative Impulse in the New Rock Underground," *Village Voice*, Aug. 18th 1975, reporting on the CBGB Festival, and *Soho Weekly News* reporting on the Artists Space festival on May 11, 1978, citing an audience member saying "They were failed . . . musicians."
27. Megan Govin, "Introduction to the Fine Arts Building," Dec. 18, 2014: https: //fineartsbuildingnewyork.tumblr.com/post/165102423267/introduction-to-the-fine-arts-building.
28. Punk Music Catalogue, https://punkmusicccatalogue.wordpress/communists.
29. Interview, Jun. 25–26, 2019.
30. Interview, Apr. 20, 2012.
31. Neil Smith, The New Urban Frontier: *Gentrification and the Revanchist City* (New York: Routledge, 1996). Virtual Garrison is mentioned in Smith's classic study of gentrification, a word that begins to find common usage with the East Village gallery explosion in the early-to-mid-80s.
32. Carlo McCormick, "Remembrance of Things Passed Over," *East Village Eye*, Aug. 1984.
33. Walter Winshield [nom de plume of Walter Robinson], "Lumps of All Kinds: Sculpture Survey at Virtual Garrison," *East Village Eye*, Jul. 1984.
34. Walter Winshield [Robinson], "Charlie Saulson," *East Village Eye*, Mar. 1985.
35. Douglas C. McGill, "Art People," *New York Times*, Oct. 4, 1985.

36. Robyn Brentano and Mark Savitt, eds. 112 *Workshop/112 Greene Street: History, Artists & Artworks* (New York: New York University Press, 1981).
37. Laurie Anderson, "About 405 13th Street," *Artforum* 12, No. 1, Sep. 1974. The show took place on May 4–14, 1973.
38. Anderson, *"About 405."*
39. Jean Dupuy, ed., *Collective Consciousness: Art Performances in the Seventies* (Performing Arts Journal Publications: New York, 1980).
40. Alan Moore, "Jean Dupuy," *Artforum* 13, No. 2, Oct. 1974.
41. Dupuy, *Collective Consciousness.*
42. Interview, Jun. 25–26, 2019.
43. Interview, April 20, 2012. Likely Julia Heyward's pieces at the Idea Warehouse and the Kitchen are being confused here.
44. Interview with Billingsley, Jan. 2, 2021.
45. Interview, Jun. 25–26, 2019.
46. Interview, Jun. 25–26, 2019.
47. Dupuy, ed., *Collective Consciousness.*
48. Email from Hovagimyan to author, Apr. 20, 2020.
49. Interview, Apr. 20, 2012.
50. Grace Glueck, "Art People," *New York Times*, Jan. 19, 1979.
51. As told to author on phone, Apr. 20, 2020.
52. Interview, Jun. 25–26, 2019.
53. Wolfgang Staehle interview with author, May 22, 2020.
54. Interview, Jun. 25–26, 2019.
55. Interview, Jun. 25–26, 2019.
56. Robert Atkins, "The Art World & I Go On Line," *Art in America*, Dec. 1995: 63.
57. William Zimmer, "An Exhibition in New Rochelle that Showcases Sheer Invention," *New York Times* [Westchester], Jan. 1,1995. See also G.H. Hovagimyan, "Tell Me About Your Mother's Tumblr," *Hyperallergic*, Feb. 27, 2013. https://hyperallergic.com/65968/tell-me-about-your-mothers-tumblr/.
58. Interview, Jun. 25–26, 2019.
59. Fiore, *112 Greene Street.*
60. *Terrorist Advertising* hypertext, nuju.net.
61. Interview, Jun. 25–26, 2019.
62. Interview, Jun. 25–26, 2019.
63. Interview, Jun. 25–26, 2019.
64. G.H. Hovagimyan interview with author, May 21, 2020
65. Press release, See also in Hovagimyan archive, Jeanne Curran and Susan R. Takata, "Definition of Concepual Art," Feb. 2004.
66. Interview, May 21, 2020.
67. Interview, May 21, 2020. See also Mark Cooley, "State of Art – A Conversation with G.H. Hovagimyan," Furtherfield newsletter, Jan. 2008: https://www.furtherfield.org/news/page/21/.
68. Interview, May 21, 2020.
69. Interview, May 21, 2020.
70. Andrew J Bottomley, *Sound Streams: A Cultural History of Radio-Internet Convergence.* (University of Michigan Press: Ann Arbor, Michigan, 2020), 79. See also, Joasia Krysa, ed. *Curating Immateriality: The Work of the Curator in the Age of Networked Systems* (Autonomedia: New York, 2006) and Dieter Daniels and Gunther Reisinger, eds., *Net Pioneers 1.0 Contextualizing Early Net-Based Art* (Sternberg Press: New York, 2009).
71. Jean-Yves Jouannais and Christophe Kihm, "Techno: Anatomie des cultures électroniques," *artpress*

19, Jan. 1998.

72. *Sound Streams*, 80.
73. G.H. Hovagimyan, "GH Works Description: Notations on works," [undated]
74. Interview, May 21, 2020.
75. Steven Henry Madoff, "Art in Cyberspace: Can It Live Without a Body," *New York Times*, Jan. 21, 1996.
76. Robert Atkins, "State of the (On-line) Art," *Art in America*, Apr. 1999.
77. Email from Hovagimyan posted on Rhizome.org, "Enter Port-MIT," Feb. 6, 1997: https://rhizome.org/community/41773/.
78. Email "the end of Art Dirt" from Hovagimyan posted on Rhizome.org, Jun. 7, 1998, accessed at https://xchange.re-lab.net/2009/mailinglist/archive1998/msg00332.html.
79. Walker Art Center, Gallery 9, Digital Art Archives.
80. Interview, Jun. 25–26, 2019.
81. Interview, Jun. 25–26, 2019.
82. Announcement, Hovagimyan portfolio clippings.
83. Austin Bunn, "Star Search," *Village Voice*, Feb. 17, 1998.
84. Artnetweb newsletter, Vol 3.02, February 5, 1998: https://artnetweb.com/newsletter/3_02.html.
85. See also "Techno: anatomie des cultures Electronique," *Art Press* 19.
86. Hovagimyan, "GH Works Description."
87. Interview, Jun. 25–26, 2019.
88. A SoaPOPera For Imacs, computers that talk and listen," Neural, Mar. 29, 2003: http://neural.it/2003/01/a-soapopera-for-imacs-computers-that-talk-and-listen/. See also, Emily Cluett, "iMac Divas," *Art & Science Journal*, 2011–2014: https://www.artandsciencejournal.com/post/108751780076/imac-divas-the-idea-of-artists-exploring-new.
89. Interview, Jun. 25–26, 2019.
90. G.H. Hovagimyan, "The International Festival of Multimedia Urban Arts," The Thing, Feb. 2, 2001. http://www.pavu.com/pavuCS/GHpress.htm
91. Interview, Jun. 25–26, 2019.
92. Heartbreak Hotel, nujus.net: http://nujus.net/~nujus/Heartbreak-new-site/index.html
93. Heartbreak Hotel, nujus.ent: http://nujus.net/~nujus/Heartbreak-new-site/heartb_descript_eng.html See also "HeartBreak Hotel: An interactive melodrama by Peter Sinclair and GH Hovagimyan," Artnetweb: http://artnetweb.com/gh/heartbreak.html/index.html.
94. HeartBreak Hotel, "Underlying Structure," Artnetweb: http://artnetweb.com/gh/heartbreak.html/heartbreak4.html
95. HeartBreak Hotel, "Underlying Structure."
96. Hovagimyan, "GH Works Description."
97. Interview, Jun. 25–26, 2019.
98. See also: Laurent Courau, "Lancement new-yorkais," *Libération*, Nov. 15, 2002; and G.H. Hovagimyan, "SHOOTER and -empyre-: Bare Life, Ghost Detainees, Exclusion and Performance," Documenta magazine (online), Jul. 15, 2007.
99. G.H. Hovagimyan, "Shooter: An Interactive Immersive Sound Installation by G.H. Hovagimyan & Peter Sinclair: A report by G.H. Hovagimyan," nujus.net: https://nujus.net/~nujus/shooter-new-site/shooter11.html.
100. "Art Port: The Whitney Museum Portal to Net Art," Whitney Museum of American Art, 2001-2006: https://artport.whitney.org/gatepages/index.shtml.
101. "Hotlist," *Artforum*, Mar. 2001.
102. Hovagimyan, "GH Works Description."
103. *(re)distributions*, curated by Patrick Lichty, Aug. 1, 2001: http://www.voyd.com/ia/.
104. Reena Jana, "Meditations on Information," Net Art News (email newsletter), *Rhizome*, Jul. 30,

2001: https://rhizome.org/editorial/2001/jul/30/meditations-on-information/.
105. G.H. Hovagimyan, Palm Rants (2001): http://nujus.net/~nujus/gh_04/gallery5.html.
106. *(re)distributions*, curated by Patrick Lichty.
107. Hovagimyan, "GH Works Description." See also Toni Sant, *Real Performance on the Pseudo Network Franklin Furnace & the Internet as an Open Medium*, PhD dissertation, Department of Performance Studies, New York University, May 2003: http://www.tonisant.com/writing/ToniSant-dissertation.pdf.
108. Hovagimyan, "GH Works Description."
109. Hovagimyan, "GH Works Description."
110. G.H. Hovagimyan, artist's statement, Apr. 13, 2006.
111. Marisa Olson, "You Probably Think This Search Is About You," *Rhizome.org Net Art News*, Apr. 14, 2006.
112. Artist's statement, Apr. 13, 2006, *Rhizome*: https://rhizome.org/editorial/2006/apr/13/vanity-search/
113. Hovagimyan, "GH Works Description." See also, "Rants and Raves," New York Foundation for the Arts Interactive, New York Foundation for the Arts, 1995–2006. Printed on May 25, 2006 in Hovagimyan papers.
114. G.H. Hovagimyan, project description: https://nujus.net/~gh/writings-web/Assembled%20Cinema%20proposal.pdf
115. Hovagimyan, "GH Works Description."
116. G.H. Hovagimyan interview on hacked interfaces with author, Galilee, PA, Aug. 8, 2020.
117. Print-out from Hovagimyan papers. "Cinema-Scope: Environment-Object-Inhabitant, Curated by G.H. Hovagimyan, July 14–16, 2006."
118. Seoul Net Festival, Digital Express Cinema4Net program, May 1–5, 2005. G.H. Hovagimyan papers.
119. Hovagimyan, "GH Works Description."
120. Hacked interfaces interview, 2020.
121. G.H. Hovagimyan papers. Festival program.
122. Hacked interfaces interview, 2020.
123. Hacked interfaces interview, 2020.
124. G.H. Hovagimyan papers.
125. Hacked interfaces interview, 2020.
126. *Love Songs from my Computer*, Alternative Museum: http://web.archive.org/web/20071017230252/http://alternativemuseum.org/exh/gh/gh.html
127. Hovagimyan, "GH Works Description."
128. *Long Songs*, Alternative Museum.
129. *Long Songs*, Alternative Museum.
130. Creative Time, *Democracy in America*, 2008: https://creativetime.org/projects/democracy-in-america/; https://creativetime.org/programs/archive/2008/democracy/.
131. Conflux publicity, Hovagimyan papers.
132. Turbulence, Pace Digital Gallery, 2009. http://csis.pace.edu/digitalgallery/turbulence/; http://turbulence.org/project/turbulence-pace-i/.
133. Hovagimyan, "GH Works Description."
134. Hovagimyan, "GH Works Description."
135. Hovagimyan, "GH Works Description."
136. Hovagimyan, "GH Works Description."
137. Hovagimyan, "GH Works Description."
138. *Triptych Party* press release, Jan. 10, 2008, Hovagimyan papers.
139. *Triptych Party II*, press release, May 16, 2009, Hovagimyan papers.
140. *Triptych Party* press release.

141. Hovagimyan, "GH Works Description."
142. Interview, Jun. 25–26, 2019.
143. Hovagimyan, "GH Works Description."
144. *((ANA)Chronisms++)* press release, TRANSFER, Feb. 1–22, 2014.
145. Hovagimyan, "GH Works Description."
146. Hovagimyan, "GH Works Description."
147. Hovagimyan, "GH Works Description."
148. Postmasters announcement. Hovagimyan papers.
149. Hovagimyan, "GH Works Description."
150. G.H. Hovagimyan residency, D6 Culture in Transit website, Apr. 2013. http://www.d6culture.org/gh-hovagimyan.html.
151. Interview, Jun. 25–26, 2019.
152. Hovagimyan, "GH Works Description."
153. Publicity, D6 Residency, Apr. 2013: http://www.d6culture.org/gh-hovagimyan.html.
154. Scott Atkinson, "3-D Karaoke coming to Flint for November Art Walk," *Mlive Flint*, Nov. 08, 2012.
155. Hovagimyan, "GH Works Description."
156. G.H. Hovagimyan interview with author on augmented reality (AR) work, fall 2020.
157. Hovagimyan, "GH Works Description."
158. "GH Hovagimyan: *(ANA)CHRONISMS* at Transfer Gallery," Net Art Net, Jan. 31, 2014: http://netartnet.net/news/announcement/item/789-anachronisms.
159. Benoit Palop, "There Will Be 'Space Oddity': *3D Karaoke* at TRANSFER Gallery Tomorrow," Vice, Jan. 31, 2014: https://www.vice.com/en/article/3d5zay/there-will-be-space-oddity-3d-karaoke-at-transfer-gallery-tomorrow.
160. Hacked interfaces interview, 2020.
161. *((ANA)Chronisms++)* press release, Cruxspace, 2014.
162. *((ANA)Chronisms++)* press release.
163. *((ANA)Chronisms++)* press release.
164. Hovagimyan on AR work, fall 2020.
165. Hovagimyan on AR work, fall 2020.
166. Claudio Gaete, "El hombre que transformará el cerro la Cruz," *El Mercurio Sabado*, Nov. 8, 2014; Oscar Aspillaga P., "Artista estadounidense construye resbalín interactivo en El Vergel, ElMartutino.cl, Jan. 12, 2014 [print outs from Hovagimyan papers]; "Creando un resbalín interactivo," TVN, Nov. 8, 2014: https://www.tvn.cl/especiales/puertodeideas/creando-un-resbalin-interactivo-con-gerry-hovagimyan-1488492.
167. Artist's statement, nujus.net.
168. Hovagimyan on AR work, fall 2020.
169. Hovagimyan phone interview with author, December 27, 2020.
170. Hovagimyan phone interview, Dec. 27, 2020.
171. Hovagimyan on AR work, fall 2020.
172. Hovagimyan on AR work, fall 2020.
173. Interview, Jun. 25–26, 2019.
174. Hovagimyan phone interview, Dec. 27, 2020.
175. Interview, Jun. 25–26, 2019.
176. Hovagimyan on AR work, fall 2020.
177. Hovagimyan on AR work, fall 2020.
178. Hovagimyan on AR work, fall 2020.
179. Interview, Jun. 25–26, 2019.
180. Interview, Jun. 25–26, 2019.
181. Hovagimyan on AR work, fall 2020.
182. Hovagimyan on AR work, fall 2020.

Appendix

Timeline

- Born June 21, 1950, Plymouth, Massachusetts
- Father drafted to army, Hovagimyan lives in Istanbul as a toddler, 1952–1954
- Moves to Riverdale, Bronx, 1954–56
- Moves to Watertown, Massachusetts, 1956–1962
- Attends high school in New Jersey: South Orange Junior High; Columbia High School, Maplewood, NJ; Cherry Hill High School, Cherry Hill, NJ; Haddenfield Memorial High School, Haddenfield, NJ, 1962–1969
- Attends Philadelphia College of Art (renamed University of the Arts), receives BFA, Philadelphia, PA, 1969–1973
- Moves to loft in Lower Manhattan at 64 Fulton Street, NY, 1973–75
- Works at 112 Greene Street gallery, NY, 1973–75
- Moves to loft in SoHo at 597 Broadway, NY, 1975–1977
- Moves to loft in TriBeCa at 474 Greenwich Street, NY, 1978
- Lives with girlfriend in Independence Plaza, TriBeCa, NY, 1979
- Marries Freda Mekul, moves to East Village, 16 Avenue A, 1980–86
- Opens Virtual Garrison, 1983–85
- Moves to TriBeCa loft at 11 Harrison Street with Joyce Castleberry, 1986
- Divorce from Mekul, 1987
- Buys property at 11 Church Road in Galilee, PA, 1989
- Marries Castleberry, 1999
- Attends master's program and receives MA, New York University, 2001–06
- Sells TriBeCa apartment and moves to Galilee, PA, 2017
- Hovagimyan is still active and working on new projects in his studio every day in Galilee, PA.

Exhibitions and Performances

1973 *About 405 E. 13th Street*, May 4–14, 1973
1974 *Control Designators*, 112 Greene Street, Sep. 21–Oct. 3, 1974
1975 *Videotapes and Performances*, The Kitchen, Feb. 18–19, 1975
Loft Show, 597 Broadway, Spring 1975
Scale 1/1, James Yu Gallery, May 1975
Thought Models, Idea Warehouse, Jun. 11–12, 1975
1977 *Rubber Room*, P.S. 1, Mar. 24–Apr. 10, 1977
Rich Sucker Rap, Artists Space, 1977
1978 *Chant à Capella*, Jean Dupuy and Davidson Gigliotti, Museum of Modern Art (1978)
The Communists, Club 57 (Apr. 7, 1978); Max's Kansas City (Apr. 23, 1978); Artists Space (May 2, 1978); Max's Kansas City (Jun. 5, 1978); CBGB (Jun. 18, 1978); Max's Kansas City (Jul. 17, 1978); Max's Kansas City (Aug. 26, 1978)
1979 *75 Warren Street*, Jan.–Feb. 1979
Tactics for Survival in the New Culture, Manifesto Show, Apr. 1979
1980 *Excerpts from a Novel*, 112 Workshop, Apr. 24, 1980

1993 BKPC *(Barbie and Ken Politically Correct)*, Thing.net; *Toys/Art/Us*, Castle Gallery, New Rochelle, NY (1994)
Sit-On, artnetweb
Giant Kosuth Price List, artnetweb (1993 & 2007)
Terrorist Advertising, Bowery & 5th St., New York, Sep. 23, 1993–Feb. 23, 1994

1994 *Hey Bozo, Use Mass Transit*, MTA & Creative Time; *Courage*, New Museum (1995); *Meme Breeders*, Eastern Connecticut State University (1996); *Billboard: Art on the Road*, Mass MoCA (1999)
Surveys & Questionnaires, Gallery 128, New York
Fibonacci Series with Calculators, artnetweb

1995 *Art Direct/Sex, Violence & Politics*, Thing.net, New York *Faux Conceptual Art*, artnetweb/Thing.net

1997 *Art Dirt*, Pseudo Online Radio, 1995–1998
Art Dirt Im-Port, Port MIT: Navigating Digital Culture, MIT List Visual Arts Center, Jan. 25–Mar. 29, 1997
A Soa(p (Op)era for Laptops/iMacs (with Peter Sinclair), Postmasters; Musée d'Art Contemporain, Marseille; Ars Electronica in Linz, Austria (1998); *Les Jaseurs*, Postmasters (1998); *Sound Artists of North America*, Musée d'Art Contemporain, Lyon (Jan. 1999); *Art et Technique: Emergence d'un Dialogue*, Espace-Exposition, Toulon (May 1999); SVA Visual Arts Museum: New York Digital Salon (1999); International Electronic Art Festival, Belfort, France (1999); *Avignon Numérique*, Avignon, France (2001); Split Festival of New Film, Split, Croatia (2002); *Burlesques Contemporains*, Jeu de Paume, Paris (2005)

1999 *Heartbreak Hotel* (with Peter Sinclair), Centre National de Création Musicale, Marseille; Interferences: International Festival of Multimedia Urban Arts, Belfort, France (Dec. 14–20, 2000); Studio for Electro-Instrumental Music, Amsterdam; Centre International de Création Vidéo, Pierre Schaeffer, Hérimoncourt, France

2001 *Shooter* (with Peter Sinclair), Postmasters, September 30, 2001; *Beta Launch*, Eyebeam, New York (2002); *Open Source 3*, La Gaîté Lyrique, Paris (2002)
The Last Noel Avant l'An 2000: Les Jaseurs Chantent [CD/solo show with Peter Sinclair], Aldébaran, Éspace d'Art Contemporain, Baillargue, France
Cocktail Party, *Whitney Art Port: Whitney Museum Portal of Net Art,* Whitney Museum of American Art, Nov. 2001; Postmasters, September 30, 2001
Palm Rants, (re)distributions
Lovers, Swingers & Shooters, Postmasters Gallery
net.ephemera, Moving Image Gallery, May 2001

2002 *Brecht Machine*, Franklin Furnace, Sep. 2002

2003 *Smart House/Dumb Interactivity*, Institute for Contemporary Culture, Royal Ontario Museum, May 2003; Award for New Media and Intermedia Performance, mediaThe foundation Inc. (2003); *Digit: Digital Media Exposition*, Tusten Theatre, Narrowsburg, NY (Apr. 2004)
Rant/Rant Back/Back Rant (with Peter Sinclair), *Open Source 3*, La Gaîté Lyrique, Paris (Sep. 2003); Split New Media Festival, Split, Croatia (Sep. 2003); Noordezon Festival, Groninger Museum, Netherlands (Aug. 2004); STEIM Institute, Amsterdam (2004); Postmasters (2004);
Les Rencontres Place Publique, Marseille/New York/Aix-en-Provence (Sep. 2004)

2004 *Vanity Search*, Computer Fine Arts Collection; Cornell University's Rose Goldsen Archive of New Media Art

2005 *Assembled Cinema*, IFC Channel (online); video_dumbo, *Authentic Fabrications* (Sep. 29. 2007);

Split Festival for New Film (2008)
HD Morphs: *Fluid Dynamics,* Seoul Net Festival, and *Glass Morphs,* Cinema-Scope: Environment-Object-Inhabitant
Podcast workshop, École National Superiére D'Art de Nice, France

2006 *Rantapod*, New York Video Festival, Lincoln Center, Jul. 2006; Festival of Pocket Films, Centre Pompidou (2007 and 2008), Digit Festival, Lackawaxen, PA; Split Film Festival, Croatia; Pixel Pops, Prague
HD_Rants (with Brian Caiazza) Dumbo Arts Festival; Art Frames at Pioneer Theater, CIRCA in San Juan, Puerto Rico, PAM at Coachella; *Guerrilla Media Vehicle*, Art Basel Miami (Dec. 6–10, 2006); *For Love & Money*, Resonance FM, Frieze Art Fair; VernissageTV; M21—The Museum of 21st Century; Fundacio Clovis Salgado/Palacio des Artes in Belo Horizonte, Brazil; Museum of Modern Art Linz, *Video as Urban Condition* (Apr. 2007); *Furious: The Angry Show* (2007), Eyedrum, Atlanta; Expanded Media, Kunstverein, Stuttgart; Computer Fine Arts Collection

2007 *Video Projections*, Artists Meeting, Art Under the Bridge Festival, Dumbo, Brooklyn, Sep. 28–30, 2007

2008 *Love Songs from My Computer*, Alternative Museum
Public Exhibition Space, Artists Meeting, Conflux Festival, Sep. 11–14, 2008
Smart Money, *Democracy in America*, Creative Time, Park Avenue Armory, Sep. 2008
YouTube Slam, Artists Meeting, Postmasters, Nov. 8. 2008

2009 *Plazaville*, Turbulence @ Pace Digital Gallery, New York, Apr. 7, 2009; Tyneside Cinema, Newcastle, UK (2009); VernissageTV, Art Cologne, Germany (Apr. 21–26, 2009)
Art Machine, Artists Meeting, Pulse Art Fair, Miami; Verge Art Fair, New York (Mar. 4–7, 2010)
Triptych Party, Artists Meeting, Postmasters, May 16, 2009

2010 *See/Saw*, *Floating World*, Building 110, LMCC Governors Island, New York City, Sep. 10–Oct. 10, 2010

2011 *Boxing Rants*, Artists Meeting, *Being & Event*, Postmasters, Jun. 26, 2011

2012 Artist in Residence, School of Visual Arts, MFA Computer Arts
Mapped Morphs (with Rhys Chatham), Postmasters, Jun. 14th, 2012
3D Karaoke, Pixel Palace Newcastle, England, Aug. 2012; Flint Public Art Project, Flint, MI (Nov. 9, 2012); Harvestworks (Mar. 1, 2013); NewBridge Project Space, Newcastle, U.K. (Apr. 2013); Valparaíso, Chile (2014); *((ANA)Chronisms++)*, TRANSFER, Brooklyn (Feb. 2014) and CRUXspace, Philadelphia (2015)

2014 *((ANA)Chronisms++)*, TRANSFER, Brooklyn, Feb. 1–22, 2014; CRUXspace, Philadephia (Feb. 1–28, 2015)
Fibonacci Spiral, Galilee, Pennsylvania (2014); Puerto de Ideas Valparaíso, Chile (Nov. 2014); Flint Public Art Project, Flint, MI (Summer, 2015)

2015 *Teenage Zombie Avatars*, *Ensign Sgr A**, Radiator Arts, Mar. 6–Apr. 10, 2015
Zipline, Chance Ecologies, Radiator Arts, Dec. 17. 2015–Jan. 20, 2016

2016 *3by3by3* (with Rhys Chatham & Raphaele Shirley), Harvestworks, Jun. 6, 2016

2017 *AR-VR*, Split Festival for New Film, Split, Croatia, Sep. 9–16, 2017

2018 *Applause Please*, *Algorithmic Landscapes of the Western Catskills*, Callicoon, NY, Oct. 6, 2018

2019 *At Home in Space*, Loft Gallery, Delaware Valley Art Alliance, Aug. 10–Sep. 14, 2019

Collections

The Alternative Museum
www.alternativemuseum.org/exh/gh/gh.html

Cornell University Library, Rose Goldsen Archive of New Media Art
www.computerfinearts.com

Walker Art Center, Digital Studies Archive
www.walkerart.org

Whitney Museum, *Whitney Art Port: Whitney Museum Portal to Net Art*
www.whitney.org/artport

Bibliography

ANDERSON, LAURIE "About 405 13th Street." *Artforum* 12, No. 1 (Sep. 1974).

ASPILLAGA P., OSCAR. "Artista estadounidense construye resbalín interactivo en *El Vergel.* elmartutino.cl, Jan. 12, 2014.

ATKINS, ROBERT. "The Art World & I Go On Line." *Art in America* (Dec. 1995).

ATKINS, ROBERT. "State of the (On-Line) Art." *Art in America* (Apr. 1999).

ATKINSON, SCOTT. "3-D Karaoke coming to Flint for November Art Walk." Mlive Flint, Nov. 08, 2012.

BEAR, LIZA. "Richard Serra & Robert Bell…Prisoner's Dilemma." *Avalanche*, May/Jun. 1974.

BOTTOMLEY, ANDREW J. *Sound Streams: A Cultural History of Radio-Internet Convergence*. Ann Arbor: University of Michigan Press, 2020.

BRENTANO, ROBYN AND MARK SAVITT, eds. *112 Workshop/112 Greene Street: History, Artists & Artworks.* New York: New York University Press, 1981.

CHRISTGAU, ROBERT. "Choices." *Village Voice*, May 8, 1978.

COOLEY, MARK. "State of Art – A Conversation with G.H. Hovagimyan." Furtherfield newsletter, Jan. 2008. https://www.furtherfield.org/news/page/21/.

DANIELS, DIETER AND GUNTHER REISINGER, eds. *Net Pioneers 1.0 Contextualizing Early Net-Based Art.* New York: Sternberg Press, 2009.

DRUCKER, JOHANNA. "Digital Reflections: The Dialogue of Art and Technology."*Art Journal* 56, No. 3, (Autumn, 1997): 46–54.

FERNBACH, ELIZA. "The edgy discomfort of G.H. Hovagimyan's rant work." Furtherfield, Oct. 20, 2008. http://archive.furtherfield.org/user/eliza-fernbach.

FIORE, JESSAMYN. *112 Greene Street.* New York: David Zwirner Books, 2012.

FOREST, FRED. *Art et Internet.* Paris: Éditions Cercle d'Art, 2008.

GAETE, CLAUDIO. "El hombre que transformará el cerro la Cruz." *El Mercurio Sabado*, Nov. 8, 2014.

GLUECK, GRACE. "Art People." *New York Times*, Apr. 15, 1977.

GLUECK, GRACE. "Art People." *New York Times*, Jan. 19, 1979.

GLUECK, GRACE. "East Village Gets on the Fast Track." *New York Times*, Jan. 13, 1985.

GOVIN, MEGAN. "Introduction to the Fine Arts Building." Dec. 18, 2014. https://fineartsbuildingnewyork.tumblr.com/post/165102423267/introduction-to-the-fine-arts-building.

HARRIS, JANE. *((ANA)chronisms++)*. TRANSFER Gallery, 2014.

JANA, REENA. "Meditations on Information." Net Art News (email newsletter), *Rhizome*, Jul. 30, 2001. https://rhizome.org/editorial/2001/jul/30/meditations-on-information/.

JANA, REENA. "Net Art with a Groove." *Wired News*, Sep. 27, 2000.

KIMMELMAN, MICHAEL. "Matta-Clark's Cross Sections of Yesterday." *New York Times*, Feb. 23, 2007.

KRYSA, JOASIA ed. *Curating Immateriality: The Work of the Curator in the Age of Networked Systems*. New York: Autonomedia, 2006.

MADOFF, STEVEN HENRY. "Art in Cyberspace: Can It Live Without a Body." *New York Times*, Jan. 21, 1996.

MCCORMICK, CARLO. "Remembrance of Things Passed Over." *East Village Eye*, Aug. 1984.

MCGILL, DOUGLAS C. "Art People." *New York Times*, Oct. 4, 1985.

MOORE, ALAN. "Loft Show at 597 Broadway." *Artforum* 19, No. 10 (Summer 1975).

MOORE, THURSTON AND BYRON COLEY. *No Wave: Post-Punk. Underground. New York. 1976–1980*. New York: Abrams, 2008.

O' DOHERTY, BRIAN. *Inside the White Cube: The Ideology of the Gallery Space*. Berkeley: University of California Press, 1999.

POPPER, FRANK. *From Technological to Virtual Art*. Boston: MIT Press, 2007.

ROBINSON, WALTER ["Winshield"]. "Lumps of All Kinds: Sculpture Survey at Virtual Garrison." *East Village Eye*, Jul. 1984.

ROBINSON, WALTER ["Winshield]. "Charlie Saulson." *East Village Eye*, Mar. 1985.

SANT, TONI. *Real Performance on the Pseudo Network Franklin Furnace & the Internet as an Open Medium*. PhD dissertation, Department of Performance Studies, New York University, May 2003. http://www.tonisant.com/writing/ToniSant-dissertation.pdf.

SMITH, NEIL. *The New Urban Frontier: Gentrification and the Revanchist City*. New York: Routledge, 1996.

SMITH, ROBERTA. "Video, in Its Infancy, Had to Crawl Before It Could Walk." *New York Times*, Jan. 24, 2003.

TRIBE, MARK. "Hotlist." *Artforum* (March 2001): 41.

WANDS, BRUCE. *Digital Creativity*. New York: John Wiley & Sons, 2002.

WOLCOTT, JAMES. "A Conservative Impulse in the New Rock Underground." *Village Voice*, Aug. 18th 1975.

ZIMMER, WILLIAM. "An Exhibition in New Rochelle That Showcases Sheer Invention." *New York Times*, Jan. 1, 1995.